ONLY ONE SURVIVED

Frances
I finally got there
after 25 years. You will
recognize many parts of
this story that we have
talked about, same story
but far different. Hope you
enjoy.

By

Les Sweeney

ONLY ONE SURVIVED

Editing, Design & Printing in the United States of America

Published & Distributed by
KITCHEN TABLE PUBLISHING
2069 Shelley Drive
Payette, Idaho

COVER: The background for the cover is a photograph taken at sundown, October 7th, 2019, at Devil's Corral in northwestern Elko County, Nevada. The Daggett family crossed the South Fork of the Owyhee River Near here in the spring of 1910.

CHILDREN of the (SHOSHONE) MIKE DAGGETT FAMILY
1911
HENNY, CLEVE, HATTIE & JOSEPHINE MIKE

Orphaned by the Donnelley Posse
on February 26, 1911

TABLE of CONTENTS

PART I

PART II

PART III

PART IV

PART V

ACKNOWLEDGEMENTS

My wife Cheri----Who spent countless years, months days hours traveling and helping me research this story!

Louis & Ester Jarneke --- (deceased)----------------------------------- Wapato, Washington
Eilene Sweeney---Payette, Idaho
Jack Murdock---- (deceased)-- Winnemucca, Nevada
Marvin Mattson-- Sparks, Nevada
Art & Sandy Harris --Midvale, Idaho
Diane Colcord-- Tilllamook, Oregon
Margaret Jones --- (deceased)------------------------------------- Yakima, Washington
Beverly Jones--- Yakima, Washington
Diane Chu ---- (deceased)--- Yakima, Washington
Shari Hillman--- Rock Creek, Idaho
David Crockett--- Rock Creek, Idaho
Bob & Marilyn Ramsey-- Filer, Idaho
Harry & Nancy Summerfield ---- (Harry deceased)------------------------- Reno, Nevada
Mark Schopper-- Reno, Nevada
Naomi Mason - Duckwater Indian Reservation---------------------------- Owyhee, Nevada
Lee Roy Arrascada ---- (deceased)--- Reno, Nevada
Walter Tranmer ---- (deceased)--- Twin Falls, Idaho
Dawn Serano ---- (deceased)------------------------------- --------------- Salt Lake City, Utah
Truman Clark ---- (deceased)-- Burley, Idaho
Frank & Lois Shields ---- (Lois deceased)------------------------------------- Reno, Nevada
Roger Jones-- Hollister, Idaho
Sally Jones-- Hollister, Idaho
Brad & Carol Hines-- Reno, Nevada
Dave Vail-- Meridian, Idaho
Dean & Nancy Sweeney--- Salem, Oregon
Gene Gray-- Payette, Idaho
Mark Parker-- Twin Falls, Idaho
Lyle Sweeney--San Francisco, California
Ci Curtis --Kansas City, Missouri
E. C. Coberly (widow of Carl Colberly)---------------------------------Susanville, California
Lois Sutton--Midvale, Idaho

AUTHORS

Dayton Hyde	Hot Springs, South Dakota
Brigham Madsen	Salt Lake City, Utah
James Varley	Twin Falls, Idaho
James Young	Reno, Nevada
Mark Schopper	Reno, Nevada
Dan Rathbun	Las Cruces, New Mexico
Greg Michno	Longmont, Colorado
Barbara Hegne	Reno, Nevada
Karen Quinton	Hollisteer, Idaho
Frances V. Leininger	Chico, Calf.
Richard Burrill	Chico, Calf.

ARCHIVES & RECORDS

Nevada State Archives	Carson City, Nevada
Recorder's Office	Winnemucca, Nevada
Recorder's Office	Reno, Nevada
National Archives	Washington,DC
Library of Congress	Washington, D.C.
Repatriation Office - Smithsonian Institute - (Eric Hollinger)	Washington, DC
Fort Hall Indian Agency - Probate Office	Fort Hall, Idaho
National Archives Microfilm Publication-M1011 GSA-1975 Record Adm.	San Bruno, CA.
American Indian Records Suppository	Lenexa, Kansas
Carson Indian School	Stewart Nevada
Idaho State Archives	Boise, Idaho

MUSEUMS & HISTORICAL SOCIETIES

Winnemucca, Nevada---Elko, Nevada---Reno, Nevada---Carson City, Nevada---
Alturas, California---Susanville, California---Twin Falls, Idaho---Burley, Idaho---
Shoshone/Bannock Tribal, Fort Hall, Idaho---Pocatello, Idaho---College of Idaho History
Center, Twin Falls, Idaho---Friends of Stricker Inc., Hansen, Idaho---Albion, Idaho---
Anderson, California--

FOREWORD

My dad came to the Diamond S Ranch at Golconda, Nevada in 1934 and as a kid growing up I had heard many stories regarding Shoshone Mike and the incident at Rabbit Creek.

A little over twenty five years ago I began reading all the material I could find regarding the incident. It wasn't long before I realized something was amiss in the stories that I had heard over the years and the stories I was reading. Something was wrong with the supposed facts, reality and the very different stories others were arriving at about the same incident.

Before embarking on the development of this story I began my own research and investigation, independent of those reflections of history, to write this story.

I approached the story in this manner in order to eliminate, as much as possible, bias from the writings of others, especially the newspapers.

In these past 25 years I have read, researched, absorbed and analyzed some 50 books, over 200 news articles, many short stories, and personal accounts and other bits of information, to get a better understanding of what the Native American has experienced since the white European Christian invaded their land.

More specifically how these stories were depicting the saga of Shoshone Mike.

Referring to only one particular page or article of the many references to get the best understanding of the White vs Indian relationship is not possible. One has to see this information as a whole to best understand this relationship and develop the truest picture of what was transpiring at the time and how it formed the mind set of the Native American Indian.

The books related specifically to this story I put on the shelf many years ago and started all from scratch in order to not be influenced by what they contained.

At the beginning of time, that time when white man landed in the Americas, the interactions with the Native American Indians, the aboriginal peoples of this nation, began to act and react differently than they had for thousands of years. Prior to this, there was no white man in the mix.

This story of an only surviving child of an Indian family slaughtered by white man, so recent as 1911 has to reflect the mind set of her grandfather, Mike Daggett, patriarch of the family.

In order to understand Mike's actions during this saga, you have to put yourself in his moccasins, with his history.

A great deal of effort was exercised in determining what the facts really were. For example, arriving at those facts took years of research, study of available information, analyzing that information, sorting through written accounts and analyzing their validity, analyzing interviews and letters, studying what made sense and what was logical and what was backed up by other information and my knowledge of the country in which this event occurred. By country I mean that parcel of Real Estate between the foot of the Sierras in the west and the foot of the Rocky Mountains on the east with the north boundary being the John Day River in Oregon and the Snake River Plains in Idaho and the south boundary being an imaginary line between Reno, Nevada and Wendover, Nevada (NGP & SRP). This also is that part of the west in which I was born, raised, educated worked, researched, hunted and played in the seventy two of my eighty four years here on this planet. I have crossed Mike's trail thousands of times.

I grew up with, knew and worked with many of the those in the generation from which the posse was made up. Although only a kid myself I saw what made them tick (their personalities the way they talked and did things).

I may not have referenced what they did or didn't do or acted but my 82 years of experience and dealing with people from all walks of life gives me the right to express my thoughts and tell this part of the story without referencing anyone, maybe not totally right but better than others who did not know this generation in this environment nor their way of life.

This story ONLY ONE SURVIVED was developed through the review of that large list of references and looking at them as a whole. One cannot get the true perspective of the relationship between the white man and the Indian, in that geographic area, the NGP & SRP, by piece/mealing or selecting bits and pieces from all the information that is out there. It has to be looked at as a whole all inclusive thoroughly analyzed and studied.

I liken my more than twenty five years on this effort to those who have researched and studied an issue or project for a period of three to five years in order to gather and analyze information to develop a Thesis for a masters or doctorate degree.

The spelling of the names of the main characters in this episode have varied as they were printed in the many written documents newspapers books etc.

"The stories told make us who we are"! John Beater - professor at Boise State University

This quote is reflected in this story many times. Our story often guides us to who we are and who we become.

PART I

CHAPTER I

IN THE BEGINNING - Genocide in America

In 1492 when the Indians discovered Columbus on their land genocide began in America, and continued for the next 500 years through 1911.

In 1492 the Indian population of America is estimated to have been about 10 million, give or take 5 million. In 1900 the Indian population had dwindled to 250 thousand, while in that same period of time the remainder, the exotic population, all other races combined went from 0 in 1492 to over 91 million. By 1900 the Native American Indian had been brought to near extinction.

What is genocide? "The deliberate extermination of a race or people".

The great egotistical white European could never accept the fact the Native American people were here first. Westward expansion brought ever greater numbers of immigrants upon the lands of the Indian, thus more conflict was inevitable and as westward migration moved forward the American Indian was driven out. If killing them seemed to be the most efficient and permanent way to get rid of them, so be it.

In the winter Indians congregated in camps, pooled food supplies and generally used the winter months as down time. It was not lost on the white-man that Indians were most vulnerable in their winter encampments. The whites took full advantage of the Indian's vulnerability and attacked when the most Indians could be killed.

Without exception, winter campaigns against Indian encampments, whether large or small, were the most effective. In either case, soldiers or often times citizens, organized to search out, kill and destroy entire camps. The goal was to kill as many Indians as possible, take or destroy, their food supplies, all shelters, blankets or whatever they had to protect themselves from the elements. When camps were attacked, women and children who did little, if any, of the fighting, would if not killed out right, run and hide. With the men killed and their camp destroyed, they had no way of survival and would die of exposure and starvation.

1

It is evidenced, in history, that no white man went into the field to fight Indians with a bow and arrows.

The military campaign, or what author Gregory Michno referred to as the *Snake Conflict of 1863 - 1868*, in the northern Great Basin and Snake River Plains, was geared to kill Indians whenever and wherever they could be found.

Officer reports usually referred to the Indians who they engaged or killed as Piautes, Bannock and Shoshone.

When the soldiers ran out of supplies they returned to military camps/supply depots, to resupply, whereas the Indian had to look to mother earth for subsistence. In winter this was not always possible and other times of the year difficult, if not impossible, as the white man had taken care of that possibility. The alternative for survival was to raid wagon trains, ranches, settlements, forts, mining camps etc.

The atrocities grew more brutal as you move from the northern US to the southern US, Mexican border. Why? because in the north Indians were an asset to the Hudson Bay Co. and were not so ill treated so less animosity. Whereas in the south the Mexican government was unstable, slave trade was rampant on both sides and Indians as human beings were looked upon as having no value except as slaves.

Most Indian agents were ruthless in dealing with the Indians. Indians were the low-life of humanity and the agents had no empathy for the Indian They stole and sold food and other supplies meant for the Indians, on the black market, while Indians died of starvation, disease and exposure. Those agents who cared about the Indians and showed some empathy were soon dismissed.

Most of those settling the west wanted the Indian gone. They didn't want them claiming any rights to land or resources that came from the land. In many cases the army actually recognized the dilemma of the Indian and made a feeble effort to protect them but were over ridden by politics in the east due to pressure from those moving west.

Indians of Great Basin and Snake River Plains were nomadic and except for their winter encampments, moved around in small bands with little need or desire to be governed by any particular chief.

Hunger, restlessness and revenge motivated young warriors to strike out on their own on deprivation raids.

The Indians could never organize, however one of the few times they did organize they killed Custer at the Little Bighorn. Had they had a little more organization and leadership and spent another hour on the battle field they could have wiped out Major Reno to the last man. But no, those that had Reno cornered looked up and saw their compadres packing up camp and moving out let Reno go knowing that army reinforcements would likely, soon be arriving.

In the book, ISHI by the statement was made "We must be the custodians of their tragedies" but even today many are in denial of the atrocities brought upon the Native American Indian.

Today one needs a hunting license to hunt big game, water fowl etc. but not to kill other animals considered vermin i.e., coyotes. Through the 19th century Indians were hunted and killed like vermin no hunting license no tags or special permits needed. This included women and children. On both sides scalps were taken as trophies. That was the mentality of the white people as well as the Indian.

The following appeared in the Silver City newspaper, Silver City, Idaho, February 1866:

The Owyhee Avalanche
Saturday Morning FEB. 17, 1866

WAR MEETINGS

A meeting of the citizens of Silver and Ruby Cities was held at the Challenge Saloon, Silver City, on Wednesday evening, 14th inst. R. T. Miller called the meeting to order.
R. Tregaskis was elected president - C. G. Whitcomb, Secretary.
A committee of five was appointed to collect money and provisions - Lytle, McGraw, Mills, Stanford and Bohannon.
Bohannon was dispatched to Boise City to confer with the Governor; and to raise money and munitions of war and men to co-operate with us.
A Committee of five was appointed to collect arms. Also, a Committee of twenty-five men to collect horses for the expedition.
A. J. Sinclair and J. A. Lytle were appointed enrolling officers.
H. Bloom was elected Treasurer.
RESOLVED, That Boise Valley and Basin be invited to co-operate with this company.
2. That anyone who has lost stock of any kind can have it by going out with this company and capturing it, but not otherwise.
3. That E. Bohannon's expenses to Boise City be paid out of money collected for this company.
4. That the proceedings of this meeting be published in the AVALANCHE.
Meeting adjourned to meet at the Challenge Saloon, Silver City, Thursday evening, 15th inst. at 7 P.M.

Thursday evening FEB. 15, 1866

Meeting came to order, President Tregaskis in the chair.

Subscription list foots up, in round numbers $1,140.

The following resolutions were adopted:

RESOLVED, Three men be appointed to select twenty five men to go Indian hunting, and all of those who can fit themselves out shall receive a nominal sum for all scalps that they may bring in, and all who cannot fit themselves out , shall be fitted out by this Committee, and when they bring in scalps, it shall be deducted out.

2. That for every buck scalp be paid one hundred dollars, and every squaw scalp fifty dollars, and twenty-five dollars for everything in the shape of an Indian under ten years of age.

3. That the Chair appoint three men to pick out the twenty-five men to go hunting Indians. The Chair appointed Massey, R. Brown and Mills.

4. That each scalp have the curl of the head, and each man shall make oath that the said scalp was taken by the company.

5. That Mr. Massey act as temporary Quartermaster.

6. That this meeting adjourn to meet at 7 o'clock tomorrow night.

G. O. Whitcomb, Sec'y.

(The men who went into the field to kill Indians were inept. No Indians were reported to have been found nor killed.

Newspapers known for their inaccuracies got this one right. The Owyhee Avalanche was responsible for recording and keeping the minutes of these meetings.)

The killing of these people was done in the most gruesome, cruel and non-caring way.

At the time, most white Europeans were in denial that this killing was somehow wrong.

The method of extermination included rifle ball, starvation, disease, exposure , poisoning and some were clubbed to death, including women and children.

Starvation was also exploited by the whites by killing of the buffalo, taking and/or driving the Indian from the lands which they depended on for subsistence.

Starvation also left them more stressed and vulnerable to disease and exposure.

In military campaigns, Indians were often captured and taken into custody and while in the custody of the military, many died. Reports brought back from an Indian campaign, often stated, *"the prisoners died or were killed while attempting escape"*.

If and when an Indian was taken prisoner they are days or maybe weeks before they could get their captives back to any kind of facilities for incarceration. The military had a most difficult time getting themselves around let alone dragging along prisoners, which may have led to the unnecessary killing of many Indians.

The American Indian came by white mans' devastating diseases quite by accident however, when the Europeans found out how deadly many of these diseases (i.e. tuberculosis, small pox, flu) were, they began infecting the Indian on purpose, including issuing infected blankets. You might say "we, non natives, here in America are here over the dead bodies of women and children".

When the Indians became bothersome and dangerous to wagon trains and settlers treaties were made with the Indians, in order to allow safe passage of the Immigrants. However, as the immigration numbers grew and their belief that more soldiers would became available after the Civil War for their protection, to remove the Indian from land the settlers wanted, the white people saw no need to honor these treaties.

All through the 19th century the white man went into what Larry McMurtry, in his book OH WHAT A SLAUGHTER, called a "killing frenzy".

If a white man wanted to get rid of an Indian he did so, drumming up an excuse later was never questioned. White perpetrators were almost never prosecuted for crimes against the Indian. If ever they were, the punishment was a joke or in those rarest of incidents where the punishment did fit the crime, there were extenuating circumstances where the white man was paying for some other offense or as a political scapegoat. Whenever the Indian tried to stand his ground and protect his family, he was treated even more savagely. The white man became incensed that the Indian should attempt to deny him of, anything he so desired of the Indian.

During the Osage Murder Trials in Oklahoma, mid 1920s, a statement was made *"The question for the jury to decide was whether a white killing an Osage Indian is murder or merely cruelty to animals"*.

Depredation on white farmers and ranchers livestock was a big issue to the white man but few cared that it was driven by hunger of their starving families and themselves. They only saw the Indian as savages and predators to be eliminated from the American scene. They were referred to as *Bucks* and *Squaws* to egotistically degrade them as human beings and further justify their treatment like animals and annihilation.

Atrocities by each side, whites against Indians and Indians against whites, were unimaginable in what was supposed to be a civilized America. Mutilation and torture were common place. Soldiers cut the genitals from women they had killed to use as

5

hat bands, scrotums from men were taken for coin pouches and other trinkets.

Although the author could find (no smoking gun) or hard evidence of these horrifying atrocities, I do not question its validity and it should be of no surprise to those who have studied and read about the mentality of the soldiers and militiamen in the field at the time. This savagery is consistent with the prejudices and disrespect for human dignity, well into the later part of the 19th century.

The Native American Indian did his part too, they were known to dismember bodies and leave them scattered about on display for the next passing white man, in revenge and as a warning. In the south it was not uncommon for white women and children to be captured, enslaved, beaten tortured and killed.

Military records reveal that infants were some times bashed against rocks to kill them. Some have questioned this cruelty. The soldiers killed women and children so for those who question this cruelty ask yourself, how do you think the women and children were killed?

Shooting and bashing in the heads of women and children didn't seem to be a major concern of this government as recently as 1890 at Wounded Knee.

You would have thought the sight of tiny bodies of children bashed in the head and blown to bits by rifle and cannon fire would have gotten the attention of someone who would try to punish those who acted with impunity but few if any ever paid for those crimes.

The Indians had no rights under white-mans' law and if ever accused of a crime he had no representation.

The Native American Indian was treated more harshly than the African American up until after the Civil War. The Indian had no monetary value. A common phrase of the whites, way up into the 20th century, was, *"the only good Indian is a dead Indian"*.

When the white-man came west he saw the land and its resources there for the taking. It did not occur to him to ask the Indian, who was living on the land, what they thought. The Indian saw the land as belonging to all Indians. The white man saw the Indian as owning no land and the Indian could not engage in any land negotiations without the approval of the white man, except to sign away rights to land, through treaties, which were never honored by the whites. The Native American Indian was not considered a

6

citizen of his own country until 1924, when he was declared so by an act of congress. They were (second/no class) citizens and it was even illegal for them to buy liquor from 1832 to 1953.

One such treaty was the "The Treaty of Ruby Valley", signed October 1, 1863, ratified by the U. S. Senate and confirmed by President Ulysses Grant in 1866. This treaty was to bring peace between the whites and the Indians. The Indians would not attack immigrants and settlers and would allow military forts, mail stations and settlements on their (Indian's) land plus mineral extraction. When this treaty was broken, white negotiators, realizing the damage they had already done to Indian lands, agreed to an annuity payment of $5,000, in the form of goods, for a period of 20 years. $5,000 for a territory, the Indians claimed ran from the Snake River, including Rock Creek and what is now Twin Falls, Idaho on the north to Death Valley, California to the south. The treaty was ignored by the whites and the United States Government surveyed and dolled out the Indian lands to the respective states and white ranchers, farmers etc.

THE ROAD ON WHICH WE CAME By Steven J. Crum.

There were whites who recognized the plight of the Indian, but they were too few in number. What little gains they made for the Red Man would be lost to the onslaught of those who were bent on extermination of the Indian including the U. S. Military, Congress or the Administration.

President Andrew Jackson was determined to rid the eastern United States of Indians! Better known as the "Trail of Tears to Oklahoma". During the Oklahoma Land Rush April 22, 1889, thousands rushed into Oklahoma to stake homestead claims on what should have been Indian lands.

Many of us seem to think of those days as long ago. But remember many of us had grandparents that were grown men and women in 1890, at the time of the slaughter at Wounded Knee.

The slaughter at Bear River, Idaho, 1863 courtesy of Col. Patrick Edward Connor was a massacre that took place close to home where this story took place. More than three reports quoted Col. Connor as making this statement when ask what to do with the children *"nits make lice"* and ordered that they all be killed.

7

There were many other brutal killings and mistreatment of the Indians, over the 500 years following the landing of the white European on the American shores, a few are included here: Navajo Trail of Tears carried out by Kit Carson, 1864; Slaughter at Sand Creek, Colorado, November 1864; Campaign of Capt. Hunt through the Owyhee Mts. of Idaho and Nevada, July to October 1866; Military Campaign in the Great Basin and Snake River Plains, 1863 to 1868; The attack and defeat of the Nez Perce 1877; Death March to Yakima from the Malhuer Reservation, 1878; action by white settlers near Squaw Creek, near Ola, Idaho, early 1880s; Yosemite Valley, Calif., 1852; Mill Creek, near Oroville, Calif., 1860s; Slaughter at Wounded Knee, South Dakota, 1890, killing of Osage Indians in the early 1920s for their money Osage County, Oklahoma and then the slaughter at Rabbit Creek, near Golconda, Nevada February 26, 1911, just to name a few.

The decade of the 1860s, was the most gruesome time in history, in the geographic area roughly described as: that area bordered on the east by the foot of the Rocky Mountains, on the west by the Sierra and Cascade Mts., on the south by the now Interstate 80 in Nevada and on the north by the John Day River in Oregon and the northern part of the Snake River Plains in Idaho. I refer to this stretch of real estate as the Northern Great Basin and the Snake River Plains (NGB & SRP). During the decade of the 1860s the military's mission, in this geographical area, was to search out and destroy the Indians and no Indian was left untouched, all Native American Indians were in one of only three situations; 1) being hunted, like vermin, by the soldiers and often by the citizens, 2) located on reservations or 3) scouts for the soldiers. There were a few, small in number, who were trusted and living among the whites but even they were killed in some instances, when they were encountered by the soldiers. Some of those scouting for the soldiers had enemies in other bands or tribes and had joined up with the soldiers to settle old scores. Chief Buffalo Horn, instigator of the Bannock War of 1878 was a scout for the soldiers in the pursuit of Chief Joseph the year before. When the soldiers were in the field hunting and killing Indians, they had only themselves to look after and take care of while the Indian, in a fight for survival, had families (women and children) to protect and care for.

In existing times there are many who are in denial and refuse to take responsibility as a white race and christians, for our actions. They can only provide excuses and, in some form of rhetoric, try to justify those barbaric actions or provide some simplistic excuse such as; they were already killing each other or they [the Natives] have a better life now than when they carried on life in their aboriginal way.

I choose not to go there but for those who do, let their conscience be their guide.

I wonder if the five or ten million who were killed or died at the hands of white man, would feel so great about their sacrifice in order that the small number who survived should enjoy this wonderful life that even today so few experience.

It was a miserable existence for the American Indian following the landing of white man on these shores. Which brings into focus the fact that, although over a period of 400 years, the possibility, that we God fearing Christians, may have brought on the near extinction of a single race through the killing of more people than any other genocidal event in recorded history.

Who told the stories of the interactions, reactions, conflicts etc. between the Indian and the white man? The white man, and he told it the way he wanted history to be heard. There was no other side of the story. Embellishment and fabrication was the norm, there was no rebuttal from the Indian. The more hatred and blame that could be heaped upon the Indian the more justification for their extermination.

Those who had experienced torture or cruelty and had lost loved ones, at the hands of the Indian, were even more motivated to embellish and fabricate stories. In their minds there could be no punishment, to the Indian, that could be considered unjust.

One of the very few stories told by the Indian occurred at Wounded Knee. This story was told by an educated Sioux Indian, Charles Eastman and backed up by photographs. The slaughter at Wounded Knee was not unlike the other atrocities/ slaughters, just better documented, largely due to photographs taken, January 1, 1891. In the book "ENCYCLOPEDIA of Indian Wars - Western Battles and Skirmishes", by Gregory F. Michno, he states *"The pattern is clear, the conclusion obvious: the way to stop Indian depredations against whites was by defeating them in battle, not offering them treaties, presents, and promises"*.

First off, these engagements had very little to do with <u>battles</u>, fights or warfare. As Michno describes these conflicts, they were more akin to slaughters than battles or fights. He also poses the question *"why did the Indians lose so many fights"?* In answering his own question he states *"In the majority of Indian battles, more important than numbers were discipline, tenacity and tactics".*

Michno forgot to mention; 1) better equipment of the soldiers and civilians. 2) The soldiers could return for more supplies. The Indians had no warehouses. 3) The Indians had their families with them. The soldiers and civilians had no such encumbrances. 4) All Indians were fighting, they had no reserves to draw from i.e. new volunteers. 5) Many of the casualties were women and children. 6) The source of his information was the white man not the Indian.

The native population and all other races were about equal, from about the time of the Revolutionary War to 1790 (approx. 4 million).

See chart on population of America - 1492 to 1900

The many stories told and books written, unwittingly describe the plight of the Indian and mentality of the white man.

When references to conflicts with Indians were described, the killing of white people i.e.. Custer, they were referred to as massacres, when referring to the killing of Indians they were referred to as battles. In most cases it was the exact opposite.

It seems we have yet to get the message. On the Borglum View Terrace, at Mount Rushmore, is located, what the Park Service refers to as the "Burkett plaque". The wording on this plaque reads as follows:

ALMIGHTY GOD, FROM THIS PULPIT OF STONE THE AMERICAN PEOPLE RENDER THANKSGIVING AND PRAISE FOR THE NEW ERA OF CIVILIZATION BROUGHT FORTH UPON THIS CONTINENT. CENTURIES OF TYRANNICAL OPPRESSION SENT TO THESE SHORES, GOD-FEARING MEN TO SEEK IN FREEDOM THE GUIDANCE OF THE BENEVOLENT HAND IN THE PROGRESS TOWARD WISDOM, GOODNESS TOWARD MEN, AND FIETY TOWARD GOD.

The facts are, these God Fearing Men brought forth their own tyrannical oppression on those already on this continent, the Native American Indian and further imported another race of people, the African American, to oppress and enslave.

One might wonder why I discuss these horrible events in such detail. The answer will become clear in the analysis of the tragic event to follow in 1910 and 1911.

POPULATION CHART

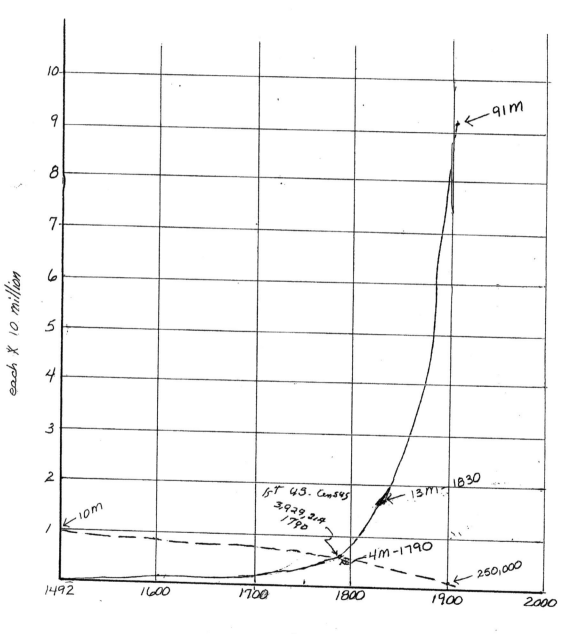

each × 10 million

10

9 ← 91m

8

7

6

5

4

3

2 — 1st U.S. Census — 13m 1830
3,929,214
1790

1 ← 10m ← 4m-1790
← 250,000

1492   1600   1700   1800   1900   2000

- - - - - Native American
_____ All other exotic Americans

11

WOUNDED KNEE SOUTH DAKOTA
January 1, 1891

Carnage left by the 7th Cavalry, at Wounded Knee, after their attack on the Indians, December 29, 1890. Charles Eastman, was asked to go to the sight of the attack, to see if there were any survivors. A blizzard struck the day after the killing and Eastman did not arrive at the scene until Jan. 1, with 100 volunteers, mostly Indians, to search for survivors and wounded. Eastman was a Sioux Indian educated as a medical Doctor.

"Fully 3 miles from the scene of the massacre we found the body of a woman completely covered with a blanket of snow and from this point on we found them scattered along as they had been relentlessly hunted down and slaughtered, fleeing for their lives".

Charles Alexander Eastman

Among the dead, along with unarmed men, women and children, were comrades of their own, from the 7th Cavalry, who were caught in the cross fire.

WOUNDED KNEE SOUTH DAKOTA

January 1, 1891

As can be seen by this photo, the 7th Cavalry left nothing for survival. However surprising as it was, Eastman found a few survivors. Others, including women and children, succumbed to the blizzard and the cold, as they ran and hid to escape the slaughter.

The white man's edict to the Indian was, become a christian, be educated and you will be assimilated into our society. Charles Eastman, a Sioux Indian, did just that. Eastman became a christian and was educated as a medical doctor. He was employed by the government, as a doctor, at the Pine Ridge Indian Agency, in South Dakota (Dakota Territory) November 1890. When he expressed empathy for the Indian, he was no longer accepted and was forced out of the government in 1893..

WOUNDED KNEE SOUTH DAKOTA

January 1, 1891

A result of the slaughter by the 7th Cavalry December 29, 1890.

Not unlike Wounded Knee, only in a much smaller scale, the slaughter at Rabbit Creek, near Golconda, Nevada, February 26, 1911, is another example of the pack mentality of the white man.

WOUNDED KNEE SOUTH DAKOTA

January 1, 1891

Mass burial after the slaughter of Indians at Wounded Knee, South Dakota.
Does this look familiar, like in a more recent time at Auschwitz or Bergen-Belsen?
Note: Trench is less than five feet deep. How much soil will be on top covering the bodies?
This burial site is located on private land and is unaccessible to the Native American Indian.

CHAPTER II

THEY WERE BANNOCK and SHOSHONE

Into this carnage of death and destruction were born two people, who became known as Mike and **Jenny** Daggett. After Mike's death he became known as SHOSHONE MIKE. Mike gave himself that name as he lay dying, after being shot by posse members, February 26, 1911, when asked "what kind of an Indian are you anyway"? He responded "me Shoshone." But he never heard himself called by the name "Shoshone Mike," he died before he ever heard the name spoken.

From the inquest after his death

In the country where he was best known for over thirty years, he was more commonly known as Indian Mike.

Mike's aboriginal name may have been (On-don-gae-te). **Jenny's** aboriginal name may have been (So pau a gah).

Indian names arrived at from records at Fort Hall, Idaho

Down through history Mike's wife's name was given as **Jenny** however Anna Hansen Hays, author of the book "BUCKSKIN AND SMOKE", referred to Mike's wife as Maggie. Anna knew the Daggett family. Could it be that was the correct name? Anna (Hansen) Hays and Carrie (Hansen) Crockett were sisters and the daughters of Mr and Mrs John Hansen who owned the Rock Creek Store for eight years, 1900 through 1908. Carrie, in a letter written to Mike's granddaughter, dated November 5, 1975, asked the granddaughter if her grand mother's name was Maggie.

Her name was **Maggie** not Jenny as will be explained later.

Mike would have been born around 1845 and Maggie around 1855.

The first documentation of their existence came about with a family interview of Carrie Crockett, in about 1972. Carrie Crockett's husband, George Crockett, arrived with his family, as a small boy of two years, at Rock Creek in the summer of 1880. That fall the Crocketts discovered that they had built their homestead cabin adjacent to the Daggett's winter camp site.

Carrie estimated Mike and Maggie's oldest son to be about seven years old, at the time.

PIONEER CHILDREN AND THEIR INDIAN FRIENDS
by Charlotte Crockett
Narrated by Carrie (Hansen) Crockett ca. 1972

On July 4, 1880 a covered wagon drawn by a weary team of horses was making its way slowly up Rock Creek Canyon. There was no road, only trails made by horsemen and the running gears of a few wagons going up to haul wood from the canyon. The occupants of the wagon, Edwin and Phoebe Crockett and their three small sons, were looking for a place to camp for the night. They had left Grouse Creek, Utah, several days before. The team was tired and night was coming on, they must find a place to camp for the night. They had passed two ranches when they saw a stream near the road, there was plenty of grass for the horses and the two cows following the wagon. Brush for firewood was plentiful, so they decided to stop, it seemed like a good place for much needed rest. Soon they had a cheerful fire going and supper, cooked over the open fire, was soon ready.

After the children, Eddie four, George two, and Mel but five months old, were in bed sleeping Edwin and Phoebe looked over the area around them and decided that this would be a good place for a permanent location , there was plenty of good land , water for irrigation could come from the creek and pasture grass was plentiful.

There was much to be done before winter to make a permanent home. There was no timber in sight for house logs, so a scouting trip must be made to locate suitable logs; however, it was not long before a one room cabin was built. Sheds and corrals for the stock came next and plenty of fire wood was gathered for the winter.

Eddie, the oldest boy, was only four years old and very curious about everything, so he needed watching to keep him out of the creek and from straying into the large brush where he could easily be lost. Pioneer living was never easy, but this family had learned to meet each day with courage and solve the problems as they came.

In the spring, getting the land cleared and a crop in, besides planting a garden took most of Edwin's time. A garden was necessary as the nearest town where all kinds of supplies could be purchased was Kelton, Utah, one hundred miles away, a long trip for horses and wagon. The care of the children was Phoebe's responsibility as well as caring for the garden, which with the housework kept Phoebe too busy to get lonely even in this remote land.

When fall came, they were surprised one morning to see some Indians making camp not far from their newly built cabin. There was no way to know if the Indians were friendly, so Phoebe was more than ever anxious about the children, especially that curious Eddie. They soon learned that this Indian family had made this there winter home for years, and that there was nothing to fear from them.

There were three boys in the Indian family, quite near the same ages of the Crockett boys, and they would come almost to the cabin as they hunted rocks and other treasures that children like to keep. Eddie, always curious, shyly approached the Indian boys, Mike and Johnie, to join them in their play; the youngest Indian boy Jim was too small to go so far from the camp. Eddie and the two boys became friends and spent most of their time together. Mike, the oldest, would sometimes come to the Crockett home for a short time, but he was shy about playing in the house. When winter came it was too cold for the little boys to get out to play together.

Mike was seven so he sometimes went with his father on short hunting trips, he would shoot birds with his small bow and arrows and fish in the creek near-by.

Spring finally came and one morning when Eddie went out to find his new friends they were gone. The Indians had left their winter camp and started back toward the higher country where they would spend the summer. Eddie was lonesome and often said "Ma, where is Mike and Johnie, will they come back to play with me?"

There were no children at either of the nearest ranches so the children were alone again to amuse themselves. George was nearly three and Eddie was trusted to see that he did not go far from the house. They would often try to help their mother in the garden, but children of that size usually do more harm than good, but Phoebe realized they had to have something to do to keep them busy so if they pulled a few vegetables instead of weeds, she just tried to show them the difference and let them play at making their own little garden.

Every fall when the weather began to get cool the Indians would be back to the old camping ground. Each year as the children grew older they learned more from each other, the Indian boys would show them how to set snares to catch cottontail rabbits and to shoot with a bow and arrow. As they grew older they all spent a lot of time fishing, the water in the creek was never very high in the fall so they were safe. The Indian boys had their ponies and all the boys would spend a lot of time riding, hunting and fishing. Every spring the salmon would come up the creek on the way to their spawning grounds. Hundreds of the large fish would be seen swimming up the creek and it was great sport to catch them. The Indian boys built a willow dam across a narrow place in the creek, then below that they would build two half dams with the ends of the willows pointing up the creek making a V shaped opening for the fish to go into. When the fish are on the way to the spawning grounds they never turn back, so it was easy to trap them. The boys would all get in the water and catch the fish with their hands, when they had all they wanted each day they would take part of the dam out and give the salmon a chance to go on up the stream, later they would rebuild the upper dam and catch more another day. They dressed their fish and smoked them for winter food, any variation of the regular diet was a welcome change to both families.

Deer were plentiful and there was no law preventing settlers from killing them for meat, at that time that was all they were used for, people were not interested in trophies, just meat for the table. Fishing and hunting were not all the things the Indian boys taught the Crockett boys, they also showed them how to dig Sego lily bulbs and cook them, when cooked they are very much like potatoes and good to eat. Another root they dug was Salsify oyster plant which when cooked tastes much like oysters.

After several years the Indians did not return to their old camping ground, the boys lost some very good friends but gained a good education in self preservation.

Mike was in his late teens to early twenties, during the 1863 to 1868 military campaign to subdue and kill Indians, in the Northern Great Basin and the Snake River Plains ((NGB & SRP).

Neither Mike nor Maggie were ever listed on the rolls of the Fort Hall Indian Reservation nor any other reservation and would have experienced first hand the ruthlessness of the military mission to subdue and rid the red-man of their ancestral lands. By the end of the 1860s nearly all the Indians that had not been killed were now on Indian Reservations.

If Mike was ever a participant in a raiding party or shot at by the soldiers during a search and destroy mission, who knows for sure, it is highly unlikely he could have avoided such an encounter.

It appears Mike and Maggie had established a routine of migrating back and forth, from Rock Creek to Gollaher Mountain in Nevada, by the early 1870s. They were not likely there before then.

On September 13, 1864, Lieutenant West with fifteen men, of the Washington Infantry were sent out to Shoshone Falls and Rock Creek to scout for Indians. They traveled up Rock Creek into the Goose Creek Mountains and back to the Snake River, without spotting any Indians, returning to their Salmon Fall Creek Camp, on September 23rd.

THE DEADLIEST INDIAN WAR IN THE WEST by Gregory Michno - page 69

The mountains Lieutenant West traveled into are located southeast of Twin Falls, Idaho and are referred to as the South Hills. They include the drainages of Rock Creek and Goose Creek. The range lies mostly in Idaho but extends south into Nevada.

It seems that the name, Goose Creek Mountains, would have been more appropriate than the South Hills, as they are known now..

In 1864 Mike would have been about twenty years old and Maggie about ten, no family started yet.

During the mid to late 1870s, the last push was made to confine **all** Indians to reservations.

The Shoshone could see the hand writing on the wall and were one of the early tribes to submit to the white mans pressure and accept their lot in life on the hell holes that were set up for them, better known as Indian Reservations. To not submit meant death and starvation, although this often occurred on the Reservations as well. The Bannocks were much more troublesome to the whites and for awhile the only time they were on the reservation, was when they went through it. This was seen as a plus by some Indian agents, as they were always short of subsistence for the people on the reservation and had the Bannocks hung around, there would have been even more starvation.

This is another example of *"the stories told make us who we are"*

John Beater Professor, Boise State University

The whites saw them as war like and to be more feared than other tribes in the area. When the soldiers encountered Indians in battle, especially if they were defeated, they would claim there were Bannock included in with the combatants.

20

By way of illustration, when Lieutenant Littlefield and Captain Wells encountered/battled a large number of Indians on Table Mountain (later called Gonfry Mountain and now Toe Jam Mountain in Elko County, Nevada) in May of 1865, Wells reported that there were Bannock Indians with the Shoshone on the mountain. I have been there at that site there is no way Captain Wells could have determined what tribe of Indians he was fighting on Table Mountain.

The other tribes saw them as more dangerous and feared. To live up to their reputation the Bannocks saw themselves as more war like and feared.

The Bannocks roamed from the Steens Mountains in Oregon, east into Wyoming where they hunted the buffalo.

The taking of Camas Prairie, located in south central Idaho, by the white farmers, and other atrocities, led to the Bannock war of 1878. Chief Buffalo Horn, who instigated the uprising, was killed early on and the war was short lived.

This was the straw that finally broke the backs of the Bannocks. Camas Prairie was the source of the Camas bulb, one of the main staple of the Indians diet. Camas Prairie was promised to the Indians by treaty but when white man decided he wanted it back, they quickly conjured up a way to take it away.

During these years of turmoil, many of the Bannocks intermingled with Shoshones to escape detection. The Shoshone were the fair haired Indians of the whites and the white man couldn't tell them apart. It made perfect sense to Mike to refuse to go to the reservation, choose a Shoshone girl for a wife and maintain the old ways of the Indian, migrate with the seasons and live off the land.

I agree with Dayton O. Hyde, in his book THE LAST FREE MAN, Mike was of the Bannock tribe. I disagree with Dayton, that Jenny/Maggie was of the Ute tribe, she was Shoshone. Also, according to Colonel J. W. Reddington, Henny, Mike's youngest daughter spoke a mixture of Shoshone and Bannock. This may or may not be true. Reddington and the newspapers had very little credibility. Reddington claimed to be a scout and courier during the Indian wars.

Nevada State Journal March 5, 1911.

The Nevada State Journal, dated January 16, 1911, ran an article which included a statement by the Colonel, stating that *"Mike was at the Indian slaughter of Bear River, in the southeast corner of Idaho, in 1863".* This was a figment of his imagination. Maggie could have been one of the few survivors, but not likely. There is no evidence that there were Bannocks at the Bear River killing.

It is not known for sure when Mike and Maggie took up winter residence in Rock Creek. The fact that they were settled into their migratory way of life by 1880 and had started a family by the early 1870s would suggest they were using this as their winter encampment before 1875.

Mike had had enough of war and wanted no part of the reservation life, so he hunkered down at Rock Creek and migrated south in the spring to the Gollaher Mountains, in Nevada, returning to Rock Creek each fall.

When Chief Buffalo Horn sparked the uprising of the Bannock War, at the end of the 1870s, Mike laid low and let that conflict blow over him. The Daggetts floated under the radar, so to speak. Maybe life was good for Mike by the early 1870s. He had settled down and made friends with white folks.

It is most likely Mike and Maggie grew up separately, each living, for the most part, a nomadic way of life. A life, not by choice, but by events of history and the constant harassment of Indians by the white immigrants. Any pattern of movement left them vulnerable to attack and elimination.

The Mike Daggett family lived peacefully among the whites for over thirty years and possibly for more than thirty five years.

ROCK CREEK LADIES CLUB at a meeting APRIL 12, 1907 at the home of MRS. WRIGHT.
Back row-AUGUSTA BROSE, MRS. LAURA ALBEE, MRS. MARY LARSEN, MRS. LUCY STRICKER,
MRS. ELLEN CLINE AND MRS. WRIGHT.
Middle row-MRS. MARY HANSEN, MRS. HANNAH PETERSEN, MRS. PHOEBE CROCKETT, MRS.
IDA RORABACK.
Front row-MISS OLLIE CLINE, MRS. MARY DOMROSE, MRS. ETHEL SAWYER.
MRS. PHOEBE CROCKETT was President

ROCK CREEK LADIES CLUB

April 12, 1907

This may be the last photo taken of Phoebe Crockett, she passed away in July of 1907. Edwin and Phoebe Crockett arrived at Rock Creek on July 4, 1880. They built a cabin and took up a homestead. The property where the original cabin was built, has remained in the Crockett family since that time. The home of David and Debbie Crockett is located near the sight of the original cabin. Unbeknown to the Crocketts they had built their cabin adjacent to the winter encampment of Indians, Mike and Maggie Daggett. The Indian family, in their annual migration had been arriving at Rock Creek in the fall and leaving in the spring.

CHAPTER III
INDIAN WAYS and SUBSISTENCE

Mike and Maggie took up residency near the mouth of Rock Creek Canyon, located twelve miles southeast of Twin Falls, Idaho, sometime in the early 1870s . This began as a winter headquarters and from here they established a migration route that led south up into the mountains and on in to Northern Nevada, more specifically Gollaher Mountain.

West and down Rock Creek, two and one half miles, from their camp, stood the small community of Rock Creek, Idaho. Included in the businesses there was the Rock Creek General Store, erected in 1894. John Hansen owned and operated the Rock Creek Store, from around 1900 until 1909. The Crockett's second oldest son, George, married Carrie Hansen the daughter of John and Marry Hansen, of Rock Creek, in 1905. The Daggetts visited here often to trade for and/ or purchase their meager needs. Mike and his family carried a charge tab at the San Jacinto store/commissary and probably had one at Rock Creek as well. There are few, if any, of the original buildings in existence today at the town of Rock Creek.

Mike was trusted by all who knew him and his family. No one in the country, which the Daggetts traveled, was concerned that they might not be paid.

The San Jacinto Commissary was located on the San Jacinto Ranch, eight miles south of Jackpot Nevada. During Mike Daggett's time the Commissary was owned by the Sparks/Harrell Co. and later the Vineyard Land & Stock Co.

 Mike was the chief or patriarch of the family. There is little evidence that any one other than Mike's immediate family, spent much time with this small band of Indians. As the family grew so did the number of members residing within the family. They were a close knit group and as the children grew up they did not venture far, except when they went to work for farmers and ranchers at seasonal jobs. Those seasonal jobs were, primarily in the hay fields or helping with the cattle, on and or near their seasonal route.

Around 1910 their numbers were fluctuating between 12 and 14. In the early to mid 1870s there may have been only Mike, his wife and two sons. By the late fall of 1880 there were several kids running around, one as old as seven.

By the time Mike and Maggie had started a family, their way of life had changed dramatically, from a mostly nomadic way of life to strictly migratory. The Daggetts existed and carried on in this manner but it may not have been, necessarily, by choice. The settling of the west by white man had put the final lance into the heart of a nomadic way of life for all Native American Indians.

In the beginning the migration route and the timing of that route, by the Daggetts, was predicated on the seasons and weather patterns but also had to coincide closely with availability of food they could hunt or gather. The highs and lows of animal population cycles and the droughts and severe winters had to be dealt with as best they could. Their survival depended upon their survival skills and their mental and physical toughness. The winter of 1889 and 1890, proceeded by the severe drought of 1889, had to have been one of those challenging times for the Daggetts. Most of the livestock ranchers in the area lost 90% of their herds. Horror stories go on and on about the winter of 1889 & 90. Most ranching operations in the Northern Great Basin and adjoining areas had similar losses, which led to near 90% bankruptcies.

Those early ranchers that brought large numbers of livestock into Mike's area of subsistence included John Sparks - 1868, Armstrong - 1868, A. D. Norton & W. G. Robison - 1871, A. J. "Barley" Harrell - 1872 and John Tinnin - early 1870s. By 1873 the Elko County ranges were considered fully stocked and by 1885 John Sparks recognized the ranges were being over grazed.

CATTLE on the COLD DESERT BY Jim Young, Range Scientist - USDA & Abbot Sparks, Nephew of John Sparks

There is some information floating around that the Daggetts spent the winter of 1909 & 1910 in the vicinity of the San Jacinto Ranch. This is not likely the Winter temps at San Jacinto often reached 10 degrees below zero while at the 5th Fork of Rock Creek those winter temps probably seldom reached down to 0.

By the 1880s Sparks and Tinnin had formed a partnership and engaged in the cattle business. They amassed a huge cattle empire that extended from the Snake River to the north, Wells, Nevada to the south, east into Utah and west to the Bruneau River in Idaho.

Subsequent owners of this vast cattle empire included Sparks & Harrell and the Vineyard Stock & Land Company which latter became Utah Construction Company (UC). They ran cattle over the entire area on which the Daggetts roamed over, migrated and subsisted. The Daggett area of operation was all within the confines of this vast area. In fact they subsisted on less than one quarter of the total cattle range.

At the time these companies were running between 40 and 50,000 head of cattle in three states.

By 1880, in the west, there had been over twenty years of invasion by the white man upon the Indian lands, like locusts, with plows and hordes of livestock.

By 1880 some 96 thousand head of cattle were running in Northeast Nevada (basically Elko county) making it ever more difficult for the Daggett family to find feed for their horses. Late in the 1800s the cattle and sheep men were in major conflict, over range, each believing one was crowding the other. If there was no room for the cattle and sheep men, where does that leave the Daggetts? They were caught in the middle. Mike was experiencing extreme pressure as farmers and ranchers squeezed him into an ever smaller and more crowded existence. Maybe that is the reason their horses were always in such poor condition.

Before the European white man arrived on the scene , North America, plant and animal life, including the Native American Indian, fluctuated. Life evolved through cycles predicated on population numbers, disease and the ever changing weather patterns, whether it be annual or long term. The effect on all life from these forces caused erratic cycles, depending upon, which stage each species was at when a particular weather event took place.

Now, adding to all of these factors, the high numbers of livestock being brought into the country was beginning to take a toll on the big game on which the Daggett family greatly depended.

The grazing pressure denuded the areas they relied on for feed for their horses, mainly around water. This included those same areas the Daggetts needed for camp sites.

All those resources the Indian depended on, fish, wildlife and vegetation, were being heavily impacted or totally destroyed.

What once were lush meadows around springs and along steams, became beat out (destroyed) meadows and bog holes.

The Indian would not ever dare to take down a beef to eat. The repercussions brought upon them would have been severe. Butchering beef led to the destruction of the Daggetts, as will be illustrated later.

In addition to the impacts from grazing cattle was the depletion of the salmon runs.

Up and until the late 1880s, the spring salmon runs also factored into their daily food requirements but by the late 1890s that source of food had nearly dried up.

The best explanations are in two quotes, compiled by Bob McQuivey, Nev. division of Wild Life, 1995 records research of Historical Records i.e. the Tuscarora, Nevada newspapers; TOWN TALK -(Volume 34, Number 130 - Saturday, April 15, 1899) *"It has been reported that salmon have been seen in the valley streams, but so far none have been caught. In years past this was a recognized sport, but for many years, owing to the dams and traps further down the river, very few salmon have been able to ascend the streams this far"* and (Volume 35, Number 148 Tuesday, May 22, 1900): *"Ed Johnson, Frank Bowen and Neil Snyder caught the first salmon of the season last Sunday on Hot Creek. These fish used to ascend the creeks around here in swarms, but the cannery traps between here and the ocean have almost completely stopped the runs, and a salmon is now almost a curiosity."*

The influx of cattle and their impact on the spawning beds had to of also been a factor in the decline of the salmon runs.

The final devastating shot to the Indians of the upper Snake and to their main food supply along the Snake, came in 1901 with the construction of the Swan Falls dam. To the upper head waters of the Snake the salmon would run no more!

The Swan Falls dam is located about twenty five miles south of Boise, Idaho, on the Snake River.

Mikes' migration route would have taken many different trails, dictated by the white man and their ever changing activities. The influx of cattle from the Texas cattle drives, beginning in the late 1860s and into the 1900s, were depleting the range of forage for his horses as well as for the stock now on the range. Feed for his horses become more scarce each year as livestock continued to pile into northeastern Nevada and southern Idaho.

As time passed and Mikes children grew older, his boys and the rest of the family began to recognize and experience their ever shrinking world with less resources and more white man intervention.

Though the surrounding farms and ranches provided seasonal employment, as they grew older it had to grate on the boys to be so governed by the white man's invasion of their land and migratory ways. It is understandable that the sons of Mike would become more embittered and resentful of the white man. Why should the white man get every thing he wanted at their expense?

The Indians, not being citizens in their own country, could not buy, sell, trade or own land, without the permission of the whites.

Each year as the family moved about the country, they would find more cattle and less feed for their horses.

Mike who grew up during the decade of the 1860s, would have been more tolerant. This life as restricting as it was, was better than being constantly hunted by the soldiers who's mission was to kill as many Indians as possible.

For over thirty five years, in-spite of their history, the Daggett family remained honest and friendly with all the white people they had contact with and who knew them. District Forester, G. A. Gutches traveled to southern Idaho, in late January or early February 1910, to investigate reports of a missing Shoshone Indian family, that being Indian Mike and his family. Gutches forwarded a report on his investigation to E. P. Holcombe, Chief Supervisor, Fort Hall Indian Agency, February 6, 1910. His investigation included, acquiring written reports and interviewing all the people he was able to contact. Each and every one he interviewed, (some of those had known the Daggetts for 20 or 30 years) and the written reports, described the family as: industrious, honest and friendly, even to the point that they were trusted to carry a tab at the San Jacinto store/commissary. Even Gay Tranmer (whom we will meet later) said they had always been friendly, in his statement to Elko Authorities September 20, 1910.

The Shoshone Mike papers from the National Archives in W. D. C. which include letters from, District Attorney of Cassia County, Idaho, T. Bailey Lee, the report by G . A. Gutches, District Forester, dated Feb. 6, 1911, written statements by Del Hardy, dated Jan. 29, 1911 and W. J. Gumble, dated Jan. 31, 1911.

Dayton O. Hyde, in his book THE LAST FREE MAN, reported that from interviewing folks around Rock Creek, Idaho and as far south as San Jacinto Ranch in Nevada, Mike and his family had many friends who knew the family well. All those who traded with the family at Rock Creek, San Jacinto, ranches in the area and other camps, knew the family to be friendly and very honest. Dayton had begun his research and interviews in the 1960s however long before Hyde's book these same reports existed. The Daggett's winter camp, on Rock Creek, where they resided five to seven months each year, was their most permanent home. They existed in this semi "nomadic" way of life. Their only alternative was an Indian reservation.

In those early years the Daggetts most likely migrated up through Rock Creek Canyon and over Deadline Ridge, after the Salmon runs in the spring, and when the Camas began to grow so they could find the bulbs. Then in the fall they came back over the top of the Mountain at the head of Rock Creek when many of the native berries were ripening, such as Choke Cherry, Service Berry, Currents and many others. In those early times Mike and family traveled by horse back, but as the family grew this mode of travel became ever more difficult so Mike acquired a wagon and from this point on they would have had to migrate back and forth through Shoshone Basin, rather than Rock Creek. There was no road up Rock Cr. and over the top of the mountain (South Hills / Deadline Ridge) until long after Mikes' time, when the C.C.C.s built the current road.

It is somewhat of a mystery as to where the Daggetts kept their horses, during the winter months, at Rock Creek. Although they may not have kept more than 8 or 10, near their winter camp, the homesteaders in Rock Creek would not have wanted the horses on their private land.

In interviews with David Crockett and Sherry Hillman, grandchildren of Carrie Crockett, and from stories passed down to them, that mystery may have two answers. One, the homesteaders and ranchers in the area ran their horses in the surrounding foot hills, during the winter, the other, there is an area known as Nellie's flat about three miles up the Fifth Fork of Rock Creek. On the steep hillside, above the flat, on the east side of the creek, a rock fence had been constructed and on the flat below, what appears to be a pit house, exists. The rock fence was about four feet high and about seventy yards long. Its construction was a major undertaking. The pit house appears to have been about ten to twelve feet across and estimated to be at least six feet deep.

The story is that an Indian lady, by the name of Nellie, a part of or related to the Indian Mike family, camped or lived here and watched after the Daggett's horses. It makes perfect sense that the Indian family would visit back and forth from their winter camp to Nellie's Flat. There is also some historical information that indicates an Indian lady, by the name of Nellie, stayed behind and did not always migrate with the family. She may have stayed in the area year around, traveled to Fort Hall, Bannock Creek or to Tacoma, Nevada to work in the store there.

In her book "BUCKSKIN AND SMOKE" Anna Hays talked extensively about Nellie the daughter of Maggie thus the daughter of Mike Daggett and how she made gloves, moccasins and other things out of Indian tanned buckskin. Without a doubt Nellie the daughter and Nellie the sister of Maggie are one and the same.

If the Daggetts wanted to have horses where they could have easy access to them, then Nellie's Flat would be the perfect place. It would be quite difficult, if not impossible, to have ready access to horses mixed up with the those of others running in the surrounding hills. Even if they did have horses out there, they would need two or three saddle horses handy to go and gather their other horses. The reasons for having horses readily available are many which would include: going to Rock Creek to trade, hunting of game in the nearby mountains, travel to meet other friends or relatives in the area, travel to part time employment on nearby ranches etc.

In addition their winter camp site, in the Fifth Fork was high enough that the inversions layers along the Snake River did not impact them. The temperatures likely ran 10 to 15 degrees warmer than down along the Snake River and the the sunny days were many more than down in the valley. The rock fence appears to have never been finished, it tied into rim rock on the lower end but was open on the upper end.

On April, 25, 1911, the superintendent of the Carson Indian School at Stewart, Nevada, C. H. Asbury, interviewed Henie, the youngest daughter of Indian Mike. From that interview, Asbury the following information: *she had an aunt, sister to her mother, living in Tacoma, Nevada and that this aunt and her husband work right there all the time about the store* (This aunt could be Nellie). And also that the Daggett family lived off the land, plus wages he and his boys earned doing seasonal work on the various farms and ranches.

Tacoma was a small station on the Southern Pacific Railroad, near the Utah line.

This information was found in a letter from Asbury, dated April 27, 1911, to the Commissioner of Indian Affairs, Washington, D. C. but never verified.

National Archives W. D. C.

They also earned money from the sale of the many items of buckaroo paraphernalia they made, such as: reatas, bridle reins and quirts (all made from rawhide), horse hair ropes, gloves and other items, made from buckskin they tanned themselves. They also traded as many of these items as they sold. To this day there is no better leather for the making of moccasins, gloves or clothing than that tanned by the Native American Indian.

The art of making reatas, quirts and bridle reins from rawhide was learned from the old Spanish Vaqueros out of California and was brought to Mike by the Buckaroos (Vaqueros) migrating from California.

In the statement Gay Tranmer made to the authorities in Elko, Nevada, September 20, 1910, Gay stated Jim (son of Mike Daggett) *"is quite a hand at all kinds of hair work and rawhide work"*. *"(he)Generally rides with a good rig, silver mounted spurs and bit"*. Henry Harris may have been an influence to the Indians in regard to their fancy buckaroo stuff.

There are references other than Gay's about the fancy equipment owned and used by the Daggetts. Their fancy gear, reflections of the California Spanish vaqueros , would set them apart from many of the other buckaroos/cowboys in that part of the country. One exception, Henry Harris the black foreman/wagon boss for the Vineyard Land & Livestock Co., also rode with a fancy vaquero outfit.

ROCK CREEK IDAHO (Old Rock Creek Station)

The building at right, was erected in 1894 as a log store and built by J. F. Tatro, the building was owned by Mr & Mrs John Hayes. Hansen bought it in 1900 and made two additions to it before moving his business to Hansen, Idaho in 1908. In its heyday it also served as a Post Office. Hansen sold it to his daughter Anna and son in law in 1909, when it was closed.

Those who traded here, during the twelve years of its operation, included the Tranmers, Girdners, Henry Harris and Indian Mike Daggett & his family. The other daughter of Hansen, Carrie Hansen married George Crockett, in about 1905. George, one of three sons, was two years old when the Crocketts took up a homestead on Rock Creek, in the summer of 1880. One day, in the fall of that year the Crocketts were surprised, when just up the creek from there newly built cabin, they saw an Indian family setting up camp. Although some what apprehensive at first, the Crocketts soon learned that the Indians were friendly and had been migrating here for a number of years, making this their winter camp. These Indians were the Mike Daggett family. They also had three sons, near the same age as the Crockett boys, the oldest, six or seven. The Daggett kids and the Crockett kids played and grew up together, at least about six months out of the year when the Daggetts were in there winter encampment. In the later part of April of 1910, their way of life ended, no more migrating to the high country in the summer and back to Rock Creek in the winter. The recorded story of (Shoshone) Mike Daggett had began.

SAN JACINTO POST OFFICE STORE/COMMISSARY
1917
POST OFFICE
SAN JACINTO

This structure, built in 1898 by the late John Sparks, one time Governor of Nevada, is located on the San Jacinto Ranch, eight miles south of Jackpot, Nevada, near highway 93. Sandstone blocks, used in construction, were quarried from a quarry 24 miles northeast of this location, at the confluence of Goose Creek and Little Goose Creek. Large iron shutters were installed on the doors and windows, for protection & security of the Post Office and store inventory. They are still operable today, 2011. Stories abound that the steel shutters were to protect against Indian raids, however the last Indian raid in the country occurred 20 years earlier.

During the late 1800s, San Jacinto was the early headquarters of the Sparks & Harrell cattle empire. They ran cattle in three states; northeast Nevada, southern Idaho and stretching into Utah. Among the people of legend, who traded here from time of construction until their death, include; Henry Harris, legendary black wagon boss and ranch foreman who worked for the different owners of the ranch and supervised white cowboys here, from the late 1800s to 1913. Henry was working for the Utah Construction Co. when he died in 1937 at age 73. Another, included Indian Mike or Mike Daggett, more famously known as (Shoshone Mike) and his family, from time of construction until late April of 1910.

SAN JACINTO STORE
ca 1943
CONOCO
UTAH CONSTRUCTION CO

April 8, 2011

35

SALMON RUNS

Scenes like this, of salmon spawning, would have been common in Rock Creek, when white man arrived in southern Idaho and during the early days of the Daggett family. Commercial fishing and fish wheels along the Colombia and Snake Rivers had had a huge impact on salmon runs by the late 1800s.

Report by Bob McQuive, Nevada Division of Wildlife, 1994 & 1995

The impact of livestock on spawning beds in the upper reaches of the Columbia River Basin also contributed to the decimated salmon runs by 1900. No salmon entered those streams to spawn above Swan Falls Dam, after its construction in 1901.

Salmon, when spawning, turned bright red and getting horses to cross these streams with a sea of salmon moving in the water may have been near impossible.

NELLIE'S FLAT

October, 2014

5TH Fork of Rock Creek Looking northeast down stream

The line that can be seen on the far hill side is a rock fence.

Arrow points to what was once a pit-house located at the lower end of the meadow.

Nellie's Flat is located on National Forest lands southeast of Twin Falls, Idaho.

ROCK FENCE
November 7, 2013

David Crockett (great grandson of Edwin & Phoebe Crockett) is standing next to the rock fence. This fence was probably constructed around 1890, give or take five or ten years, by Indian Mike Daggett and his family. The fence, which looks to have been about four feet high ties into a rim rock on the lower end and a rock out cropping on the upper end. The upper end of Nellies Flat and the Fifth Fork of Rock Creek, can be seen in the upper right of the photo.

The Daggetts camped on Rock Creek during the winter and migrated south into Nevada in the spring then returning in the fall. Nellies Flat would have been the ideal place to keep their horses during the winter months.

Large Pit or Depression

V

REMNANTS of a PIT-HOUSE
November 7, 2013

A living structure (Pit House) once occupied this site and served as a dwelling for the Daggett family from the late 1800s to 1910. It appears to have been 10 to 12 feet across and about 6 feet deep. The structure most likely had a woven willow type roof with sod on top. It is located, at the lower end of Nellies Flat, about two miles up the Fifth Fork of Rock Creek, near Twin Falls, Idaho. Nellies Flat is actually a meadow that runs along the creek in an area where the canyon opens up to 80 to 100 yards wide. This flat or meadow got its name from an Indian lady, by the name of Nellie, who lived here part time, watching after the horses of Indian Mike / Mike Daggett. Nellie is believed to be part of the Indian Mike family, either the older daughter of Mike or a sister to Mike's wife Maggie. A rock fence is located across the creek on the steep hill side. Although rather strange in its location, it was used to control the horses of the Indians, either to keep them up on the bench between the rims or down on the flat along the creek or both, during the fall and winter season when they migrated back from Gollaher Mountain. The story of Nellies Flat was passed down from one generation of the Crockett family to the next.

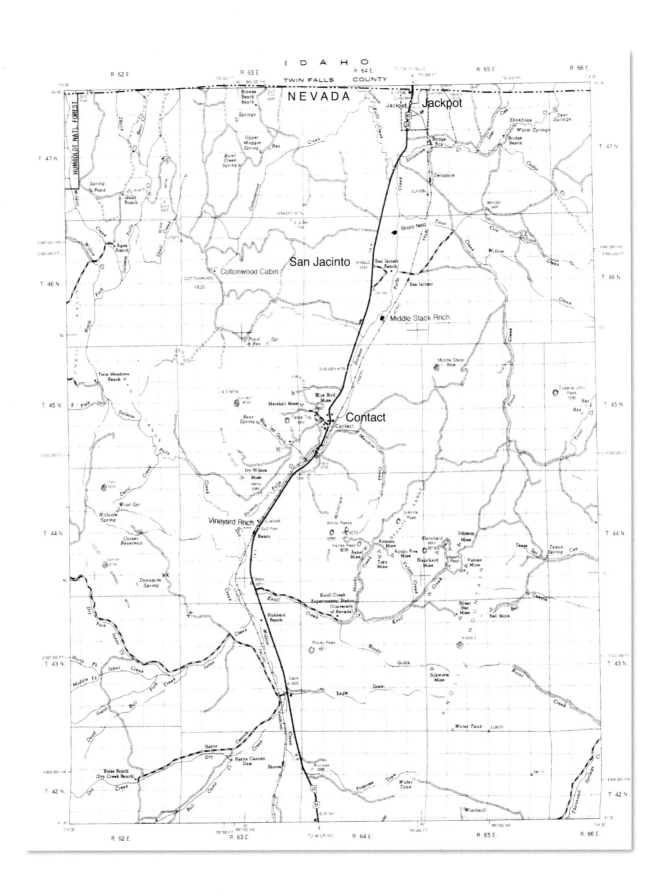

40

Courtesy Herrett Center - College of Idaho - Twin Falls, Idaho

CLAY POT (SHOSHONE)
This artifact measures approximately eleven inches across at the top.

The above pot, found by irrigators near the Daggett's winter camp on Rock Creek SE of Twin Falls, Idaho, was donated to the Harrett Center, by the Crockett family.
Staff at the Herrett Center and the Crockett family, who have owned the property, where it was found, since the 1880s, do not believe this vessel was used by the Daggetts.
I am not so sure. Clay pots are quite fragile and difficult to transport on horses. Indians in times past would leave or hide grinding stones and this type of vessel at more permanent camp sites, to come back to, as they migrated back and forth from winter to summer camps.
It is most likely the Daggetts did the same,during those early days, before they acquired more modern cook ware and before they had a wagon for transport.

CHAPTER IV
NO ONE WOULD EVER RETURN

In the early spring of 1910 the Daggetts were looking forward to beginning their annual migration south. Green grass was beginning to grow allowing the horses to start putting on much needed weight, after a winter of meager rations of scarce and dry grasses.

More birds were arriving each day, setting up a deluge of different songs, each unique to the different species. Songs of the Blackbirds and the Meadowlarks were the most noticeable and could be heard over the rest. To the Indian this meant it was time for them to also start their migration.

In the early spring of 1910, around the first of April, the 12 or 13 members of the Daggett family packed their belongings into their old wagon and left their winter camp in Rock Creek. Behind they would leave wickiup frames and other items they would not need until fall.

There is one member of the family that was never accounted for (Nellie). We know she existed. But who was she? Was she a daughter of Mike and his wife or a sister to one or the other?

BUCKSKIN AND SMOKE by Anna Hanse Hays

There is some speculation as to the exact location of the Daggett's winter camp on Rock Creek. In an interview with Carrie Crockett, Dayton Hyde interpreted the information to mean that the camp was located in the willows along the creek, a few hundred yards up stream from the Crockett house. David Crockett remembers his father telling him the Daggetts lived in a dug-out on the hill side a few hundred yards to the south of where Dayton understood the camp to be. They are probably both right. In the early years when the salmon were running it made perfect sense to have at least part of their camp on the creek when processing fish. The depression on the hill side above the highway, going up Rock Creek, looks exactly as it might after it had been abandoned for one hundred years. This sight is located on David's property and the highway right of way.

At first it seemed unusual that the Daggetts would leave Rock Creek so early in the spring when the salmon runs were just getting started, but history has an explanation. By the very late 1800s few salmon ascended the upper tributaries of the Snake River. No reason for the Daggetts to dally now, when spring broke just get on with it and start their migration south to the high country.

After more than thirty five winters in Rock Creek, unbeknown to them, they were leaving their winter camp forever. Not one of the family would ever return. All but one, a new baby born in early April after the family had reached Gollaher Mountain, would be dead within three years.

The one exception might be a daughter of Mike and Maggie's, Lizard Daggett. It is reported she married Lige Harris, a black man, who worked for the Vineyard Land & Stock Co. (V. L. & S. Co.) and was residing at Tacoma, Nevada but there is no documentation of this being true. She mysteriously disappeared from the scene in 1910. She did not leave Gollaher Mountain with the rest of the family in late April. She may have spent the winter of 1909 and 1910 at Tecoma with her aunt. In a letter to the Commission of Indian Affairs, dated April 27, 1911, C. H. Asbury, Superintendent at the Carson Training School, stated "Mike's wife *had a sister living at Tacoma, Nevada and that she and her husband work there about the store"*. Asbury came by this information from an interview with Mike and Maggie's youngest daughter, Henie.

(This aunt could be Nellie) There are two names floating around in history that were supposed to be daughters of Mike and Maggie, they being Lizard and Snake. This could be true however there is no reliable documentation that they had daughters with these names. Some of this information came from Dayton Hyde in his book THE LAST FREEMAN.

Lige shows up on the 1910 census in the household of his brother Henry Harris, buckaroo boss for the V. L. & S. Co., but Lizard Daggett Harris, does not show up on the census. This is not necessarily surprising since Indians were counted from the rolls of the reservations where they were all supposed to be enrolled. Since none of the Daggetts were enrolled on any reservation she would not show up there either.

44

Lige Harris also disappeared from the scene after the 1910 census and then showed up in the 1920 census, in Los Angeles, married to a black lady, 1st name, Mamie.

No record has been found, to date, of a daughter of Mike's by the name of Lizard nor any record that she even existed, other than at Fort Hall on a list that is supposed to be of the Daggett family and a reference in the Shoshone Mike papers at the National Archives in Washington D. C. and by Dayton Hyde. Dayton got his information from his interviews with folks in Twin Falls area who knew the Daggetts. A great niece of Lige and Mamie's, Geraldine Wilson as a little girl of eight or nine years old, remembers her aunt as black and that they, Lige & Mamie, were married late in life. T. Baily Lee, district attorney for Cassia County stated "one of Mike;s daughters was in love with Henry Harris" but that doesn't pan out either. Another brother of Henry's, Charles, who worked for Henry at San Jacinto disappeared from the scene and all records, between 1900 and 1910. Maybe Lizard, if she existed, and Charles disappeared together and lay somewhere in an unmarked and forgotten grave.

On or before the 10th of April the Daggett family should have made their way to Indian Mike Spring or Chicken Spring, on their southerly migration route.

Indian Mike Spring and Chicken Spring are located on the north end of Gollaher Mountain.

The grandfather of Roger Jones, of Rogerson, Idaho, had told Roger that he had often seen the Daggetts camped at Chicken Spring. These two springs are located about two miles apart and one or the other would have been a regular stop on their annual migration route from Rock Creek to Gollaher Mountain.

Interview with Roger Jones - 2009

I believe it was at Chicken Spring, that a baby girl, the youngest of the Daggett family was born to Mike's daughter, Snake, (if that was her name) on or about the 12th of April 1910.

Two years after her birth the Superintendent, Evan Estep, at the Fort Hall Indian Reservation, in Idaho, arrived at the baby's birth date after asking Mike's youngest daughter when the baby was born. He was told *"when the flowers started to bloom"* so Mr Estep gave the little girl his date of birth April 12, 1910.

There is no historical record that indicates any of the Daggett family ever gave her a name.

She never new where she was born and it is sad she was never able to return here to see this wonderful place. She passed away fifteen years before we were able to determine this to be her place of birth.

The Prosecuting Attorney for Cassia County, Idaho, T. Bailey Lee, stated that In November of 1910 three Indians reported to him, at his office, that fourteen members of the Shoshone tribe had been slaughtered by white men and that four of those missing Indians were his wife and three children.

I believe one of those Indians to be Jim Mosho, the husband of the mother and father of the missing children.

In a report by District Foster G. A. Gutches, February 6, 1911, he wrote that Jim Mosho made a statement to him that there were twelve members in the Daggett family when he (Jim Mosho) visited the family in the summer of 1909 including three small children. Since the information given was basically the same as was given to Lee earlier it is assumed the father of the baby is Jim Mosho. From here forward the baby girl will be referred to as Baby Mosho.

G.A. Gutches was the District. Forester for the Dept. of the Interior, U. S. Indian Service, Fort Hall Indian Agency at Rossfork, Idaho.

Later in this story an attempt will be made to unravel a very confusing history of family and relations.

Mother and daughter could not linger long for the family was on a mission to gather some of their horses on Gollaher Mountain. They were believed to have about thirty head of horses running in the area of Gollaher Mountain. The horses of the Indians were intermingled with other horses in the area. These horses were owned by ranchers in the area and other individuals. In addition there were also wild horses (mustangs) running with the branded horses.

Within days of the baby's birth, (Baby Mosho), the life and the world the family lived in, would be turned upside down.

Indian Mike Sp. & Chicken Sp.

V

GOLLAHER MOUNTAIN, (NEVADA)

[EXTENDING ACROSS THE PICTURE, IN THE DISTANCE]

June 2005

Indian Mike Creek, Indian Mike Spring and Chicken Spring are located at the foot of

Gollaher Mountain (center)

This photo taken (looking southeast) from the top of Deadline Ridge, Idaho.

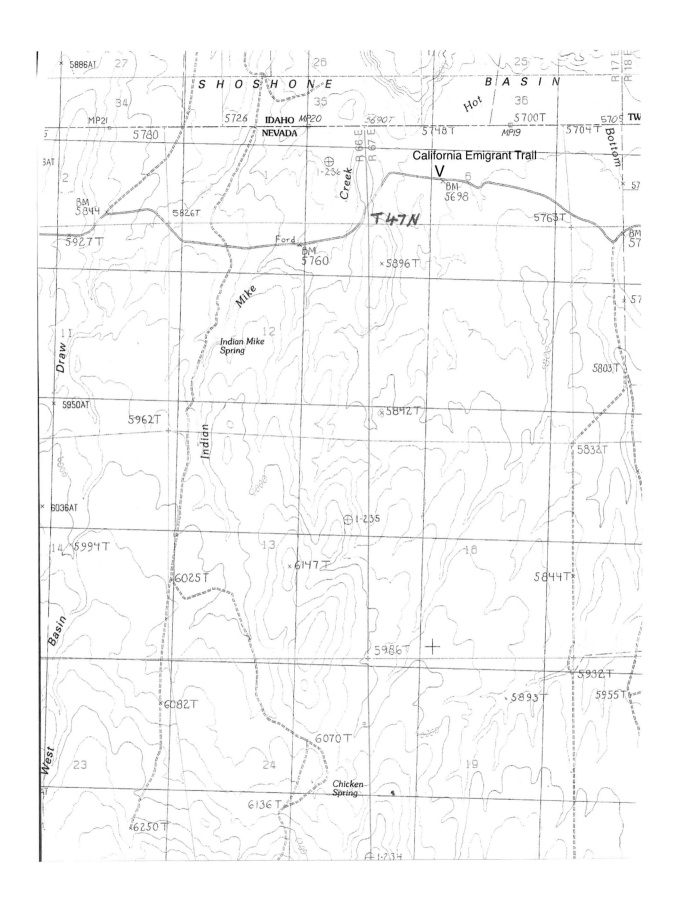

CHICKEN SPRING

June, 2011

I believe Chicken Spring, to be the birth place of a new member of the family, on or about the 12th of April 1910. For now she will be known as Baby Mosho, born free, in this solitary and peaceful location, as all those Native Americans before her.

There is no record of her having a name until June of 1911 when, at the Stewart Indian School near Carson City, Nevada, she was given a name.

INDIAN MIKE SPRING
June 2011

Looking northeast toward Deadline Ridge in Idaho.

Indian Mike Spring empties into Indian Mike Creek

Both were named after Indian Mike. The Mike Daggett family roamed this country from

the early to mid 1870s until April of 1910.

CHAPTER V

A TRAGEDY UNFOLDING

Between the 1st part, and the middle of April 1910, two seemingly innocuous events, that will lead to a very tragic end, are born.

The point of beginning for each, were separated by a mere twenty miles. One in Twin Falls, Idaho and the other at the mouth of Rock Creek, just twenty miles southeast of Twin Falls.

Their goal is the same, run (gather) horses on Gollaher Mountain in the far northeast corner of Nevada. Ironically, in the end, they will end up camped within a couple of miles of each other, the Tranmer outfit on Cow Creek and Mike Daggett's outfit on Willow Creek.

The Tranmer outfit, headed up by Gay Tranmer, called the *Tranmer & Co.* leave Twin Falls sometime around the tenth of April.

How do we know it was known as the Tranmer & Co.? Because Gay had a charge account at A. E. Organ's Saloon, in Imlay, Nevada, under the name *Tranmer & Co.*

Page 356 - testimony of A. E. Organ, at Nimrod Urie's murder trial in Winnemucca, Nevada, April 19, 1911

The Tranmer party was made up of Gay Tranmer age 33, Frank Tranmer age 43, Nimrod Urie age 22, Ed Diffendarfer age 31, Gordon Girdner age 25, Girdner's wife, Harriet, age 23, Girdner's 2 old daughter Lenore and 16 year old Frank Dopp (stepson of Frank Tranmer). Dopp was taken along to wrangle horses. The saddle horses had to be herded during the day while grazing as there were other horses in the area and there were no fences or pastures to hold them in other than a corral at night. Dopp worked for and If Gay owed Dopp $150, as reported, then he would have been working for Gay for at least five or six months.

G. A. Gutches report on missing Shoshone Indians Feb. 6,1911 - National Archives W. D. C.

Although inaccurate as to time frames, according to Uries' statement, January 9, 1911, before Judge E. J. L. Taber and District Attorney, James Dysart, both of Elko, Nevada

and Sheriff Lamb, of Humboldt County, Nevada, they got their outfit together (at Twin Falls) and then headed for Gollaher Mountain.

Urie's statement gave some details of their progress as they traveled from Twin Falls to Cow Creek on the west side of Gollaher Mountain.

Urie and Diffendarfer had left Bliss, Idaho earlier, having been invited by Gay, to meet the Tranmer horse running outfit in Twin Falls. A quote from Urie's statement:

"First day out they pulled from Twin Falls to Gay Tranmer's ranch, stayed there a few days (give them 4 days) *then they pulled to Duck Springs (1 day), and from there to the Point Ranch* (1 short day, two and one half miles) *they stayed there about a week* (give them 7 days). *Then they pulled to Bridge Ranch, then they pulled to Cedar Creek. and the next day we pulled to where Gay had his corrals built"* (on Cow Creek), give them 3 days, total 17 days. *"We saw some horses down in the canyon in a quaking asp grove".* According to statements by both Urie and Tranmer, this was the 5th or 6th of May. Working backwards by 17 days, they would have left Twin Falls around the 20th of April. In a written statement by W. J. Gumble dated January 31, 1911, *"he saw Gay, Dopp, Girdner and others at the Point Ranch about the 17th of April".* Also, according to Gumble, *"he saw Herb Tranmer, Frank Tranmer, Jim Rake and one other about twenty five miles north of the Point Ranch on the same day",* (easy ride to the Point Ranch in five or six hours). This group told Gumble, they were headed to Jarbridge to work in the mines.

Statement of W J Gumble, national archives W. D. C.

Its an uncertainty as to who traveled together to the Point Ranch but it appears the Tranmer outfit rendezvoused there. They most likely would have one or two with the camp wagon and 2 or 3 trailing saddle horses. Others could have joined in (caught up) along the way, most likely at Gay Tranmer's place and/or the Point Ranch.

If the statements above were all true it would have taken the Tranmer outfit seventeen or eighteen days to make the trip from the Point Ranch to the Tranmer corral on Cow Creek, an easy three day trip, even with a wagon. This shows the time frames related by Tranmer and Urie to be totally fabricated. They were on a mission to run horses there was absolutly no logical reason to remain at the Point Ranch for two weeks. Therefore, the Tranmer outfit arrived at Cow Creek on or about the 20th of April rather than leaving Twin Falls on that date. The reason for the fabricated dates will be discussed later.

When arriving at their camp site, the normal activity would be to, set up camp, repair the horse corral, if needed, and then do what ever was necessary to repair the horse trap/ corral, in preparation for gathering horses and then start gathering horses.

Other notes of interest:

1 - *"Gay Tranmer, Gordon Girdner, and Frank Tranmer went to Twin Falls Monday."*
Twin Falls Times, Rock Creek News, gossip column, March 15th, 1910

2 -*"On Soldier Creek, which runs into Deep Creek, W. G. Tranmer has a ranch on which he raises alfalfa"*
Twin Falls Times, May 1,1908)

3 - James Deiro, grandson of Gordon Girdner, said his mother Lenore, told him *"they rode there (Cow Creek) in a covered wagon."*
Interview withJames Deiro, on March 30, 2011,

A wagon loaded with gear and supplies for eight people would have been quite heavy and required a team of four to six horses or mules to pull. Lenore at age two could not have remembered this wagon but what she told her son was based on stories she heard from her mother and father. The covered wagon would not be a lot unlike those of the early immigrants traveling west from Missouri in the eighteen hundreds.

The Daggett family broke from their winter camp in Rock Creek, around the first part of April and unhurriedly begin their annual migration south into Nevada. No need for haste as horses are in poor condition from inadequate winter feed and they will be living off the land where game and other resources are available, such as the camas bulbs.

By 1910, due to the large influx of cattle in the west, over the last forty years, feed on the winter ranges would have been depleted by cattle numbers in excess of the carrying capacity of the range. They would, however, want to begin running horses sometime in early spring since horses that have wintered out are also in poor condition and easier to handle (catch) than fat slick ones that have had the advantage of fresh spring/summer feed in late spring and early summer.

The Daggetts would likely travel five to fifteen miles in a day day and remain at any one camp site two to five days, depending primarily on available feed for horses, but other factors may also influence their routine such as water availability, temporary employment at one of the ranches, availability of camas roots etc. Before moving from one camp to another they would scout ahead therefore they would know what lay ahead before they started out for the next camp.

At camps where they spent any length of time, they would construct "wickiups" for shelter. A dome structure, framed from willows tied together and covered with canvas or maybe deer hides, not likely deer hides after the late 1800s.

Indian Mike Spring, named after Mike Daggett, and Chicken Spring were the locations where the Daggetts would most likely spend some time. They were out-of-the-way places each with a large meadow that should provide plenty of feed for their horses and plenty of good water for Indians and horses, providing cattle hadn't been in ahead of them and eaten all the feed. Either location is a beautiful place for Mike's granddaughter to have been born. In early spring new life is sprouting everywhere, green grass, flowers of all kinds, leaves and new shoots sprouting from the many shrubs and willows, birds of all kinds building nests in preparation for a new generation and the shear peacefulness of it all.

This would have been the perfect place for the family to stop on their southward migration, to await the arrival of an addition to the family, before continuing on to Willow Creek, another of their regular camp sites. That new baby was born on or about the 12th of April 1910.

Their camp on Willow Creek was a mere six miles, by the way the crow flies, from San Jacinto and only a two days journey from there camp at Chicken Spring or Indian Mike Spring.

By the time they reached their Willow Creek camp, the Daggetts would have traveled nearly 75 miles since leaving their winter camp on Rock Creek.

On their trek south to their Willow Creek Camp they would encounter Willow Creek about one and one half miles down stream from their usual camp site and closer to San Jacinto. It only makes sense that they camp on the creek for a time to allow part of the group to travel to the commissary at San Jacinto. Leaving from the lower site on Willow Creek would save three miles of foot travel carrying supplies on their backs.

In addition, water in Willow Creek ran past this point through late spring, most years, thus providing water for their camp.

As related by Dell Hardy, in a written statement dated January 29, 1911:

"The latter part of April I saw two bucks, two Squaws and a papoose, (this was Mike's outfit after grub) some two miles east of San Jacinto Ranch. These Indians were on

foot. Allie Paterson told me and Dave Paterson that the Indians came afoot after grub because their horses were too poor to ride".

Shoshone Mike papers National Archives W. D. C.

These Indians would be **Snake** the mother of the new baby (papoose in a cradle board), the other squaw would probably be Henny, the 15 year old daughter of Mike and Maggie. The two bucks were probably two of Mike's younger sons ranging in age 12 to 16.

Allie was the clerk and/or the Post Master at the San Jacinto store/commissary and post office, where the Daggetts often traded, sold and/or purchased goods.

Written statement by W. J. Gumble dated January 31, 1911.

"I saw the Indians tracks about April 16th where they had gone on foot to San Jacinto from camp and back. I found some Indian trinkets on the road. From this I would naturally suppose the horses were in bad condition and unfit for use".

- Shoshone Mike papers National Archives W. D. C.

The question here is, did the Indians normally ride to San Jacinto for grub or trade?

In those days it was not uncommon for the chief (patriarch) to send the squaws for grub or trade, while they rode the horses off to some other event, whatever that might be.

According to these statements of Hardy and Gumble, the Daggetts were seen in the vicinity of San Jacinto, probably between April 20th and April 25th although Gumble said he saw where they had gone to San Jacinto around April 16th, most likely a little later than this but the 16th is possible. I think the 16th may have be a typing error and should have been the 26th. They were headed to San Jacinto to sell and/or trade, their Indian wares for needed supplies and then return to camp.

This time frame, approximately ten days, (12th to the 20th of April) would allow time for celebration of the new addition to the family and rest for mother and child, before proceeding south to their Willow Creek Camp.

Tranmer and Co. and the Daggetts would have had to crossed over one or the others wagon tracks on their way to their respective camps. That early in the spring there would have been no reason for other wagons to be in that area of Gollaher Mountain. Evidence and time frames would indicate the Tranmer outfit crossed through to Cow Creek prior to the Daggetts coming around the foot of Gollaher Mountain, on their way to Willow Creek therefore the Indians crossed over the wagon tracks of the horse runners. The Indians now realize they are not alone on Gollaher Mountain.

The Willow Creek camp was semi-permanent. How long they planned to stay here is rather hard to determine.

After they had set up camp they would begin scouting the area for horses and setting up or repairing an existing corral to gather horses into.

From here they could also travel to the nearby ranches for employment in the hay fields or cow camps, hunt game in the higher country and travel to San Jacinto for supplies.

From what menial records there are, it appears that Mike's boys were well experienced in the handling of horses and cattle.

After gathering a few horses of their own, it would be time for those old enough to head to the cow camps. There, employment would be available, as the ranchers would be branding calves and moving cattle onto the summer ranges followed, by work in the hay fields.

The Indians may have remained here until early fall. The hay harvested and stacked, their summer employment in the hay fields would come to an end.

Frost in the mornings and ice in the water buckets would be the signal to prepare for the trip back to their winter camp on Rock Creek.

At the end of the haying season, ranchers would begin the process of gathering cattle off the summer range. Some of these cattle would be brought to the various ranches where they could be fed hay for the winter. Others would be driven to the desert winter ranges where they would remain until spring. In the spring the cycle would start all over again.

Some of the older boys probably stayed on at the various ranches until the cattle had been gathered. They then would catch up with the family later in the fall, either on the way back to Rock Creek or at their winter camp on Rock Creek.

In the later years I believe Mike and the women stayed in camp for most of the period, hand crafting their many wares for trade and sale.

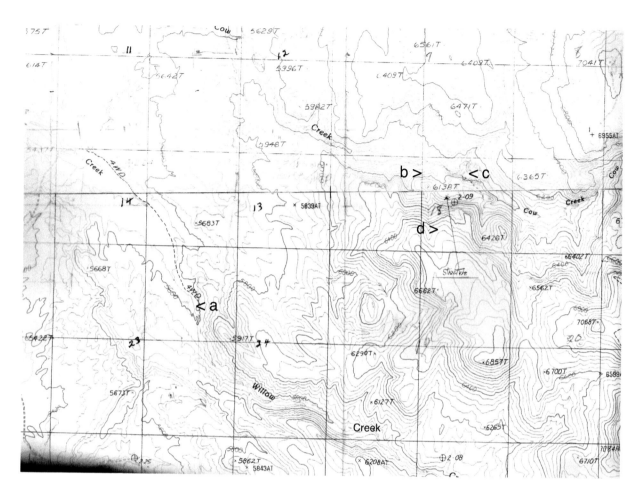

AREA of TRANMER/DAGGETT CONFLICT

Late April 1910

a - Daggett's Willow Creek Camp Site - April 1910
    (12 miles SE of Jackpot, Nevada and 8 miles NE of the San Jacinto ranch)

b - Vicinity of Tranmer camp on Cow Creek.

c - One of the Tranmer corrals (approx. location).

d - Hidden Valley - location of protective rock structures.

CHAPTER VI

ALTERCATION AT COW CREEK

The Tranmer bunch start running horses on or about the 20th of April.

When the Daggett clan began to scout around is a little more fuzzy. It appears that the day they ran into the Tranmer horse runners was about the 1st day they started their own scouting for horses which would be about the 25th of April 1910. It is at that time they ran into the Tranmer gang and their corral full of horses with altered brands.

The story, as related by Gay Tranmer, <u>September 20, 1910</u> is as follows:

"We were riding for Buck Rice an Idaho Stockman (P. O. address Rock Creek, Idaho) looking for horses. I own some horses myself. Rice wanted me to get his horses while I was after my own. We moved in there May 5th, 1910, got in there and set up camp. Ed Diffendarfer and N.R. Urie were with me helping to get the horses. We went to a place about 21 miles northeast of Contact to start in. Gollaher Mountain is where we camped. We got there on the 5th.

On the morning of the 6th we started up to where we were going to build a fence to hold our saddle horses. We went afoot. While we were looking around up there we were on a rim rock. We looked right down into a canyon of quaking asp and see a bunch of horses down in there.

Besides us three there was a man named Gordon Girdner and his wife and also the boy that was killed, Frank Dopp. Dopp was 16 years old and a nice boy. Mother and stepfather live in Idaho. Their post offic address is Rock Creek. Frank Tranmer is the stepfather. Mrs. Girdner and the boy stayed at the camp, while we were scouting around. We supposed it was those Indians' camp that we saw down in the canyon but they had always been friendly and we did not expect any trouble.

These Indians had lived around in there for years. We knew them personally and had worked with them running horses. They had been employed at various times by white men to help run horses. There was one family of them, that's all we know of. There were five men, and then there was the old lady and I think two young squaws. Then there were some three or four younger Indians in the family. It was known as the family of old Mike. Some say old Mikes's name is Daggett. But generally known as Mike. I don't know the name of the old woman. The oldest boy is named Jim. The next one is Jake. The next Charlie. And then there is another boy that old Mike called Sagebrush but he has another name. So there are five men in the family. Mike the father and his four sons.

Old Mike is a man I should judge 65 or 70 years old. Medium heavy set, kind of stooped. Generally wears overalls mostly ragged. Face wrinkled from age. Slightly bow legged. Talks English a little bit, but there's a lot of Indian about old Mike. Jim, the oldest son, is low heavy set about five feet seven. About 33 years old. Wears his hair cut off square around the front, and the back of it is braided and around his neck. Weighs about 165. Slightly bow legged and wears high heeled boots generally. Is quite a hand at all kinds of hair work and rawhide work. Speaks good English when you can get him to talk. Generally rides with good rig, silver mounted spurs and bit. Not near as dark complected as the other three boys. Kind of low sullen look. More of round face than other boys.

Jake is tall and kind of slim. About 6 feet. Very dark. Looks very much like Charlie, Roman nose, big mouth.

Charlie almost same as Jake. Is little younger than Jake. About same height.

Sagebrush. Don't know much about him. They say he is very dark complected and tall. Doesn't go around white folks very much.

When we saw these Indians two of them had fancy breast straps on their horses. All these young Indians stay around Old Mike. Jim usually rides brown mares. Jake has a sorrel mare and a bay mare, small with hip knocked down.

We walked down and looked at some of their horses. While we were looking at them Charlie rode up. Some of these horses had disfigured brands. Some of the others had brands that were not disfigured, and belonged to stockmen in Nevada and Idaho. I don't think any of them were Indian horses. There were many fresh irons, all different, all kinds of curliecues and everything else. Pretty near all different brands and couldn't make them out.

There was about thirty head in the bunch that we looked at. I started to talk to Charlie and he wouldn't talk very much. He says "You see some of your horses down there?" I supposed he was referring to the bunch of thirty. I started to look at them. I walked a little away from him towards the horses, and the other boys told me when I looked around that Charlie had gone back to camp. The other boys told me that in leaving he said to them "Gay (which is my name)come down little wickyup down there." I supposed he meant by this that my horses were down below where they had a corral and horses in them. We started to walk around the trail at the edge of the brush and he met us before we got down to the corral. He had a Winchester and he shot right down at the side of me. He says "Me killum you". I commenced to argue the point with him and asked him what he wanted to kill me for. I supposed that as soon as we got away from where they were camped it would be all right. While we were talking Jim rode up. I talked to Jim and asked him what they wanted to kill us for. He pointed his six shooter at each one of us deliberately and each time he would point the pistol at one us he would repeat, "Me kill- um you--me killum you--me killum you-- me killum you." And then he added, " Me killum all white man that come up here." I argued the point with him. He rode off to the brush. We started like we were going to our camp. Charlie then headed us off with his gun and pointed us up the hill.

After he had driven us up the hill about a quarter of a mile we got in close to some rocks and he stopped in a kind of hole and we went on about 100 yards. I saw him point his gun up towards us. I told the boys they had better get behind some rocks. Three of us got behind one big rock there. Girdner got behind some rocks to the left of us. We just got behind the rocks when Charlie began to shoot at us. He shot two or three shots before we made any attempt to shoot. Then I started to shoot at him with a Winchester and shot two shots at him when he started to go up around the ridge to head us off from camp. Then I shot again and shot at the horse. When I shot, the horse stopped and he jumped off behind some rocks. He shot two or three more shots at us and then we didn't see him any longer. I shot one more shot when he was behind the rock. Then we started to camp. We were afraid they would get down to camp before we could. Girdner, when we got to see him, was about a half mile ahead of us. The Indians run around then and commenced to shoot at Girdner before we got down to him. We run on into the creek then and went down the creek to our camp. They fired two shots at us before we got to the creek. Jim I am certain was there, not certain which of the others. Jim and Charlie was all I saw, unless I crippled Charlie which I think I did. In that event there was another besides Charlie and Jim, because I saw two after the time when I might have crippled Charlie, Jim and one other. When they were shooting at Girdner there, one of them rode around across the draw to where the boy was killed. Girdner said he heard two shots fired over there. The boy did not know anything about the trouble we had been having. He had remained at camp with Mrs. Girdner, and had just started out to round up the saddle horses a few minutes before I got to camp.

After we got into camp the Indians kept on shooting down into our camp. While we were in camp we saw one Indian going back up from where the boy was killed. I think this was the Indian with Jim, because Jim had a pistol and I think Jim waited up above and was shooting down at the camp when the other one went down and shot the boy. Ed Diffendarfer went to Contact for grain about 1:30 P. M. We never saw anything more of the Indians until about 2 o'clock, when they began shooting again. They moved around onto a hill north of camp and they commenced shooting at me. They fired four shots at me I was horseback and about a quarter of a mile from camp. I run on up to camp, and then they fired two or three shots at Urie. Then Urie shot at them three times. Then they shot back six or seven times. Then they moved over on the hill south of us again. Then they shot five or six times. Last shot was so close to my head that I could feel the air. This was about seven o'clock in the evening, when the last shot was fired. Mrs. Girdner said she counted 25 or 27 shots fired that afternoon by the Indians. They were ambushed all the time when they were shooting. The boys afterwards went up and looked at one ambush. There were rocks in a cedar tree.

The next day we began to look for the boy, and looked for him every day for a week. Finally we found him about a quarter of a mile from camp. There was one bullet hole through his brain and another one through his body,near or through the heart. Either of the shots without the other would have produced instantaneous death. They were unquestionably rifle shots. The wound in the body went clean through, and bored a large hole while the other entered the skull in front, and after passing through the brain came out through the skull towards the rear and higher up on the head.

Charlie might be crippled now, because when we went back to the place where I shot him, we found a piece of overalls with two holes, and covered with blood. It was the part of the overalls below the knee. There were also the ashes of a camp fire there, and it looked as if the rocks had been scraped away to make a bed.

The boy knew the Indians--had played with them as children. He had no arms or weapons with him and was entirely defenseless and unaware of the trouble we had been having. The Indian that killed him no doubt went right up to him and shot him twice in cold blood. The Indians had been stealing horses and were no doubt sore because we went in there and saw them.

George Grimm, Deputy sheriff of Elko County, went with us after the Indians, but owing to storms and other things, we had to abandon the pursuit, having nothing to indicate where the Indians had gone, and being without money".

No evidence Mike's outfit ever had a pistol, they didn't have money to spend on a useless pistol. Rifles for hunting big game - Yes. Tranmer story bogus.

Gay stated *"There were many fresh irons, all different, all kinds of curliecues and everything else".* If they were altering brands they would be readable especially fresh brands other wise why alter.

In latter research it was reported that the Indians had left Gollaher Mountain with twenty or twenty five head of horses and also that the Indians had horses branded with a B.

In his statement Gay also said one of the reasons they had to abandoned pursuit of the Indians was due to storms. It is highly unlikely storms or other things could have wiped out all sign, over night, of a family of twelve leaving the area and taking with them an estimated twenty head of horses. Grimm had made at least two trips to Cow Creek from Contact with five different men. In doing so they would have had to of crossed over the trail/tracks the Daggetts made in their exit of the area.

Nimrod Urie made a statement, in Winnemucca, Nevada, before Judge E. J. L. Taber and James Dysart, District Attorney and Sheriff Lamb on <u>January 9, 1911</u>, regarding a run-in with Indians. This statement was made after he and Frank Tranmer were arrested by Sheriff Lamb, for the murder of the Quilicies. Mr and Mrs Quilicie were murdered during a robbery of their bar in Imaly, Nevada January, 1911.

His story, also, begins when they got their horse running camp set up at Gollaher Mt. (Cow Creek), on may 5th.

Urie's statement:

"This was May, I believe. I think we pulled in there May 5th. Gay says we will go up here and see where we are to build a fence across the canyon. He took his rifle along with him and Girdner had his six-shooter, and I and Diffendarfer did not have any guns with us. In fact Diffendarfer did not have a gun. I had a gun, but did not have it with me. My gun was left at the camp. We went up there to where we was going to build the fence and we saw some horses down in the canyon in a quaking asp grove. We went part way down the hill and saw one of the Indians just out of the brush. We went on down and was looking at these horses. This Indian rode on up and asked us what we wanted there. He asked us if we was looking for some of Gay's horses. He tried to tell us, as near as I could understand, that he had some of them there, or knew about them or something of that kind. They was about thirty head of horses there in the grove. The Indian then said "There's a little housey down here, Gay" or something like that. We started down toward the corral and the Indian went ahead of us. He rode quite fast as he road down, and met us about half way between the corral and this bunch of horses that we had just left. He met us there, and he rode up to Gay and shot down alongside of him and asked him what he wanted. He told him that he had stolen some of his horses that is, the Indian told Gay that he had stolen one of his (the Indian's) horses. This was the tall Indian Charlie.

Then he pointed his rifle at Gay and told him that he was going to kill him. Gay asked him what he wanted to kill him for, and he said, "you stealum my buckskin colt." Then this other Indian Jim rode up, and he told Gay "You stealum my buckskin colt." Gay told them that he hadn't seen the colt. Jim said "That'll be all right--in a day or two you come down again." Then Gay told him about building this fence across the canyon that run right close to their corral. That seemed to make them kind of mad and they said, We guess we killum you now." Jim only said it once. Charlie was the worst. Gay says "Well guess we go." We started up the hill the way we had come down, and this Charlie followed us. When we got part way up the hill Gay looked around and saw the Indian drawing his rifle on us. I and Ed and Gay were there together --the three of us, and

64

Girdner was off to the right of us. Gay turned around and saw this Indian and told us to get behind them rocks. We all three of us got behind a big rock that was there, and the Indian shot. Then Gay shot at the Indian twice while he was standing there. Then the Indian rode around a little grove there and got off his horse and got behind some rocks. The Indian shot again. Then I think Gay shot two shots at this Indian while he (the Indian) was laying behind those rocks. Then Gay told us to get there in that quaking asp grove and see if we couldn't get to the top of the hill and get out of sight. We got to the top of the hill and waited a little bit and then he came up. We started back then toward our camp. When we got back four or five hundred yards we saw Girdner ahead of us. He was ahead of us perhaps a quarter of a mile. We went on down and came up on a ridge, and these Indians was right ahead of us, they had gone around and headed us off before we got to camp.

One Indian stayed where he was on the ridge right on the east side of the camp. The other Indian got on his horse and rode around like he was going around to head us off. We heard two or three shots that was fired and supposed that they were shot at Girdner. Then we started down towards the creek and this Indian that stayed there he shot at us once while we was crossing the flat where we was going to go across the creek.

Then Gay said to me and Ed, I will get into camp as quick as I can to keep him from getting into camp where the woman and kid is. He was referring to Mrs Girdner and her baby. I and Ed told him alright, and that we would try to keep out of sight until we could go down through the brush and get to camp ourselves. We got into camp and Girdner came into camp just about the same time that we did. Gay asked the woman where Frank was, and she said he had just gone out after the horses, and that he said he would be back just as quick as he could get back to wash out some saddle blankets. We went out to the edge of the brush and we could see this Indian up on top of this ridge. The first we saw of the other was when he run up the hill to where his horse was tied. He got on his horse and rode up the hill hollering and riding toward the other Indian. Then Ed he got ready and went to Contact to get the Sheriff.

We didn't see any more of the Indians then till about two o'clock. They came around on a point north of camp and commenced to shoot at Gay. He was at the corral ahorseback putting the horses in the corral. He was putting the saddle horses in the corral. These were the same horses that Frank Dopp had gone out to get, and they had come down the hill, and Gay had gone to put them in the corral.

Then Gay, as soon as they started to shoot at him, started to ride toward the camp so he could get in the trees. I think they shot about six shots at him while he was riding from the corral to the grove where the camp was. I had the rifle, and I thought I would shoot at them to keep them from shooting at him as I was kind of in the trees and I shot at them once. Then they went higher up on the ridge where there was a cedar tree, and they shot three or four shots from there.

Then they came around on the ridge east of camp again and they shot down from there several times and finally, the last shot that was fired, one of the Indians had come down from this ridge about two hundred yards away and shot at Gay, who had his head up over some rocks. He missed Gay's head about two inches. That was the last shot, and this was about seven o'clock in the evening. I and Gay stayed there in the rocks for half an hour after this last shot was fired, and then we went back down in the camp, and went down to the corral and got saddle horses and took Girdner and his wife down the creek and then I and Gay came back up to camp. That night he watched the camp and I watched the saddle horses in the corral. The next morning we saddled up a couple of horses and rode out on the hill and went down to where Girdner and his wife were.

We started to come back up to camp, and Ed and Nigger Henry and Grim rode into camp. We rode into camp and got some dinner and that day we started to look around. Grim thought he had better go back to the ranch and get some of the buckaroos and some more Winchesters. Next day they came out and we went up and looked around the Indian corrals and went up to where Gay had shot at this Indian and we saw where he had got off his horse and got behind these rocks --saw blood , a dutch oven, pieces of overalls, and some empty cartridges.

This same day we went to the Rancho Grande. The next day we came back. They went into San Jacinto that evening and we went on down to camp.

It was about a week after this fighting with the Indians that we found Frank Dopp's body. Gay found the body. Him and Girdner was building a wing on to the corral and Gay was driving (dragging) poles over from the grove to this wing. While he was making one trip he saw Frank's body laying by a bush on the side of the hill".

Indians recognizing colt in the corral with altered brand could trigger an altercation. Urie said *"we went to Rancho Grande".* Who was we and why would any of the horse runners leave Girdner's wife and child there with out maximum protection (all of the horse runners) if there were wild Indians in the country shooting people?

Both G. Tranmer and N. Urie stated the confrontation with the Indians took place on May 6th, 1910. They both stated that they, Deputy Sheriff Grimm and others searched the area for three or four days. This is also supported by Gutches in his report.

District Forester, G. A. Gutches' report of Feb. 6, 1911 to E. P. Holcombe, Chief Supervisor, Denver, Colorado - National Archives W. D. C.

They also stated that the Indians were shooting from above from about 2 pm until 7 pm. This needs some further thought. Was this the period of time the Indians were caring for and burying their brother?

Were they keeping the Tranmer gang pinned down while they attended to such matters?

Asbury interviewed Henie Daggett April 27, 1911 and according to Asbury, Henie told him they left the area that same night and that her brother Jack was the one who was shot and killed. Gay stated he thought he had hit Charlie.

Asbury's report from April 27, 1911 - National Archives W. D. C.

After they had searched for Dopp and the Indians, finding neither, George Grimm left for Elko, Nevada to report the incident to the Sheriff. He obtained a warrant for the arrest of the Indians. This warrant was signed on May 5, 1910.

Warrant - Ledgers Northeastern Nevada Museum Elko, Nevada

The warrant was signed a day before Urie and Tranmer said the incident occurred, this being after three or four days in the field searching for Dopp and the Indians. Therefore, their date of the 6th, on which the confrontation took place is pure fabrication.

Urie stated, Ed went to Contact, Nevada to report the incident to the Sheriff. Gay Tranmer stated Ed went after grain. I believe the the word grain was mistaken for the name Grimm, there was no reason for Ed Diffendarfer to go for grain.

In the meantime, the rest of the crew moved the Girdners down the creek to a safer location. Gay and Urie went back up the creek to guard the horses and the camp for the night. Ed returned the following day with Deputy Constable George Grimm along with Henry Harris, black foreman and buckaroo boss for the Vineyard Land Stock Co. By 1910 Harris had become a legend along the Idaho/Nevada border, was considered one of the most trusted and capable men in the country. He knew the area around Cow Creek, he knew the Indians, he knew the horses, he knew the Tranmers and probably all of the crew there with Gay Tranmer. It was no accident Grimm chose Henry to accompany him to investigate.

Statement by Urie and **HENRY HARRIS - 1865 - 1937** biography by Les Sweeney

The probable Tranmer reaction when Harris arrived with Grimm & Ed was

"Ah shit they brought Nigger Henry back with them"!

During that afternoon Grimm, Harris and supposedly the Tranmer outfit, searched for the Dopp boy and the Indians. Finding nothing Grimm and Harris returned to Contact, that same day, for more help.

Grimm deputized Dave Paterson, Byron Godfroy and Joe Stewart and returned the following day to continue the search for Dopp and the Indians. These three men were working for Henry Harris at the San Jacinto Ranch.

These four, Grimm, Paterson, Godfroy, and Stewart, with the help of the horse runners, searched that day then it was reported they continued on to Rancho Grande for the night.

Also on this day a portion of a pant leg, with two holes in it, a dutch oven, remnants of a fire, a place where rocks had been cleared away providing a place to lay down and blood was found, all where Gay thought he had hit Charlie Daggett, (this bit of information came from Gay Tranmer and Nimrod Urie).

They returned to Cow Creek from Rancho Grande the following day, engaged in additional searching before again returning to Contact, with no luck in finding Dopp or any sign of Indians. Gay Tranmer stated *"we looked for Dopp and looked every day for a week"*. No body was found by May 5th, if the above were true.

According to Urie's and Gay's stories this would be May 9th.

The following day, after getting back to Contact, Grimm proceeded to Wells where he caught the train to Elko, this being the 5th of May. This date is derived from the Wells newspaper the Nevada State Herald, dated May 6th, 1910. Any information gleaned from newspapers of the day has to be suspect as to its accuracy, however they weren't clairvoyant, they couldn't write about a story that had not yet happened.

At least five days have now passed since the altercation. If they searched for one more day before returning to Contact, on the third day out, it is more likely that six days have passed. Deputy Grimm could not have left the Rancho Grande Ranch nor Cow Creek and arrived in Elko, in time to sign a warrant, on the same day. Grimm had a 90 mile horseback ride to get to Wells to catch the train to Elko.

Gutches, in his report said they made an effort to search the surrounding area for a few days and then disbanded which would account for at least three days.

This pushes the date of the altercation even further back, to the 30th of April.

Gay had identified, to Deputy Grimm, three of the Daggett boys as being those involved in the incident: they were Charlie, Jake and Jim. There is no mention of Sagebrush nor Mike, only that they were part of the Daggett family.

Gay had grown up with the Daggett boys, on Rock Creek, and had known them his entire life.

Upon arriving in Elko, George Grimm swore out a complaint charging; Indian Jim, Indian Jake, Indian Charlie, Indian Mike and John Doe, an Indian, with a felony to wit: murder of Dopp. A warrant was issued and given to George B. Grimm, a Deputy Constable, for the arrest of the Daggetts. The warrant was signed May 5, 1910, corresponding with the Nevada State Herald reported date of May 5th, when Grimm took the train to Elko, Nevada.

Although no body had yet been found and only three Indians identified as being at the scene of the altercation this legal action, charging five indians with murder, was taken based on the statements of the Tranmer gang.

It is unclear, at this point, who did what but news articles reported Deputy Grimm traveled to Fort Hall in search of the Daggetts. Other reports indicated that local ranchers formed a posse to search for the Indians and Dopp.

The Twin Falls Times - May 12, 1910

However this article is so contaminated with inaccuracies that it can serve no purpose as to historical facts, only the lunacy and the prejudices of the time.

Dopp's body was found eight days later within one quarter of a mile of the Tranmer camp and near their corral on Cow Creek. Gay Tranmer stated he found the body of Dopp about a quarter of a mile from camp. According to Urie's statement, Gay found the Dopp body while dragging poles to the Tranmer corral.

It was reported by Gutches that the boy was found within 75 paces of the Tranmer Corral. Del Hardy stated he heard Joe Stewart say *"it would be almost impossible not to see Dopp from the corral"*.

Information gleaned from written statements by: Gay Tranmer September 20, 1910; Nimrod Urie January 9, 1911; Del Hardy January 29, 1911; written report by G. A. Guthes February 6, 1911

How could Frank Dopp, missing for eight days, be killed within sight of the corral and none of the Tranmer outfit having found him?

Answer, they did know. When the Daggett boys killed Dopp, they not only created a problem for themselves but also for the Tranmer outfit. The disfigured brands were not of the Indians making but of Tranmer and Co.

Accusing the Indians of stealing twenty or thirty horses made no sense. Where are they going to go with them? Their world has been limited to; from the mouth of Rock Creek, southeast of Twin Falls to Gollaher Mountain. Every one in that area knew them and they had no market for stolen horses.

There is also some question as to why, or if, the Indians had weapons with them when encountering the Tranmer gang. Running horses with a big heavy rifle hanging on the saddle would be extremely difficult and what reason would they have to carry a rille to gather horses? After the shooting of their brother the Indians boys may have had to go back to camp for weapons, to attack the Tranmer outfit,. There is some evidence of this in the statements of Urie and Tranmer in September and January when they stated that the Indians came back late in the day and began shooting at the camp form above.

After the one brother was shot did one of the brothers abandon the other two brothers, one injured, to go back to camp for help? With the Tranmer Co. armed that would be a tough decision. Maybe they hunkered down & stayed with their brother until he died,

70

buried him in the rocks and at this point they may have decided to deal with the situation themselves thus they then went after the Tranmer gang killing Dopp,assuming the Indians had a rifle.

In statements by Hardy and Gumble when referring to the fact that the Indians were on foot to trade at the San Jacinto store, the reason they were on foot was: *the horses were unfit for use and too poor to ride*. Which opens up another possibility that the Indians were on foot when they encountered the Tranmer outfit.

In analyzing Gay's and Urie's stories on what happened at Cow Creek it is difficult putting it all together, as it actually happened. One of the things that make it hard is that both are covering their butts over changing the brands on horses.

Urie had not likely ever been there before so remembering some details of the incident, after eight months, is difficult and putting that together with deception muddies the water. Urie is fairly young and immature, whereas the Tranmers and Gridner are the opposite they have been around a while and probably this is not the first time they have been doing things that were illegal. Therefore a little better at deception and leading others off the trail. Diffendarffer seems to be in between and hopes the Tranmer brothers can keep him out of trouble if he just lays low for while, which seems to be what he did.

It is too bad the authorities didn't put more pressure on Urie, I think he would have caved in and spilled the beans.

Another thing, Urie is trying not to bring the wrath of God down on him from the others of the gang especially the Tranmers. Girdner was a strong willed person and Urie may have been more than just a little afraid of him also.

Gay is covering his butt and in doing so has to cover everyone else's too, yet he is not under the stress the same as Urie, he isn't facing murder charges.

In review

1 - Tranmer & Co. arrived at their horse running camp at Cow Creek on or about April 20, 1910, Gay's brother, Frank, included.

2 - The horse runners had fixed up a corral and had gathered about 30 head of horses, mostly branded by about April 25, 1910.

3 - The Tranmer outfit was unaware there was any one else in that part of the country, however the Daggetts knew someone was in the area and had gone to see about their own horse gathering possibilities. In addition they wanted to see who, besides themselves, were in the area and what they were up to.

4 - The Indians encountered the Tranmer outfit with a corral full of horses in a canyon on Cow Creek. The corral was located in a grove of Aspen trees and the horse runners were changing brands on horses.

5 - An altercation ensued resulting in the deaths of one of the Daggett boys and Dopp. Gay Tranmer gave the following account of this site to Elko County Ditarict Attorney, E. J.Taber in Elko, Nevada September 20, 1910. *"Charlie might be crippled now, because when we went back to the place where I shot him, we found a piece of overalls with two holes, and covered with blood. It was the part of the overalls below the knee. There were also the ashes of a camp fire there, and it looked as if the rocks had been scraped away to make a bed".*

Nimrod Urie gave the following account of this site to Elko County Sheriff S. Lamb and E. L. Taber in Winnemucca, Nevada January 9, 1911. *"He (the Indian boy) had got off his horse and got behind these rocks --saw blood , a dutch oven, pieces of overalls, and some empty cartridges".*

6 - One of the Tranmers either Gay or Frank, shot Jack Daggett wounding him in the leg and severing the main artery and possibly shattering bones in the lower leg.

Maybe Frank Tranmer shot the Indian boy and the reason he wasn't put at the Cow Creek site by Gay nor Urie.

Hard to shoot the Indian boy in the leg without hitting his horse. He most likely was not on his horse when he was shot as was related by Urie.

In retaliation two or three of the other sons of Mike Daggett returned to the scene and shot Frank Dopp the 16 year old kid that was wrangling horses for the Tranmer outfit.

7 - It could not be ascertained whether there were two or three Daggett boys at the site where the confrontation took place.

Tranmer and Urie stated they had a running battle with the Indians in an area with large rocks and an area there cleared of rocks they supposed that the Indian boy was laid.

There is an area comprised of large boulders that fits their descriptions, located in a hidden valley adjacent to Cow Creek.

There is also a site next to a large boulder there where an area has been cleared of rock and a small wall built of rock, for protection.

The most likely scenario is that Jack died there and was buried in the rocks near by.

8 - The Indians had killed a white boy and they must now leave the area immediately and they did.

9 - Tranmer & Co. had a body on their hands and a corral full of horses with altered brands. Both problems had to be taken care of. They could not afford to have the Sheriff or his posse there investigating the Dopp killing and the whereabouts of the Indians. The disposal of the horses took 1st priority.

10 - The horses were taken to the head of Badger Creek, two large pits opened up in the bottom of the wash/head-cut, a total of 25 head of horses shot and tumbled in and then covered with dirt.

11 - Since the incident was supposed to have happened the day before, Dopp's body had to be hidden otherwise no fresh body to present.

12 - When Deputy Grimm arrived with Henry Harris the 1st day and others the following two days, they were told the area, where the body was actually located, had been throughly searched by them, the Tranmer outfit.

13 - By the middle of May Dopp's body had yet to be be found. Eight days later when it was difficult, impossible at the time, to determine the length of time that had passed since Dopp's death, he was miraculously found, by Gay Tranmer, near the Tranmer corral.

14 - It was the Tranmer and Co. and not the Indians that were altering brands in an attempt to steal horses.

15 -The Daggetts knew nothing of the buried horses and only stole horses on their departure from Gollaher Mountain. The Daggetts didn't have the luxury of taking time to bury horses, they had to get out of the area.

16 - In accusing the Indians of stealing horses, where would they go? They had no market or access to the outside world; only white man had that.

73

17 - The Elko authorities made no effort to solve the case or to determine the guilt or innocence of the Daggett boys. There was no indication the Elko County Sheriff, I. G. Clark nor Elko County District Attorney E. J. L. Taber, took any interest in the case.

18 - T. Baily Lee, District Attorney of Cassia County, exercised everything in his power to get the Elko authorities to act but to no avail.

It wasn't until September 20, 1910, in Elko, that D. A. Taber took the statement of Gay Tranmer. No one questioned Gay as to its validity. The Sheriff, it appears, was inept and I wonder about D. A. Taber. The statement of Nimrod Urie wasn't taken until January 1911 by now, Judge E. J. L. Taber; the newly elected Elko County District Attorney, James Dysart and Humboldt County Sheriff Lamb. Urie's statement was not taken until after Urie and Frank Tranmer had been arrested for a murder.

19 - The statement of Nimrod Urie, though flawed, had to have some credibility as to camp and corral locations, because those could be checked out as to their actual physical location on the ground.

20 - Both Urie and Gay Tranmer's statements said "they arrived at Cow Cr. about 5th or 6th of May".

A warrant was issued and given to Deputy George Grimm on the 5th of May, for the arrest of the four adult males of the Daggett family. He had already spent three or four days investigating and searching for Dopp before arriving in Elko and acquiring the warrant.

Tranmer & Co. were lying in an attempt to separate themselves from the time of the altercation and when the horses were buried, suggesting that those two incidents had occurred ten days before the Tranmer outfit ever arrived at Cow Creek.

21 - The buried horses were found about the 25th of May.

22 - The Daggetts normally spent the months between April and October on and around Gollaher Mountain. In 1910 their migration to the Mountain had ended early, around the 25th of April.

23 - Whatever happened the Indians were long gone or had at least disappeared by the time George Grimm and Henry Harris arrived at the Tranmer camp on the first day of their search.

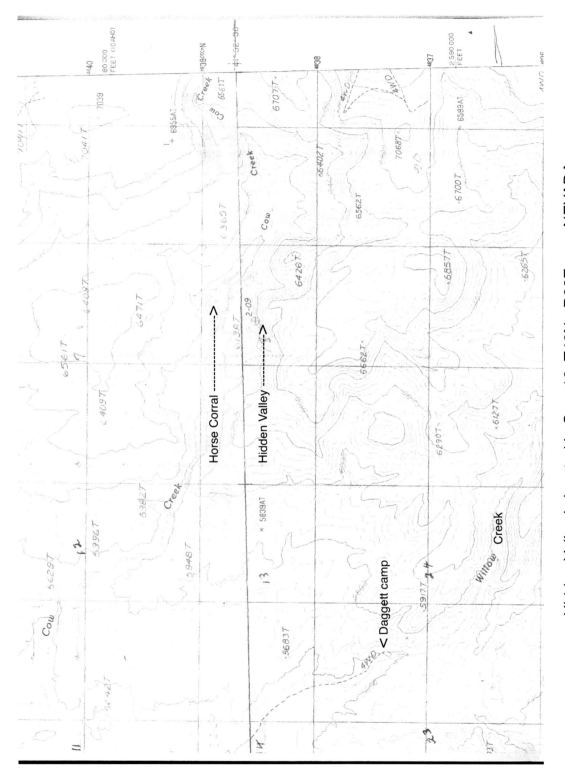

Hidden Valley is located in Sec. 18. T46N   R66E   -   NEVADA

Postcard photo: courtesy Bethene Brewer, from Newton (Tom) Harrell collection

Henry Harris's Outfit

1910
San Jacinto Ranch, Nevada

From left, on horse back, Henry Harris(black buckaroo boss), 2nd from left, on white horse, Lige Harris, Henry's brother. The 1910 census shows the following white buckaroos were working for Henry: Joe Stewart, David Patterson, Otto Pagar, Tony Vail, Bryan Godfray, & Jamie H. Baker.

It is quite likely, that five of those listed above are in this photo. Stewart, Patterson and Godfray were deputized and returned with Deputy Grimm on the following day, after Grimm and Harris had made their initial investigation, to further search for Frank Dopp and the Daggett family.

ELKO COUNTY SHERIFF'S OFFICE - ELKO, NEVADA
1907

Fm left: W. S. Elmore, Joseph Harris, George Grimm and I. G. Clark.

Harris was elected sheriff in 1910 & served from 1911 to 1936. On or about the 30th of April 1910, Grimm enlisted Henry Harris to go with him to the Tranmer horse running camp at Gollaher Mt to investigate the disappearance of Frank Dopp. The Tranmer outfit told Grimm, the sons of Indian Mike Daggett had attacked them and was also responsible for the disappearance of Dopp. Grimm was Deputy Constable at Contact, Nev. Clark was the Sheriff but made no effort to investigate the killing of Dopp nor the burial of 25 head of horses at the head of Badger Creek on Gollaher Mt. The buried horses, connected to the Tranmer outfit, were found around the 25th of May 1910. When Joe Harris took over as Sheriff in January of 1911, he vowed to make a thorough investigation of the whole incident. However an event that occurred on Feb. 26,1911 caused the new Sheriff to abandon his promise to investigate the incident any further.

77

SITE of DAGGETT'S CAMP on WILLOW CREEK
2009

This, I believe, was the location of the Daggett camp when the altercation with the Tranmer gang took place and the location from which the Daggetts left around the 25th of April 1910. How do we know this? 1) The Daggetts had built a corral at their camp, from trees and brush. In the center of the picture you can see Aspen trees and on the hill above and to the right, a Juniper tree. A very hot range fire burned this area in 2007 however trees did survive and were part of the landscape in 1910. The stream channel has cut down lowering the water table but these few Aspen are still hanging on. The hills to the right and out of the picture have scattered Juniper. Therefore materials were available for constructing a corral and at that time the water table was high enough to sustain small aspen groves and meadows along the creek. 2) On or about the 25th of April four members of the family were seen walking to San Jacinto for "grub", walking, the folks at the store assumed because their horses were too poor to ride. The distance from this camp to San Jacinto is about 8 miles. I believe the Indians had walked from where they first struck Willow Creek, 2 miles down from where this photo was taken, thus the total trip would have been 4 miles shorter. 3) There camp was close enough to Cow Creek, where the Tranmer Gang was set up, so as to allow three of the boys to ride there, on poor horses.

UPPER RESERVOIR - COW CREEK

May 17, 2019

(This photo taken 119 years after the incident)

The dam was breached (3), at this location, many years ago leaving sediment followed by the invasion of a large patch of willows as can be seen here. The dam (1) was built at the head of a small canyon. Prior to the building of the dam this area would have been an Aspen grove that continued down the canyon. That portion of the grove, above the dam, disappeared when material was needed to construct the dam. The tops of Aspen trees (2) can be seen, far left center, in the canyon below the dam. In this grove is believed to be the site of the corral where brands were being altered and where the confrontation between the Tranmer outfit and the Indians took place. The body of Frank Dopp is likely buried near here. A body laying out from the last part of April until late in May would have been in an extended state of decomposition and very hard to move, especially if it was very far to access a wagon.

ASPEN TREES in COW CREEK CANYON
April 20, 2015

Cow Creek just below upper reservoir (washed out years ago). I believe one of the Tranmer horse corrals was located up stream about 50 yards and to the right, out of the picture,.

Aspen trees can been seen in the bottom of the canyon. Gay Tranmer and Urie both spoke of a corral in the canyon in the Quaking Aspen trees. On the ridge near by there are (Juniper) Cedar trees that they also spoke of.

The hidden valley is over the ridge to the left, out of the picture.

HIDDEN VALLEY

MAY 2015

Looking west across Hidden Valley

Person standing left center is standing at protective structure.

Far left center, not shown in the photo, is located the site/rock I believe to be the site
where the wounded Indian boy was laying.

CLEARED AREA
April 2015

1 - Cleared area as described by Gay Tranmer
2- Remnants of a rock wall estimated to have been 20" to 30" in height.

Gay Tralnmer's statement to Elko County District Attorney E. J. L. Taber in Elko, Nevada September 20, 1910: *"Charlie might be crippled now, because when we went back to the place where I shot him, we found a piece of overalls with two holes, and covered with blood.*
It was the part of the overalls below the knee. There were also the ashes of a camp fire there, and it looked as if the rocks had been scraped away to make a bed".

HIDDEN VLLEY
Looking east

April 2015

> 1 - Rocky area that fits the description, laid out by Nimrod Urie and Gay Tranmer, where Gay may have shot the Indian boy he thought was Charlie Daggett.

> 2 - Cleared area that fits the description made by Gay Tranmer.

> 3 - Remnants of a rock wall that would have been high enough to protect a person lying here (estimated to be enough rock to build a two foot wall.

Nimrod Urie's statement to Taber and Humboldt County Sheriff Sela Lamb at Winnemucca, Nevada January 9,1911: *"Went up to where Gay had shot at this Indian and saw where he had got off his horse and got behind these rocks saw blood, a dutch oven, pieces of overalls and some empty cartridges"*.
The dutch oven may have been used to mix a poultice for the injured Indian boy,

RIFLE PIT/PROTECTIVE STRUCTURE

April 2015

This rifle pit or protective structure is located in the Hidden Valley, where it is believed one of the Indian boys could have held the Tranmer gang at bay while they attended to their wounded brother.

There seems to be no other reason for this structure to be at this location. If it were a blind from which the Indians could shoot game there would need to be other natural or man made barriers that would funnel the game near enough to be taken with a bow and arrow. There are no other such barriers or structures in the area.

HIDDEN VALLEY

April, 2015

< 1 - Rock where, at its base, there is a cleared area believed to be the site that was cleared to lay the wounded Indian boy.

< 2 - Location of rock protective structure where one of the Indian boys could have held the Tranmer gang at bay while they attended to there wounded brother and later buried him in the rocks nearby.

HIDDEN VALLEY
May 2015

1 V - Looking east across the Hidden Valley at the top of the ridge in back ground.

2 > - Rock where cleared area and wall is located.

3 > - Location of rock protective structure where one of the Indian boys could have held the Tranmer gang at bay while they attended to there wounded brother and later buried him in the rocks nearby.

226

In the Justice's Court of _____ Township, County of _____ , State of _____

No. _____

State of Nevada **Plaintiff**	Action _____
vs.	Demand, $ _____
A L Cummings	
	Attorney for Plaintiff
Defendant	Attorney for Defendant

DATE 1910		PROCEEDINGS
No 132 May	9	On this 22 day of April 1910 personaly appeard Bangert McKinney and Swore to a complaint charging the defendant A L Cummings with obtaining money by false pretences to wit One Hundred dollars a Warrant was issued and given to complaining witness
no 133 May	5	State of Nevada vs Indian Jim. Indian Julius Indian Charley Indian Mike and John Doe an Indian — On this 5th day of May 1910 personaly appeard George B Grimm and Swore to a complaint charging the defendants with a felony to wit Murder a warrant was issued and given to George B Grimm a deputy Constable

87

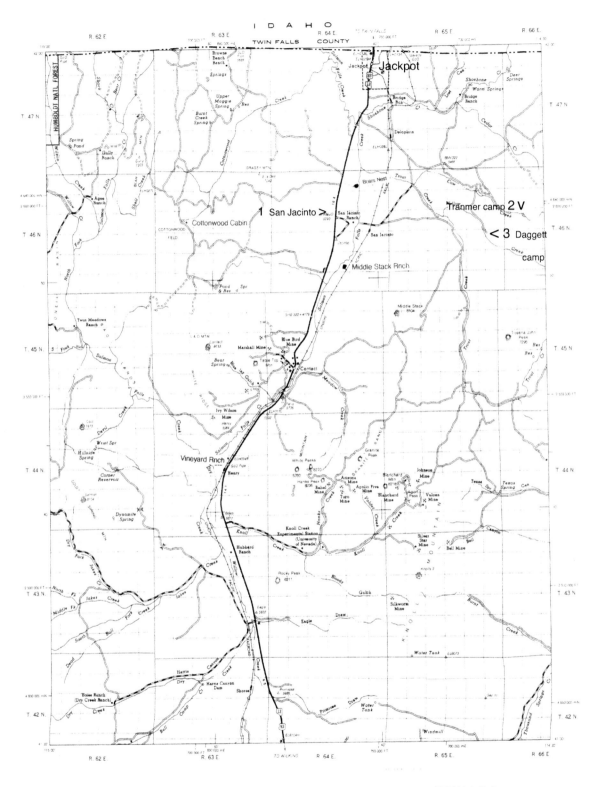

CHAPTER VII
PITS (BURIED HORSES)

From about the middle of May, when Dopp's body was found, until about the 25th of May when two very large pits were discovered, each containing several horses,there was little if any activity regarding the incident. These pits were located near the head of Badger Creek and described by Dell Hardy, in his statement given January 29, 1911, as follows: "*One pit was about 30 feet long, 6 feet wide on one end and 8 on the other. We dug two feet to the horses and would judge the pit to be five or six feet deep.*

The other pit was about eight feet long and three or four feet wide. This was the pit that was undermined. These pits are about six miles south of Little Goose Creek corral at the south end of April Fool Point", (near the head of Badger Creek).

When these pits were first discovered by Jack Haden and further examined by Del Hardy, Frank Dale, Charlie Wilson, Earl Haden and others, they had not made the connection with the Tranmer/Indian Mike incident at Cow Creek.

Hayden was an employee of the Vineyard Land & Cattle Co. and according to Hardy was camped about three quarters of a mile down from the pits, containing the horses. These men would have been very much puzzled as to why anyone would go to that extent to bury horses.

Dell Hardy, Jack Haden and Frank Dale went immediately to the site of the buried horses and dug down about two feet to several horses, identifying four individual horses, in an attempt to determine exactly what it was that Jack Haden had found. It was obvious some sort of crime had been committed. No one would go to this effort just to have something to do on a Sunday afternoon.

Del Hardy went to the H D Ranch to report their strange findings. He located Adam Peterson at the upper H D Ranch who in turn said he would report their findings to authorities.

About the first of June, Jack Haden, Earl Haden, Charlie Wilson and others went to the site and pulled out four or five horses from the pit. By that time another larger pit, containing horses, had been found near by.

There was never any mention of what brands might have been found on any of the buried horses. After over a month of being buried, that being the month of May, the extent of decay, on buried horses, may have made brand identification difficult if not impossible.

The one pit being undermined and the fact that these pits were large enough to contain a total of twenty five head of horses, when all the horses were finally removed, suggests that they were located in head cuts or eroded portions of Badger Creek. This, along with being the later part of April, when the soil was soft for digging, explains why whoever buried these horses, however poorly, were able to do so in a relatively short period of time, estimated to be about four days.

Sites exist in Badger Creek Canyon, where the soil could be excavated, deep enough, to contain a number of horses.

photo above

According to Hardy, sixteen head of horses were eventually removed from the larger pit and nine head from the smaller pit, in September 1910.

There were three sawn T-bones with the horses in the larger pit. The fact that these T-bones were sawn would indicate white man's handy work. Mike's outfit probably didn't have a meat saw with them. Indians usually cut meat from bone and Indian of the past had always removed meat from the carcass in this manner.

These pits, located in the bottom of Badger Creek, would be subject to erosion of the soil placed on top of the horse carcasses and by late May, when Jack Haden made the discover of the pits, sufficient soil had eroded away to expose the horses buried there. Therefore he knew what the pits contained, horses! In addition, the horses, now buried since late April, would have been subject to a great deal of decay. It would have been impossible to read brands on the horses by the time they had all been pulled out, in September.

Had the horses been buried in a "true" pit they would have been quite difficult to extract. However, in a wash, quite easy, it would be a down hill pull or at the worst level.

In District Forester, G. A. Gutches' report of February 6, 1911 Gutches concluded that all of the horses were finally removed from the pits about the 21st of October.

When word finally got out about the pits and what they contained, speculation and doubt began to surface as to the story related by Nimrod Urie, Gay Tranmer and other members of the Tranmer outfit.

Urie's & Gay's statement & Gutche's report on where and when Dopp's body was found - National Archives W. D. C.

The Tranmer gang and other whites of Elko, Nevada said the Indians killed and buried the horses. Based on Tranmer's story, how could this be? If the Tranmer gang had reported the incident that day, May 1st, and Ed Diffendarfer, Deputy Grimm, with Henry Harris, returning the next day, began looking for the Dopp boy and the Indians, it would have been impossible for the Indians to be there, burying twenty five head of horses, without being seen. In addition, the group saw no Indian camp or family (twelve in all) with twenty or thirty head of horses. The Indians had left the country.

Tranmer statement, *"owing to storms and other things, we had to abandon the pursuit, having nothing to indicate where the Indians had gone and being without money"*.

A family of twelve, with that many horses would have left signs or tracks that would have been visible for several days and would not have been obliterated overnight.

There would have had to have been heavy overnight storms to erase all sign. There was no indication nor statement by either Urie or Gay to that effect. However, if the incident had taken place five or six days earlier, which I believe to be the case, then tracking would have been much more difficult, with some storms and other horse tracks obliterating sign or travel in the area.

91

Another factor to be considered is; if the Tranmer bunch was leading the investigation, who knows where they led others to search and what information they were offering as to where the gang had already searched. Since no one there at the time doubted their story it provided a great amount of opportunity for cover up and misguide search efforts. Burying twenty five head of horses took a monumental effort and several days time. Even if the gang found a wash, they still had to do some digging and find enough dirt to cover the carcasses. The burying of the horses had to be done before any posse or others showed up looking for a body or Indians.

Being this early in the spring would suggest that Mike's band had gone earlier than usual to Gollaher Mt. and came upon the branding of horses (rebranding if you will or changing existing brands) by the Tranmer horse runners.

Mike and his boys may have gone there to gather some of there own horses and found the Tranmer gang changing brands on Indian horses. They undoubtedly had horses in the area as there was little room down in Rock Creek nor the 5th Fork of Rock Creek to winter more than a dozen or so horses. By this time white man's livestock were also wintering in Rock Creek.

Gutches was led to believe the Daggetts had twenty to thirty head of horses in the area. Mike Daggett's sons were probably less tolerant than Mike and were tired of being pushed around by white man, thus more apt to react negatively to someone trying to steal their horses, assuming some of the horses with the altered brands were those of the Daggetts.

The statements of Hardy and Gumble, the facts and logic, surrounding this case, do not match with the statements of Gay Tranmer and Nimrod Urie.

For starters the dates of the altercation, as related by Gay and Urie, were a total fabrication. A warrant had been issued for the arrest of the Daggetts on May 5th. Therefore the altercation took place no later than May 1st of 1910 and not on the 5th as they reported.

Secondly, it made no sense for the Tranmer outfit to remain at the Point Ranch for a week. They were seen at the Point Ranch on April 17th, therefore they arrived Cow Creek on or about the 20th.

Thirdly, the statements of Gumble, Hardy and others who knew Mike Daggett and his family gave credence to the fact that the Daggetts were honest, trusted at the San Jacinto store/commissary on their word and had never been known to cause any trouble or steal livestock or anything else. Therefore on or about the 25th of April it was the Indians who had come upon the Tranmer outfit with a corral full of horses, with disfigured brands and not as Gay and Urie had reported.

The discovery, around the 25th of May, 1910, of buried horses on Badger Creek, further substantiated these findings.

The Wells Nevada State Herald newspaper, of May 6, 1910, include an article stating *"the killing took place one day last week"*.

The Elko Independent newspaper, dated Friday May 13, 1910, included an article stating *"the killing took place April 25th"*. Keeping in mind the inaccuracies of news articles in papers of the time, they may have gotten this date right and is additional evidence that the April 25th date was the date the altercation took place.

Another reason the gang would fabricate the time frames; The tracks of twenty five head of horses needed time to fade, i.e. other horses in the area to track over them and possibly weather conditions, snow or rain would help.

Dell Hardy stated, *"There was no evidence of a struggle of any sort about the pit I was at."*

Gutches report, *"Horses feet were doubled under, horses were piled in very compactly"* thus less pit more horses.

Horses had to be halter broke and somewhat gentle in order to get each one up to the pits shot and to have them topple in without signs of a struggle. It would have also been difficult for the Indians to take horses out of the corral and be able to drive them along when they headed west without their being somewhat gentle. It would be near impossible with the whole family packed up and not able to move very fast.

The question I could never answer, whose horses were they?

CHAPTER VIII

HORSE THIEVES

On that fateful day in late April of 1910 the lives of Mike and his family changed forever when, at Cow Creek, on the west side of Gollaher Mountain, they clashed with the Tranmer outfit, who were altering brands on horses.

It is difficult to determine exactly what happened but some kind of an altercation between the Indians and the horse runners, took place resulting in the death of one of Mike's boys, either Charlie or Jack, and Frank Dopp. According to Gay Tranmer and census records, Frank Dopp was sixteen years of age.

It appears from Gay Tranmer's statement and what information Asbury was able to get from Henny, Charlie and Jack were the two youngest of Mike's grown sons.

Both boys, Tranmer's horse wrangler, Dopp, and the Indian boy, were most likely in their middle teens.

It is reported by C. H. Asbury, Superintendent, Stewart Indian School, that Mike's boys killed Frankie Dopp in retaliation for the shooting of their brother.

Asbury report, April 27, 1911 (Asbury was Superintendent of the Carson Training School at Stewart, Nevada) - National Archives - W. D. C.

When Mike's boys killed the Dopp boy, they not only created a problem for themselves, but also for the Tranmer gang. Tranmer and Co. now have a body to contend with. They need to notify authorities but this brings people to the area and also a posse. If they are to blame the Indians, what are they to do?

First get rid of the evidence. How to do this? Kill and bury the horses they have changed the brands on, which they did. Secondly they had the body of Frank Dopp to deal with. Since Ed Diffendarfer had ridden to Contact, Nevada and reported to Deputy Constable George Grimm that the altercation had taken place yesterday and since Dopp's body would have aged while they were burying the horses there would be no fresh body to show investigators/posse.

The solution, hide the body and steer searchers away from the area where he was hidden. The body of Dopp could not be revealed until sufficient time had passed so no one could tell how long the boy had been dead. In his written statement, September 20, 1910, Gay Tranmer stated, *"we looked for him for a week"*.

Eight days after Deputy Grimm had made his investigation, at Cow Creek, the boy's body miraculously appeared on the hill side near their corral and only one quarter mile from the Tranmer camp. This information also came from the Gay Tranmer statement: Dell Hardy reported that Joe Stewart had told him *"I heard Joe Stewart say that it would be almost impossible not to see the boy from the corral where the body of the boy was found eight days after the killing"*.

Written statement by Dell Hardy-on Jan, 29, 1911 - National Archives W. D. C.

Although Gay and Urie did not put Frank Tranmer at the corral altering brands, in their statements they were connected in every other way, from March 1910 through January 1911.

Frank Tranmer, Gay Tranmer and Gordon Girdner were together in Twin Falls March 10, 1910.

Twin Falls Times dated March 15, 1910

Frank Tranmer, Herb Tranmer and one other man were seen together about the middle of April 1910 twenty five miles north of the Point Ranch, which is located about fifteen miles north of the Idaho/Nevada state line.

Statement of W. J. Gumble dated January 31, 1911 - National Archives W. D. C.

Frank Tranmer's wife, Jeanette, Frank Dopp's mother, accused him and the rest of the gang of killing her son and stealing horses.

Casia County Dist. Att., T. Baily Lee's letter to Elko, County Dist. Att., E. J. Taber dated Jan. 14, 1911 - National Archives W. D. C.

In the Report on Missing Shoshone Indians, by G. A. Gutches, District Forester, February 1911, stated: *"On Sept. 20, 1910, Diffendarfer, Urie, F. Tranmer and Gay Tranmer came into the District Attorney's Office at Elko and Gay Tranmer made the enclosed statement"* (Gay Tranmer's statement).

Report on Missing Shoshone Indians by Gutches, page 3 and INFORMATION WANTED - The Murder of Frank Dopp by Gay Tranmer - National Archives W. D. C.

In a written statement made by Urie ten January 1911, and read in court at his trial states *"I knew Frank Tranmer since last April"*.

The Tranmer outfit was in Imaly, Nevada during the month of December of 1910, they included, Ed Diffendarfer, Nimrod Urie, Frank and Gay Tranmer. There is some evidence that Gordon Gridner was also there at some point.

Nimrod Urie's Statement at his trial in Winnemucca, Nevada - Date Thursday April 20, 1911

The horse thieves lay blame on the Indians for the killing of Frankie Dopp and said "they" caught the Indians changing brands on horses.

Knowing the consequences of crossing the white man, the Indians immediately left the country, which might suggest that they might have been the true culprits. However, the Cassia County D. A.,local ranchers and others who knew Mike and his family, did not believe the allegations against Mike's band. Mike had lived in peace and had not committed any crimes of any kind or indicated any propensity to do so for thirty five or more years.

In fact there had been no problems of any kind with Mike's band during this time.

Everyone who knew Mike and his family, knew them as friendly and very honest people.

The Last Free Man by Dayton O Hyde and Statements of Hardy, Gumble and the Gutches report - National Archives. W. D. C.

However, in fear for their lives, Mike and his family must now leave the land they had subsisted on for all these thirty five years.

At this point let us fast forward to get some insight on the type of people who were in this Tranmer outfit really were.

A young couple by the name of Quilicies were robbed and murdered at their bar in Imaly, Nevada. On January 9, 1911 two men were caught and later convicted of that crime. They were Frank Tranmer and Nimrod Urie.

Now the authorities in Elko County began to realize that maybe the Idaho folks were right after all and Mike's band were innocent of the crime of stealing horses.

In a letter, dated November 24, 1911, to the the Attorney General in Washington D. C., T. Bailey Lee, Prosecuting Attorney for Cassia County, Idaho, alleges that Frank Tranmer's wife accused Frank and the others of having a bad reputation and of stealing cattle and had killed her son to prevent exposure. This was not true the Indians had killed Frank Dopp. Frank and Jeanette had been married a little over three years.

In G. A. Gutches report of February 6, 1911, he states:

"The men implicated in the quarrel with the Indians have a reputation of being all around bad men and horse thieves. At the present time Frank Tranmer and N. R. Urie are held at Winnemucca for murder. Gay Tranmer is under bond to appear before the Dist. Court at Twin Falls this month. He refused to pay the mother of the murdered boy $150 due him in wages at the time of the murder. Girdner is wanted for selling mortgaged property".

In addition if Gay owed Frank Dopp $150 it would appear Dopp hadn't been paid for five or six months or more. In 1910, a young kid wrangling horses would not have been paid more than $20 or $30 dollars per month and possibly less.

In a side note, Gay had some kind of run in with a Mrs. Walters in 1908.

Twin Falls Times - Rock Creek News, Fri. May 1, 1908 - The trial between Gay Tranmer & Mrs. W. Walters will begin in Rock Cr. Wednesday.

Another thing that shines a light on this gang's reputation, as to guilt or innocence; after the Gollaher Mountain incident, none of the gang went back to the Rock Creek/Twin Falls area until the next year. The whereabouts of Gay during December of 1910 is not known. No record was found indicating that Gay had gone back home to Rock Creek before May 2,1912.

Twin Falls Times - Rock Creek News, Thur. May 2, 1912 - Gay Tranmer and Del Hardy were in from Rogerson Sat.

Twin Falls Times - 11-14-12 - Rock Creek News - Gay Tranmer is going to leave for Nevada Tue. where he will spend the winter.

Rather strange considering every member of the Tranmer gang had friends and family there, of which they had none in Nevada as will be explained later.

The effort by the Elko County authorities to investigate the incident at Gollaher Mt. was dismal at best. No effort to investigate the the possible killing of the Daggett boy was ever attempted, either by the Elko authorities, federal law enforcement nor the Bureau of Indian Affairs. No statement was taken from Gay Tranmer until Sept. 20, 1911 and no statement was taken from Urie until mid January 1911, at Winnemucca, Nevada, after he had been arrested by Sheriff Lamb for his part in the killing of the Quilicies at Imaly, Nevada.

The fifteen year old girl, youngest of Mike's daughters, was not with her brothers when the altercation occurred but still could have provided a good deal of information about the incident at Gollaher Mountain, when she was interviewed by Superintendent Asbury at the jail in Washoe County, Nevada, April 27, 1911but there was little or no effort there either. He made some strides in that direction in his interview with her but he did not pursue it in detail

Information from Gay, Urie & Gutchs Shoshone Mike papers National Archives W. D. C.

To understand what took place on Gollaher Mountain one has to analyze the statements of Gay Tranmer and Nimrod Urie and the inconsistencies therein. To best do this, ask the questions and then analyze their statements and answer those questions.

Question # 1 Why would they lie about dates and time frames?

Ans. To put as much distance as possible between the actual dates and their claimed dates of the whole episode, especially since, according to them, Mikes' outfit was supposed to have already corralled horses and changed some brands. Changing, drawing over or mutilating brands on twenty five head of horses could take at least a day plus it also took time to gather these horses. They set blame on the Indians for the changing of brands, so it was necessary to distance themselves from the actual dates as much as possible.

Question # 2 Why did it take so long to find Dopp's body, when it was practically in sight of the corral and only a short distance away. Where was Dopp killed? Did they move and conceal his body?

Statement of Hardy National Archives W. D. C.

Ans. The killing of Dopp put both parties in a dilemma. Mike's boys would be shot on sight, if caught, and the Tranmer gang had horses with mutilated brands to dispose of before authorities could be called to the scene. It took some time to bury twenty five head of horses. Dopp's body was aging while they were burying horses.

Horses having been disposed of, it was time to call in authorities but now they have no fresh body. Dopp has to be hidden away until aging is no longer a problem. Keeping him in rather good shape is not a big problem this time of year. By covering Dopp in the daytime and cooling him at night, like keeping a beef, they could control the aging to a great degree. Then, when it could no longer be determined how long Dopp had been

99

dead, he suddenly appeared on the hillside. Questions never fully answered include Where was Dopp killed? Did they move and conceal his body?

Question # 3 Why couldn't Deputy Grimm and Henry Harris, with the help of the Tranmer gang, find Indians or horses the next day after the confrontation?

The next day would have been around the 1st of May.

The Daggett family would need fifteen or twenty horses to move a family of twelve and all of their belongings plus, according to Henny's statement, they also took some loose horses along. With the loose horses they took along, the total number of horses would be approximately twenty five.

C. H. Asbury's interview of Heney - dated April 27, 1911 - National Archives W. D. C.

There would have had to of been a lot of fresh horse tracks left by twenty or thirty head of horses leading away from any corral or camp, in the area. The ground is soft in April making horse tracks easy to see, especially that time of year.

Ans. a) Because the Daggetts had left days earlier, around the 25th of April. b) The Tranmer outfit was directing and assisting in the search and at that time there was no reason to suspect a Tranmer cover up. c) Deputy Grimm and his crew didn't try very hard, only part of 3 days.

Gay stated that the weather had obliterated the tracks, however, the tracks of 25 or 30 head of horses obliterated in one day, nearly impossible. It would have taken a heavy rain to erase that many tracks in that short period of time, one day.

Question # 4 What happened to the horses with the disfigured brands?

Ans. On about the 25th of May, 25 head of horses were found buried in two large pits, at the head of Badger Creek. These pits were located some six miles southeast of the corrals where the confrontation took place.

At first it was thought by other Indians and Cassia County D.A., T. Baily Lee, that Mike's outfit might be buried under the horses. This was found not to be true when all of the horses were removed from the pits during the later part of September, 1910.

Hardy statement and letters of T. Baily Lee - National Archives - W. D. C.

In the interview by Asbury, with Henny, she also said "they took some horses when they left the area, but knew nothing of the buried horses".

Asbury's report of April 27, 1911 - National Archives W. D. C.

Question # 5 Who buried the horses and why?

Ans. Not the Indians, they were leaving the country after killing Dopp. They needed live horses not dead ones.

Asbury's report of April 27, 1911 - National Archives W. D. C.

Buried horses would not have been the biggest problem for the Indians; Dopp was, they buried no horses. Even if they had horses with altered brands, Dopp was a much bigger problem.

They had to leave the country, they didn't have the luxury of taking time to bury twenty five head of horses.

On the other hand, if you have a dead body on your hands and horses with altered brands that can be traced to you, being the only other party at the scene, the Tranmer gang needed to do whatever necessary to hide and or destroy the evidence.

Destroying evidence would have been a high priority before they could call in the authorities to deal with the Dopp killing. The Tranmer gang could explain away the killing of the Daggett boy as self defense but not horses with altered brands that could be traced to them.

Some of the horses the Indians left with were branded with a (B) on the left hip/thigh. Who this brand belonged to is somewhat of a mystery. Later in February of 1911, horses with this brand were found to be in the possession of the Daggetts at Little High Rock Canyon in Washoe County, Nevada and near Rabbit Creek in Humboldt County, Nevada.

Inquests at The Denio Camp February 15, 1911 and Golconda during the 1st part of March 1911

The Daggetts stole some horses when they left Gollaher Mountain, evidently from the corral where the altercation with the Tranmer gang took place.

The question is did some of the horses taken, by the Indians, from the Tranmer corral, have a (B) branded on the left hip/thigh and if some were branded with a (B), were they Indian horses or did they belong to some one else?

As to who branded horses with a (B) on the left hip, the possibilities are several. In those days the grazing of livestock was free with as many animals as the other ranchers grazing livestock in the area would let you get away with. A man by the name of Buck Rice was referred to by Gay and Urie as having horses in the area. Urie stated they

101

were to hold Bucks Rice's horses if they caught any. Gay stated they were going to gather horses for Buck Rice.

Who knows what the true story is. Maybe the (B) brand on the left hip belonged to Rice however Alex Kunkel, collector of brands and branding irons, says Buck Rice's horse brand was a pot hook or upside down J. Alex owns a ranch near Hollister, Idaho, which is near the ranch that belonged to Buck Rice.

The most likely scenario is, the horses branded with the (B) on the left thigh belonged to the Daggetts.

Question # 6 Was one or both of these brands being altered?

Ans. Very likely both, one of the Tranmer gang, Ed Diffendarfer, branded with a backwards BE joined (ǝE), on the left hip. This brand was registered to Diffendarfer in Idaho (page 110 of the Idaho brand book 1916).

Altering a (B) to Diffendarfer's brand would be very easy, it would only require adding 3 legs to the B (ǝE) with the 3 legs pointing to the right.

If the Indians branded with a (B) on the left hip, Stealing Indian horses would have been wrought with less risk than stealing white man's horses and if the Indians caught them doing it could be the catalyst that led to the confrontation.

If the pot hook, the horse brand of Rice, was large enough and located on the left hip, it too could be easily made into a backwards. ǝE

The folks in Idaho knew all along, something was wrong with the Tranmer/Urie statements.

Certainly the District Attorney, T. Baily Lee, of Cassia County, Idaho, thought there was something amiss. When Lee got word of the incident he went to great lengths to get the Elko authorities to take some action because it was out of his jurisdiction.

He asked that Gay Tranmer be arrested and questioned about the incident at Gollaher Mountain and in addition he suggested they track down Gordon Girdner in Washington State and get a statement from him as to what really had taken place, at Gollaher Mountain.

Lee's letter to Taber, dated Jan. 14, 1911 - National Archives W.D.C.

Girdner was in the State of Washington. He showed up there in Yakima, Washington on the 1910 US census. Girdner took his family and traveled to Yakima sometime during the summer or fall of 1910.

Frank Tranmer and Nimrod Urie were both sentenced to be hanged for the killing of the Quilicies in Imlay but both sentences were commuted to life. Frank died in prison in 1918 and Nimrod was paroled after serving only thirteen years.

The only written accounts of the altercation with Mike Daggett's boys were given by Gay Tranmer, Sept 20, 1910 at Elko Nevada and Nimrod Urie, which appears to have been made in late January of 1911 at Winnemucca, Nevada. Urie's statement was made before Judge E. J. L. Taber, District Attorney, James Dysant and Humboldt County Sheriff Lamb. Urie made a similar statement at his trial.

Sheriff Lamb didn't become involved in Urie's life until the murders of the Quilicies at Imlay, Nevada on January 6, 1911.

According to their statements the altercation with the Daggetts took place at the Tranmer horse corals, located southeast of the Tranmer camp.

Chapter VI, Altercation at Cow Creek

In the corner's inquest for Menina Quilici, page 2 of Urie's testimony Urie stated he met Frank Tranmer at Tranmer Ranch last spring when he, Gay Tranmer, Ed Diffendarfer, and Gordon Girdner were headed up to run (gather) horses. He stated "he never heard any more until they started down here (Imlay), when he heard Frank was in jail in Elko, then he ran into Frank in Imaly and he helped run horses." Urie only mentioned Ed Diffindarfer running horses.

Page 18 of his testimony

Note: It is pretty hard for only two guys to run horses. Urie said Frank came down to the Blakslee ranch, near Imlay, Nevada to help run horses. Now there are three men to run horses. He also stated there was trunk at that ranch (near Imaly) belonging to Gay Tranmer. It had in it a sling shot belonging to Girdner and keys belonging to Gay. There continues to be this close connection between Gay Tranmer, Frank Tranmer, Nimrod Urie, Ed Diffindarfer and Gordon Girdner all the way from Twin Falls Idaho to Imaly, Nevada.

The whole gang was from the Twin Falls area they included Gay Tranmer, Ed Diffendarfer, Nimrod Urie, Frank Dopp (horse wrangler), Frank Tranmer (brother of Gay and step father of Dopp).. Most were born and raised there. Now they are all in the Winnemucca/Imlay area or have a connection there. The explanation is fairly simple, they were distancing themselves from the Gollaher Mountain incident.

A man, by the name of Truman Clark and Gay Tranmer worked for Truman's dad on the Conover Place at Roseworth, south of Buhl, Idaho. They worked together there, feeding cattle and putting up hay, during the winter of 1931 & 32, the summer of 1932 and the winter of 1932 & 33. In an interview with Truman October 19, 2004, I asked him about the incident at Gollaher Mountain. He said this is the first time he had ever heard of it.

I interviewed Gay's son, Walter Tranmer, on June 9, 2007, he too had never heard of the incident.

Where most people (old timers) liked to tell of their run-ins with the Indians, Gay Tranmer had shed it from his mind. It appears Gay did not ever want to see the images of or hear of altered brands nor buried horses again.

Although there is no hard evidence of what actually happened at Cow Creek, a likely scenario could be as follows:

Three of Mike's boys ran onto the Tranmer gang altering brands on horses. The Indians were looking to gather some of their own and hopefully catch some unbranded horses. There may have been some kind of close encounter or confrontation. The Tranmer outfit ran the Indians off, shot at them, maybe not kill or hit one but close enough to scare them off. One, who they thought was Charlie, was hit. They, or someone, evidently Gay, shot too close and hit Charlie evidently severing the femoral artery, from which he died.

Mike's boys were not likely armed, the last thing they needed was to have to haul around a couple heavy, awkward, rifles, while attempting to gather horses.

The Indians buried Charlie somewhere between Cow Creek, where the Tranmer outfit was camped and Willow Creek, where the Indians were camped. This burial was probably under rocks in a rock pile or boulder field.

Two of the three boys returned with rifle or rifles to Cow Creek overlooking the Tranmer camp. In seeking revenge for the killing of their brother they fired into the camp killing the Dopp boy.

Mike's history tells him that when you kill a white man, you and your family will pay the consequences, (in blood).

These boys have created one hell of problem for the family, but they stick together, as a family and all leave the country together, heading west.

They have also created one hell of a problem for the Tranmer gang. They now have a dead body and a corral full of horses with altered brands. So, stow the body in the shade, run the freshly branded horses out of the country, kill and bury them. Then call in the law, regurgitate their story and find Dopp nine days later.

When Mike's boys returned to Cow Creek they also separated the Tranmer outfit from some of their horses plus some, that did not have fresh brands, from the horse trap, totaling at least twelve horses.

How about Girdner's wife and two year old daughter? Did someone stay with her or did she stay in camp by herself, with the baby, while the gang were killing and burying horses over a period of four to five days. Taking her to the head of Badger Cr. while trailing, killing and burying horses would have been almost impossible. So what did they do? They couldn't leave her and baby there alone with wild Indians running around the country, they needed all hands to bury horses.

Somehow the Tranmer outfit knew the Indians had left the country.

The Daggetts didn't try to bury any horses to hide evidenced. All the evidence to cause them trouble was in the form of the young Frank Dopp. They broke camp, loaded almost everything they owned on horses, and leaving their wagon behind, got the hell out of there, with as much haste as they could muster, as was stated by Mike's 15 year old daughter to Asbury, April 27, 1911. The last thing the Indians needed was to take the time to bury twenty five head of horses.

The Indians did not bury any horses, as claimed by the Tranmer bunch.

What did the Tranmer horse runners know about the Indians disappearance? They couldn't have taken Girdner's wife and two year old daughter with them to bury horses, therefore they must have known the Indians were gone.

105

A question not yet answered is; did the Tranmer outfit go to Gollaher Mountain to steal horses or did that opportunity arise after the got there?

Another question; if Gay Tranmer had a corral already constructed at Gollaher Mountain, had he stolen horses there before?

It should be noted that neither Gay Tranmer nor Nimrod Urie ever mentioned Cow Creek in their statements. Without question they knew where they were which further illustrates their effort to distance themselves from the goings on at Cow Creek.

When Gay made his statement in Elko, no one bothered to ask any questions, after all the accused were Indians. And why did they not contact the Elko authorities before September 20, 1910, the date Gay made his statement? The most likely answer is the horses had been uncovered and they felt they had better make a statement.

They blamed Indians, so if Indians were changing brands why not call the Sheriff or at least turn them in?

Ans. - It would draw too much attention to themselves.

What were they doing all summer and was Frank Tranmer in fact in jail in Elko, as Urie said he had heard? The answer to these two questions is unknown.

What did the Tranmer gang know about the Daggetts vacating Gollaher Mt.? They must have known but no hard evidence was found that they knew.

The tracks of twenty five head of horses being driven to the pits in Badger Creek would have been easy to follow. This is another reason the gang needed more time.

More time would allow other horses in the area and storms to obliterate the tracks.

What was the Tranmer gang doing in Elko? Authorities in Elko were inept and believed their bull shit story. Idaho folks who knew them did not, except for the newspapers and they got it wrong.

Tranmer outfit had to have miraculously found Dopp's body so no one would show up looking for it and discover the buried horses.

Why would the Tranmer outfit go to such great lengths to hide evidence of horse stealing? Before autos and tractors became the main source of transportation and horse power for farming and commerce, horses were extremely valuable and up and into the early 20th century you could lose your life if caught stealing a horse or horses.

There is a history of horse thieves losing their lives in Idaho when suspected of stealing horses right up and through 1903.

[In April of 1892, posse from Market Lake , Idaho , shot and killed two horse thieves in Jackson Hole, Wyoming, and in May of 1903, two men tried to run off 14 horses from a construction camp at Milner, near Twin Fall. One of them drowned in the Snake while trying to escape from the angry crowd chasing him and the other was caught and nearly lynched "before cooler heads prevailed."]

FIRST CHILD BORN IN TWIN FALLS COUNTY AND

"EARLY PIONEER" OF TWIN FALLS AREA
WILLIAM G. TRANMER
Pictured Here With Wife Phoebe
Born 22 May, 1877 at Rock Creek, Idaho
(Near the Stricker Ranch Stage Stop) South of Hansen
Died 10 July, 1952, Age 75 Years

Twin Falls Historical Society

GAY TRANMER
ca 1916

In 1916 Gay at age 39, married 16 year old Phoebe.

Tranmer assembled a horse running crew in the early part of April, 1910 to run horses on Gollaher Mountain, Nevada, thus was born the Saga of Shoshone Mike. Three of Mike's boys encountered the Tranmer crew altering brands on horses, which led to an altercation, resulting in the death of one of Mike's sons, Jake, and the death of Frank Dopp, horse wrangler for the Tranmer crew and step son of Gay's brother Frank.

The Daggetts, fearing reprisals from the white community, left there in late April 1910.

Height	1 m	78.9	Head length	19.3	L Foot	26.0		blue	Age	44	Born in	18
Stretch	1 m	82.0	Head width	14.7—	L Mid F	12.1		Class 2-3	Apparent Age			
Trunk		96.3	Cheek width	13.9	L Lit F	9.5	Color L Eye	Areola r-j-m	Nativity		Illinois	
Curv			R Ear length	6.5	L Cubit	47.7		Periph =i-m	Occupation		Vaquero	
Eng. Height		70¼	Remarks relative to Measurements					Pecul				

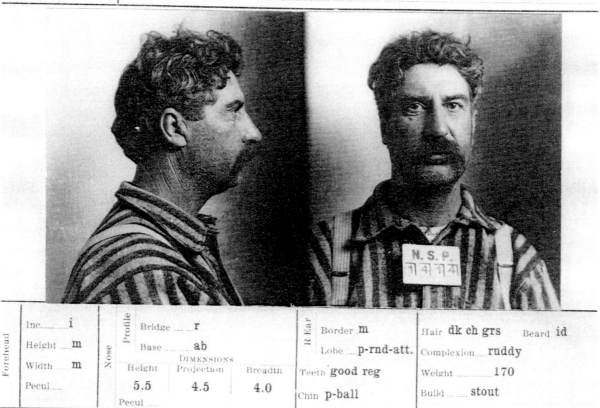

Forehead	Inc i	Profile	Bridge r				R Ear	Border m	Hair dk ch grs	Beard id
	Height m	Nose	Base ab					Lobe p-rnd-att.	Complexion ruddy	
	Width m		DIMENSIONS					Teeth good reg	Weight 170	
			Height	Projection	Breadth					
	Pecul		5.5	4.5	4.0			Chin p-ball	Build stout	
			Pecul							

NEVADA STATE POLICE
CARSON CITY. NEVADA

Examined 7-18-11
By Stone

FRANK TRANMER

July 18, 1911

Nevada State Prison - Carson City, Nevada

Note: Charles **Stone**, of the Nevada State Police, was with the posse that were involved in the incident that took place February 26, 1911 near Golconda, Nevada.

NIMROD URIE

Entering
Winnemucca Jail
January 1911

Entering Nevada State
Prison
1911

At the Nevada State Prison
Believed to be on or before
Nov. 26, 1923
when he was discharged
from prison

GIRDNERS

ca 1921

Gordon, Lenore, Harriet and Bill -

Gordon was a friend of the Tranmer brothers and a member of the Tranmer outfit altering brands on horses at Cow Creek. Harriet, a rather petite young lady of twenty three, was taken along as the cook. Lenore, only two, was also along and in the camp of the horse runners. In latter years it is reported that Harriet took Lenore and hid out, in fear for their lives, from a angry and drunken Gordon. Harriet was under constant fear for her life if she ever revealed what she knew about the Gollaher Mt. incident. She did eventually escape and divorce Gordon.

BUCK RICE (Shoshone Basin)

ca 1918

Buck Rice owned a large number of horses around the country. A good number of those, he wintered on and around Gollaher Mountain.

When the Tranmer horse runners began gathering horses there around the 20th of April, 1910, they would have encountered some of Rice's horses.

Pot hook   Ꝺ

CHAPTER IX
MIKE'S STATE OF MIND

The Daggetts have vanished from Gollaher Mountain.

According to the Tranmer outfit they were caught red handed stealing horses and they killed Frank Dopp. The Indians have crossed the white man. What happens when Indians cross the white man? When it is this serious, he is run down and killed, family and all. Mike, Maggie and the older boys have seen this first hand. In fact, growing up in the 19th century, they have seen it many times, no justice for Indians, innocent until proven guilty only applies to white man, not Indians.

Mike and his family have left the country, their homeland, for fear of what treachery might be brought upon them, at the hands of the white man.

The new baby, only weeks old, will spend the next ten and a half months laced in a cradle board as the family traveled west, to the Sacramento River and then back east into Nevada, their journey ending on the 26th of February 26, 1911. She would live in that cradle board, experiencing the extreme heat and the extreme cold, their shelters being nonexistent except for a few blankets and a tarp, the exception was at Little High Rock Canyon where the family constructed a Wikiiup for shelter.

The environment, through which they will travel, included wood ticks, gnats, mosquitos, rattle snakes and other critters. If you were to travel over that same route, today, which the Daggetts passed, you would find much of the country has changed very little and those same critters still inhabit the area.

To review Mike's state of mind let us regress a bit and review history that Mike had been a part of and other episodes of history he most surely was aware of. This time frame in history should give us some insight into what was weighing heavily on his mind when the decision was made to leave Gollaher Mountain.

For a period of about thirty years, beginning in the 1850s and culminating at Wounded Knee, the Indians in Mike's world and time were hunted down and slaughtered, you might say a "wholesale killing took place". Military campaigns were conducted for the specific purpose of killing Indians. As the white man entered into Mike's world, they spread out, taking whatever land and the resources from that land that they wanted. They were incensed that the Indian should fight back. Gregory Michno's work, that he refers to as the "Snake Conflict", 1863 to 1868, is a basic and defining illustration of a planned annihilation of the Indian. Mincho researched military letters and reports for the information he used in writing his book "Snake Conflict". Very little was taken from other sources.

In an attempt to hang on to their homeland and avoid starvation, the Indian fought back, savagely and with their own cruelty, but they were no match for the advancing white man. Throughout the last half of the 19th century, any accusation of theft or other crime by an Indian, whether real or not, was a license to kill an Indian without further investigation.

Mike grew up during the decade of the 1860s. During that decade Mike and Maggie lived within the geographic area (NGB & SRP) generally described as the area along the Snake River between the Rocky Mountains the Sierra/Cascades Mountains.

In that decade Mike would have been in one of three situations; Scouts for the soldiers, on a reservation or being hunted by the soldiers.

Mike and his wife grew up in this atmosphere of "no Indian should exist where white man wanted to be".

Were the Daggetts correct in their assumption, that their chances of survival now, are slim to none?

The facts stated again here from Chapter I, IN THE BEGINNING, you be the judge:

1) In January of 1863 General Patrick Connor led an attack on the Shoshone in their lodges on Bear River, in southern Idaho. After 4 hours of terror and mayhem an estimated 250 Shoshone villagers lay dead, including women and children. The general had a large ego and wanted to be fighting in the civil war but instead he was relegated to watching Mormons and Indians from his post near Salt Lake. When he heard about the Indians in their winter encampment at Bear River, he decided to march up there and clean them out.

"The Shoshone Frontier and the Bear River Massacre" by Brigham Madson

2) In February of 1866 the mining interests of Silver City Idaho organized a group of

volunteers and raised money for them to go and pursue the Indian and kill him wherever he could be found. A bounty to be paid for every man woman and child killed.

3) In 1866 a report by Capt. Hunt of the 1st Cavalry, logged four months of operations against Indians throughout the Owyhee country, from the Snake River in Idaho to Paradise Valley, Nevada. The Captain left Camp Lions, near Jordan Valley, Oregon, in July and returned in October. His mission, kill Indians. The total number Indians, estimated to have been killed, approximately eighteen. He specifically identifies five killed in one engagement and seven in another. In a 3rd engagement he says a number were killed.

Not a lot of Indians were killed for such a long campaign however one is too many when they were guilty of no crime. There is little doubt that they included women and children.

The Journal of Captain Hunt National Archives - W. D. C.

4) The Bannock War of 1878, led to the wholesale slaughter of Bannock Indians and those Piaute and Shoshone Indians who joined Chief Buffalo Horn. Buffalo Horn was the instigator of the Bannock War.

5) In the death march to Yakima, in December of 1878, 550 Indians were rounded up, as prisoners, at the Malheur Reservation and taken to Fort Simco, Yakima, Washington in the bitter cold of mid December. In the following years less than 200 returned to Fort Hall and other reservations in northern Nevada, southern Idaho and southeast Oregon, most died of white man diseases and exposure.

The white mans version on the forced move was to protect these Indians from the waring Bannock Tribe. The Indians version is; they were taken to Yakima as prisoners.

"SURVIVORS of the BANNOCK WAR" by Benson Gibson Page 32 and THE SHOSHONE of the DUCK VALLEY INDIANS RESERVATION by Whitney Mc Kinney

6) The slaughter at Wounded Knee in 1890, another senseless and tasteless killing of Indians, when the Soldiers slaughtered a whole encampment of Indians, including women and children.

"THE SOULE of the INDIAN" By Charles Eastman

The list of atrocities, that Mike would have seen or been aware of, if not there in person, goes on and on.

7) And then finally, a warrant was issued, on May 5, 1910, for all five of the grown men in the Daggett family, even though only three were seen at the site of the altercation.

Chapter VI - Altercation at Cow Creek

Write-ups going around in the media included the following:

1 -- "He, H. Clark, [the Sheriff of Elko County] investigated and found that the Indians had stolen some 80 head of horses and after collecting same in the Shoshone Basin, Twin Falls County, ran them over the line. He sent word to citizens to *"kill all the Indians, and every Indian that may be found roaming the Idaho country"*.

From the Twin Falls Times dated May 12, 1910.

2 -- From Elko County D. A., E. J. Taber, dated Sept. 27, 1910 to Commission of Indian Affairs W.D.C. *"If they [the Indians] had been caught right after the crime was committed, I am afraid the law would never have had a chance to deal with them as the people in the vicinity were worked up to a high pitch"*. This statement appeared in several newspapers at the time, which included The Daly Elko Independent, Elko Weekly Independent, and the Humboldt Star.

National Archives Washington, D C.

3 -- Telegram to Nevada State Journal, on or about February 24, 1911, from Washoe County Sheriff, Ferrel: *"I want to add one Indian scalp to my collection and I am going to get it. This is the only place (Tuscarora, Nevada) I can send any news at present. I want Indians more than anything else and bring this chase to a close"*.

THE INDIAN MASSACRE OF 1911 By Effie Mona Mack Page 60

4 --"So intense is the feeling here against the Murderers that it is freely said they will never reach a jail even if taken alive".

OAKLAND TRIBUNE - February 13, 1911

Finally, on February 26, 1911, his fears became reality when Mike and seven of his family were killed near Golconda, Nevada.

These experiences were to shape his thoughts as to what lay ahead and guide him in such a manner that he and his family would live, with the white man, under a cloud of uncertainty and survive. Mike realized, from these life long experiences, to deprive white man of anything white man wanted could sooner or later, could lead to severe consequences to he and his family. He had to be looking over his shoulder the entire

65 years of his life, in fear white man might decide that the Daggetts mere existence may need to end.

After the killing of Frank Dopp at Gollaher Mountain, the Daggetts knew that their chance of survival, for the long term, were dim or non existent.

The stage was now set for a long trek across the wastelands of southern Idaho and northern Nevada. The Daggetts would not look on them as wastelands, they had been here before, hiding from the white man. It was a proven point when somehow they managed to negotiate a trail across three states, from Gollaher Mountain, Nevada to north central California and back into north central Nevada, with the alleged contact with white man no more than half a dozen times, during the 500 mile trek over a period of nine and half months.

In addition to having been there before they would camp and scout ahead thus they knew where and what lay ahead at the next camp site before moving on.

The Daggetts did not have an opportunity to lay in supplies for a long trip before leaving Gollaher Mountain, so raiding cow camps along the way makes sense.

Asbury's interview of Heney April 1911 - National Archives Washington D.C..

Why Mike and his family continued westward to the Sacramento River is not known.

Why in fall of 1910 they turned and started back eastward toward their old stomping ground is also a mystery. They had to have been driven by some force we do not relate to or comprehend.

CHAPTER X

THERE WERE DOUBTS AND THEN THERE WERE DOUBTS

Early on in this tragic story of Indians vs horse runners the Elko County authorities were doing a lot of posturing and making accusations against the Indians but little else. The newspapers, Twin Falls Times, Wells Nevada State Herald, Elko Independent, among others, led the foray, railing against the Indians and convicting the Daggetts before they really knew who was involved. They were accepting the word of the Tranmer horse runners without ever speaking with an Indian.

Others, who knew one or both parties involved, had some reservations about the Tranmer story.

Then, over the next nine months, the wheels of justice turned very slowly as a multitude of letters and other correspondence between the Indian agencies, both local and in Washington D. C, Elko authorities, Cassia County Idaho District Attorney, T. Bailey Lee and the Attorney General's office in Washington D. C. flowed back and forth.

As the different agencies and organizations began to slowly sort out the different facets of this episode, both federal and local, the heat began to build on the Tranmer outfit.

On January 6, 1911, a most heinous crime was committed in the double murder of Jean and Marina Quilici, who owned a saloon at Imlay, Nevada. The Quilicis were both shot in the back, during a robbery of their saloon, Jean died immediately and Mrs. Quilici died the following day.

The Humboldt County Sheriff, S. G. Lamb, with Indian tracker John (Skinny) Pascal in tow, took two men suspected of the crime, into custody, at the Blakesley Ranch, on the Humboldt River and a short distance from Imlay. The two suspects were Frank Tranmer and Nimrod Urie.

All five of the horse runners were connected to Gay Tranmer at the Blakeslee Ranch, near Imlay. Ed Diffendarfer was still in the area but Gordon Girdner had left the country for Yakima, Washington. Gay Tranmer was conspicuous by his absence and both Nimrod Urie and Frank Tranmer were in the Winnemucca jail. No one seemed to know the whereabouts of Gay.

Cassia County District Attorney, T. Baily Lee and C. H. Asbury, Superintendent at the Carson Training School at Stewart, Nevada were both calling for his arrest.

Tranmer and Urie were tried separately for the murders. Each was convicted and sentenced to death. Tranmer died in the Nevada State Prison, September 17, 1918. Urie was released from prison in December of 1923 and married November 20, 1927.

Urie's defense was that Frank Tranmer had threatened to kill him if he did not participate in the robbery and that Tranmer did the actual shooting.

Urie had confessed before trial, after Sheriff Lamb assured him of his safety as Tranmer was locked up and couldn't get to him.

Urie, however, never wavered from his story regarding the tragedy on Cow Creek on Gollaher Mountain, the spring before. He continued to maintain that the Indians were the ones stealing horses.

However, no one interrogated him about the buried horses or altered brands. He may have been as afraid of Gay Tranmer as he was of Frank. Gay wasn't locked up.

It also must be pointed out that Skinny Pascal testified at these trials.

Transcript of the Urie trial and the Nevada State Archives.

The killing of the Quilicis in Imlay, Nevada, by Frank Tranmer and Nimrod Urie, brought more doubt on the Tranmer story and magnified the heat on the horse runners.

All were connected to Frank and Urie at the Blakesley Ranch, in one way or another.

Urie testified that there were items that belonged to Gay Tranmer and Gordon Girdner in a trunk there and that Ed Diffendarfer and Gay Tranmer had been staying there.

Gay Tranmer had a charge account at Ed Slaughter's saloon, in Imlay, under the name "Gay Tranmer & Co." on which Frank Tranmer had made some charges.

The heat was on the Tranmer & Co. and building up until just thirteen days (January 19, 1911) after the Quilici murders, the Daggetts made a huge mistake in the killing of four stockmen in Little High Rock Canyon, located in northeast Nevada, destroying any chance of surviving the killing of Frank Dopp.

The Quilici affair had put a whole new light on the altercation at Cow Creek back on April 25, 1910. However the killing at Little High Rock turned the whole thing upside down again saving Gay Tranmer's butt and leading to the destruction of the Daggetts.

The killing at Little High Rock didn't come to light until the 10th of February 1911. The true identity of who did the killing wasn't known until the 26th of February, 1911, when the Daggett family was wiped out near Golconda, Nevada, by an overzealous, incompetent, so called posse.

The Indians had no inclination of all that had transpired since they had left Gollaher Mountain. As of January 19, it was too late. In fact all the Daggett family, except four of the children, died, never knowing how close they may have come to being exonerated. There were accusations by rumor of other killings supposedly done by the Daggetts but that is what they were, rumors, with no validity.

One or three of the Daggett boys may have had to answer for the killing of Frank Dopp, but there was no reason to kill any other members of the family, other than they were Indians.

All through the months of May, June, July and August, no effort was made by the Elko authorities to investigate the Gollaher Mountain incident. The D. A. didn't care, the Sheriff, was totally incompetent and didn't care. Nothing transpired, even at the goading of the Cassia County, Idaho D. A., T. Baily Lee. In the end, this pitiful effort led to the near destruction of Indian Mike and his family. Had newly elected Sheriff, Joe Harris, been Sheriff from the beginning, back in April, maybe something would have been done, but Gollaher Mountain was a long ways from Elko, and after all only an Indian and some white kid from Idaho were alleged to have been killed.

Where was the Tranmer outfit from the middle of May to the middle of September? One bit of information suggested they might have been involved in robbing a train near Ogden Utah, where a porter was killed. Further research revealed that not to be true.

Although they all had friends and family in and around Twin Falls, there is no evidence any one of the Tranmer outfit returned to the area during the remainder of the year. Only Ed and Gay returned later.

The time of Gay's return to the area is in question, he was not there as of December 1910. He may have gone back to the area sometime in early January 1911.

The first documentation on him being back in the Twin Falls area was May of 1912.

Ed Diffendarfer had family there, but Ed's ties there are a little more obscure. Ed hadn't returned by 1913, but did have his brand registered in Idaho in 1916. In 1913 Sheriff Lamb, from Winnemucca, had to retrieved him from Ogden, Utah to testify in the Frank Tranmer trial.

Gordon Girdner's family lived in Twin Falls and his father was foreman of a horse ranch there. No matter Gordon took his family to Yakima, Washington and never returned.

Why did Frank Tranmer, who was married to Frank Dopp's mother, not go back to the Rock Creek/Twin Falls area if he was innocent and not a part of the branding of horses and the killing of the Indian boy, since it was his stepson that was killed by the Indians. One would think he would go back to his wife in Twin Falls.

Frank Tranmer and Urie were arrested about Jan. 10, 1911 for the killing of the Quilicies in Imlay, Nevada. They were both convicted and sent to the Nevada State Prison. Frank died there in 1918. Nimrod Urie returned to Twin Falls 13 years later, after being paroled.

Frank Dopp never returned he was killed near the Tranmer corrals by the Daggett boys.

Gay Tranmer, mastermind and instigator of the horse running operation, got off unscathed. He was the only one of the eight people, involved in the horse running at Cow Creek that did. The killing of the ranchers at Little High Rock and the Daggetts at Rabbit Creek saved Gay's butt!

The incident at Cow Creek, on Gollaher Mountain, Nevada, gave birth to the "Saga of Shoshone Mike and the eventual death of twenty two people.

In an interview with Truman Clark, in September of 2004, at Buhl, Idaho, shortly before he passed away, he said he and Gay Tranmer worked together for Truman's dad for about a year and a half, putting up hay and feeding cattle. Truman said Gay never mentioned the run-in with Indians on Gohaller Mt. nor did he mention any other-run with Indians.

In an interview with, Gay's son, Walter Tranmer, June 8, 2007, shortly before Walter passed away, said he knew nothing of the incident, "but that his father could talk Indian". Gay had no intention of ever bringing up the subject, he had gotten away with stealing horses and killing one of the Daggett boys.

122

On the flip side, eight members of the Donnelley posse, from Surprise Valley that killed eight of the Daggett Family on February 26, 1911, bragged about their involvement for years. These men, however, were acquitted by an inquest jury.

CHAPTER XI

AT GOLLAHER Mt.

Between the first of May, 1910 and Feb. 7, 1911.

To best illustrate what was going on between the first of May, 1910 and February 7, 1911, regarding solving the mystery at Gollaher Mountain, I offer excerpts from official letters, written during that period, which include my observation and comments **(in bold letters)** as to their significance and accuracy.

Letters from the National Archives, W. D. C.

1910

May 5th -- **Complaint filed by George Grimm,** charging Indians Jim, Jake, Charlie, Mike and John Doe an Indian, with murder. A warrant was issued and given to Grimm to serve.

Grimm was listed as "Deputy Constable" on the Warrant. If he was the Constable of Contact, what authority did he have out in the county? What is a Deputy Constable? Not sure but evidently he was wearing two hats. He was a Deputy Sheriff and the Constable of Contact and had jurisdiction in the county and the town of Contact.

MAY 26th -- A letter was forwarded to C. H. Asbury, Superintendent Carson Training School, Stewart, Nevada **from/by** Superintendent Haggett of Western Shoshone.

This letter was not found in the National Archives. But it is assumed to describe the crime at Gollaher Mt.

JULY 27th -- To Commissioner of Indian Affairs, W. D. C. **from** C. H. Asbury.

Received above letter on June 6th. forwarded by Superintendent Haggett. Enclosed sketch of location and news clipping. Rc'd paper but nothing in it and the files had not been kept so I could not search them. After second request of Elko County Sheriff, I. G. Clark, I received this:

" will say that we have not been able to learn anything till yet, but we are working on the case, and may learn something of it later, we are in doubt whether the Indians done it or not, if any thing new is learned will advise you"

I wrote to Humboldt County Sheriff, he knew nothing of the case.

I wrote to Supt. Haggett again, asking him to advise me of any of interest, but heard nothing.

I wrote to Supt. at Fort Hall.....reply signed by Special Agent Mc Chesney, no info but would keep a watch for the Indians.

I wrote to postmaster at Contact, Nev. June 30, no reply yet.

Don't plan to travel to that part of the country since the local authorities are taking no interest in the matter.

AUGUST 5th -- To Asbury **from** John R. T. Reeves, Acting Chief, Land Division. Rc'd your letter of July 27 regarding alleged murder by Indians as outlined in news clipping from Carson City May 8th. *No need to incur any additional expense. Report to this office anything new.*

AUGUST 14 -- To Dept. of Interior U. S. Indian Service, Stewart, Nev. **from** W. A. Kent, *Post Master at Contact. "Pardon delay in answer but had to await return of Coroner".* **(The body was found way back in the middle of May)**

Indians ranged Cedar Cr., Bull Cr., Cow Cr., Trout Cr., Willow Cr. and southern Idaho. Party of 3 men and a boy, headed by Gay Tranmer of Rk. Cr. Id. went to get horses on Cow Cr., but on going there ran into the indian camp, not knowing they were there. The indians were found with a bunch of horses which had evidently been stolen because the old brands were obliterated by theirs. As soon as the presence of the white men was discovered by the indians they were held up to the point of their guns and ordered to leave the country at once. And as soon as the white men left they were followed up by the indians and fired upon several times before they escaped to camp which was fired into also. The boy of the camp was attracted by the shooting and went out in the hills to find the cause when he ran into the Indians and was shot dead,where he was found by Sheriff's posse a few days later. The indians have not been located since but were supposed to have buried their horses about 12 miles north east of Ranch

O'Grande which is in northeast Elko Co. Nev. There are three or four Indians in the party. They are supposed to be now near Steeple Rock Mt. Ida. - near Pocatello, Id. Write to the Supt. Fort Hall Reservation and you may get more information.

Kent had the happenings and location wrong but he had gotten the information from the coroner, who had gotten info. from the Tranmer outfit. Two questions: who was the coroner, Deputy Grimm? And who found the body? Gay Tranmer said he did, in his statement to DA Taber, Sept. 20, at Elko.

The ledger, documenting the the actions of Grimm and the coroner, was turned in at the Elko County Court House as many others were, when municipalities around the county folded and no longer existed. Those ledgers no longer exist. They were either lost, thrown away or taken by some one.

AUGUST 17th -- To Commission of Indian Affairs D. C. **from** Asbury

Referring to letters of May 26 and Aug. 5th. Enclosed letter just received from the Postmaster at Contact in response to my letter to him of June 30. I sent copy to Fort Hall.

SEPT. 27 -- To U.S. Comm. of Indian Affairs, DC **From** E.J Taber, Elko County. D.A. Enclosing statement of fact connected with the cold-blooded murder of boy (Dopp) by Indians. Also sent to sheriffs Id., Utah, Wy., and Montana. "Wish US Gov. would help us get hold of these Indians. *The murder was so atrocious that it calls for vengeance. I have no personal interest whatever in the matter, but as district att. I would be glad to catch these Indians and prosecute them". ["If they had been caught right after the crime was committed, I am afraid the law would never have had a chance to deal with them, as the people in the vicinity were worked up to a high pitch"].*

The region where the crime was committed is sparsely settled and not easy of access, though by no means inaccessible. The Indians are well known to many of the whites asking for help to locate Indians.

Note Taber labels the incident as *"STATEMENT OF FACT" and "ATROCIOUS"* . **All based on Gay's statement, no questions asked. Also note quote in brackets. The bigger questions are, where were the horse runners between the middle of May until the 20th of Sept. and why no statements from the Tranmer outfit until Sept. 20th? Why was there no statement from any of the others who were there?**

127

OCT.12 -- To Taber **from** F.H. Abbott, Asst. Commissioner of Indian Affairs, W.D.C. *Your letter of Sept. 27 is the first information the office has had regarding such a crime. Send a supply of circulars (Gay's statement) and we will send out to Superintendents of Indian Reservations in the vicinity.*

OCT. 16th -- To Abbott **from** E.P. Carville, Dept. DA, Elko. Circulars are in the mail.

OCT. 29 -- To Spear, Wadsworth; Hoover, McDermitt; Haggett, Owyhee; Wadsworth, Fort Hall; Hall, Whiterocks, Utah; Griffith, Fort Bidwell, Calif. **from** John Francis. Alleged, by Gay, the murder took place on May 6th. Send any information to Taber. Related Gay's statement, Head of family Mike Daggett, 4 sons, 3 squaws.

NOV. 9 -- To Comm. Indian Affairs, DC **from** John B. Hoover, Supt. Fort Mc Dermitt. *"Some of my Indians saw the suspected parties traveling west through Cedarville, Calif. last July. They had some twenty horses and whenever anyone approached to look at the horses or examine the brands, he was told to go away or he would be killed. I have just written this information to Mr Griffith, Supt. Fort Bidwell School, Fort Bidwell, Calif."* **Interesting letter, how did Mc Dermitt Indians know there were some 20 horses, unless they saw them? They obviously did. About the brands, why would the Mc Dermitt Indians be looking for brands? They didn't know about the brand issue until asked by Hoover. I believe the Indians were entertaining themselves and, saw a chance to blow a little smoke (add a little wood to the fire). I do not believe they were threatened by Mike's outfit.**

NOV. 24 -- To Att. Gen. DC **from** T. Bailey Lee, Pros. Att. Cassia Cnty. Idaho. *Three Indians have just left my office, they reported 14 of their kin, members of the Shoshone Tribe and for the most part women and children, have been slaughtered by white men, and their remains concealed or burned. Latter part of July rumors of cowboys encountering horse stealing Indians. Fight ensued white boy killed Indian wounded. Boy's body found later, Indians gone. Frank Tranmer who told the story disappeared, the dead boys mother immediately announced her belief that Tranmer who had borne a bad reputation had, in conjunction with others, been caught by her son while stealing cattle and killed to prevent exposure. Ranchers went with constable to the area, found wagon and trenches. It is now discovered that 2 other unsavory* *characters had left the country. Nevada officers have done nothing not even investigated the trenches where the 14 Indians are surely buried. The wife and children of informants are among the missing Indians. They can get no action from the Nevada authorities. My hands are tied the state line blocks me. Can you place someone here to ferret this thing out.*

It is interesting that Lee knew nothing of the event until rumors came in in July. The Dopp boy and the Tranmers were from Rock Cr., right in the middle of Lee's jurisdiction. Fourteen Indians was correct if Lizard & new baby were included. Did those relatives know of the new baby? They hadn't seen the Daggett family since the summer before which would have been about 8 months.

List of family members Part I - Chapter II

It also should be noted that Lee was given the information about the missing relatives, in person, while much of the other info is second hand. Also note Frank Tranmer told the story and then disappeared. His wife, Dopps mother, accused Frank of being involved and then he evidently disappeared (more evidence Frank was with Gay & others at Cow Cr). However it was Gay who told the story. Lee had as much trouble keeping the stories straight as every one else. He had one part right, the Nevada authorities did nothing!!

NOV. 26 -- To Taber **from** C.F. Hanke, 2nd Ass. Comm. Asking for more circulars and alerting him of the Nov. 9 letter regarding Indians going through Cedarville.

NOV. 30 -- To Hanke **from** Carville *I will get circulars out.*

NOV. 30 -- To Secretary of Interior **from** Fowler. Enclosed Lee's letter. *Have written Lee requesting info alleged murders on territory exclusive jurisdiction of US. will case come within federal law? Lee letter also sent to US Att. for the Dist. of Nev.*

NOV. 30 -- To Taber **from** AG Fowler. News clipping and confirm letters sent.

Shoshone Mike papers National Archies W. D. C.

DEC. 8 -- To Comm. Indian Affairs D C **from** Asbury. Ref. letters. May 26 and Aug. 5 and news clipping Reno Gazette Dec. 7. *Lee called attention to Dept. of Justice that there is evidence white horse thieves had killed Indians and buried horses. Elko dispatch, they knew nothing more. Not much credit to this report and might explain* *indifference of local officials and the lack of information among the people of that location.*

Sheriff Clark & DA Taber had conflicting stories and plenty to act on, but obviously didn't care. Besides it would have been a long hard horseback ride, in December, from the railroad at Wells 90 miles to Gollaher Mt. This may be the big reason Elko authorities were making no attempt to sort out the facts.

DEC. 12 -- To Comm. Indian Affairs DC **from** Thos. J King Jr., Superintendent, Cheyenne River Agency. Enclosed clipping Dec. 7 Washington Star. *Give me description of the 3 men Lee mentioned and will try to apprehend.*

DEC. 20 -- To King **from** FH Abbott. *No description of the 3 men. Not sure crimes committed. Information Sept. 27 from Taber, murder of Dopp by Indians, as related by Gay Tranmer. Tranmers mixed up. Thinks Gay and Frank are one and the same. Looking for definite info to forward.*

DEC. 20 -- To Taber **from** Abbott. **(Asking Taber to investigate the allegations of Lee)** Regarding letter Nov. 30 from your office here is copy of Lee letter differing from Gay's story. Still confused over the brothers Gay and Frank, Abbott ask Taber to look into the allegations of Lee and if not can you account for the Indians. *Can you check the trenches and give us results of your findings. If Lee's accusations are correct hope you will leave no stone unturned in apprehending killers.*

Ass. Commissioner Abbott turning up the heat on the Elko authorities.

DEC. 20 -- To E.P. Holcombe, Chief Supervisor, Denver, Colorado **from** Abbott. Enclosed copy of letter Nov. 30 from acting AG regarding murder of 14 Indians and letter from Lee same subject. Investigate earliest and report.

DEC. 21 -- To AG **from** Frank Moros First Ass. Sect. Rc'd Nov. 30 letter Acting AG enclosing Lee letter. Indian office is investigating, will communicate any info. Appreciate your action.

DEC. 29 -- To Sect. Interior **from** Fowler. Rc'd letter from Nev. US Att. saying he has to rely on reports from your office. Will forward info from you to DA.

1911

JAN. 3 -- To AG, DC **from** Lee. More info for the Att. General.

Outrage took place about 15 miles southwest of the 3 corners, Utah, Nev. and Idaho and understands it is Forest Reserve. Indians receiving rations from Gov. Agency and were out hunting with families when attacked.

Lee was right about location but had bad info on the Forest Reserve part. There was no Forest Reserve in that part of Nevada. There is no evidence the Daggetts ever received rations. They were not registered at any reservation.

JAN. 9 -- Urie's statement, taken by Sheriff Lamb, DA Dysart & now, judge Taber.

JAN. 10 -- To Comm. Indian Affairs, DC **from** Taber, now the district judge, (James Dysart is now the new DA) *extraordinary situation which becomes more dramatic as time goes on. Not aware people in Idaho were satisfied that it was the white men who killed Dopp and they may have killed the Indians.*

Had Taber not gotten Lee letter, sent to him on Dec. 20th?

Press report 14 Shoshones killed by white horse thieves, horses and Indians buried in trenches. Day or so later the papers of Nev. were filled with big head lines and Nevada officers were doing nothing absolutely nothing etc. going on assumption that Indians had killed the boy as related by Gay Tranmer. Matter first reported by George Grimm, deputy Sheriff at Contact. *Grimm reported to me substantially as Gay, but of course Grimm got info. from Gay and the men who were in his party. Heard Gay owed boy $200.00 don't know if that is true. Week or so ago train robbery between here and Ogden which robbers killed the porter and robbed passengers and escaped.*

Check. SL papers for this story. Done - no connection.

A few days later murder of the Quilicies at Imlay. *Surprised when Frank and Uries names showed up in the paper as the men arrested for the killing. Don't know yet if Tranmer is Frank or Gay. "It was Gay Tranmer that sat in my office here in Elko with the man Ed Diffendarfer (see printed circular) and gave me the story which I had printed and sent to you and to so many Sheriffs, hoping that we could catch the Indians."*

"Now it appears that it is some of these very white men that are accused by the boy's mother and others in Idaho of having killed the boy".

Writing to Lee, Glad he reported to AG we may be able to solve mystery. Also writing to officers in Winn. so they will know of this other affair. Think officers here will ready to take up these matters. JC Harris is now the sheriff. Sheriff told me last night he was going to go dig up the horses to see if Indians under them.

January 10, no one is going to get to the head of Badger Cr. to dig up horses this time of year, besides they were supposed to have been dug up last Sept. Where is the communication? Also no mention of the Elko County Sheriff, by name, until after Harris elected Sheriff. Not aware of Lee letter forwarded to him Dec. 10th nearly 3 weeks ago?

JAN. 13 -- To Comm. Indian Affairs DC **from** Asbury. Enclosed news clipping from Jan. 11, Urie's confession and account as related by Tranmer and Urie. Frank T. and Urie arrested in connection with the Quilici murders in Imlay.

Clipping with letter dated Jan. 28th - NationalArchives W. D. C.

JAN. 14 -- To Sect. Int. **from** US AG Fowler. Forwarding Lee letter of Jan. 3 and also US Att. for Nev. to communicate directly with Lee and possible Grand Jury investigation.

JAN. 14 -- To Taber **from** Lee. *Mills of the Gods may yet grind exceedingly fine. Facts appear, Gay told you he, Urie and the dead boy, Dopp, were attacked by Indians during May; he identifies these as friendly Indians with whom Dopp played as a boy and that these Indians had some horses.*

Dopp was soon thereafter found dead in the vicinity. Dopp' mother, (Jeanette) immediately accused Gay, Frank, Urie and others of killing the boy in order to destroy evidence of horse stealing.

Where did Lee get this info? was it second hand?

Urie and Frank disappeared. *In August 2 enormous trenches were found in the vicinity, trenches partially examined and some 20 dead horses were counted, no evidence of horses having been dragged any distance, apparently shot at the side of the pits and tumbled in, an old wagon was found later on. 14 Shoshone, residence of Rock Cr., same as identified by Gay had an old wagon and several horses. In May they went over into Nev. to trail around for the summer. Not one came back, white neighbors at Rock Cr. have heard no word of them. They have relatives living on Banner (Bannock) Cr. some 14 miles below American Fall, Id.*

Went to Nev. for the summer & white neighbors at Rock Cr. hadn't heard from them. Further evidence they did not winter in Nev.

(Bannock CR. is 14 miles south of American Falls)

None of the relatives have been able to get word of the missing Indians although they have scoured the country for them. [3 of the Banner Cr. Indians came to me asking help, and one of them is the husband and father of one of the missing Indian women and three children also missing.]

Ref. Nov. 24th letter to AG from Lee.

The Imlay murderers are J. Frank Tranmer and Urie, the men who first appear connected with the Indian attack. Gay is reported out of the county.

Now this tell the whole story. There is not a question of doubt that these Tranmers, Urie, and possibly Walter Sparks (nephew of ex governor Sparks, and supposed to be the third man connected with the Imlay murders) and others were out stealing horses, and coming upon the Indians either tried to steal their horses, or feared exposure and killed the entire band, including the boy whom they feared. The Indians have vanished and of course are dead. Daggetts could not have left the country w/o communicating w/ their Banner Cr relatives, that they plan to go into Nev., when weather permits and dig into trenches for bodies.

1st heard of trenches when in Goose Cr. country last August. Informants said they heard San Jacinto ranch men found them and planned to excavate. We took no action until Indians came in Dec., saying they could get no help anywhere and had been told Nev. Sheriff ordered them killed.

Since writing AG received communications from around Oakly and Rock Cr., who are unified in proclaiming the Tranmer and Urie Gang the real murderers.

Gay in as deep as anyone, and is of the kind of scoundrel that would turn State's evidence to save his neck. Gay already tied whole bunch in by story given you.

Regrettable trenches not opened before now and brands examined. "The missing Indians were well behaved, old residents or Rock Cr. and had many friends among the whites. They worked for their neighbors and were generally respected but as Carlyle might say "they are clean gone" and it is impossible that they could have made the attack Gay said they did, killed the white boy, and gotten out of the country with out leaving some sign or trace of their travel. I believe evidence is at the bottom of pits and if such shred of evidence can be found, I can conceive of no way in which the gang enumerated by Gay can escape the rope".

Lee had gotten a lot of his info second hand and from some who thought they knew but he did have better information and grasp of the situation than those actually investigating, especially the Post Master at Contact who was right in the middle of it & didn't get the facts right. Lee said the Indians that came to him said *"white men, they had talked to, told them the Elko Sheriff had ordered the Indians killed".* Lee told them that couldn't be the case which was most likely true, however that is exactly what was stated in an article in the, Twin Falls Times newspaper, dated May 12, 1910.

As I've stated many times the news papers of the day had little credibility.

The information regarding the wife and 3 children of one of the Bannock Cr. Indians came directly from the Indians when they visited with Lee. This is an interesting part of the story.

The number of Indians in the Daggett family is accurate as will be seen later in this saga.

JAN. 18 -- To Asbury **from** S. C. Lamb. *Didn't know much about the Elko incident until arrest of Urie and F. Tranmer for the murder of the Quilicies. Communication from Taber saying he always suspected Tranmer, Urie and some of their pals were guilty of the crime in Elko County. Invited Taber and Dysart to Winn. to get a confession out of Urie. They were unable to get anything out of him that was any different, he still claims Indians killed Dopp.*

Taber <u>did not</u> always suspect the Tranmer outfit. In fact Taber still lay blame on the Indians up until January 10th.

Letter from Taber to Commissioner of Indian Affairs, W. D. C., dated Jan. 10, 1911 - National Archives W. D. C.

That was easy for Urie because the Indians did kill Dopp but they never pressed him for the buried horses or altered brands.

JAN. 20th -- To Asbury **from** Lee. *Absolutely sure Urie and Tranmer are mixed up in the Indian murder in Elko. Will find from the evidence taken last summer in a preliminary hearing Gay specifically states that Urie and Diffindarfer were with him when the Indians attacked them. I see Urie confessed to Imlay murder and was forced to go along by Ed and Frank, that they had been together last summer after horses. Urie if pressed will tell whole story. Everything I dig into connects Urie, Frank, Gay, and Ed to the disappearance of the Indians and the killing of Dopp. Last week, in Twin Falls, Gay's mother, Sarah P. Tranmer, jumped me for my interest in this business and assured me that these men were attacked by those Rock Cr. Indians and young Dopp killed. She had not then heard of the Imlay murder, but I kept tabs on her having already received notice of it from Taber and the next day when the thing came out in the papers there was a gathering of relatives at the house where she was staying and she disappeared. I know this if my own knowledge for I watched her. If the Elko officers will dig in those pits where these horses are lying they will find trace of those Indians for they are wiped off the earth and it is the talk of an imbecile to suppose that a band of Indians could make such an attack as these men claim, kill one of their number and get away without some one knowing where they went.*

Their relatives over on Banner Cr. would not be scouring heaven and earth for them if they were alive either.

We have the guilty men in the names I have mentioned and no time should be lost in apprehending Gay Tranmer".

Lee hung onto the idea that the Indians were buried under the horses, which was not true but he knew Gay was guilty of something which he was but could not get Elko authorities to arrest or detain Gay for questioning. He was right on that point, Gay was guilty of something (altering brands on horses and the rest were all tied in). Also of killing the Indian boy. If Elko authorities were as tenacious as Lee they probably would have gotten to the bottom of the whole thing and the remainder of the crew would have served time for stealing horses.

JAN 26th -- Statement by Lee basically repeating what he already covered in previous letters.

Frank Tranmer had been killed by Indians and the others had come back to Rock Cr. and summoned a posse to back after the Indians and that the Elko Sheriff was coming north to meet them.

All false!

Several weeks later I spoke to men standing on the street and they told me they thought it was the ranchers (Tranmer outfit) had concocted the Indian story.

These Indians have been living on Rock Cr. for over 20 years, were docile law abiding good Indians, owned ranches and stock **(false horses only),** *were respected by the white neighbors and never harmed anybody. Dopp played with them as a child and they were fond of him. One of the young squaws now missing was in love with Nigger Henry, spoken of by Urie as present at the attack. This woman would never have left the country without letting this man know of it.*

There is no evidence there was any connection between Henry Harris and any of Mike's daughters. One was 15 the other had children and a husband, the other if she existed may have been connected to Henry's brother Liege but no evidence of that has ever been found.

Henry Harris - 165 - 1937. by Les Sweeney

JAN. 28 -- To Comm. of Indians Affairs DC **from** Asbury. Suggesting that a federal officer go into the field with Elko officials to investigate the pits to gather evidence incase Urie and Tranmer are not convicted. Lee is entirely convinced they killed the Indians.

A thorough investigation should have been done, by the Elko County. Sheriff, over 6 months earlier. They would have found no dead Indians but would have had some incriminating evidence to confront the Tranmer gang.

JAN. 28 -- To Asbury **from** Abbott, Ass. Comm. Comm. in contact with Taber and Dept. of Int. and Dept. Justice now on board. Copy of Jan. 10 letter, from Taber enclosed.

JAN 28 -- To Taber **from** Abbott. Acknowledgement of Jan. 10 letter. Wants info found, when trenches investigated. *If bodies are found I hope Elko will do all possible to see that perps are punished. News clipping from Reno Gazette, Jan 11, and Jan. 13 letter enclosed. appears Urie and F. J. Tranmer committed the crime.*

News clippings, dated May 10, Eastern papers, from Wells Herald, Elko Independent, dated June 9 and Reno Gazette, dated Dec. 7th, i- National Archives W. D. C.

Again, using news papers as some sort of a factual document, rather than checking it out for themselves or putting an investigator in the field.

FEB. 2 -- To A. G, **from** Frank Morse, 1st Ass. Sec. Acknowledgement of receiving letters, Act. A G, Jan. 14, Lee letter, Asbury letter dated Jan. 13, news clipping and letter from Taber dated Jan. 10. *It appears Indians were murdered by horse-thieves, 2 of which have been arrested in connection with the Quilici murders.*

Feb. 6 -- To Sect. Int. **from** A G Fowler. Acknowledge receipt of letter with additional info concerning murder of 14 Indians and arrest of Urie and Tranmer, this info forwarded to US Att. for Dist. of Nev.

FEB. 6 -- To E. P. Holcombe, Chief Supervisor, Fort Hall Indian Agency, Rossfork, Id. **from** G. A. Gutches, Dist. Forester. Forwarding report on the alleged murder of the Shoshone Indians and statements of parties familiar with the case.

My opinion Urie's and Tranmer's statements are false. Gen. opinion Indians caught Tranmer's outfit stealing horses, they killed the Indians and boy fearing he would give the crime away.

Information secured confirms this theory. Hardly possible the Indians could remain in hiding so long.

Indians not registered at Fort Hall but were wards of the government therefore duty to throughly investigate this affair. Make a thorough search when the snow is gone. Pits should be examined by proper authorities, statements secured from the Girdners and all efforts to solve the case. I will wait further orders at Reeds Hotel, Ogden, Utah. Telegram relating to orders from Farr received.

***WHAT TELEGRAM ?* Although they were wrong, due to Lee's insistence the noose was tightening around the neck of the Tranmer gang. Gutches finally made the case that some one needed to get on the scene and examine the case. Again over 6 months late. It had to be the Elko County sheriff, Clark, that hadn't done his job. Didn't care or was incompetent, probably both.**

FEB 6 -- GUTCHES REPORT:

For this report Gutches met with and or interviewed a number of people including: Cassia County D. A., T. Baily Lee; Del Hardy and W. J. Gumble which he also got a written statement from each; Elko County D. A., E. J. Taber; Elko County Sheriff, I. G. Clark and several ranchers and their employees. He made no on the ground investigation. He couldn't, in Jan. and early Feb.

Daggetts left Fort Hall 20 years ago, settled on small ranch near Rock Cr. , ranch was their headquarters but lived greater part of the year in northern Nev. in vicinity of San Jacinto and head waters of Little Goose Cr.,area ranged by the Vineyard Land & Cattle Co., family spent winter 1909 & 10 in vicinity of San Jacinto and traded at the Co. store. Last time the Indians seen at store was last week of April, except as related by Gay and Urie.

They did not reside at Fort Hall nor did they spend the winter in the vicinity of San Jacinto or head waters of Goose Cr., at 5,000 feet +, elevation, winters are too harsh. They migrated back to Rock Cr. each fall.

The Daggetts moved around under the radar, they didn't bother any one, didn't ask for anything, didn't create any sort of commotion, people hardly noticed them. They made their way by themselves, self sufficient and a burden on no one, until they ran into the Tranmer outfit, changing brands on horses.

According to Jim Mosho, who visited the family during the summer of 1909, consisted of old Mike his wife, four sons ages 17 to 40, three grown daughters, and three small children, 12 people. Sons names, Jack, Jim, and the two youngest Jake and Charlie.

This info had to have come from D. A. Lee. Jim Mosho was one of the Indians that visited Lee, Nov. 24 and may be the one who claimed his wife and three children were with the Daggetts when they disappeared.

Ranchers and employees all spoke very highly of these Indians. They were honest, industrious and never known to steal stock. They worked for the stockmen, trusted at Co. Store and always paid their bills. Daggetts owned 30 or 40 horses fall of 1909 but tough winter w/o hay, they lost some of their horses and remainder so poor they had to walk to San Jacinto for provisions. Ranchers estimated they now have about 30 head. Cattlemen state their horses too poor to rustle horses.

May not be too poor, they were able to leave camp and go far enough to get tangled up with the Tranmer gang, or did they walk?

The statements of Gay and Urie show that Gay Tranmer, N. R. Urie, Ed Diffendarfer. Frank Dopp, Gordon Girdner, Mrs Girdner and baby arrived Cow Cr. May 5th. They came to run horses, Mrs Girdner was the cook. They went to the Indian Camp on the 6th where the fight took place, as described by Urie. Diffendarfer went to Contact, Nevada on the 6th for Deputy Sheriff Geo. Grimm, returned on 7th with Grimm and Nigger Henry. Grimm returned to Contact and deputized Dave Paterson, Byron Godfroy and Joe Stewart to aid in finding Dopp and arrest the Indians. They made an effort to search the surrounding country for a few days then disbanded. The body of Dopp found 9 days latter, within 75 paces of the Tranmer Corral.

We know Gay and Urie lied. Grimm signed a complaint against the Indians and a warrant issued for their arrest, on the 5th, after all of the above had taken place. Their reason for lying, was to separate themselves from the incident as much as possible. The body was 75 paces from the Tranmer corral and not found, that is because the gang saw to it that no one searched that area. Easy, all they had to do is say we searched that area already.

No records according to present sheriff (Harris) to show that the Deputy reported this affair to the proper Officials. Nothing was done by the Sheriff or D. A. and as far as the records show they had no knowledge of the Affair until months later.

Not true, the warrant for the arrest had been signed back on May 5th and both the Silver State news paper, in Wells and the Elko Free Press, ran stories covering the event at the time & the Elko D. A. sent circulars out Oct. 16th.

Sept. 20, Diffendarfer, Urie, F. Tranmer and Guy (Gay) Tranmer came into the D. A.'s Office at Elko and Guy (Gay) Tranmer made the inclosed statement. Mr Taber told me that he had heard something of the affair about two weeks previous. He notified the Indian Office and sent Tranmers statement to the neighboring sheriffs. The Office forwarded the inclosed circular to Superintendents of Indian schools in this country. Nothing further was done.

Note: Frank Tranmer included in this group. Absolutely no reason to believe he was not there! Taber hadn't heard anything of the affair until after the 1st of

**Sept.? By the 27th of July, Asbury had already heard from the Elko County.
sheriff after a second request, Deputy Grimm had signed the complaint on May
5th and the story was in newspapers including Wells Silver State and Elko Free
Free Press. One thing they did have right, "nothing further was done".**

*Pits containing horses were discovered about May 25, by Jack Haden and the facts
were given in his statement. It is apparent his word did not reach the Sheriff of D. A. as
they did not know of the pits until Dec. 8 and did not believe the story at this late date as
Elko Free Press, Dec. 8 shows. No action taken by Elko authorities.*

**Where were they, during the 1st part of May, when warrant was issued and story
was in the local papers? And again no action was taken by the sheriff.**

*Ranchers in vicinity of Rock Cr. took up collection and sent Theo. Burr, C. Chambers
and C. S. Selliken, private citizens to excavate the pits. Pits were opened up about Oct.
21. One 30 ft. long, 8 ft. wide, 3 & 1/2 ft. on one end and 6 ft. deep at the other. Dug by
pick and shovel in hard dirt.* **No hard dirt at site of pits in April.** *It contained 16
horses and three sawn T-bones. Horses feet were doubled under, horses were piled in
very compactly. Other pit, quarter mile distance. Opening nearly round and 8 ft. across.
It was 8 ft. deep and under mined. 9 horses were taken out of this pit.*

*An Indian camp and a corral were only a few feet distance. Four Indian saddles and an
old American tree belonging to Indian Mike were found in a tree nearby, also parts of an
old gun and a folding chair which was nearly new were found near the pit. The old tree
is at Rancho Grande and the remainder of the articles were carried away by Trapper
Red (Mr Burr). It is doubtful if these pits were thoroughly examined. A third pit has
been reported but it could not be located.*

**Descriptions of pits don't match those of Hardy's but are close. Sawn T-bones,
an interesting point. Mike didn't likely have a saw. Indian camp few feet away not
accurate. Indian camp, with all those articles, was on Willow Cr., 5 or 6 miles
north west of buried horses on head of Badger Cr. The horses, after laying there
and or buried, all summer would be in such a state of decomposition that no
brands could be read. District forester Gutches doubted the pits were throughly
examined, which could be true. He thought the pits, Indian camp and corral were
next to each other. Information he probably got from Gumble. Gumble got his**

140

first info about pits from some one else and mistakenly thought they were near the Indian camp. Later when he found the camp he made no mention of pits. There were 3 corrals and 2 camps, total and could have easily been mixed up if he had not been to each one in person.

The men implicated in quarrel with Indians have bad reputation being all around bad men and horse thieves. At present F. Tranmer and Urie in Winn. held on murder charges. Gay Tranmer is under bond to appear before the Dist. court in Twin Falls this month. He refused to pay the mother of Dopp $150 due him in wages, at the time of the murder. Girdner is wanted for selling mortgaged property.

Gutches got that right, they were bad men - Frank and Urie up for murder, Gay to appear in court for not paying mother of Dopp back wages and Girdner wanted for selling mortgaged property. Dopp must have been working for Gay for several months, and not payed, to owe that much in back wages, in 1910. This info might be available in Twin Falls court records. I do not believe Gay went back to that part of Idaho earlier than Dec. 1910 or later. Girdner was in Yakima, Washington, by now and there is no evidence he ever went back.

Alleged murder took place on public land in Nev. and does not come under federal law. Prosecution belongs the state authorities but they have taken no action.

Family missing since last May. Recommend Office make through search for bodies as all evidence points to foul play.

One very important witness Gutches never interviewed, was Henry Harris, black buckaroo boss for the Vineyard Land & Stock Co. Henry was head quartered at the San Jacinto Ranch. Harris knew the following better than any one in Idaho or Nevada: 1) the Indians, 2) the horse runners, 3) the horses, 4) that part of the country where the incident took place (Gollaher Mountain) and 5) had gone with Deputy Grimm to Cow Creek on the 1st day of investigation which was the beginning of the saga of Shoshone Mike. Why would Gutches interview Harris? What would a black guy know?

CHAPTER XII

The INCIDENT AT COW CREEK IN REVIEW

1 - Tranmer & Co. arrived at their horse running camp at Cow Creek on or about April 20, 1910, Gay's brother, Frank, included.

2 - The horse runners had fixed up a corral and had gathered about 30 head of horses, mostly branded by about April 25, 1910.

3 - The Tranmer outfit was unaware there was any one else in that part of the country, however the Daggetts knew someone was in the area and had gone to see about their own horse gathering possibilities. In addition they wanted to see who, besides themselves, were in the area and what they were up to.

4 - The Indians encountered the Tranmer outfit with a corral full of horses in a canyon on Cow Creek. The corral was located in a grove of Aspen trees and the horse runners were changing brands on horses.

Map - Chapter VII, Altercation at Cow Creek

5 - An altercation ensued resulting in the deaths of one of the Daggett boys and Frank Dopp.

6 - One of the Tranmers either Gay or Frank, shot Jack Daggett wounding him in the leg and severing the main artery and possibly shattering bones in the lower leg.

In retaliation two or three of the other sons of Mike Daggett returned to the scene and shot Frank Dopp the 16 year old kid that was wrangling horses for the Tranmer outfit.

7 - It could not be ascertained whether there were two or three Daggett boys at the site where the confrontation took place. In any event they got Jack to a place next to a large boulder, cleared the area of rock and built a small wall of rock for protection. The most likely scenario is that Jack died there and was buried in the rocks near by.

8 - The Indians had killed a white boy and they must now leave the area immediately and they did.

9 - Tranmer & Co. had a body on their hands and a corral full of horses with altered brands. Both problems had to be taken care of. They could not afford to have the Sheriff or his posse there investigating the Dopp killing and the whereabouts of the Indians. The disposal of the horses took 1st priority.

10 - The horses were taken to the head of Badger Creek, two large pits opened up in the bottom of the wash/head-cut, a total of 25 head of horses shot and tumbled in and then covered with dirt.

11 - Since the incident was to have happened the day before, Dopp's body had to be hidden because they had no fresh body to present.

12 - When Deputy Grimm arrived with Henry Harris the 1st day and others the next 2 days, they were told the area, where the body was actually located, had been throughly searched by them, the gang.

13 - Eight days later when it was difficult, impossible at the time, to determine the length of time that had passed since Dopp's death, he was miraculously found, by Gay Tranmer, near the Tranmer corral.

14 - It was the Tranmer and Co. and not the Indians that were altering brands in an attempt to steal horses.

15 -The Daggetts knew nothing of the buried horses and only stole horses on their departure from Gollaher Mountain. The Daggetts didn't have the luxury of taking time to bury horses, they had to get out of the area.

16 - In accusing the Indians of stealing horses, where would they go? They had no market or access to the outside world; only white man had that.

17 - The Elko authorities made no effort to solve the case or to determine the guilt or innocence of the Daggett boys.

18 - T. Baily Lee, District Attorney of Cassia County, exercised everything in his power to get the Elko authorities to act but to no avail!

It wasn't until September 20, 1910, in Elko, that D. A. Taber took the statement of Gay Tranmer. No one questioned Gay as to its validity. The Sheriff, it appears, was inept and I wonder about D. A. Taber. The statement of Nimrod Urie wasn't taken until January 1911 by now, Judge E. J. L. Taber; the newly elected Elko County District Attorney, James Dysart and Humboldt County Sheriff Lamb. Urie's statement was not taken until after Urie and Frank Tranmer had been arrested for a murder in Imlay, Nevada.

19 - The statement of Nimrod Urie, though flawed, had to have some credibility as to camp and corral locations, because those could be checked out on the ground.

20 - Both Urie and Gay Tranmer's statements said "they arrived at Cow Cr. about 5th or 6th of May. Again this was an attempt to separate themselves from the time horses were buried which they now knew had been found. This would allow that the horses were buried ten days before the Tranmer outfit ever arrived at Cow Creek however we already know they were lying. A warrant was issued and given to Deputy George Grimm on the 5th of May, in Elko, for the arrest of the four adult males of the Daggett family.

Grimm had already spent about six days investigating and searching for Dopp before arriving in Elko and acquiring the warrant.

21 - The buried horses were found about the 25th of May.

22 - The Daggetts normally spent the months between April and October on and around Gollaher Mountain.

In 1910 their migration to the Mountain had ended early, around the 25th of April.

PART II

CHAPTER I

LEAVING GOLLAHER MOUNTAIN FOREVER

The Daggett family was about to embark on a journey not of their choosing, maybe not unlike what Mike was a part of in the 1860s. Maybe he had been there before, running and hiding from the white man, intermittent fighting skirmishes with the soldiers and the occasional raiding and killing of the white man to quench his hunger and anger. Maybe he had starved out like all the others but rather than choose reservation life he and (Maggie) chose to find a niche in which the white man would allow them to exist. Maybe they had hoped that was all behind them after all it had been over thirty years since the last Indian uprising, in Mike's world, when Chief Buffalo Horn led the Indians into the Bannock War.

Whatever the past this is a new chapter in their lives. It must have been significantly clear to the Daggetts that they would never return to Gollaher Mountain. Where they were going, they knew only that it was away from their home range, Rock Creek to Gollaher Mountain.

They would be traveling cross-country on horseback and there was no way a wagon could be taken along. Their wagon was left behind at Willow Creek on the west side and at the foot of Gollaher Mountain. It was found there by W. J. Gumble about the 1st of June.

Statement of W. J. Gumble, January 31, 1911 - National Archives W. D. C.

In leaving Gollaher Mountain Mike and his family headed west across some of the most desolate and uninhabited lands of the west, northern Nevada and southern Idaho. They traveled west through southern Idaho, across northern Nevada and then southwest into northern California and all the way to the Sacramento River.

In passing through Idaho and Nevada they would have crossed the width of the Owyhee Desert and the northern end of the Black Rock Desert.

Their route is described more specifically later in this chapter.

Interview of Henny by Asbury, April 27, 1911 - National Archives W. D. C.

Their route across Idaho and Nevada remains, even to this day, one of the largest areas in the west that looks the most like it did in 1910.

The westward journey of Mike's band across the Owyhee Desert from Gollaher Mountain, as I describe it, is quite in contrast to that of Modoc County Sheriff A. E. Smith from information he gave to E. M. Wilson, who wrote THE LAST STAND OF SHOSHONE MIKE and that of Dayton Hyde, author of the book "THE LAST FREE MAN". They say the Daggetts traveled southeast then south as far as Ely, Nevada, then west to the Pyramid Lake Reservation and then northwest into California.

This was not the case. Far more likely they traveled through country Mike knew well. Maybe unforgiving to the white man but Mike would have been right at home.

There are reasons Mike would have been familiar with the country over which they were about to pass. In years past he would have been part of hunting expeditions and forays up the tributaries of the Snake and Qwyhee Rivers following the salmon runs. This was Bannock Country so there would have been many reasons for his familiarity with the country. The Bannock traveled from Wyoming to the Steens Mountains in war and in search of game.

In war, again we are talking primarily about the 1860s when the Indian was hunted winter and summer and day and night by the soldiers.

The youngest member of the family was less than three weeks old when they set out on this long and perilous trek. Therefore at this point in time, with Jack Daggett dead and one daughter unaccounted for (at least in my mind) the Daggett family consisted of twelve members.

Daggett family, mid April 1910

With what was left of his family and a new baby granddaughter Mike and his family headed west into a great unknown as far as what lay before them.

When the Daggetts headed west from Gollaher Mountain the exact route they took remains for the most part a mystery.

Due to snow conditions they could not have gone over the Jarbridge Mountains, in Nevada, that early in the spring. The most logical route would take them northwest into Idaho, then back southwest into Nevada, north of the Duck Valley Indian Reservation (Owyhee) across the Owyhee Desert out of the tributaries of the Snake River

148

Watershed and into the Great Basin. The least difficult route from the Snake River Watershed into the Great Basin would be over a low almost undetectable pass. Four or five miles west beyond this low pass they would have crossed the south fork of the Little Humboldt River just above the Little Humboldt Ranch.

They are now at the upper end of Clover Valley on the east side of Humboldt County, Nevada. From here they could move diagonally southwest across Clover Valley to the lowest pass in the next range of mountains between the Dry Hills and the Osgood Range. Then proceed northwest a couple of miles then due west across Eden Valley to Paradise Valley through Stewart Gap in the Hot Springs Range. From here the most logical route would be south then west, north of Toll Gate, across Sand Pass, north of Winnemucca, around the south end of the Slumbering Hills then northwest to Willow Creek past one of the Lay Brothers ranches and over a northerly pass on Jackson Mountain to Jackson Creek passing by another of the Lay Brothers ranches, located on the east arm of the Black Rock Desert.

After additional research and review of information regarding the travel of the Daggetts, the following winter, I have changed my mind. I think they crossed over the south end of the Jackson Range rather than the north end.

There is reference made to a harness trade or proposed trade at the Lay Ranch at the foot of Jackson Mountain, as described in the Humboldt Star February 24, 1911.

"Last July Indians stopped at Lay Ranch in Jackson Mountain and traded for some old harness".

Newspaper articles are always speculative as to their accuracy but this bit of information to come out of nowhere seemed odd except, the Daggetts did leave their camp on Gollaher Mountain, with a set of harness, at least there is no evidence they left it behind.

From a point near or at the Lay Brother's ranch they most likely traveled south about fifteen miles along the east side of the Jackson Range then west over the south end of the Jacksons continuing west straight across the east arm and over the lower end of the Black Rock Range coming out onto the west arm of the Black Rock Desert about four miles northwest of Double Hot Springs. At this point they would strike the old Applegate Trail following it along to the mouth of Fly Canyon, up along Fly Canyon past High Rock

149

Lake to the mouth of Little High Rock Canyon, up Little High Rock Canyon and on across to Cedarville, California.

John B. Hoover, Superintendent at the Fort Mc Dermitt Indian School in Nevada, reported, by letter dated November 9, 1910, to Commission of Indian Affairs in Washington D. C. that the Daggetts had traveled through Cedarville, California last July with some 20 head of horses. This number of horses corresponds with information gained by C. H. Asbury, Superintendent at the Carson Indian School, Stewart, Nevada, from his interview with Henny Daggett on April 25, 1911 and a report by G. A. Gutches, District Forester which stated "the Indians owned 30 to 40 head of horses in the fall of 1909".

Letter, Asbury to Commission of Indian Affairs April 27, 1911 and report of G. A. Gutches, February 6, 1911. National Archives - W. D. C.

From Cedarville they traveled west over the Warner Mountains and then southwest to the Sacramento Valley.

Where the Daggetts went after leaving Cedarville in July is somewhat speculative. In July they could have crossed over the mountains most anywhere the higher the cooler.

The next credible sighting of the Indians was by O. D. Van Norman in November of 1910. That contact with the Daggett family, in Hog Ranch Canyon, was revealed to the Silver State news paper February 23, 1911 and then again to the Humboldt Star, February 24, 1911. In both cases the information came through Washoe County Sheriff Ferrell. This information, gleaned from O. D. Van Norman, occurred three days before the killing of the Daggett family at Rabbit Creek and before they knew for sure who the Indians were. O. D's. description of the family was too accurate for him to not have seen them in person.

It should be noted, Van Norman did not describe the encounter as unfriendly nor threatening only that they wanted to trade him a palomino colt for a usable horse. The Indian family desperately needed horses after losing most of theirs in the deep snow, while crossing over the Sierra Mountains. Had O. D. mentioned anything of a threatening nature the newspaper would have been all over it. All of over 200+ news

150

articles of the time dramatized and exaggerated the story. The encounter involved an attempted horse trade with O. D.

Hog Ranch Creek empties into Little High Rock Canyon at its head, about three miles east of the Denio Camp and less than two miles above where the Indian family set up their winter camp.

The following is a part of a letter from C. H. Asbury, Superintendent at the Carson Indian School at Stewart, Nevada to the Commissioner of Indian Affairs in Washington D. C., dated April 27, 1911, wherein Asbury interviewed Henny Daggett, through an interpreter.

"They, the Daggetts, left that section [Gollaher Mountain] and on leaving stole several horses taking them out of the corral or pasture and riding some and driving some loose. They gradually worked their way westward, keeping away from the settlers, stealing beef as it was needed for their food, also taking provisions from sheep or cattle camps, in fact, any place they could get it. In this way they went clear through into the central part of California, evidently to the Sacramento River where they found abundant fruit in the orchards and melons in the fields to which they helped themselves. Toward winter they started back east over the main range of the Sierra Nevada Mountains and in going over the mountains at this time, they lost most of their horses as they became poor and weak and in the deep snow they could not travel. They had gotten back into the western part of Nevada where they were camped in an isolated place".

Asbury Report to Commission of Indian Affairs April 27, 1911 National Archives, W. D. C.

This is the only creditable information ever gleaned from Henny other than the approximate birth date of baby Mosho.

All points to their spending some time in the Sacramento Valley in the vicinity of Oroville, California and leaving there around the end of October or first part of November. If the family went as far as the vicinity of Oroville they would have been able to hear the same train whistle as Ishi, the last Indian of his tribe that showed up at the slaughter house in Oroville, California, in November of 1911, looking for something to eat.

From the book "**ISHI** In Two Worlds" by Theodora Kroeber

In 2010 a book **VINA'S HISTORY - In Photos and Stories** was written and published by Francis V. Leininger. One of those stories included in her book was from her good friend Ruth L. (Speegle) Boring Jones. Ruth's family had a homestead on Deer Creek northeast of Vina, California which was also about Forty miles northwest of Oroville, California and a short distance from the Sacramento River. Ruth said that in 1910 when she was ten years old an old Indian came up to their cabin on the Homestead wanting to trade her mother gloves and moccasins for food. He introduced himself as Shoshone Mike. Mike never knew his name was Shoshone Mike so this part of the story is not true. Ruth told this story after she had read the book THE LAST FREE MAN by Dayton Hyde. She most likely did see an Indian come on to the homestead but it probably would not have been, Mike.

No one knew, for sure, what had happened to the Daggett family from the time they left Gollaher Mountain in late April 1910, until they were run down near Golconda, Nevada February 26, 1911.

There were letters of correspondence going back and forth between county officials, in several states and some of the Indian agencies, including Washington D. C., from early May 1910 until October 1910. This correspondence reflected the interest the agencies had in trying to determine what had actually happened to the Indian family.

Then on October 16, 1910, a circular went out to Indian agencies and law enforcement offices in Nevada, Utah, Idaho, Oregon and California advising them to be on the lookout for these particular Indians.

The only response to the circular was that report from John B. Hoover in November. No one seemed to give his report any credence, nothing was done.

The family of twelve, with an estimated twenty horses, had traveled all the way from northeastern Nevada to north central California and back into Nevada without anyone other than Hoover having reported their existence.

It was not until after the bodies of the four sheepmen were found at Little High Rock Canyon and the Indians were run down near Golconda that stories began to float in. These stories were further embellished and exaggerated by the newspapers of the day. That kind of press got peoples attention and sold papers.

After February of 1911 everybody got in on the act and stories were floating around about one incident or another and each time those stories were told they became more dramatic and less truthful almost to absurdity.

152

The crux of the whole thing is; the Indians were able to float under the radar, so to speak, because they were not the bad Indians that the white people wanted them to be and did not commit all the crimes they were alleged to have committed. Most of those stories were a figment of folk's imagination and grew with each telling.

Why they left that part of California is not known. Apparently it was too crowded there and they headed back towards the Owyhee country of which they were most familiar. Another explanation might be in the statement of Henie, Mike Daggett's daughter, when she told Asbury, Indian Agent at Carson Indian School, that they, the Indians helped them selves to melons etc. in the gardens in the Valley. In early fall after harvest there may not have been anything else to eat or scavenge thus they headed back to where they were familiar with the country and knew how to subsist from the land.

In leaving the Sacramento Valley in the late fall they proceeded back east over the Sierra Mountains basically retracing their spring route, in the direction of their winter headquarters on Rock Creek, where they had wintered for the past nearly 35 years.

I say basically retracing their spring route because it appears that they may have traveled back east from the Sierra Mountains, over the lower end of the Warner Mountains, rather than over the pass leading into Cedarville as was reported by Hoover in November of 1910.

During their trek west from Gollaher Mountain,into Idaho then back into Nevada the family would camp then scout ahead in search of a new camp site. The length of time spent at each camp was determined by the availability of feed for there horses, their own need of something to eat, weather conditions and the time it took to find a camp site that met these requirements. They also had to decide on their route of travel to avoid detection and unnecessary travel. In this way they knew exactly where and how far they had to travel, the routes they would take and what the new camp site provided. In essence they had made that entire journey, over a period of ten months, without being detected. The only creditable exceptions were their contacts with: 1- one of the Lay ranches on Jackson Mountain, 2- Indians from the Mc Dermitt reservation as they passed through Cedarville, California and 3- O. D. Van Norman in Hog Ranch Canyon.

153

On the return trip east they were taking the most logical and direct route for that time of year, (January and February) towards home back in Idaho. There is no evidence of back tracking or wondering around trying to find their way. They had been there before. From the above it seems evident that they traveled west into California then southwest into the Sacramento Valley possibly to a part of the valley near Oroville, California.

I believe while in search of a winter camp site, from their camp in Hog Ranch Canyon, they found a very secluded place high on the north rim of Little High Rock Canyon. That site was about one and one half miles down from the head of the canyon.

From all indications and for a practical matter they probably left Hog Ranch Canyon and arrived under the high rim of Little High Rock Canyon in late November or early December. This would not have been a very difficult move the weather was exceptionally mild and the distance rather short, five to ten miles, depending upon where they were in Hog Ranch Canyon. Although the site was not all that roomy it would serve well for a winter camp site so they hauled all their belongings up the side of the canyon, built a wickiup of willows and set up camp for the winter.

Wickiup photo by Matthews

The move into the canyon was not so much as a hideout but as a winter camp that also served well as a hideout. The site is a depression against the face of the rim where they could set up their camp and not be visible from anywhere in the area unless one walked right up within a few feet of the camp. It also faced south, directly into the sun making it quite comfortable when the sun shined. Finding this site would have been their only bit of good luck from the time they left Gollaher Mt. until the end of their journey. There are probably not one in a hundred canyons in this part of the country that has such a secluded and protected site where one can see out without being seen plus taking full advantage of warmth from the winter sun.

For a family of twelve their camp site was quite small, their wickiup (or tepee as described by Matthews on plate # 1) taking up the greater part of the available space in the depression.

To gain access to the main canyon floor the Daggetts constructed a trail switching back and forth from their camp site all the way down to the bottom of the canyon. The upper portion can be followed today, over one hundred years later, until it gradually succumbs

154

to soil, loose rock movement and erosion on the talus slope. This steep trail was their main avenue over which they carried willows and other materials to construct their wickiup, hauled meat from butchered beef, sage brush and sage brush bark. The bark was used as mats on which to lay in order to maintain surveillance of the canyon and surrounding area.

Baby Mosho now about eight months old likely spent a lot of her time in her cradle board leaning against the face of the rim in the sun. Hattie about four years old, would likely be allowed to play around the crowded camp site but not allowed to play up on the rocks from which the older boys used as a lookout.

Once camp was set up the next order of business was to keep from starving. This problem was solved by gathering beef/cattle on the canyon floor at the foot of the trail from which they accessed their camp. It was very unlikely there were cattle at this location waiting to be butchered therefore the Daggetts probably gathered cattle from down the canyon and drove them up to this site. Based on the amount of beef found later on at or near the Indian's camp, they would have had to have killed and butchered at least five or six head.

Their horses, in very poor condition and exhausted (some were lost, from the long trip through the snow and lack of feed over the Sierras) needed a rest. Their obvious intent was to rest up until the green grass of spring was sufficient to get the horses in shape to carry them back to the Owyhee country or beyond to ck across the Sierra Nevada Mountains only four, very poor and emaciated, reGollaher Mountain.

Of the horses that the Daggetts managed to get bamained alive by mid January, the others had perished from starvation. It seems that there should have been adequate feed in the bottom of Little High Rock Canyon to maintain a small number of horses after all cattle were surviving in the canyon. The explanation for allowing their horses to starve, they were hiding their horses on the bench between the lower and upper rim of the canyon. This bench is too small in acreage to furnish adequate feed for even the four horses let alone additional animals. The only historical evidence that any of the dead horses were found on the canyon floor was when Captain Donnelly of the State Police reported that someone told him there were seven dead horses in the canyon branded with a B on the left stifle.

155

If cattle could survive in the canyon then why not horses?

Inquest at Denio Camp, February 15, 1911

Too few horses and too weakened to carry a family of twelve, any further, the Daggetts were now in a desperate situation. They were trapped against the high rim of Little High Rock Canyon with no means of escape.

The family had to be weighing their alternatives as to where and how were they going to acquire enough horses to proceed to the Owyhee country and maybe back to Gollaher Mountain. If not back to Gollaher Mountain then where?

Horses at Denio Camp and horses at sheep camps on the winter range at the edge of the Black Rock Desert, had to have been possibilities they were agonizing over.

On January 18, 1911 their "hideout/winter camp", such as it was, became compromised when Bertrand Indiano a sheepman, who had sheep on the winter range at the edge of the Black Rock Desert passed by where the Indians had been killing and butchering beef. Indiano came across the site of the butchered beef as he traveled up Little High Rock Canyon from his sheep camp and heading to Eagleville. Historical information indicates Indiano was on his way to Eagleville, California to obtain supplies to take back to his winter sheep camp on the edge of the Black Rock Desert.

The beef carcasses Indiano saw were located just below the Indian camp on the floor of the canyon. The Daggetts were drying and curing beef for future as well as current needs.

The Daggetts were on high alert after Indiano had passed their camp site. They knew some one would be coming back. But not a lot they could do about it, their horses were too few and too week to take the family and their possessions from their perch under the rim at Little High Rock Canyon.

However following Indiano's discovery of the beef carcasses the Daggett's dilemma of having enough horses to carry them on eastward took care of itself.

On that fatal day of January 19, 1911 with three other stockmen in tow Indiano returned to the site where he had seen the butchered beef carcasses the day before.

G. L Matthew's photos Feb. 15, 1911 - Plate No 2 and Jan. 21, 2008 by Les Sweeney Chptr. 2

156

THE DAGGETT FAMILY MID-APRIL 1910

		DB	DD
Mike Daggett	father	1845	1911
Maggie Daggett	mother	1855	1911
Jim Daggett	son	1873	1911
Pete Daggett	son	1875	1911
Charlie Daggett	son	1882	1911
Jack Daggett	son	1890	1910
Jake? Daggett	son	1899	1911
Willie Daggett (Sagebrush?) *	grandson	1901	1911
Henny Daggett	daughter	1896	1912
Snake Daggett (Mosho)?	daughter	1882	1911
Cleveland Mosho	*grandson	1905	1913
Hattie Mosho	*granddaughter	1907	1912
Baby Mosho	*granddaughter	1910	1992

* Children of Snake

Year of birth approximate, except for Hattie and Baby Mosho

There is some question as to who died at Gollaher Mt. Charlie Daggett or Jack Daggett.

The make up of the Daggett family was arrived at after review of; statement of Gay Tranmer, Asbury's interview with Henie Daggett and records at Fort Hall, Idaho.

Great Basin thatched wickiup

WICKIUP FRAME
February 15, 1911
Wickiup frame abandoned in Little High Rock when the Daggett family left there on or
about January 19, 1911

DAGGETT'S CAMP SITE

May 19, 2004

Site located next to the upper rim, in Little High Rock Canyon. This depression scarcely had room for the wickiup, let alone all of the belongings of a family of twelve. The flat part of the depression, measured not more than twenty feet by thirty feet. Note the jagged crack in the rock upper center of picture and compare to photo taken in 1911. Also note lack of snow in the 1911 photo, due to the warmth of the sun against the rock face. On that same day, February 15, 1911, down in the canyon there was an estimated eight inches of snow.

CHAPTER II

KILLING AT LITTLE HIGH ROCK CANYON

The winter of 1911 had turned into a nightmare for both the folks of Surprise Valley and the Daggett family.

On January 17, 1911, three stockmen (Peter Erramouspe, John Laxague, both sheepmen and Harry Cambron, part owner and manager of the H. C. Cattle Co.) departed Eagleville, California to check their livestock on the winter range at the edge of the Black Rock Desert. Their route would take them almost due east via Home Camp some 18 miles from Eagleville, then southeast, approximately 25 miles to Billie Denio's Camp and another 15 miles through Little High Rock Canyon to High Rock Lake near the edge of the Black Rock Desert.

Sheldon Recreation map - 1: 250,000 & writings of Frank Perry 1949 & Mort West 1934 and numerous other sources.

The H. C. Cattle Co. owned Home Camp and they owned sheep as well as cattle.

Land of Bunch Grass Sage & Sun by Ralph Parman (Parman owned Soldier Meadows during 1920s)

On January 18th, Cambron, Laxague and Erramouspe arrived at the Denio Camp, located about four miles west of the head of Little High Rock Canyon.

Coincidentally a sheepman by the name of Bittram (Bertrand) Indiano, who also had sheep in the Black Rock area, arrived at Denio's on the same day after having traveled up Little High Rock Canyon, from his winter camp.

On the way up the canyon, Indiano had come across cattle that had been recently butchered. They were in the bottom of the canyon and about one and one half miles down from the head of the canyon.

At that point, in the canyon, unbeknown to Indiano, he was directly below the Daggett family's camp situated under the high, south facing rim, about 350 feet above and 300 yards distant from him, as he stood on the canyon floor. After some contemplation of what he had found, he continued on toward Billie Denio's, some four and a half miles to the west.

When he reached Denio Camp he described his findings, which led to considerable discussion between the four stockmen/sheepmen and Bill Denio regarding the situation with the butchered cattle.

By the next morning, on the 19th, the three sheepmen from Eagleville had convinced a reluctant Indiano to accompany them back to where he had seen the butchered animals the day before.

The reluctance of Indiano to go back to the site of the butchered beef is understandable. It delays him a day in getting to Eagleville, secondly he would have been more than just a little spooked at what he had seen in the canyon and thirdly he was no friend of Harry Cambron. The H.C. Cattle Co. had filed suit against Indiano the summer before, June 10, 1910, asking for $1,000 in damages caused by the grazing of over 3,000 head of sheep on H.C. Cattle Co. land.

In the Second Judicial District Court of the State of Nevada (Washoe County) dated June 10,1910

Ironically had the 120 acres, which Idiano's sheep trespassed on, been totally destroyed the value of that land may not have totaled more than $1,000.

Had it not been for the other two Basque sheepmen, Erramouspe and Laxague, Indiano would not likely have gone back. The butchered cattle weren't of any great concern to Indiano, he owned no cattle.

There may have been a discussion at Denio camp the evening before, that proposed the possibility of traveling by the north rim to reach the butchered beef, rather than riding openly and blindly down Little High Rock Canyon. They probably recognized the possibility of being ambushed in the bottom of the canyon, so they may have considered accessing the site of the butchered beef by way of the north rim. However, there is only one access route from the north rim to the middle rim and onto the canyon floor, in this section of the canyon.

Three weeks later when the posse arrived at the site where the beef were killed, they determined that the four men had come down from the north rim to access the canyon floor. However, if they were ever serious about accessing the canyon via the north rim, at some point, before reaching the head of the canyon, the group changed their mind and decided to travel down the main canyon.

Descending from the top of the north rim would have been a dangerous route, with snow and ice on the steep hillsides covering boulder fields and rock slides.

Coming down from above would take them down a small but treacherous side canyon, especially treacherous in winter snow conditions, although it spills out right at the location of the butchered beef. In fact coming down this side canyon would be impossible due to small rims and a boulder field.

Any travel down this side canyon would have to be down one side or the other, both being very steep.

In fact the only access to this small canyon from the north rim is from the west side. It begins as a box canyon and to cross to the east side requires crossing at the head near the rim forming the box. Once in the canyon there are only two ways to continue to the main canyon, one; on the east side next to the main rim, until reaching a point directly above the cut in the lower rim and then proceeding down a very steep talus slope to the main canyon floor. The east route was used by the Indians as they traveled back and forth from their camp site to the floor of the main canyon.

The Daggetts had moved their whole outfit through this cut with at least eight head of horses which included the four horses of the stockmen. The Indians came down this steep trail after the sheepmen had passed into the canyon and had been killed.

After three weeks and a snow storm it would have been impossible to determine if the stockmen had passed there or just their horses, with the Daggett's camp on board, thereby obliterating any tracks the stockmen may have made.

The other, is by the west side paralleling along the steep hillside. Here again the stockmen would have to negotiate boulder fields and steep rock slides.

It is not absolutely certain that one could determine where the four stockmen accessed the canyon floor but coming down the main canyon bottom had to have been their route.

The four men did not pass from the rim above to the side canyon and proceed down through the deep cut, as reported by Captain Donnelley and others.

**ref. explanation of Plate No. 2, photo taken by G.L. Matthews and the written account by Frank Perry published in the Nev. Historical Society Quarterly Volume 15, Issue #4 winter 1972 pages 25 and 26.

As the four stockmen approached the butchered animals the hair on the back of their necks had to be standing up and it had to be with great apprehension that they closed on the beef carcasses.

On the other side of the equation the butchered beef had been discovered and now the Daggett's campsite, in addition to their problems way back on Gollaher Mountain, which led to them being here in the first place, was in jeopardy of being revealed. They had to have expected a visit from someone after Indiano had came upon the cattle carcasses ,but were probably quite surprised that it was the next day.

It was obvious to the the Daggetts at this point that the stockmen knew of the butchered beef and had located their camp since it was just above the talus slope and a few yards to the east.

Testimony at inquest, Washoe County court records No. 807, page 4, chapter - "Posse Organized"

By the 19th of January they had only 4 or 5 horses alive the rest had perished from starvation. The Daggett family, trapped under the rim and in desperate need of horses for transportation, somehow, someway, had to acquire horses. They now had an opportunity to acquire those needed horses.

With the discovery of their campsite and the butchered beef their need to leave was even more urgent. They knew that they were in trouble with these men alive but were they desperate enough to kill? Put yourself in their moccasins, what would you have done?

They had been pushed into this miserable situation through no fault of their own. The Daggett boys had nothing to look forward to but more hardship, uncertainty and death. They could only blame the white man for this sorry state of affairs and would not have hesitated to take their frustration out on the four stock men. This would, partially, account for the many gun shot wounds in each body and mutilation (removing the mustache of Erramouspe) if that actually occurred.

Inquest at Denio Camp, February 15, 1911

It was very clear to them that they absolutely could not afford to allow any of the sheepmen to escape. Allowing them to survive was not an option Their location would be compromised nor could they fail to get control of the four horses they so desperately needed.

As the Daggetts saw it, their only alternative was to first get control of the horses and then kill the stockmen.

As the four ranchers approached the location of the butchered beef, the Indians suddenly appeared, confronting the four with rifles and relieving them of their horses. To be safe they would have moved the horses back a fair distance before the shooting started.

Speculation can get wild here. Harry Cambron was the only one of the four that had a weapon, a small 32 caliber pistol that would fit in the pocket of his chaps.

Did Mike's outfit just start shooting or did Cambron, not knowing how many Indians there were nor how many weapons they had, feel the group's best chance was for him to make an effort to protect himself and get to his pistol but was shot before he could do so.

If two of the sheepmen were shot in the head with a pistol, as Morrison reported, it would indicate Cambron had gotten to his pistol. The reason to shoot the two in the head indicates they were not dead after being shot down with rifles. The Indians may not have known how to chamber a cartridge in a semi automatic pistol.

The most likely scenario, Cambron had gotten to his pistol and chambered a shell or had a round already in the chamber when he was shot. Then the Indians picked up the pistol and shot the two wounded sheepmen in the head.

Since Cambron had not likely taken the pistol with him for any particular reason he may not have had more than ten rounds of ammunition and those being in the clip in the pistol.

Or maybe someone in the group started mouthing off and got the whole bunch shot. In any event it didn't matter, they were already doomed. The four men were shot to death by the Daggetts, on the north side of the canyon floor, about 100 yards west of the break "natural gate" in the lower canyon rim. There is no reason to believe the Indians offered any mercy to the ranchers, as they cut the ranchers down in a burst of rifle fire. Someone was going to pay for this miserable situation they were in. If one was to speculate, it would be that the stockmen were killed by the same two Indians that killed Frank Dopp on Gollaher Mountain, last April and that Indian Mike Daggett, grandfather and patriarch of the family, did none of the shooting in either case.

It would have been logical for Bill Denio to accompany the others down to the butchered beef and ride back with Indiano, but for some unknown reason he did not, lucky for him. The Daggett family knew there was no question now as to how much trouble they were in. What are the alternatives? These had already been mapped out, only one viable now, drag the bodies down to the creek in the bottom of the canyon, where they could be concealed in the snow and hope they would not be found for a good long time; load

165

up the four fresh horses along with their own very poor, starving ones and make a run for the Owyhee Desert, 200 miles to the east.

So they did just that, packed up all their belongings and what ever beef they could load onto eight horses and leaving very little behind, as they did last April when they left Gollaher Mountain, slid down from their perch under the high north rim of Little High Rock Canyon, onto the canyon floor below. I say slid because that is about how they would have to exit their camp, it was too steep to do other wise, even with switch-backs built into the trail.

They had, at most, four live horses of their own at this time, but now with the four of the stockmen, they had eight to move a family of twelve.

We must remember it was the white man that caused the Daggetts to be here in this desperate miserable situation in the first place, 300 miles from their winter home in Rock Creek Canyon, Idaho, the winter camp they had come back to each winter for the past thirty to thirty five years.

Carrie Crockett interview in the early 1970s

Since the Indians were so desperately in need of horses one would ask why did they not kill Indiano and take his horse? They did not know that there was going to be an opportunity to acquire four horses on the following day.

The most likely answer to that question is the Indians were not at all prepared for Indiano's arrival. They were not in a position to get control of his horse. The option to get control of Indiano's horse and to kill Indiano did not present itself. Both had to occur, they could not afford to lose the horse nor allow Indiano to get out alive.

On the 20th of January the Daggetts departed down Little High Rock Canyon, with nearly all the family on foot and set out for the Owyhee country, nearly a 200 mile trek. Probably the only one riding was the second to the youngest, Hattie.

The youngest of the Daggett family rode in a cradle board on her mothers' back. There is almost no doubt her mother walked and carried her the entire distance.

There were not enough horses to carry all their belongings and family members too. Their hope was that by the time the bodies were discovered they will have made it to some safe haven, however I doubt they had any specific destination in mind, only a dream to follow in hopes of finding this magical place, possibly on the Owyhee Desert.

166

No such luck as it turned out, due to the lack of horses and the fact that they were nearly all on foot, they were a few days short.

Before leaving Little High Rock Canyon the Daggetts striped the cloths, not soaked in blood, from the dead men to alter and make warm clothing for the children.

Fragments of clothing found on the trail indicated they made alterations as they traveled east into the rising sun.

Based on Dr. Morrison's report, describing entrance and exit wounds in the bodies of the four men, there is a logical explanation of what occurred. Bullets entering the men at an angle indicate three of the men were turning away from their killers, to the left, in a defensive motion, thus hitting the ranchers in different parts of their bodies, as they were shot down in rapid succession. All four went down from the first volley of rifle fire. Cambron, Erramouspe and Indiano, did not die immediately so they were shot in the head. Bullet wounds in the lower body (hip area) of Cambron and Erramouspe, would indicate the Indians were leveraging shells into those rifles and firing as rapidly as possible, from hip level. It appears the Indians shot Laxague and Indiano in the upper body first and then turned their fire on the other two, Cambron and Erramouspe, at hip level, and after the later two went down they were shot in the upper body and the head.

Dr. Morrison's report Page 7 & 8, chapter "Posse Organized" and inquest conducted at Denio camp

Note: Later, February 15, 1911, when Captain Donnelley of the State Police investigated the killings, he reported the four stockmen were ambushed from the willows on the south side of the canyon and others have told the same story but this could not have been.

They could not have done that by ambushing these men from the willows across the canyon, as reported by Donnelley and others. The Indians had, at most, two repeating rifles, a 40-82 and a 38-55, both Winchesters, and a shot gun.

At the inquests held in Winnemucca, March 1 through March 4, 1911, these were the only weapons (fire arms) positively identified in evidence, as belonging to the Indians.

Record of the Proceedings on Coroner's Inquest in the Sixth Judicial District Court, No. 356 and 357 Humboldt County, Nevada

Had they surprised the horses, as well as the four men, and started blasting away with these high powered weapons, from ambush, in that narrow canyon and men started tumbling off their mounts, the horses would have stampeded and the Indians would have lost them all. The rifle fire from the Indians heavy rifles would have made one hell of a noise and God awful booming vibration, ricocheting and echoing off those canyon walls.

It is certain the Indians had control of the horses before the shooting began and the thunderous booming began to echo off those canyon walls. There was no ambush from the willows.

Also note, none of the men were shot in the back. Had the Indians started shooting from ambush, the horses would have whirled and headed back up the canyon. To bring all the stockmen down they would have had to shoot someone in the back.

From the Morrison report, it appears Cambron was shot in the right temple and Erramouspe behind the right ear, no exit wounds were noted, indicating these two were shot with Cambron's 32 caliber pistol. Those bullets may still be with the remains, in the coffins, at the Cedarville, California cemetery.

Laxague had a bruise to his right eye, probably from a rifle butt. Indiano was shot twice in the head, both bullets exiting. With little doubt, those two wounds were the result of being shot by a high-powered rifle.

Morrison report, Nevada State Archives

Over the years it has been suggested, on several occasions, that rustlers killed the four stockmen and the Indians just happened along and gathered up personal belongings. This is not true for several reasons: 1) The Daggett camp was located directly above and only about 300 yards from where the four men were murdered 2) The Daggetts had clothing from the dead men 3) They could not have stretched the arms over the heads of frozen bodies and removed clothing (the bodies would have frozen the 1st night and it is difficult to remove clothing from cold bodies let alone frozen ones) 4) photos and other evidence suggests clothing was removed intact and not cut from the bodies 5) Horses would not have stood around waiting for the Indians to gather them up, they, the horses would have been long gone 6) Had the murderers been rustlers or outlaws, they would not have left Cambron's automatic pistol nor four horses for someone to come by and pick up.

The fact that the Indians did not kill O. D. Van Norman at Hog Creek nor take his horse or horses, steal horses from Denio Camp which they could see from the high hill at the mouth of Hog Creek Canyon nor kill or steal from any of the sheep camps near High Rock Lake, tells you that was not their method of operation.

The killing of the four sheepmen came about in desperation. They had avoided killing people and stealing horses as long as possible. However, as time passed, more horses perished and their situation become more desperate, it is quite likely one of those alternatives would have been acted on.

At the end of the trail the Daggetts had seven horses. They had lost one horse that had died on the trail, just short of the summit, leading out of Paradise Valley and down into Edan Valley. That horse was branded with a B on the left thigh.

Inquest Proceedings at Golconda, Nevada March 2 through March 4, 1911

LITTLE HIGH ROCK WHERE BODIES WERE FOUND

PLATE No. 2, Is a general view of the canyon, looking in an easterly direction. The four men came off the upper rim-rock to the left of the camp, and through a narrow break in the lower rim-rock and over the slide, as shown in the left of the picture, to where the beef was found by Indiano, which was near where the three horses are standing in the center of the picture.

From the confession of the young squaw that was captured, it was learned that the four men were seen by the Indians from their lookout near camp some time before coming over the upper rim-rock and some of the Indian bucks secreted themselves in the willows near where the bodies were found, and shot the four men when they came to examine the beef the Indians had killed. A cap and other remnants of clothing were found near this point, which led to the finding one the bodies thrown in a narrow creek-bed surrounded by willows at the "X" in the picture. In the front of the picture may be seen two men with one of the bodies on a stretcher, starting up the canyon to where the sleigh was in waiting one and a half miles distant. (See Plate 3)

G. L. Matthews

170

LITTLE HIGH ROCK CANYON
JAN. 21, 2008

Snow depth here, averaged about six inches in the bottom of the canyon. In 1911 it appears to be about eight inches. The four ranchers did not likely come down over the slide and through the narrow break in the lower rim. They would have been easier to kill on the steep slope and much easier to hide in the side canyon, above the lower rim. The Indians did not kill the four ranchers from ambush in the willows. The Indians desperately needed those horses since they only had four, very poor, starving and week horses of their own to move all the belongings for a family of twelve. The others had died of starvation. The Indians could not afford a surprise attack and start blasting away in that canyon with those heavy rifles. and they would have lost them all. When rifles started booming and bodies falling off their mounts the horses would have stampeded, there would have been no horses left in that canyon, for Indians. The Indians had absolute control of the horses before the killing started.

171

PLATE NO. 1, This view is of the deserted tepee, and the location is marked "Camp" in plate No. 2. About 25 or 30 feet to the left of the tepee was a couple of large rocks which were used as a lookout, and from which point they could guard the canyon in all directions. Leading from the tepee to this lookout was a trail covered with sagebrush bark and behind the rocks forming the lookout was also a bed of sagebrush bark, on which one would lie concealed and guard the canyon from all directions. This camp was located in a depression and could not be seen for only a short distance. The deserted camp, together with finding the combings of an Indian woman's hair, Indian arrow heads snow shoes and other Indian curios, was considered conclusive evidence that the four stockmen had been murdered by Indians.

By G. L. Matthews Feb, 15, 1911

SITE of INDIAN CAMP

October 2005

Arrow points to the location of the Daggett camp in Little Rock Canyon.
The camp occupied a depression at the base of the rim and next to the shale rock.

DAGGETT CAMP SITE

JANUARY 22, 2008

White arrow points to depression where Daggetts had their camp.
Snow conditions are very similar to ground cover February 15, 1911,

CHAPTER III

MISSING ON THE BLACK ROCK

By the time two weeks had passed since the departure of the three stockmen, major concern for their safety had been generated and the community was beginning to buzz with speculation as to why they had not returned, within the expected time. The round trip should not have taken more than about ten days before returning to their homes. Speculation as to their extended time away swirled around all sorts of scenarios. Were they caught in a blizzard and froze or lost, poisoned from canned food, killed by outlaws for their horses and equipment and so on. They were missing on the Black Rock.

Then late on the 7th of February the camp tender for Bertrand Indiano, arrived in Eagleville with the following news:

Indiano had left camp on January 18th and had not returned. It is reasonable for the camp tender to to expect his boss to be back with supplies within seven or eight days. (Based on the telegram below the camp tender worked for the Humphry-Cambron Cattle Co. but his name was never found in any reliable records.)

On arriving at Denio Camp, located three and one half miles from the head of Little Rock Canyon, the camp-tender learned from the Denios that Cambron, Laxague, Erramouspe and Indiano had arrived at Denio Camp on the same day, January 18th. That the four had departed there together on the 19th, with Indiano leading the way to show them where, on the previous day, he had seen the recently butchered beef.

From Denio Camp it is three miles to the head of Little High Rock Canyon and one and a half miles on down the canyon to where Indiano had seen the carcasses of butchered beef.

The fact that none of the four had ever arrived at any of the winter camps was of grave concern to those back home in Surprise Valley. Based on the writings of West and Perry one of those camps was near High Rock Lake.

The four missing men, being prominent ranchers in the Valley, were well known in that corner of California and now the whole valley is in a buzz with speculation and concern.

Indiano had just come up from his winter camp so it was expected he would have gone back to Denio's, after showing the other three the butchered beef, and continued on to Eagleville. Bill Denio must have wondered why Indiano had not returned and may have been the reason for his journey down Little High Rock two days after the four had left his camp. This information was given by Warren Fruits at the Inquest for the stockmen, on February 15th.

Upon receiving this information in Eagleville, word was sent by wire to H. Humphrey, of Humphrey - Cambron Cattle Co., that his camp tender had arrived last evening, February 7th and that the four men were missing.

Humphrey-Cambron Cattle Co., Reno, Nevada: "Your camp tender just came in Cambron, Indiano, Lexague and Erramouspe left Denio Camp to go seven miles away to the sheep on January 19th. But never reached them. They have not been seen since. A posse has been formed here to leave at once to find them. The sheep are reported alright." "Operator Eagleville, Cal." From the Reno Evening Gazette February 8th 1911.

On the morning of February 8th, a search party of five men; Warren Fruits, Dave Bryant, George Holmes, Joe Reeder, Pete Etchart and probably Mort West, departed Eagleville for Little Rock High Canyon via Home Camp, and Denio Camp, in search of the four ranchers, who had now been gone for three weeks. They arrived at Denio's on February the 8th. On the 9th, Bill Denio accompanied them down the canyon to show them where the butchered animals were located. Denio had himself gone there two days after the four left his camp on the 19th of January. At about 10 am on the 9th, Warren Fruits found the bodies partially covered with snow, a mile and a half down from the head of Little High Rock Canyon.

Inquest testimony of Warren Fruit, Feb. 15, 1911, at Denio Camp. Note: he did not include West in his testimony.

It was reported that Warren Fruit unloaded his rifle, firing into the air. If anyone found the bodies the signal was supposed to be three shots Warren must have gotten a little excited when he came across the bodies, as might be expected.

Warren and Dave Bryant beat it back to Eagleville to report what they had found. They arrived in Eagleville in time to get the news in the February 10th issue of the Nevada State Journal. The February 10th issue of the Reno Evening Gazette came out without this news. They had to have ridden all night to get the information out in time for the February 10th issue of the Nevada State Journal.

CHAPTER IV
POSSE ORGANIZED

Captain J. P. Donnelley, head of the Nevada State Police, in Carson City, Nevada and Washoe County Sheriff W. C. Ferrel, at Reno, Nevada, had already started planning for the trip to Eagleville in anticipation of the Warren Fruits search party results. Captain Donnelly had a special train held up in Reno for the journey.

Word came on February 11, 1911 and they left Reno, Nevada on that day, headed for Alturas, California on the O&C Railroad. Those on board included: from the Nevada State Police, Capt. J. P. Donnelley, Sergeant C. H. Stone, Sergeant P. M. Newguard and Private Buck; Washoe County Sheriff - W. C. Farrell; Justice of the Peace, acting Corner of the County of Washoe, Nevada, Lee J. Davis and Dr. S. K. Morrison.

Reno Evening Gazette (REG) - Feb. 17, 1911

They arrived in Alturas on Sunday the 12th of February, in the early morning.

REG and Nevada State Journal (NSJ) February 13, 1911

From Alturas the lawmen, that now included Modoc County Sheriff, A. E. Smith, traveled east over the Warner Mountains to Cedarville, California where they were joined by Photographer G.L. Matthews, then continued 16 miles south to Eagleville, California.

At Eagleville, on February 13, they made preparations to recover the bodies of the stockmen from Little High Rock Canyon.

The RENO EVENING GAZETTE of February 13, 1911, carried a message from a wire sent by Davies that: "posse leaving Eagleville by 9 a. m." Probably not by 9 a. m. they were still charging out rifles and supplies on that day. By the time they got packed up and lined out, they would have been lucky to get out of there by noon.

Donnelley also reported that they were leaving in a blinding snowstorm. This may account for them not arriving at Denio's until late Tuesday the 14th.

By the time the State Police arrived in Eagleville, the town was already in turmoil. Between February 7th and the 13th, 7 different men charged out equipment and supplies to the H.C.C. Cattle Co., at the T. H. JOHNSTONE Co. General Store in Eagleville, for the man hunt. The charges were made nine different times, the 1st was on the 7th and the remainder on the 10th, 11th, 12th and 13th. The charges ranged

177

from tobacco to six rifles and included pack equipment, groceries, grain, horse feed, shovels, rope, 45 boxes of ammunition and one pistol.

The first charge, on February 7th, was made by Joe Reeder, a member of the first group, that left for Little High Rock, in search of the missing ranchers.

Ben Cambron, brother of one of the missing sheepmen, made several charges of equipment and supplies. On the 13th, Mort West, one member of the posse, charged out tobacco, 24 boxes of shells, for 3 different rifles.(25-35, 30-30 & 30 US Winchester). More confusion and another example of a chaotic scene, buckaroos and ranch hands ordering stuff and making decisions and no law enforcement people involved. This is an interesting order and date, it included ammunition for a US 30 Winchester. A US- 30 Winchester shows up later in this saga. Frank Perry, a member of the posse, stated in his story that he and Mort West left early, for Little High Rock Canyon, before the State Police arrived. It is a little hard to understand how the State Police could be in Eagleville, get a wire out by 9 am and West and Perry having checked out ammunition etc. and be headed out before State Police arrived.

Charles Demick, Superintendent of the Quinn River Division of the Miller & Lux cattle empire and his crew; Henry Hughes, Fred Murphy, Ed Hogel, Sid Street, Fred Hill and Gilbert Jackson, charged out six rifles and one pistol, as follows:

February 10, 1911

1 - One 25-35 - Charged out by Fred Murphey - Returned March 2, 1911.

2 - One 25-35 - Charged out by Ray (Ed) Hogle - Returned March 8,1911.

3 - One 30 US Winchester (28 inch barrel) - Charged out by Henry Hughes - No record of it being returned.

February 13, 1911

4 - One 25-35 (26 inch barrel) - Charged out by Sid Street - Returned March 2, 1911.

5 - One 30-30 - Charged out by Fred Hill - Returned March 8th or shortly after.

6 - One 30-30 (26 inch barrel) Charged out by Jackson - Returned by Chas Demick March 2, 1911.

One - 44 Colt pistol & 3 boxes shells - Charged to Chas Demick, Returned March 2nd.

It should be noted here that Demick and his crew all checked out weapons they evidently had none of there own. Conclusion no need for buckaroos to have weapons in this day and age.

Fred Murphy, Sid Street, Gilbert Jackson, Fred Hill and Jim Batey, all part of Demick's outfit, had started out with the posse on the trail of the Indians but went no further than Soldier Meadows. These six turned in equipment and rifles shortly after arriving back at Eagleville.

All rifles and the pistol, were recorded returned by March 8th or shortly thereafter except for the 30 US Winchester, signed out to Henry Hughes. Only two of the seven weapons charged out at the T. H. JOHNSTONE Co. General Store, were carried all the way to the end of the manhunt. They were the 30-US Winchester, carried by Henry Hughes and a 25-35 charged out by Ed Hogle.

This must have been like what we call a "Three Ring Circus" only without anyone in charge or any coordination. This was the beginning of what turned out to be a fiasco of an uncontrolled vigilante posse. Was Capt. Donnelly of the Nevada State Police incompetent? By the time this man hunt ended it was obvious he was in over his head and had lost control of the situation from the very beginning.

The uncontrolled actions and the mentality of the posse, led partially, if not totally, to the murder of the women and children at the end of the hunt.

The posse arrived at Home Camp, located about fifteen miles east of the Nevada/California state line and some eighteen miles from Eagleville, on February 13th. On the following day they continued on to Denio Camp, a distance of about 25 miles.

On the morning of February 15th, the posse proceeded to the site of the killing in Little High Rock Canyon, recovered the bodies of the ranchers and brought them out to Denio Camp. Night had descended on Denio Camp by the time the recovery crew arrived there with the bodies of the stockmen and the coroner Lee Davis had to hold the inquest with only the light of a kerosene lamp. The bodies were brought out from the head of Little High Rock Canyon to Denio Camp by Dick Cook. Dick Cook, a rancher from Surprise Valley, had brought out a sleigh with a four horse team to transport the bodies of the sheepmen back to Eagleville.

Writings by Frank Perry, 1949, and charges at the general store (grain for Dick Cook's team - page 18)

Davis summoned the following eight men to act as jurors and arrive at a verdict as to the death of the four men found dead in Little High Rock Canyon: Jack Ferguson, Henry Hughes, Fred Hill, R. T. Cook, P. M. Newgard, James Grery, Frank Buck and F. A. Murphy.

Called to testify before the jury were the following three men: Captain J. P. Donnelly, Warren Fruit and Dr. S. K. Morrison.

INQUEST # 807

INQUEST OF 4 STOCK MEN AT DENIO'S   *Feb. 15, 1911*

Capt. JP Donnley *being sworn upon his oath says.*

A- I am Supt. of Nevada State Police

Q- Did you visit the scene of the crime where four men was murdered in Little High Rock Canyon if so please state the result of your investigation

A- I went in the canyon on the 15th. We found bodies of four men murdered and they were lying in a pile in a depression

Q- Did you examine surrounding country

A- I did and found an Indian camp under the rim rock it looked as thou it had been occupied some months & looks as thou it had been recently occupied.

Q- How far was it from where the men were found to the Indian camp

A- About 300 yards

Q- Do you know where the men were killed?

A- I believe they were killed at the bottom of the canyon about 30 yards from where we found the bodies you could see where the bodies were found

we could see where the bodies were dragged and we found a cap and a couple of sox we also found a dead horse near the Indian camp it was branded (B) on the left stifle. It looked like an Indian pony. We couldn't find any wounds on the horses

I know there was four and have been told there were seven dead in the canyon, none of these horses belonged to the murdered men.

Q- What photographs were taken there today

A- There was a photograph taken of the Indian camp, and one of the bodies before they were disturbed

Q- What leads you to believe this an Indian camp?

A- By the articles found at the (camp site?) and construction of wikiup or camp, Indian snow shoes, pants sewed with sinew and animals made of mud. Also arrow heads rawhide string, meat, they had a trail padded with sage bark from this wikiup to their look out

Q- Do you think this deed was committed by Indians

A- I do beyond a doubt

[rest of statement missing!!]

Warren Fruit *being sworn upon his oath says*

He resides in Eagleville, Modock Co. Cal. and that he was well acquainted with John Laxague, Harry Cambron, Pete Aramosby, B Indiana

Q- What time did these men leave Eagleville

A- 16th or 17th Jan. 11

Q- Where were they going

A- To look for their sheep

Q- When did you next see them

A- I found them dead in Little High Rock Canyon on Feby 9th at 10 o'clock a.m.

Q- Who was with you

A- George Holmes, Joe Reeder, Billy Denio, and Pete Etchart [was just behind me]

Q- Please describe how you found these men and their position and condition as near as possible

A- We started out from Eagleville to hunt these men they had been missing 22 days. We knew that they had gone to Little High Rock Canyon. We went to Bill Denios' and he said that Indiano had told him of seeing some cattle that had been butchered in the canyon that at first he doubted Indiano, but 2 days later he had himself found the cattle and he would go and show us where the beef was cached he went and showed us the

181

beef and then we found more, about five head had been butchered (they were Miller & Lux cattle)

We looked around a wile and about 30 or 40 feet from where the cattle were found we found the four men they were lying in a small depression or creek bed all in a pile and quite a lot of the clothing was gone. The shoes had been taken from all of them. but the felt boots had been left on one of the men. John Laxague had on a green sweater and it had been pulled over his head. As soon as we made the discovery Dan Bryant and I came to Eagleville and reported and the officers at Reno were notified by wire.

Q- Describe the location of Little High Rock Canyon, as near as you can

A- It is about 50 miles almost East from Eagleville,Cal. and lies in Washoe County Nevada and about 45 miles east of the Nevada - Cal. line

Q- Can you give me approximately the	age	nativity	married	children
A- Cambron	27	Cal	no	
Indiana	34	French(Basque)	no	
Laxague	35	" "	yes	3
Aramosby	45	" "	yes	2

Q- And what date do you think these men were killed

A- Jany 19th, 1911

Q- How many men do you think there was in the party that butchered the cattle

A- Couldn't say for shore but we all agreed that there was about 5 in the party

Q- Do you think it was Indians

A- My opinion is it was not Indians the camp was not like an Indians camp

Q- Did you go up to the old wickiup

A- no

Signed - Warren Fruit

Subscribed & sworn to before me   *Signed - Lee J Davis*

Dr. S.K. Morrison *being sworn on his oath says*

Q- What is your name and profession

A- SK Morrison Physician & surgeon

182

Q- And your Co. Physician Washo Co.

A- yes

Q- Were you called on to hold a post mortem examination upon the remains of the four men found dead in Little High Rock Canyon

A- Yes

Q- What was the result of the autopsy

A- I found four bodies thoroughly frozen

No 1	Harry Cambron	shot 4 times
No 2	Peter Erramouspe	upper lip removed 3 shots
No 3	John Laxague	arm wound
No 4	Burttrum Indiana	Several wounds in face other wounds

Signed - S K Morrison

Subscribed and Sworn to, before me   Feby 15th 1911   --

Signed - Lee J Davis

To G. W. Perkins, Chairman, the Honorable Board of County Commissioners, Reno, Washoe County, Nevada:

Dear Sir --- as requested by you, I made the trip from Reno to Little High Rock Canyon, which is located in the northern end of this county, and hereby submit the following report of conditions as I found them.

I found the bodies of four men which were thoroughly frozen and the four frozen together in a dry creek bed surrounded by willows about a mile and a half from the entrance of Little High Rock Canyon and about four miles from Denio's Ranch. These bodies were separated from each other with great difficulty and were carried on stretchers to the mouth of the canyon where they were placed on a sleigh and taken to Denio's Ranch where the inquest was held.

BODY NO. 1. -- Identified as Harry Cambron. Height, 5 feet 11 inches, Weight, 176 pounds.

The under shirt and shirt were pulled over the head entirely covering the same, arms were extended over the head. The only clothing on the lower limbs was the under-draws which were pulled down below the knees, all other clothing missing.

There was an inch cut over the knuckle of the middle finger of the right hand. He had been shot four times. One bullet passed from the seventh rib auxiliary line on the right side passing through the liver and lungs and coming out two inches above the left nipple. Another bullet passed through the left buttock and thigh. Another through the left elbow and a 38- caliber pistol bullet entering the head behind the right ear. It was impossible to tell the entrance from the exit wounds on account of the area around the wounds being gnawed by the snow mice.

BODY NO. 2. -- Identified as Pete Arramauspe. Height, 5 feet 8 inches, Weight 170 pounds.

The clothing that was left on this body consisted of an undershirt from which the sleeves had been cut, drawers and overalls on the lower limbs and a sock and a felt boot on the

184

left foot, Right foot being bare. The upper lip contained a heavy black mustache which was removed with a knife after death. He was shot four times . One pistol bullet entered the head two and a half inches behind the right eye. A rifle ball passing through the chest entering two inches above and one inch below the left nipple on the left side and exit two inches below left shoulder blade. Another rifle ball entering left thigh at its outer side passing through the thigh, through the scrotum and through the right thigh cutting the right femoral artery, and another rifle ball passing through the right thigh four inches below the buttock coming out on the anterior surface of the right thigh.

BODY NO. 3. -- Identified as John B. Laxague. Height 5 feet 10 inches. Weight about 186 pounds. The undershirt, shirt and knit jacket were pulled over his head and arms and extended over the head. No other clothing remained.

The right eye was blackened, which was probably post mortem. He was shot once, the bullet entering one and a half inches above the right nipple, passing diagonally through the chest, coming out through the left side of the back four inches below the shoulder blade and two inches from the spine yet the entrance and exit of this wound had been gnawed buy the mice making it impossible to state positively which wound was the entrance and which was the exit.

BODY NO. 4 -- Identified as B. Indiana. Height 5 feet 9 inches Weight, 185 pounds. The clothing remaining on the body consisted of an undershirt, shirt and knit jacket and drawers which were pulled down around the ankles. There was no other clothing.

He had been shot three times, twice in the head and once through the shoulders. One bullet entered the point of the chin, coming out one inch below the left eye, another bullet entering just below the left eye, passing through the brain, coming out on the back of the skull in the occipital region on the right side. The left eye was displaced from its socket by the last named wound. The lower eyelid the upper lip and the region between these two was practically shot away.

In the occipital region where this first bullet made its exit the skull was fractured for an area of two inches by one inch and the fragments of bone had fallen into the brain due to the tissue which held them in place being gnawed away by mice. Another rifle bullet

passed through the upper part of the chest entering the top of the left shoulder and
passing out through the top of right shoulder.
It was impossible to remove the two bullets which remained in the head on account of
the mutilation which it would have necessitated because of their frozen condition.

Respectfully submitted
SIDNEY K. MORRISON, M. D.

Copy has been filed with the district attorney.

There are some interesting inconsistencies in Morrison's report, leading one to believe he put the report together later, from notes taken at the inquest or it was transcribed incorrectly. Examples include; in his testimony at the inquest he stated Erramouspe was shot three times. In his report he stated Erramouspe was shot four times, also in his report Morrison stated Indiano was shot twice in the head, both bullets passing through the head. Later in same report he stated it was impossible to remove the bullets from the head because of mutilation.

Body silhouettes page 201 through 204

Recovering the frozen and bullet ridden bodies to take home and the participation in the inquest at Denio Camp, had to be a gruesome task. It would have been especially difficult since nearly all, except the State Police, knew the stockmen personally and was probably a contributing factor in the actions of members of the posse later on, at the end of the trail.

At this point, February 16, 1911, there were at least 30 men in the posse/recovery crew plus the photographer.

There is no evidence that the three men, Erramouspe, Cambron, and Laxague had a pack horse with them. No need for a pack horse since there were line camps at Home Camp and at Denio Camp. The main camps, on the winter are usually supplied in the fall, so no need here either. New railroad construction had reached Gerlach, Nevada in 1906 so if supplies were needed at the main camps they are brought in from there as has been alluded to in several accounts. There are no high passes nor snow country to pass through to access Gerlach from their winter camps.

And there is no evidence Indiano had a pack horse or a pack string, so we are left to conclude one of three possibilities, 1) He wasn't headed in for supplies, 2) He had pack animals near Eagleville to bring back supplies on the return trip or 3) Pack animals or pack string were left at Denio Camp when he headed back down Little High Rock Canyon with the other three sheepmen to show them where he had seen the beef carcasses.

His plan was to return to Denio Camp and then continue on to Eagleville.

Only 4 horses were identified as missing along with other items as described in the Reno Evening Gazette and the Humboldt Star, February 17, 1911.

1-Bay horse, white stripe on face, white feet, weight 1100 lbs. 5 years old and branded HP on left shoulder, 76 on left side.

Ferguson testified, March 9th, that the horse with the HP on left thigh and 76 on left side was property of Harry Cambron

1-Bay horse, white star on forehead, stripe on nose, quarter circle on left shoulder, JA on left side.

1-Sorrel horse, light main & tail, white face, Wt. 1100 lbs, LT on right thigh.

(LT was the brand of Lawrence Thomas Sweeney, grandfather of author.

1-Black Oregon horse 7 or 8 years old, no brand known.

This horse was most likely Indiano's horse as only the Denios had seen the horse and would not have been looking for brands already difficult to see due to long winter hair. Although the newspapers of the day were suspect as to their accuracy, they would try to get this information as accurate as possible. It is concluded that the two bay horses were branded on the left thigh, not left side and the black horse was meant to be identified as a Morgan horse not an Oregon horse. A Morgan horse has identifiable characteristics where as an "Oregon horse" serves no purpose in identification.

Some stories have surfaced claiming the Indians had taken a white horse, belonging to Harry Cambron, when they departed Little High Rock Canyon. This is not true, the only horses taken by the Indians were as listed above.

Other items listed as missing included the following:

1-Gold, open faced watch, No. 13978232 or 13997831.

1-Silver hunting case watch, C. H. Cambron's name on the back.

1-Savage Automatic Pistol, 32 caliber, number either 14160 or 13711.

Testimony at the inquest on March 1st and 2nd, respectively, by Stone & Parsons, identified the Savage revolver, now in court, by the No. 26474 as the one taken at the Indian camp. Interesting, these numbers didn't come near matching those listed above, or those on Harry Cambron's missing pistol.

George Holmes - Testified he found a Waltham watch, 15 Jewels - No. 10973688 in evidence. Where did it go?

Ironically, at almost this same time, Frank Tranmer and Nimrod Urie who were involved in the Gollaher Mountain episode, were in the Humboldt County jail for the murder of the Quillicies at Imlay, Nevada. The Elko County authorities, having now put all this together, were having second thoughts as to who might really be the guilty party at Gollaher Mountain and were no longer out to kill all and any Indians. Sadly, Mike and his family had no knowledge of these developments and it now appeared the Elko authorities were prepared to investigate further.

However, that investigation never came to be, even after the slaughter of the Daggetts at Rabbit Creek, the Elko authorities, the newly elected Sheriff Harris and former District Attorney, E. J. L. Taber, now a judge, made no effort to investigate further. After all no one of significance had died at Gollaher Mt., just some kid (Frank Dopp) from Twin Falls, Idaho, with the Tranmer Gang and an Indian boy (Jack Daggett). Other additional circumstances that led to their complacency, will be discussed later.

The many books, news articles, stories etc. that have been written and told about this incident in history, have all missed the mark on weather and snow conditions encountered. All claim the winter of 1909 / 1910 was the most severe on record.

At the time, newspaper stories and other accounts, including Captain Donnelley's Nevada State Police report claimed there to be three to four feet of crusted snow on the ground in that part of the country, at that time and one of the coldest winters on record. Since they could not have traveled that distance, in that short period of time, in those snow conditions, those reports were wrong. In fact, it was warm and rainy through about the middle of January. However in the mountains and in the higher elevations there would have been a lot of snow.

On the other hand by the 8th of February, much of the snow that fell in January, on the lower country, had melted off. There might have been drifts that deep on the 6,000 foot pass between Eagleville and Home Camp but not crusted snow on the level ground.

Also see THE NEW ERA, (Alturas, California newspaper) weather reports for Nov., Dec. 1910, Jan. and Feb. 1911 and the Reno Evening Gazette.

Dec. 19, 1910 -- weather report for Nov. temperature varied from low of 7 degrees on the 1st to 76 degrees on the 25th. The average minimum was 26 degrees.

Jan. 11th -- weather report for Dec. mildest since weather reports have been kept.

Feb. 8th -- weather report for Jan. temperature ranged from 54 degrees on the 7th. to 21 degrees on the 23rd, total amount of snow 32 inches with rain mixed in but most of snow melted off by Feb. 8th.

Reno Evening Gazette, Feb. 8th, 1911 -- H. G. Humphrey of the H. C. Cattle Co.quote "snow at that time only a foot and a half feet deep, but fearfully cold.

Reno Evening Gazette, Feb. 10, 1911 -- H. G. Humphrey's quote "snow not very deep".

Feb. 15th -- THE NEW ERA, "N.C.O. Rail Road snowbound again".

The N. C. O. Rail Road ran west of the Warner Mountains and there could have been places where the cuts for the railroad had drifted in.

In fact, there was only about ten or eleven inches at Denio Camp and about eight inches on the floor of Little High Rock Canyon.

Photos dated Feb. 15, 1911 and Jan. 21, 2008

The snow conditions February 16 1911 and January 23, 2008 are very similar. The snow depth at the Denio camp was only eight inches deep and six inches deep in Little High Rock Canyon, in January 2008. In comparing the pictures taken February 16th 1911 with the 2008 photos, it appears that there could have been, at most, two or three more inches February 16, 1911 than there was January 23, 2008 and no whereas near the snow depths and snow conditions (three to four feet of crusted snow) as reported by media, from statements of the posse, and others interviewed, including Frank Perry in his written account.

The estimated snow depths: Home camp 12 to 16 inches,

The Humboldt Star reported February 1911 as colder than normal. The Temperature ranged from 52 degrees on the tenth to 4 degrees on the 16th. Although colder than normal still much warmer than reported in books and newspaper stories.

Weather reports in the newspapers were as accurate as they could make them. There was every reason to report as accurate as possible and no reason not to.

G. L. Matthews Photo February 13, 1911   PLATE No. 7

POSSE LEAVING EAGLEVILLE, CALIFORNIA IN A SNOWSTORM

I believe this to be the contingent that arrived from Carson City via Reno, Alturas, Cedarville. Those in this picture probably include; Capt. Donnelly, Sgt. Newguard, Sgt. Stone and Private Buck, of the Nevada State Police; Washoe county Sheriff, Ferrel, Dr. Morrison, coroner Davis, from Reno and Modoc County Sheriff, Smith. They were on there way to recover the bodies of Harry Cambron, Peter Erramouspe, J. B. Laxague & B. Indiano

This is actually only ten of some thirty or more men, who left Eagleville to recover the bodies of the four ranchers, in Little High Rock Canyon.

The posse arrived at Home Camp, located eighteen miles east of Eagleville, in Nevada, on the evening of the 13th and then on to Camp Denio, the next day. On the following day, Feb. 15, they traveled into the canyon and brought the bodies back out to Denio Camp. An inquest was held that evening at Denio Camp, in the dark. On the morning of the 16th, at least fifteen members of the recovery team, headed back down Little High Rock, in pursuit of whom they believed to be Indians. The Indians had left their camp, under the rim, back on January 20th. The remainder returned to Eagleville with the bodies of the four ranchers.

When the bodies of the four sheep men were returned to Eagleville they were placed in the Church, seen in the background, to thaw just three days after this photo was taken. It was reported that blood remained on the floor of the Church for many years afterward.

191

CHURCH in EAGLEVILLE Calf.

October 27, 2013

Church where the frozen bodies of the sheepmen were taken to thaw, Feb. 16, 1911.
It is reported that as the bodies thawed blood ran out on the floor and the stains
remained there for many years afterwards.
Services are still held here today, 2019.

G. L. Matthews photo - Feb. 16, 1911   PLATE No. 5

DENIO CAMP

"This picture shows a general view of Camp Denio, five miles west of where the murder was committed. In the foreground can be seen the corral with some 50 head of horses. To feed those horses it was necessary to haul hay some 10 miles, and owing to bad roads 500 pounds was a sufficient load for four horses. The first building back of the corral is a small bunk house probably 10 feet square. The other building in the distance is Mr Denio's house, about 12 x 16. In this building was cooked and served excellent meals for at least 50 persons and for which Mr. and Mrs. Denio refused to accept pay. Much is due them for their generous hospitality".

G. L. Matthews

CAMP DENIO -
Jan. 21, 2008

Building in the center of picture was not there in 1911. To the left of the tree and almost under it, in center of picture, a rock foundation remains today, location of the Denio house. The barley visible, bit of debris in front of the house, lies the collapsed bunk house. Also just to the left of the collapsed bunk house, note car tracks in the snow. Snow depth here is eight inches. In comparing the 1911 picture, I would judge there to be two to three inches more snow in 1911. Oral history and written stories, paint a much different picture, claiming this to be the most severe winter on record with snow depths in the area to be three to four feet deep and crusted. As can be seen in comparing the two pictures, those stories are not true. For example Frank Perry Wrote: *"We all took our turn at helping out, with chores, cutting wood, washing dishes, etc. we had plenty to eat but not enough beds. With three feet of snow and crusted over, it was quite a chore to gather sagebrush and keep a fire going all night to keep us warm".* This was at Denio Camp, Feb. 14 and 15, 1911.

G. L. Matthew's Photo - Feb. 15, 1911   PLATE No. 2

LITTLE HIGH ROCK WHERE BODIES WERE FOUND

PLATE No. 2, Is a general view of the canyon, looking in an easterly direction. The four men came off the upper rim-rock to the left of the camp, and through a narrow break in the lower rim-rock and over the slide as shown in the left of the picture, to where the beef was found by Indiano, which was near where the three horses are standing in the center of the picture.

From the confession of the young squaw that was captured, it was learned that the four men were seen by the Indians from their lookout near camp some time before coming over the upper rim-rock and some of the Indian bucks secreted themselves in the willows near where the bodies were found, and shot the four men when they came to examine the beef the Indians had killed. A cap and other remnants of clothing were found near this point, which led to the finding on the bodies thrown in a narrow creek-bed surrounded by willows at the "X" in the picture. In the front of the picture may be seen two men with one of the bodies on a stretcher, starting up the canyon to where the sleigh was in waiting one and a half miles distant. (See Plate 3)

G. L. Matthews

195

G. L. Matthews Photo Feb. 15, 1911   PLATE No. 4

PLATE # 4.   This plate shows the bodies as they were found in the creek-bed, as they had been placed there and left by the Indians. The bodies were in a good state of preservation having been frozen solid shortly after being placed there and owing to severe cold weather had remained frozen, and it was with some difficulty the bodies were pried apart. The place where they were found was surrounded by brush and the bodies could not have been seen unless one had gotten within 15 or 20 feet of them.

G. L. Matthews

MONUMENT in LITTLE ROCK CANYON
MAY 2005

In the lower left of the picture, at my feet, is a monument that has fallen down, due to neglect over the past one hundred years. In the stream bed below is the exact location where the bodies of the stock men, Harry Cambron, John Laxague, Burtrand Indiano and Peter Erramouspe, were found by Warren Fruits, on February 9, 1911.

By comparing this photo with Plate # 2 taken by G. L. Matthews, February 15, 1911, one can identify the large arrow shaped rock, above and to my left. On that old photo is marked an X at this location. Most streams meander and move over a long period of time. The stream at this location, has moved only a few feet in the past one hundred years.

197

G. L. Matthews Photo Feb. 15, 1911   PLATE No.3

PLATE # 3.   This plate shows the bodies after they had been carried on stretchers up the canyon through brush and over rocks for one & one half miles, being the nearest available point to which the 1 horse team and sleigh could be brought . From there the bodies were taken to Denio's, where the inquest was held by the aid of a light of a sagebrush fire and a lantern, with the mercury several degrees below zero.

G. L. Matthews

198

POSSE / RECOVERY CREW at DENIO CAMP
Feb. 16, 1911

Appears to be about thirty men in this picture. Some will return to Eagleville with the bodies of the four ranchers and the others will take to the trail of the Indians.

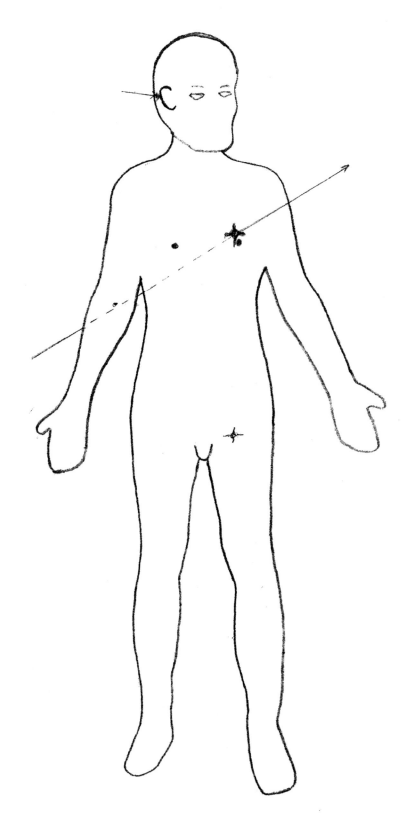

Body # **1**   Harry Cambron

200

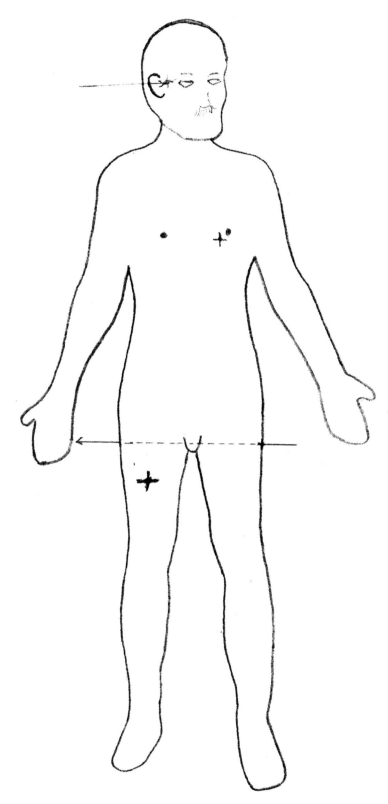

Body # **2**   Pete Erramouspe

201

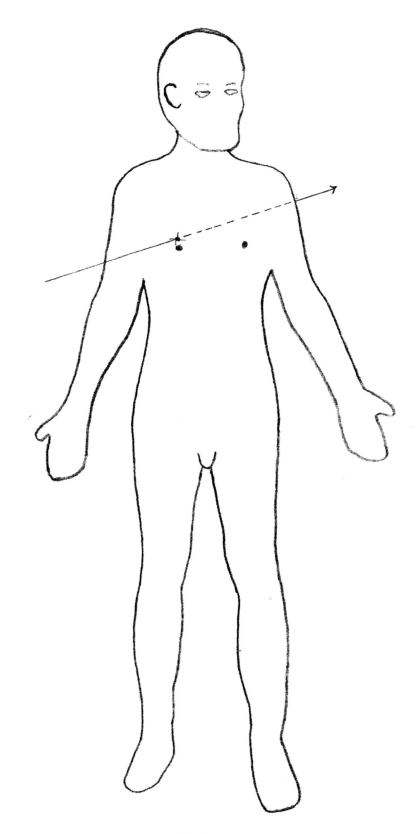

Body # **3** John Laxague

202

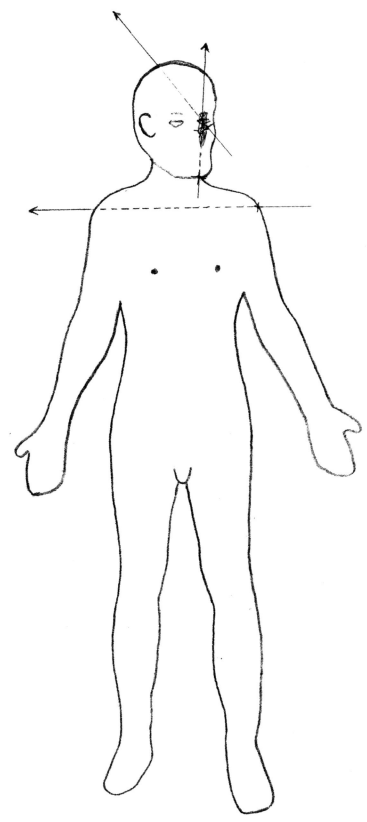

Body # **4**   Bertrand Indiano

203

CHAPTER V

CROSSING THE BLACK ROCK

Embarking on this trip to the east, in the dead of winter, the Daggetts would traverse some of the most desolate part of the west, most of which has changed little to this day.

Photos-starting at page 11

The family probably pressed hard on the 1st leg of their journey to get beyond the sheep camps, reported to be in the area of High Rock Lake, and traveled at night to avoid detection.

They would have traveled in silence, each with their own thoughts. Indians are not known for a lot of unnecessary conversation. What communication there was would be limited to a few utterances as to their direction of travel, checking on the welfare of the children, condition of the packs or horses or other things critical to their welfare or mode of travel. The youngest member, now ten months old, would have made her own displeasures known whenever she became hungry, uncomfortable from long hours in a cradle board or a soiled diaper, if they had diapers. Hattie, only 4 years old, would have some of the same issues. She was too young to walk or to heavy to be carried so she would have been riding on one of the horses, either on a pack slung on the side or possibly riding with her mother. Their mother may have ridden much of the way, with the baby on her back in the cradle board and Hattie riding in front or behind her. Did Cleave, who was six or seven years old, ride or walk the whole way, probably some of both. In the early days of the trip the family would have been moving with great urgency and for Cleave to keep up he would have to ride.

The only constant sounds would be from the horses hooves in the snow, squeaky during the cold times when temperatures were below freezing and a crunching sound as temperatures alternated from freezing at night to thawing during the day. They would have experienced both. When they encountered areas of frozen ground, where there was no snow, the plodding of the horses would have sounded like the non-rhythmic beating of distant drums.

Using the best information available which includes newspaper articles, (with much skepticism), Frank Perry's account, inquest testimony, other written accounts and analyzing the most practical route, I have determined that the following is a pretty accurate description of the route the Daggetts took in their journey from the camp site in Little High Rock Canyon, east to Rabbit Creek.

If Perry's account is correct about the Indians crossing High Rock Lake on the ice, at night, it would indicate they embarked on their long journey east late afternoon or evening of January 19, 1911 and this route parallels the route they used when traveling west the spring and summer before, between the last part of April 1910 and July 1910. Traveling at night with snow on the ground would have been quite possible as the moon was three quarters to one half visible between January 19th and the 22nd of 1911, providing skies were clear, no clouds. By the 6th of February 1911 the moon was back to about half. So again from about the 6th to the 21st of February, with snow on the ground and no clouds, traveling at night would have been fairly easy providing you could see the mountain ranges ahead.

The children must endure freezing winter conditions one experiences in January and February, without shelter other than a tarp a few blankets and horse blankets. The only natural shelter they will encounter across this barren land will be depressions in the landscape or in a wash, if void of water. During very cold windy conditions one of the most miserable places you can be is on horse back. Little Hattie, who was too heavy to carry and too young to walk had to have experienced those miserable conditions. They would have needed to wrap her up in lot of blankets and clothes to keep her warm especially on a windy day. Try to visualize how they must have tried to keep her safe on the horse.

They proceeded down Little High Rock Canyon about ten miles, across High Rock Lake on the ice and on to Fly Canyon. At this point they probably picked up the old Immigrant Trail, paralleling Fly Canyon, traveled about seven miles to Mud Meadows and then, skirting along the west side of the Black Rock Range continued south on the Lassen Trail for about 15 miles to a point three or four miles northeast of Double Hot Springs, located on the east side of the west fork of the Black Rock Desert.

From this point on the west side of the Black Rock Range they will head east about three miles over a low pass on this range of mountains on to the west side of the east fork of the Black Rock Desert. They are now about fifteen miles south of the Piaute

Meadows Ranch and approximately ten miles north of the desert playa and would have traveled a total of 40 miles. From this point Mike's outfit traveled east across the east arm of the desert. They likely crossed at a slight angle to the south which would land them in the vicinity of Rattlesnake Canyon at the foot of the Jackson Mountains on the far side of the east arm of the Black Rock Desert, a distance of about fifteen miles. This part of the desert offers little if any shelter and no feed for the horses in fact very little vegetation. For the most part scrub greasewood can be found with mounds of dirt gathered around each plant, deposited by the wind. There are a few willows along Quinn River itself and scattered patches of salt grass in the bottom and sides next to and adjacent to the high water line but too little feed for a number of horses for any length of time.

In crossing the east arm of the desert they set their sites on the lower end of the Jacksons in order to access the mountains where they could find a low pass or knew where there was a low pass that they had found the summer before on the south end near the head of Rattlesnake Canyon or Black Canyon.

Based on historical information it appears that after reaching the summit at the lower end of the Jackson Mountains they followed the ridge line in a northeasterly direction and then traveling down Shawnee Creek to the edge of Desert Valley on the west side and then heading east and a little south keeping north of the Jungo Hills

John De Long interview March 22, 2014 (local rancher who's family has lived in the area sine before 1900)

Then continuing east across the sand dunes at the south end of Slumbering Hills near or a little south of Sombrero Peak.

From this point they continued easterly to Sand Pass.

Why cross here rather than follow the route to the north that they had taken the spring/ summer before, by the Lay Brothers ranch on Willow Creek? They are leaving the scene of the killing at Little High Rock Canyon and they are not about to travel close to any ranches if they can possible avoid it and the distance is shorter if they are headed for a low pass over the Osgood Mountains.

Passing by the Lay ranch on the east side of the Jacksons at Willow Creek, takes on an interesting part of the saga.

As stated earlier, an article in the Humboldt Star newspaper refers to a group of Indians stopping during the previous spring at one of the Lay ranches and wanting to trade for some old harness.

Again newspaper stories do not have a lot of validity, however in this case there is a connection.

In addition Mort West mentioned in his writings that the Indians had stopped at one of the Lay ranches the spring before and worked for time breaking horses. I don't think the Indians stopped anywhere long enough to go to work breaking any horses they were putting as much distance as possible between them and Gollaher Mountain. However Mort's writings offer another connection to the Lay ranches.

At this point they headed east again through Sand Pass to the Hot Springs Range and then north along the foothills on the west side of this range to a low pass 5 miles northeast of the old Stewart Ranch.

From here they traveled east to the Osgood Range then south, about two miles, up a small canyon and over the summit into another small canyon which, at times, contains an intermittent stream leading to Rabbit Creek.

Finally, in the protection of a small draw leading to the south into the main canyon or tributary to Rabbit Creek the Indian family made a more permanent camp. For the 1st time since leaving their camp under the rim in Little High Rock Canyon they stopped for what they expected to be a few days rest and to contemplate what lay ahead. At this site they built a small shelter and probably would have expanded on it had they had time.

Proceeding further now was hopeless. Horses and Indians were starving and exhausted and could travel no further. They had been on the trail for 38 days since leaving Little High Rock Canyon on the 19th of January and had traveled a approximately 200 miles, in the snow and cold.

The Indian family of twelve made up of only 3 grown men, in their prime of life, the other nine were grand parents and women and children, the children ranging in ages from ten months to twelve years. For the most part the family walked the entire distance, from Little High Rock Canyon to Rabbit Creek, in the dead of winter, in moccasins made of leather and rags, in the snow and wet, for a distance of 200 miles.

Two hundred miles in 38 days equates to about 4 or 5 miles per day. Progressing at this slow rate tells us that they were camping for a few days and then scouting ahead for camp sites and to avoid other human activity whether they be cattlemen, sheepmen or miners. In addition packing up the family family belongings and moving a short distance each day would have been an impossible task. When moving they were moving about ten to fifteen miles on any given day.

The Indians were retracing their route and in the same manner as they had traveled the spring and summer before.

Their only hope now was to rest up, horses and Indians, and allow the horses to gain some strength on green grass that would be starting to grow this time of the year.

By the time they had reached Rabbit Creek their blankets and cloths had become rags, some or maybe all were the same blankets they had when they left Gollaher Mountain nearly ten months ago.

In traveling east, the family had taken the easiest and most logical route in the direction of their home range, there was no backing tracking, they had been there before. The only variance in this manner of travel would be to avoid other human activity.

The Daggetts had been on the trail from January 19 through February 26, crossing the most desolate part of Nevada, in the middle of the winter, in subfreezing temperatures. During the period the Indian family was on the trail, temperatures could have dropped below zero and most likely ranged in the low teens at night, especially during the first couple weeks of their journey. They had no shelter except for blankets and possibly a canvas tarp, and scant amount of feed for their horses. The family subsisted, almost entirely on dried beef with the possibility of an occasional rabbit or possibly fresh beef if they had encountered any cattle in their travel.

If one wants to experience what the Daggetts experienced that winter in 1911, go out in your yard in the winter with snow on the ground, at about zero to fifteen degrees, clear off the snow as best you can, throw down some saddle blankets, grab a large piece of dried beef for nourishment (no seasoning), wrap yourself up in some old blankets, settle in for the night and see how it works out.

If the Daggetts did not know before they knew after killing the four sheepmen there was no way the white man was going to allow them to survive and who knows what they had in mind at this point. Had they had the chance how far would they travel eastward and to where? There were four dead behind them and certain capture and death in front of them.

Whatever those plans were, they never came to be, eighteen armed men descended upon them, in their meager camp, near Rabbit Creek, north of Golconda, Nevada on February 26, 1911.

Twelve photographs were mounted for display by Mrs. J. R. Starkey. The display was donated to the National Guard Armory of Winnemucca by Mrs. Starkey August 19th, 1938 and remained there for many years.

Those photos will be seen in following pages with my comments, on some, in bold letters.

EAST ARM of the BLACK ROCK

Jan. 20, 2008

Looking east across the east arm of the Black Rock Desert at Jackson Mountain, just north of where the Daggett family crossed, on or about the 23rd of January 1911. The Indian family crossed here in the dead of winter. When stopping to rest their only shelter being blankets and possibly a tarp. The three youngest children Cleveland, Hattie and the baby, were just seven years, four years and ten months, respectfully. They had been on the trail 38 days when the posse finally ran them down at Rabbit Creek, northeast of Golconda, Nevada, February 26, 1911.

BLACK ROCK DESERT

March 23, 2014

Looking west across the east arm of the Black Rock Desert near where the Daggett
family and part of the posse crossed from west to east during the winter of 1911.

To the left of the white soils on the hills in the background is a low pass over which they
probably passed or the the next pass to the south. In between this pass and the
mountain in the far back ground lies the west arm of the Black Rock Desert.

From the point from which this picture was taken to the foot of the hills on the far side is
fifteen miles. The Indian family crossed here in late January of 1911.

(The annual Burning Man Celebration takes place on the Black Rock Playa about thirty
five miles southwest of where the Indians and part of the Donnelley posse crossed.)

WINTER CAMP WELL

March 23, 2014

C. C. C. project from the 1930s

When the Daggett family arrived at the west side of the the Jackson Mountains on the east side of the east arm of the Black Rock Desert, in late January on 1911, they would have crossed at approximately this location.

Four members of the posse, Sgt. Newgard, Frank Perry, Jack Ferguson and Jim Tahem crossed on the tracks of the Indians, February 19, 1911 and they too would have arrived at this approximate location. Perry in his writings, in 1949, stated that they had found a tent, when they arrived here on the east side of the desert.

The hills in the background, at a distance of plus 15 miles, is the lower end of the Black Rock Range and at the top center of the picture would be the location of the pass where the Indians and posse crossed from the west arm of the Black Rock Desert which would be about four miles north of Double Hot Springs.

SOMBRERO PEAK
May 2014

This photo was taken from Sand Pass, near Highway 95 north of Winnemucca, Nevada, looking west. The Daggett family and Donnelley's posse passed to the left which would be south of Sombrero Peak in February 1911. This is another example of how little the country has changed since 1911.

Mountain left center is Blue Mountain.

HOT SPRINGS RANGE & OSGOOD MOUNTAINS

May 20, 2014

Photo taken looking east across the south end of Paradise Valley at the Hot Springs Range. Stewart Pass is about in the center of photo.

The mountains far right, tops showing with the snow, are the Osgood Mountains.

The Indians traveled along the foot of the Hot Spring Range on the far side of the valley then east over the pass and across Eden Valley. At that point they are at the Osgood Mountains. From there they traveled over a low pass into the Rabbit Creek drainage.

The posse followed along the Indian's trail on the the 25th of Feb.

MINE TAILINGS POND

June 2008

Tailings in this pond are from the Getchell Mine. The pond is located about two miles northeast of the mine.

The small white building, center, is situated about on top of where the Daggett's camp was on February 26, 1911.

This tailings pond covers the entire area where the Donnelley posse encountered and killed the Indians.

#16

These are the filthy vermin cloths of captured Indians washed and hung out to dry. All clothing of captured Indians were practically rags and made from the cloths of the four murdered stockmen.

By Mrs. J. R. Starkey

Humboldt County Museum Photo

LAST CAMP of the DAGGETTS
February 28, 1911

Located in a small tributary to Rabbit Creek

When the Indian family descended from a low pass, separating Eden Valley from Clover Valley, on the 25th of Feb. 1911 it appeared they attempted to set up a little more elaborate camp than they normally did. They had no other alternative, they and their horses were exhausted, they could go no further. Their hope would be to give all a much needed rest, allow the horses to regain some strength and to some how replenish there own meager food supply. Time permitting they all could get a rest. The green grass was starting to grow so hopefully horses could begin to gain some strength. The far larger problem was how were they going to feed themselves. This dilemma was short lived. At noon on the following day twenty armed men descended upon their camp and by 3 P.M. all but four children of the Daggett family were dead.

218

CHAPTER VI

ON THE TRAIL OF THE DAGGETTS

On February 16th, the morning after the inquest at Denio's, February 16th, Dick Cook and part of the posse returned to Eagleville with the four bodies.

How did Cook travel over the high pass, between Eagleville and Denio Camp in the winter, with a four horse team and sleigh? It would have been extremely difficult if not impossible. Answer, he didn't he traveled by way of Lost Creek and Duck Lake.

Writings of Mort West - Mark Shopper

The remaining men (23 identified) departed Denios to take up the trail of the Daggetts. They included:

1--Capt. Donnelley, J. P. - age 51 - Carson City Nev. - Supt. of Nev. State Police
2--Newgard P. M. - age 32 - Carson City Nev. - Sergeant Nev. State Police
3--Stone, Charles H. - age 35 - Carson City Nev. - Sergeant, Nev. State Police
4--Buck, Frank - age ? - Private, State police
5--Smith, A. E. - age 45 - Alturas, Calif., - Sheriff of Modoc County, Calif.
6--Ferrell, Charles P. - age ? - Reno, Nev. - Sheriff Washoe County, Nev.
7--Cambron, Ben F. - age 40 - Constantia, Calif. - Stockman
8--Ferguson, Jack age - 34 - Eagleville, Cal. - Stockman
9--Perry, Frank - age - 22 - Eagleville, Calif. - Teamster
10--Parsons, Wm. M. - age - 27 - Eagleville, Calif. - Buckaroo
11--Fruit, Warren - age - 21 - Eagleville, Calif. - Buckaroo
12-- Van Norman, Otto - age - 28 - Grass Valley, Nev. - Farming
13--Reeder, Joseph - age - 33 - Gerlach, Nev. - Miner
14--Hughes, Henry - age - 33 - Eagleville, Calif. - Rancher
15--Holmes, George - age - 46 - Eagleville, Calif. - Carpenter
16--West, Mort - age - 24 - Eagleville, Calif. - Buckaroo
17--Hogle, Edward - age - 31 - Eagleville, Calif. - Buckaroo
18--Charles Demick - Manger of the Quinn River Division for Miller & Lux Ranches
       (turned back at the Quinn River Crossing Ranch)
19--Fred Murphy
20--Sid Street
21--Gilbert Jackson
22-- Jim Batty.
23-- Fred C. Hill
(Murphy, Street, Jackson, Batty and apparently Hill, turned back at Soldier Meadows). Jim Tahem, buckaroo for Miller & Lux who joined the posse at Soldier Meadows turned back at the Lay Ranch on Jackson Creek.

They were poorly organized poorly led, a posse of "disorganized vigilantes" and from all accounts, they were following the lead of Sheriff Smith and Ben Cambron.

The mind set of Ben Cambron was revenge for the killing of his brother, with little thought of bringing the perpetrators to justice through the legal system. He probably should not have been on the posse and Smith was out of his jurisdiction.

The goal of those that went down into Little High Rock Canyon was three fold: one, recover the bodies and return them to Eagleville, two, determine who the killers were and three, go after those responsible.

After investigating the scene it was determined the four sheepmen had been murdered and that the guilty party were Indians.

The generation that came before many of these on the posse, or at least the generation before that, grew up killing Indians. Those members on the posse from Surprise Valley, California, had listened to the stories told by the old timers about killing Indians back in the 1860's, so it was easy to transition back to those days and now they had an opportunity to act on their childhood fantasies of killing Indians. Killing Indians like that earlier generation. They are truly going to be Indian fighters now and they are on the trail feeding off each other. The horrible murders of the sheepmen, they knew, and the act of bringing the shot up bodies out of Little High Rock made it all that much easier to fall into that mind set.

The killers were determined to be Indians so it made their mission that much more justifiable and easier to convince others that justice meant the Indians needed killing. After hearing of this brutal killing of the sheepmen at Little High Rock residents of Surprise Valley saw justification for whatever atrocities may be committed at the end of the hunt. The murderers had to answer for what they had done.

Consequently this egotistical vigilante group set out on the trail of the Daggett family with questionable law enforcement leadership and with the mind set, we are going to get us an Indian.

Other than Capt. Donnelley's report, of which the details were never found, the only members of the posse who ever wrote about the pursuit of the Daggetts were Frank Perry and Mort West.

Mort West wrote his version in 1934 some 23 years afterwards and Frank Perry wrote his version 1949, 38 years later. There were errors and misinformation in their writings and it is easy to criticize them for that but without their written accounts we would know far less about this unfortunate incident.

The posse followed the Daggett's trail down Little High Rock Canyon then exiting Little High Rock Canyon and crossing near High Rock Lake. At this point they would have picked up the old Applegate Trail at the head of Fly Canyon and followed it to Mud Meadows. At Mud Meadows the posse turned north to the Soldiers Meadow Ranch where they laid over a day, February 17th, to shoe horses and prepare for the task ahead. The Soldier Meadows Ranch was owned by the (Pacific Live Stock Company) more commonly known as "Miller & Lux".

The posse must not have been very well prepared to pursue the Indians if after only one day on the trail they had to spend another whole day at Soldier Meadows in preparation for the days ahead.

An Indian by the name of Jim Tahem who worked for Charles Demick (Miller and Lux), joined the posse at Soldier Meadows. He was probably selected by Demick to join the posse because he was familiar with that part of the country between Surprise Valley and the Jackson Mountains.

On the 18th the Posse returned to the trail of the Daggetts at Mud Meadows and continued along the Applegate Trail as it paralleled the west fork of the Black Rock Desert to within about four miles of Double Hot Springs then broke to the east over the south end of the Black Rock Range to the west fork of the Black Rock Desert. At this point they left the trail and headed north about 15 miles to the Piaute Meadows Ranch to stay for the night. The Piaute Meadows Ranch also belonged to the Miller & Lux cattle empire. In fact, Soldier Meadows, Piaute Meadows and the Quinn River Ranches all belonged to the Miller & Lux Cattle empire of Henry Miller and Charles Lux.

On the 19th Capt. Donnelley took all but Frank Perry, Jim Tahem, Sergeant Newgard and Jack Ferguson and continued on northeast to Quinn River Ranch (Quinn River Crossing) where the main crossing and only bridge across Quinn River was located. Capt. Donnelley traveled to Quinn River Crossing for a couple of reasons; one there was telegraph capability at Amos Nevada from which they could alert the Humboldt

County Sheriff, Selah Graham Lamb. One of the posse members was dispatched to Amos to send that message to Lamb. (Amos was little less than 20 miles from Quinn River Crossing), secondly going north offered a much better crossing of Quinn River and thirdly they were not sure which direction the Indians had gone when reaching the Jackson Mountains.

These four, Perry, Taham, Newgard and Ferguson returned fifteen miles to the south where they turned east across the desert on the trail of the Indians.

Frank Perry's account written in 1949

According to Frank Perry they crossed Quinn River with some difficulty. They had to break the ice and swim their horses to cross the river. They continued east to the east side of the Black Rock Desert and west side of the Jackson Mountains where they found a tent with hay in it and shelter for the night.

The tent was located on the road leading from Sulphur, Nevada to the Lay brother's ranch on Jackson Creek and probably used by the local ranchers either the Lay Brothers, Miller & Lux buckaroos or the Bidart sheep outfit, as a line camp.

In later years the Civil Conservation Corp (C.C.C.) drilled a well at or near this location. A cabin was built on this site by the rancher Bill De Long and used as a line camp or winter camp from which it got its current name, "Winter Camp". In the days before horse trailers it was necessary for someone to stay here part time to move cattle onto the mountain in the spring, off in the fall and watch over them on the winter range.

On the 20th Perry and company departed their line camp tent and headed north ending up at the Lay Ranch on Jackson Creek a distance of about fifteen miles.

Perry's account of having to break ice and swim their horses to cross Quinn River seemed a little far fetched however on the 21st of January 2008 I visited Quinn River at the approximate location of their crossing in 1911 and found that one could almost step across the stream however there were large chunks of ice, three inches thick, laying up on the river bank, 6 feet above the bottom of the river thus the water could have been high enough to swim a horse in December or January of 2008. So much for my skepticism.

Perry also indicated the trail of the Daggetts across the east arm of the Black Rock was fairly easy to follow. The Indians had crossed on the snow and the horses hooves had

222

packed the snow which resulted in the snow in the track being packed and did not melt as fast as the snow surrounding each track therefore leaving a quite visible trail. This is a common occurrence in February, the snow starts to melt this time of year and melts the soft snow first.

When Capt. Donnelley reached the Quinn River Crossing he immediately sent word to Sheriff Lamb, via Amos advising him of the direction the Daggetts were taking when he last saw the Indian trail at the west edge of the Black Rock Range. The Indian trail pointed west and a little south toward the Jackson Mountains and would probably pass into the area of Rattlesnake Canyon about fifteen miles south of Jackson Creek. Donnelley would have advised the Sheriff that Sergeant Newgard, along with three others, had gone back south from Piaute Meadows to pick up the Indian trail and follow it west across the desert. Tahem who knew the country would have been the one who pointed out that the trail was headed toward Rattlesnake Canyon. The other three in this party had never been in this part of the country before and would have no idea where the passes were across the desert on the Jackson Mountains.

In talking to Louis Bidart of Winnemucca, Nevada on April 3, 2014, he told me that his dad was running sheep at the south end of the Jackson Range and had seen the Indians pass through but at the time he was not aware that they had killed anyone so he did not pay them much attention. This is more confirmation that neither the ranchers nor anyone else in the area, had been made aware of the killings at Little High Rock prior to the Indians passing through that part of the country. In fact no one knew it before February 10th and by that time the Indians were probably well past the Jackson Mountains in the vicinity of the Sand Dunes.

Lamb along with his brother, Keis, and Skinny Pascal, Piaute Indian tracker, took the train from Winnemucca to Sulphur, Nevada. There they unloaded their horses and headed north on the west side of the Jackson Mountains toward Lay's Jackson Creek Ranch to intercept the tribe or their trail. However no interception, the Indians had proceeded west into the area of Rattlesnake Canyon and Sheriff Lamb had apparently missed their tracks. It appears they caught up with Perry and company at Jackson Creek. Capt. Donnelley and the rest of the posse had traveled about eighteen miles south from Quinn River Crossing to Jackson Creek as they all rendezvoused there.

This was on the 20th of February. Sheriff Lamb, Keis and Pascal would have traveled almost thirty five miles in-route from Sulphur to Jackson Creek.

There is some speculation that the four members of the posse, Perry, Tahem, Ferguson and Newgard, that followed the Indian trail across the east arm of the Black Rock Desert did not really want to catch up with the Indians in the canyons on the south end of the Jacksons and thought it wiser to head north up to the Lay Ranch at Jackson Creek where they would join the main contingent of the posse. The shot up bodies of the sheepmen they helped carry out of Little High Rock five days earlier were well etched in their minds. Bravery takes on a whole different priority when there are only four men, versus eighteen, that are about to contact the Indians.

The thoughts of my brother Pat Sweeney when we visited that point on the trail, March 23, 2014.

However they also were without vitals or shelter so they had to get somewhere fairly soon to get something to eat.

It is not clear where the posse now including Lamb, Keis plus the Piaute Indian tracker, Pascal, all got together but they did on the 21st of February somewhere in the vicinity the Lay Bros. ranch on Jackson Creek. The posse now in tact headed over the north end of the Jackson Mountains via a pass at the head of Jackson Creek.

Tahem did not follow the posse over the pass. He dropped out and proceeded to Quinn River Crossing. Charles Demick, foreman of the Quinn River Division of the Miller & Lux empire never accompanied the posse beyond Quinn River Crossing.

Now with everybody all in one bunch and accounted for they proceeded on to another of the Lay brothers ranches on the east side of the Jackson Mountains located on Willow Creek where they stayed the night. They had traveled about forty five miles.

On the 22nd the posse again split up.

Newgard, Perry, Ferguson and Tahem, the four members of the posse that followed the Indian trail across the desert to the west side of the Jacksons, provided the information regarding the place where the Indians entered the Jacksons on the west side. This gave the posse a good reference point from which to search on the east side.

Two days after Newgard and his group had quit the trail in the area of Rattlesnake Canyon, on the west side of the Jackson range, the posse scattered out from Lay's

Willow Creek ranch and headed south and southeast into an area of sand dunes in search of the Indian trail to find where it exited on the east side of the mountain.

Even though the posse had this reference point, they had a difficult time finding the trail due largely to a lack of leadership and confusion. When they broke up into smaller groups they also had difficulty staying in touch (keeping track of each group). Evidently part of the posse picked up the Indian trail and some missed it. Perry being one of those who found the trail but in the confusion wound up staying out all night while all the others guided by Sheriff Lamb continued on to Winnemucca, Nevada.

The lack of organization resulted in the posse not getting back together until that night,February 22nd, except for Frank Perry who remained in the sand dunes until morning. Perry had traveled east through the sand dunes, on the Indian trail until it got dark. He found an old well with a pile of lumber and a "goods box" that he emptied of sand, turned it against the wind and settled in for the night. He stated he didn't want to build a fire that night in the event it might attract Indians if they were in the area.

Frank Perry 1949

Perry had probably found an old stage stop on the stage road connecting Silver City, Idaho with Winnemucca, Nevada which ran west of Winnemucca Mountain.

Meanwhile Sheriff Lamb had escorted the rest into Winnemucca, about a thirty five or forty mile ride from Willow Creek. This was on the 22nd of February.

Perry caught up with the rest of the posse at Tollhouse the next day, February 23rd. Tollhouse or what used to be Tollhouse, is located eleven miles north of Winnemucca, Nevada.

According to Mort West the posse had traveled south that morning from Lay's Willow Creek Ranch scouting the snow line but no one found the trail, however in the afternoon he and Frank Perry found the Indian trail.

In Perry's writings he listed Captain Donnelley, Ben Cambron, Sheriff Smith, Jack Ferguson and himself as finding the Indian trail, no mention of Mort West.

Some of the old timers that are familiar with this story and the Lay ranches, claimed some of the ranch people saw the Indians and hid from them because they were bad Indians. This is not likely to be true as no one there knew of the killing at Gollaher Mt. or at Little High Rock at the time the Indians passed by Jackson Mountain. If they had seen the Indian family they could not have looked too scary. There were twelve in all, made up of a grandfather at age 65, three adult males and the rest women and children. There are several references to the Daggetts having been at one of the Lay Ranches the spring before trying to trade for harness. As stated before this has a high probability of being true. They had abandoned a wagon at Gollaher Mountain last April and there is no indication or reference to harness being left behind. It would have been foolish to leave harness behind when it could have been so easily taken along, they had 15 or 20 head of horses. Harness could be used to tie their belongings to or used as a kind of pack saddle or used to trade for something they needed more as they apparently did or tried to do, at one of the Lay ranches. The reports that they tried to trade harness at one of the Lay ranches is additional evidence that the Daggetts traveled this way on there way west the spring or summer before.

The harness trade was probably mentioned to the posse at one of the Lay Ranches. It wasn't something you would expect from some one traveling across country on horse back and not likely given much credence by the posse. The fact that it was likely and that the Indians had their harness with them made it quite factual. It would also be odd that any one traveling across country on horse back would also be traveling with a set of harness without a wagon attached.

Washoe County Sheriff Ferrel and Private Buck of the Nevada State Police left the posse at the edge of the sand dunes and traveled south to Sulfur, Nevada. they caught the train to Winnemucca, Nevada and then on to Elko, Nevada to form another posse to intercept the Indians if they headed east through Squaw Valley, located in eastern Elko County. They also intended to alert the Duck Valley Indian Police at the Duck Valley Indian Reservation in that they might show up there. The reservation is located on the Idaho/Nevada line north of Mountain City, Nevada.

The Silver State and the Humboldt Star newspapers of Winnemucca reported that Washoe County Sheriff Ferrell and Private Buck of the State Police arrived from Jungo, Nevada on the train this afternoon (Feb. 23rd) and proceeded on to Elko, Nev.

If this is true then evidently after the posse picked up the Indian's trail where the Indians exited the Jackson Mts. they followed it to where it passed the south end of the Silver State Range (Slumbering Hills). At this point, Sheriff Lamb, Ferrill and Capt. Donnelley

226

had determined that the indians were headed for the Owyhee country so Sheriff Ferrill and Private Buck were dispatched to catch the train at Jungo, Nevada and proceed to Elko to organize another posse to intercept the Indians if they got that far.

It was also on this day, February 23rd that it was revealed, from Sheriff Ferrel, to the newspapers that O. D. Van Norman had had that encounter with the Indians at Hog Ranch Canyon back in November. He identified the Daggetts accurately enough to know that he had seen them

2-23-11 Silver State & 2-24-11 Humboldt Star Newspapers - Winnemucca, Nev. and R.E.G. Feb. 24, 1911

On the 23rd the posse regrouped again at Tollhouse and headed east then northeast toward the Stewart Ranch at the southeast corner of Paradise Valley, all the while being on the trail of Mike's outfit which was by now becoming quite fresh.

It appears Sheriff Lamb and his brother, Keis stayed in Winnemucca while the rest of the posse including Pascal, the Indian tracker, took the trail again via Tollhouse then returned that night to Golconda, Nevada. The Indians had crossed the southern end of Paradise Valley between Tollhouse and Paradise Hill then traveled north about 4 miles before turning east over the pass of the Hot Springs Range leading into Eden Valley. Evidently some of the group had a little too much to drink in Winnemucca on the evening of the 22nd as very little was accomplished by the posse on the 23rd.

February 24th found the posse headed north out of Golconda toward the Stewart Ranch, a distance of about 23 miles.

The movements, who was involved, where and when from February 23rd through the 25th become a little muddy or maybe confusing and a lot muddy.

Reports by Perry and others are also somewhat confusing and conflicting. Apparently the posse spent most of the 24th between Golconda and a pass on the Hot Springs Range, located about 3 miles northeast of the Stewart Ranch. They found where the Daggetts had crossed over this pass and, in fact, had lost a horse on the approach to the pass. The horse had most likely died of starvation and fatigue thus leaving the Daggetts with only seven horses.

From here the trail led east across Eden Valley to a shallow draw and up to the summit on the Osgood Mountains, overlooking another draw or small canyon that leads east into Rabbit Creek. This drainage does not join with Rabbit Creek until it nearly reaches

Kelly Creek, some 7 or 8 miles to the southeast and at this point Rabbit Creek is well into Clover Valley.

The posse had evidently followed the Indian trail up Lying Canyon to the summit or nearly to the summit overlooking Eden Valley, during the 25th of February.

The constable from the community of Paradise Valley, Nevada, Charles Byrnes, had received a poster from the State Police to watch for certain men and certain horses. He learned from a phone message that the same horses had been seen in Lying Canyon so on Saturday morning he left Paradise to investigate.

Testimony of Charles Byrnes - March 3, 1911

Byrnes and four men that were with him, including Mearl W. Prussia, had already reached Lying Canyon ahead of the posse and had inspected a camp site of the Daggetts in the canyon. Byrnes found hot cinders where the Indians had built a campfire the day before or had possibly vacated the camp that morning. It is here where the Paradise men met the Surprise Valley posse for the 1st time.

Supposedly a prospector in the area had spotted the Daggetts and notified Lamb who in turn notified Capt. Donnelley at Golconda.

Recollection of Frank Perry 38 years after the incident

This could be true or whoever left the message for Byrnes also contacted the Sheriff and the Sheriff left the message for Byrnes.

It is not clear who of Donnelley's posse were present when they met Byrnes and his crew. It may not have included Mort West and some of the others. Part of the posse had left Golconda in the early morning hours of the 25th without notifying the others.

Frank Perry and Mort West recollections

Something strange was going on. Of those who left early appeared to include Sergeants Charles Stone and P. M. Newgard of the State Police, Frank Perry and Jack Ferguson.

After the two groups, Donnelley's and Byrnes's, had gotten together they planned for the next day, February 26th. By the afternoon of the 25th they all scattered back to Paradise Valley, Willow Point and the Stewart Ranch. It is not clear if the group left behind at Golconda had caught up with the main posse in Lying Canyon or if they joined up at the Stewart Ranch.

More confusion, but on the 26th most of the gang had finally gotten together at the approach to the summit leading to Rabbit Creek and headed over.

About one half mile over the pass and around the south side of the second butte they stopped to look down onto the forks of two draws making up the main draw leading to Rabbit Creek.

At about 400 yards from where the posse stopped to scan the area below, they spotted smoke from a camp fire and horses grazing near by. On the 26th of February of 1911, the posse had finally overtaken the Daggett family and had located their camp.

Inquest testimony at Golconda, Nevada, March 3 and 4, 1911

The "Vigilante Posse" had caught up with the Indian family about twenty miles northeast of Golconda, Nevada, in this dry stream bed, a tributary to Rabbit Creek which in turn is a tributary to Kelley Creek.

As time went on the camp sites of Mike's tribe had gotten closer and closer together. The Indians and their horses were hungry and exhausted as attested to many times. They were in open country, with little or no cover, and miles from any place to hide, however they could go no further.

By this time the State Police and the two sheriffs had lost their professionalism, if they ever had any, and taken on the mental state of the Surprise Valley bunch.

Donnelley and Deputy Byrnes had not yet arrived to where they look down at the camp site. They were trailing behind the others, Donnelley in a light wagon, (spring wagon) Byrnes on horse back. Donnelley had stayed at Willow Point and the main posse stayed the night at the Stewart Ranch, about two miles closer to the trail. This was one of two reasons Donnelley was not with the posse when they engaged the Indians, the other being that he couldn't travel as fast in a wagon as the others could on horse back. Mearl Prussia testified that he started out with Constable Byrnes and joined the posse at the Stewart Ranch on the 26th. Perry, in his writings years later stated he was riding with Byrnes and Donnelley but caught up with the posse by the time they spotted the Daggett camp. Does this mean he stayed at Willow Point too?

More confusion as to who stayed where and who left from where and when.

Testimony at the inquest for the eight members of the Daggett family killed at Rabbit Creek

To straighten it out, as best I can, I offer the following: On the night of February 25, 1911 Donnelley stayed at Willow Point and the main contingent of the posse stayed at the Stewart Ranch, two miles closer to the trail. The main contingent on the posse may not have arrived at the Stewart Ranch until the wee hours of the morning on the 26th. Capt. Donnelley was joined by Byrnes and Prussia at Willow Point on the morning of the 26th. They had traveled from Paradise that morning. For some reason three of the men that were with Byrnes on the 25th never returned with him on the 26th. Evidently after meeting this large group of Capt. Donnelley's posse, the day before, someone decided more men were not needed, they could tell by the tracks most of the band was made up of women and children.

Prussia, who had accompanied Byrnes the day before, evidently went with Byrnes, on the morning of the 26th, to Willow Point and then caught up with the main contingent under the command of Sergeant Newgard at the Stewart Ranch before the posse got under way that morning. Donnelley and Byrnes trailed behind, Donnelley in a wagon and Byrnes was on horse back, staying behind with Donnelley.

The only intelligent decision Captain Donnelley made during the whole fiasco was obtaining a wagon for the last day's pursuit of the Indians. It was obvious from the day before that the band was made up mostly of women and children and the posse would overtake them on the following day. They were going to need a wagon to transport women and children. Mort West in his writings 20 years later criticized Donnelley for trailing Indians in a wagon rather on horseback. West did not see the big picture. He made no connection to what was going on.

Sheriff Smith testified he started from the Willow Creek Ranch on the 26th. He probably meant Willow Point but I'm not even sure of that.

Mike's temporary camp was located 2 1/4 miles northeast of the current location of the Getchell Mine, which did not exist in 1911. A tailings pond, from the current mining operation now fills at least one mile of the canyon where the Indians were camped and killed.

On the trail of the Indians was for the most part gleaned from the story written by Frank Perry. Perry's account has enough inaccuracies that it makes much of his account

230

suspect. In recounting what others had told him and what he had no personal knowledge, he was way off.

There was much to do about the hardship the members of the posse endured while pursuing the Daggetts across the harsh wastelands of northern Nevada during the last part of February 1911 but little or no mention of the hardships the Indians had to endure. Stories told over the past one hundred years have exaggerated and embellished the real life drama as to how tough the posse members were and the extreme winter conditions they endured. The temperatures didn't likely fall below twelve or fifteen degrees.

Frank Perry and Mort West, in their writings spoke of there being no room in bunkhouses for every one to sleep, eluding to the fact that some slept in hay stacks. Sleeping in a haystack with a saddle blanket over you is much better than sleeping in an overcrowded bunkhouse on the cold floor. The Daggett family had neither they slept out in the open on frozen ground.

Each member of the posse had his own well fed horse, responsible only for themselves, and had shelter nearly every night. All were in the prime of their lives most were in their twenties and thirties, the exception being, Capt. Donnelley who was fifty one and three others were in their early forties.

Whereas the Indians had horses that were in poor condition, except for the four they had taken from the stockmen. They had no shelter from the cold and wind except for what they might find in a shallow draw and what they could get with the use of saddle blankets. Out of twelve persons only four were considered adult men, The others were women and children, the three youngest being seven, four, the youngest being less than a year old and a girl of about fifteen.

The posse was on the trail for a mere 10 days,from mid to late February, they had hot meals at least once each day, in most cases 2 hot meals.

The Daggetts had been on the trail for 37 days, across the most desolate part of Nevada in the middle of the winter, in subfreezing temperatures. It may have fallen below zero in January. The Indian family had no hot meals and no shelter. They subsisted almost entirely on dried beef.

The hardship stories made up by the posse members and others over the years are embarrassing when compared to the hardships the Daggett family endured

> > > > > Approximate rout of the Indians
- - - - - Approximate rout of the posse which includes different posse members taking different routs and some joining and leaving the main group.

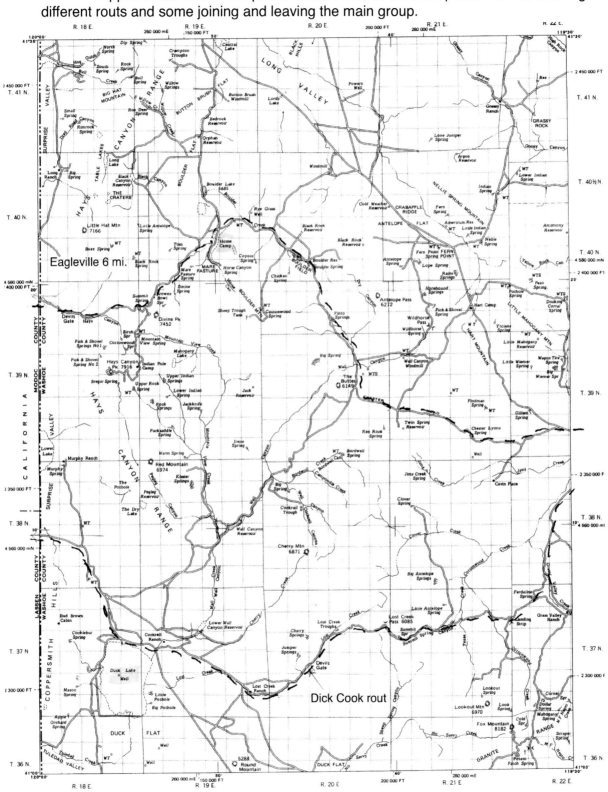

> > > > > Approximate rout of the Indians
- - - - - Approximate rout of the posse which includes different posse members taking different routs and some joining and leaving the main group.

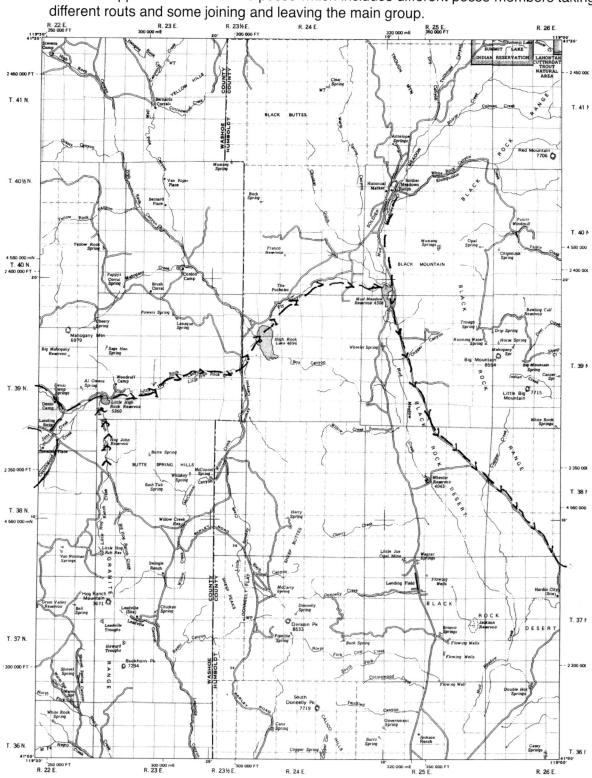

> > > > > Approximate rout of the Indians

▬ ▬ ▬ ▬ ▬ Approximate rout of the posse which includes different posse members taking different routs and some joining and leaving the main group.

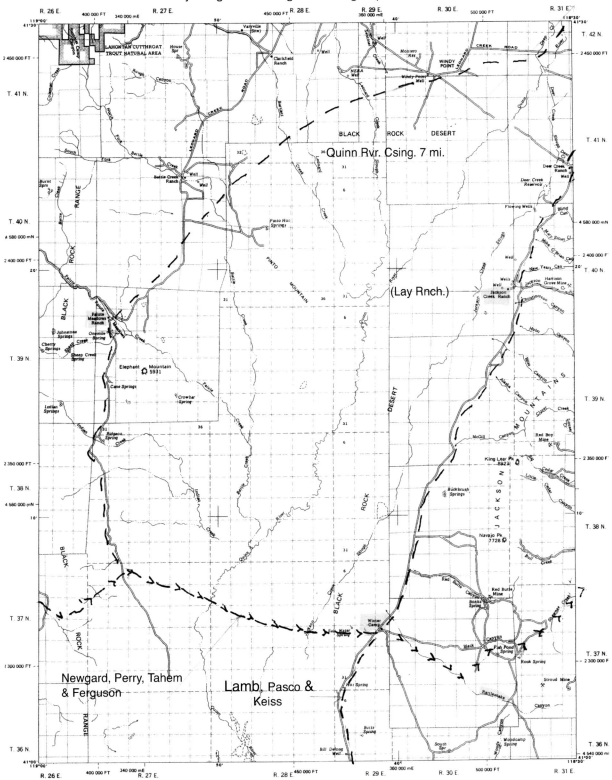

Quinn Rvr. Csing. 7 mi.

(Lay Rnch.)

Newgard, Perry, Tahem & Ferguson

Lamb, Pasco & Keiss

235

> > > > > Approximate rout of the Indians

▪ ▪ ▪ ▪ ▪ Approximate rout of the posse which includes different posse members taking different routs and some joining and leaving the main group.

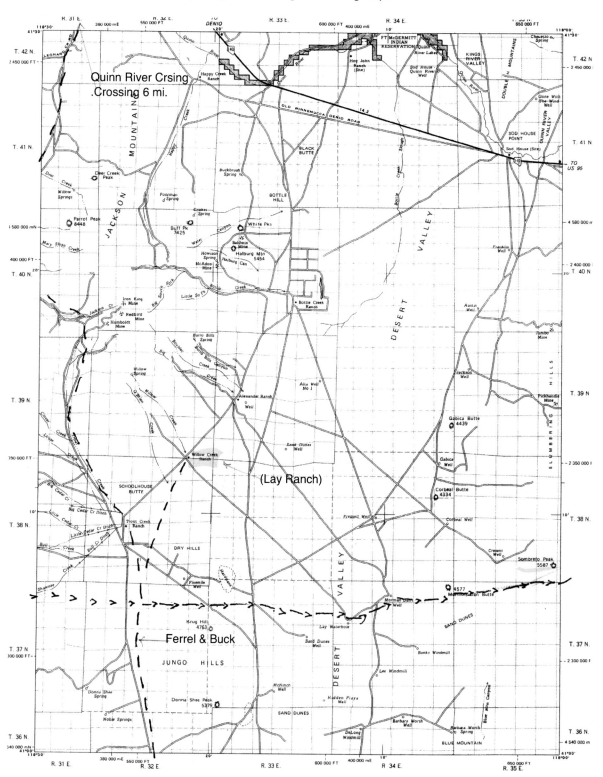

> > > > > Approximate rout of the Indians

- - - - - Approximate rout of the posse which includes different posse members taking different routs and some joining and leaving the main group.

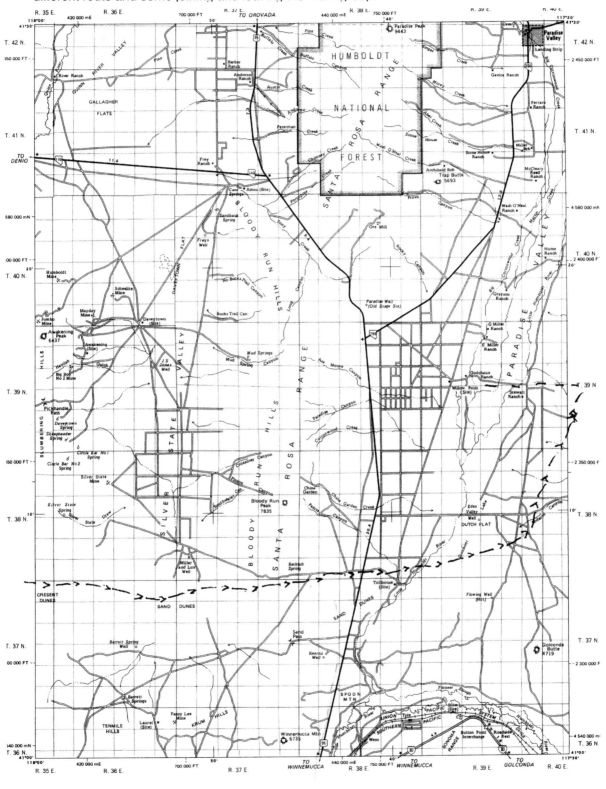

237

> > > > > Approximate rout of the Indians

▪ ▪ ▪ ▪ ▪ Approximate rout of the posse which includes different posse members taking different routs and some joining and leaving the main group.

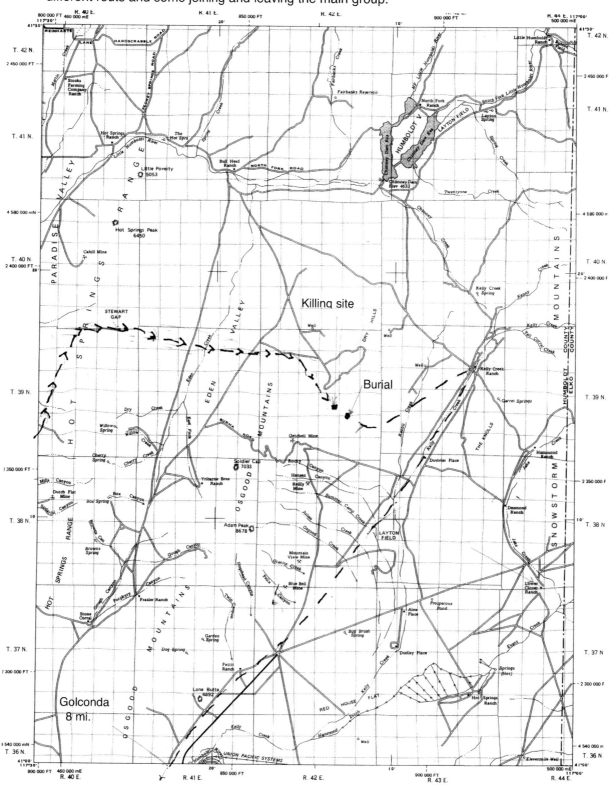

238

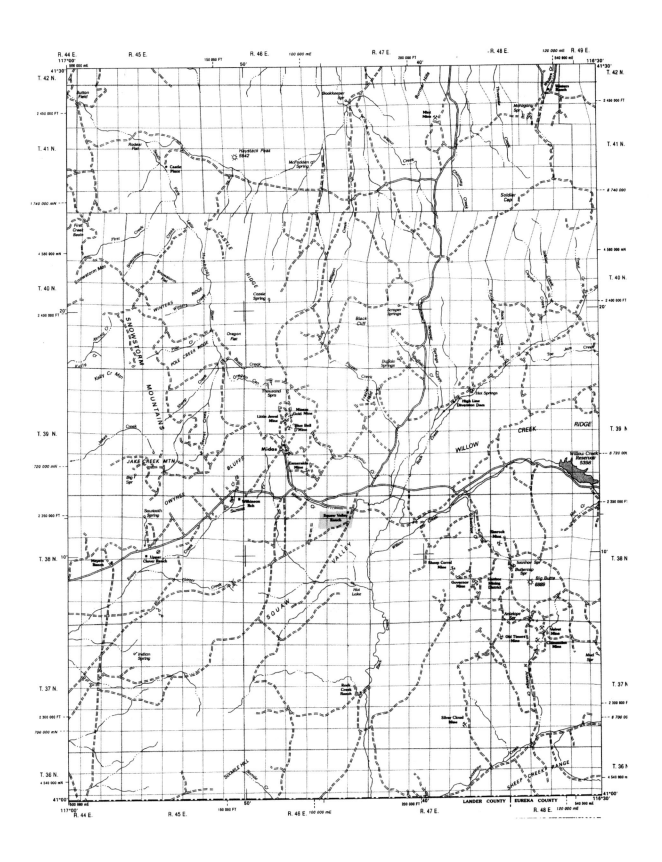

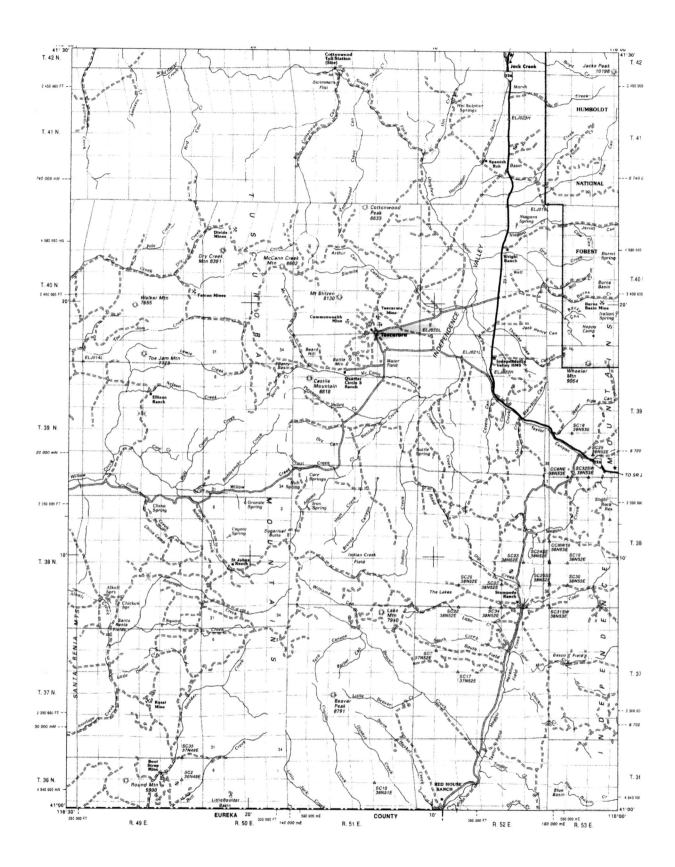

240

PART III

CHAPTER 1

KILLING OF THE DAGGETTS AT RABBIT CREEK - Feb. 26, 1911

On February 26, 1911 the posse departed Paradise Valley, some from the Stewart Ranch and some from Willow Point. Byrnes and Prussia left Paradise Valley and joined Donnelley and others at the Willow Point Ranch. Other members of the posse may have departed from Golconda. They all got together at the Stewart Ranch around seven in the morning and proceeded east following the Indian's trail over the pass leading into Eden Valley. They continued southeasterly across Eden Valley to a small canyon and then up over the pass into a drainage that leads to Rabbit Creek. The posse had picked up the Indians trail and followed it all the way to their camp in the Rabbit Creek drainage.

Although there were 20 members of the posse on the trail of the Indian family on February 26, 1911, two, Washoe County Sheriff Ferrill and Private Buck of the State Police had gone on to Elko to form a posse to intercept the Indians if they had gotten as far as Squaw Valley or the Owyhee Desert. This left eighteen posse members at the scene when they caught up to the Indians.

Captain Donnelley was not present when the posse emerged at the location of the Indian camp, he was trailing behind in the light wagon (spring wagon). The Capt. had delegated Sergeant Newgard to be in charge.

Although difficult to ascertain for sure, it appears the posse had gone around on the south side of the second butte as they descended into the drainage to Rabbit Creek. The posse gathered on the southeast side of that butte and looked down the draw and saw smoke from the Daggett's camp. Seven head of horses were also spotted grazing beyond the camp.

According to the testimony of the posse members at the inquests, held March 1, 3, & 4, 1911, the following chain of events took place on that day, February 26, 1911.

241

While the posse members gathered there on the side of the butte surveying what appeared to be the Indian's camp a young Indian girl, believed to be the daughter of Mike, saw the posse on the hillside about one quarter of a mile (400 or more yards) above their camp and sounded the alarm. Mike Daggett, with a rifle and two of his boys ran out from their makeshift camp to face the men who had been pursuing them for the past eleven days.

Someone in the posse shouted *"they are getting their guns"*. They all dismounted and formed a firing line at the orders of Sergeant Newgard. Newgard ordered Pascal to call to the Indians in the Indian language, telling them to surrender. Other members of the posse did the same in English. In answer there came a shot or shooting from the Indians. At that point firing began all along the line at the three members of the Daggett family that had come out from the camp and the fight was on.

The young squaw who had sounded the alarm also tried to retrieve some of their horses.

Evidently when Captain Donnelley arrived on the scene someone told him that a young squaw tried to retrieve the horses. Donnelley testified that *at his orders he had the Indian's horses gathered and two shot.* Three posse members began shooting horses and at least two and possibly three horses were killed. There is no explanation as to why he had some horses gathered and others shot. By now the whole situation is becoming unraveled and chaos is setting in.

One of the horses that was shot and killed matched the description of the horse branded with the LT on the left thigh. That brand belonged to Lawrence Thomas Sweeney of Fort Bidwell, California. It is somewhat of a mystery how the sheep men come to have this horse, probably purchased or traded for at some time. My grandfather lived on the upper end of Surprise Valley some 40 miles from Eagleville. He was acquainted with nearly everyone involved in this incident, including Ed Hogle. Lawrence Sweeney drove the stage, for a time, between Madeline, California through Eagleville to Adel, Oregon.

Two of the three Indians that came out from the camp fell at the first volley, one of those being Mike. Mike fell about 100 yards from their camp, the other, one of Mike's sons, fell about 20 yards from their camp and the 3rd ran back to the camp.

At the inquest for the Indians, held March 3 &4, 1911, except for Newgard, all of the members of the posse who testified and were there when the first shot was fired, stated that the first shot came from the Indians but no one identified which of the three Indians that came out of their camp to face the posse fired that first shot. Modoc County Sheriff Smith stated he did not know who fired the first shot. Then later during his testimony he said the first shot came from the Indians. Smith also stated that they were about 450 yards from the Indians when the posse started their advance. At this time the Indian trailer, Pasco, was asked to ask the Indians to submit. Smith also stated *"he shouted for the Indians to throw up their hands but the Indians wouldn't"*.

Newgard, who according to Donnelley was in charge, also stated *"he did not know who fired the first shot"*.

Also, each member testified that Skinny Pasco and other members of the posse *"hollered to the Indians to submit but were answered with shots from the Indians"*. Following the killing of Mike and one of his sons, other members of the family began shooting from their camp, including areas of concealment near the camp. According to testimony the fight with the Indians raged on for three hours.

Although difficult to determine exactly what was going on after Mike and the one son was killed, it appears that the two remaining sons of Mike, were the family members who were firing at the posse from the camp. One of those sons could have been only a teenager.

The act of holding the posse at bay for some time allowed the women and children to attempt an escape down the wash.

Warren Fruit specifically testified that *"they battled the Indians for two hours at the upper camp and then for another hour down where the women and children were killed"*.

Reeder said *"after the two Indians dropped the other Indians sneaked down the canyon we stayed there and held our positions for awhile"*.

The Indians that tried to escape down the canyon were overtaken by the posse members about one mile down from their makeshift camp.

Seven of the eighteen members of the posse remained at the makeshift camp of the Indians where Mike and one of his sons were killed while eleven proceeded down the wash in pursuit of the women and children.

Each member of the posse (15) that testified, testified that *"the Indians were ordered to surrender numerous times but they refused and continued to attempt escape"*.

Merl Prussia and Pascal were not called on to testify at the inquest for Hogle.

According to testimony, while under fire the posse pursued the Indians until they were cornered. *"The Daggett family fought with rifles, pistols, bows & arrows and a spear. The "squaws" were fighting with pistols, bow and arrows, a spear and beating on a drum"*.

"Near the end of the fight 3 bucks lay dead in the wash, the two older squaws were shooting arrows and pistols the young squaw was running up at the different posse members and jabbing at them with a spear". According to testimony, *"the posse continued to push forward in pursuit of the Indians when posse member Ed Hogle, who had moved out ahead of the others, was mortally wounded by one of the Indian bucks"*.

There were only eleven posse members at the scene where Hogle and the women and children were killed.

"As Hogle fell backwards the buck who shot him broke from cover and started running down the wash whereupon they all (posse members) opened fire on him". He fell by the body of one of the other bucks." *"The two older squaws and the two children were also inadvertently killed at this time while shooting at the bucks"*.

Some testified they may have been killed while shooting in the brush at the bucks. Others said they were mixed up so that it was hard to tell the bucks from the squaws. The battle was now over. According to posse members, Ed Hogle had been shot by one of he Indians with Harry Cambron's pistol. That pistol had been taken from the killing scene at Little High Rock Canyon.

Eight Indians including women and children had been killed by the posse. Two lay dead near the Daggett's camp the remaining six lay in the wash about one mile down, where the battle ended.

At that place two Indians lay dead, twelve or fifteen yards down the wash from there two boys ten to twelve years old lay dead and ten or twelve yards beyond the two boys lay the bodies of the two women. The young girl with the spear had ran to her mother or sister and was holding her and wailing. Apparently Baby Mosho was still in the cradle board and the four year old girl was standing among the carnage. The boy, six or seven years, old tried to run away but was caught by Ferguson.

A 40-82 Winchester rifle and cartridge belt was found next to Mike and, according to Joe Reeder, a long pistol was found near the buck that had fallen a short distance from where Mike lay mortally wounded. A 38-55 Winchester rifle was found at the Indian camp and a shotgun was found down the wash not far from where the six Indians were killed. Two members of the posse said Cambron's pistol was found at the camp others said it was found in the wash near the buck that killed Hogle. Two posse members, Reeder and Hughes, testified that there was a box magazine Winchester, a 30 US Winchester and another pistol found but were not identified as to what location they were found nor were they in evidence at the inquest held March 1st, 3rd or 4th nor were they in the photo labeled "Indian weapons".

When asked by the jury, "did the Indians resist arrest"? Each posse member responded, *"they did"*. When asked "did the Indians try to escape"? Each posse member answered *"they did".*

Chapter V Inquest Ed Hogle - March 1, 1911.

In thoroughly analyzing the testimony of the posse, the newspaper accounts and what little was written about the incident by two members of the posse, twenty and thirty years later, respectfully, the conclusion of the inquest jury, as outlined above, made no logical sense.

The only members of the posse who wrote about the incident were Mort West and Frank Perry.

Captain Donnelley submitted a brief report.

The actions of Mike in running from the camp with a rifle to face the posse was the action any normal person would take to protect his family. This action, he hoped, would allow his family to escape down the canyon. However out there alone and firing at the posse, fifteen men with rifles bunched together, was suicidal at 200 to 400 yards distance as some of them testified. It would have been hard for Mike to have missed everyone and their fifteen horses at that distance. Mike could not have fired more than one or two shots if he fired any shots before he was cut down by twelve or fourteen rifles. In fact there is no evidence that he killed any one during that thirty year period of time between July of 1880 and February 26, 1911 when he was killed at Rabbit Creek. The same two boys that killed Dopp, are most likely to have been the two that killed the sheep men at Little High Rock, January. 19, 1911.

Testimony of the posse members was that "a shot was fired" (from the Indian's side) but no one specifically saw one of the three Indians, that ran from the camp, fire a shot. When that shot was fired all hell broke loose and firing began all along the line.

Mike and one of his boys went down immediately. The other son ran back to camp to usher the family down the canyon, hopefully to some kind of safety.

Sgt. Newgard supposedly ordered Skinny Pascal to go down and ask the Indians to surrender and other members of the posse also shouted the same order in English. Pascal never got closer than a couple hundred yards of the Daggetts. Frank Perry, in his writings thirty years later, said they were about 450 yards from the Indians in a windy snow squall and it was impossible to communicate at any distance.

As Perry wrote years later, *"communications were impossible in those conditions"*. Winnemucca weather records showed that snow had fallen on that day, February 26. All of Perry's account of trailing and killing the Daggetts, written in 1949, cannot be taken as true fact as there are many parts of his story that are not true. However in studying the context in which he writes, other facts that are known and a review of inquest testimony, I believe this part of the story to be true. Other members of the posse testified they were about two to four hundred yards from the Indians when shooting began. None of those who testified placed the distance between the posse and Indians closer than 200 yards.

Common sense tells you that you do not ride or walk up within 200 yards of an enemy's rifle muzzle and try to communicate with the person behind the trigger, especially since the posse had just ten days earlier carried the bodies of four men out of Little High Rock Canyon. There was no question in the minds of the posse that anyone other than these Indians had shot and killed the men at Little High Rock Canyon.

Several posse members testified that they shouted or hollered to the Indians to submit but communicating with someone at a distance of at least two lengths of a football field, in any condition, let alone this condition would be impossible. Perry was right, there were no communications as claimed.

If the posse members were close enough to communicate, how was it that no one in the posse identified which of the three Indians shot first? If the Indians were too far distant to identify which Indian shot first then how could any of the posse members have communicated the request to submit? These two questions leave in doubt who shot first.

This also raises another possibility. With the very loud noise from fifteen rifles firing all along the line and no one sure which Indian fired first, there is a good possibility that someone in the posse fired first and that Mike and his son were cut down without ever firing a shot.

At some point the remaining ten members of the family, two grown sons and the women and children tried to escape down the canyon. This was to no avail, about a mile down the draw or small canyon they were overtaken by eleven members of the posse and more killing of Indians began.

It is a little hard to understand how the fight/battle could have raged on for three hours when only two of the ten remaining are adult males and the other eight are women and children.

From a practical standpoint, records available and testimony at inquest the most likely scenario; one or both of the two adult men now still standing, were firing at the posse from the Daggett camp while the women and children attempted to escape down the wash. The weapons they had available were the 38-55 Winchester a shot gun and a 32 caliber automatic pistol. It appears the 38-55 was fired until it ran out of ammunition or jammed. There is no evidence it was carried beyond the make-shift camp. The shot gun was picked up further down the wash, indicating it too was out of ammunition.

It was first thought that the pistol was picked up somewhere in the vicinity of where the last six of the Daggetts fell. However there is no direct evidence or testimony that it was fired or had ammunition available at this point. There was no clear evidence from testimony indicating who had possession of the pistol, if anyone, when the six Indians and Hogle were killed. Stone and Parsons testified it was picked up at the Indian's camp approximately one mile up the wash from which most, if not all, of the gun fire came.

There was never any evidence that the son that went down with Mike had a gun. Only one posse member testified that he had a long pistol, but that pistol was not in evidence at the inquest nor in the photo labeled "weapons of the Indians". Mike did have a rifle and shells, as was testified to by nine members of the posse. This rifle and shells were in evidence at the inquest. The shotgun and the 38-55 were also in evidence at the inquest and in the photo labeled "weapons of the Daggetts".

In addition to the firearms noted above, a spear, two bows and numerous arrows were in evidence and included in the photo labeled "weapons of the Daggetts".

Harry Cambron's 32 cal. pistol was in evidence at the inquest but not identifiable in the photo of the Daggett weapons.

To recap the scene of the encounter with the Indians; Mike, one grown son and one of the two rifles of the Indians are now out of commission. With two adult males down, the only remaining members of the family of twelve, are two adult males, a grandmother, a mother with Baby Mosho on her back in a cradle board, a fifteen year old girl, two adolescent boys, ten to twelve years old, and the two smaller children, Hattie four years and Cleve six years old, a total of ten family members alive.

Age of children derived from letter; From C. H. Asbury, Superintendent on the Carson Training School at Stewart, Nevada to Commission of Indians Affairs, Washington D. C. - National Archives.

This small contingent of the Daggett family were unable to get to their horses, of which at least two possibly three had been shot and killed by the posse, proceeded down the canyon on foot. They ran down the wash/canyon for about a mile before they were finally over taken by the Donnelley Posse.

Meanwhile two or three members of the posse were rummaging through the camp vacated by the Indians a short time before, scattering the family possessions in every direction looking for hidden Indians.

THE LAST INDIAN UPRISING IN THE U. S. By Frank Perry's & testimony at the inquest.

When posse members finally discovered that the remainder of the Daggett family were trying to escape down the canyon, a couple of the posse members got on horseback and quickly proceeded down there and headed them off.

One mile below their camp the Indians were brought to bay and their route of escape cut off. Here the Canyon opens up leaving the Indians with very little cover and where six more of the Daggett family were killed. That included all of those except for the fifteen year old girl and the three smallest children.

When the inquest jury asked each posse member *"why was it necessary to kill the women and children"* the answer was *"they were killed while shooting at the bucks"*. What was left of the Daggett family had gone as far as they could, which was quite a distance considering that the little four year old had to run or be carried and the mother of baby Mosho was carrying the ten month old baby on her back in a cradle board.

At first it was thought that the ten members of the family may have had some sort of firearm but by further analyzing the inquest testimony, it is determined that the only weapons they had were, two bows, arrows and a ceremonial staff with a metal blade attached to the end. They were ill equipped to defend themselves against eleven rifles. The shotgun had been dropped in the wash some distance above where the last six members of the family were killed. It was likely out of ammunition and abandoned, there was no need for it now. The dropping of the shotgun further up the wash may also have been to show the posse that they were unarmed.

No posse member testified that he saw a weapon other than a pistol at the location where the six members of the family were killed. Through an intensive review of the inquest the statements of the posse members it was found to be so convoluted, false and contradictory that it pointed to no evidence that there could have been a firearm at that location.The pistol was never at the lower site. It was found at the make-shift camp as Charles Stone and Bill Parsons testified. The Indians had no firearms at the lower site where the six family members were killed.

The Daggetts knew that the time they feared most, DEATH, had come. The bows and arrows and a ceremonial staff with a blade attached could hardly be considered lethal weapons against eleven high powered repeating rifles. The flimsy bow and arrows of the Daggetts could only be used for the hunting of rabbits and other small game.

The grandmother, mother and little children were huddled together at the lower point in the draw. The two adolescent boys and two adult males were within a few yards of the family huddled together. When the killing was over, all bodies were within a total of about 40 or 50 yards of each other.

The wash or small canyon ran in a southeast direction. The northeast side of that portion of the draw/wash/canyon where the six members of the Daggett family were killed, was steep and exposed. Any Indian trying to escape up that slope would have been totally exposed to the posse. Therefore the Indians were in the wash as described by the posse. The posse members were advancing along the bank on the southwest side of the wash where there was some brush for cover.

From the testimony of the posse at the inquest, the two adult male Indians were lying close together and on the north side of the wash. The two young boys were lying close together in the middle of the wash. The two women were lying close together on the south side of the wash, all within a distance of 30 to 40 yards. The women were not in the line of fire when shooting at the adult males and could only have been intentionally shot and not shot by accident. One posse member testified, *"The squaws were acting as combatants and it was impossible to avoid killing them as I believe the squaws were killed by bullets intended for the bucks, they were mixed up so"*.

Think on that one for a moment when you consider other testimony and the location of the six bodies in the wash. There were no adult males mixed up with the women and children.

Statements of the posse; *"the squaws may have been killed when shooting into the brush at the bucks"* also the inquest jury asked of posse member (Henry Hughes) *"could the squaws been killed by bullets passing through the bucks"*? The answer *"yes"*. Whenever a buck stuck his head up or they saw him, everybody fired at him. Their explanation was they didn't know who it was. As a matter of fact the posse members there were indiscriminately firing away at every Indian regardless of age or gender, they were murdering Indians one at a time. It is a miracle that the fifteen year old girl nor one of the smaller children was not shot.

The last of the killing was when one of the Indian boys quite, possibly the ten year old was flushed out and killed as he ran down towards the women and other children who were huddled together in the wash.

In the photograph taken of the family in death it can be seen that a young Indian boy or girl that appears to be no more than eight or ten years old, has a portion of his head shot away. He was shot in the back by about ten riflemen and blown face down in the sand. They testified at this point that the grandmother and the mother with baby Mosho on her back were also killed. A posse member was also killed at this time.

Ed Hogle, the only posse member to lose his life, was killed at about the time the shooting ceased. He was pushing ahead to make sure to get himself an Indian. It was nearing the last days in our history when an Indian could be shot down for sport. In fact about thirty years beyond those days.

Not one member of the posse testified they actually saw the young Indian shoot Ed Hogle. They testified they heard a shot and saw the buck running down the wash so they all opened fire.

Testimony at March 1, 1911 inquest (Ed Hogle)

Ed was shot by one of the other posse members by accident. They were all approaching the gulch not knowing how many Indians might be alive or if they were armed. Each posse member would have been on hair trigger alert, shells in the chambers, safeties off, fingers on triggers and etched in each of their minds the four shot-up bodies of the sheepmen at Little High Rock.

Two men, O.D. Van Norman and Frank Perry were out about 30 or 40 yards from the main group, Perry on the upper end of the group and O.D. on the lower end. It appears that at least one or both were watching the women and children huddled in the canyon to prevent them from escaping.

One of those two men got buck fever, no pun intended, and just touched off a shell killing Ed Hogle by mistake. This suspicion is further backed up by an article in the Humboldt Star paper which stated that the bullet that killed Ed Hogle, *"went in the upper left shoulder near the collar bone and came out underneath the right arm, probably touching the heart"*.

Humboldt Star news paper dated March 1, 1911

251

This same story came out in the Elko Independent Weekly dated March 4, 1911. Since all of the news media of the day is so wrought with fabrication and misinformation, the only way to prove Ed was shot in this manner is to exhume his body from his grave at the Anderson Cemetery in Anderson, California. However I believe the newspaper may have gotten this one right.

Hogle was approaching the wash, ahead of the others, in a crouched position. If the Indian who was down in the wash, who had supposedly shot Hogle from almost point blank range, the bullet would have had to pass straight through Hogle's body and not enter high in the shoulder and exit under the arm pit.

When Hogle was shot one of the Indian children ran from that spot and they all shot him in the back. Inquest testimony indicated they all opened fire on the buck (Indian boy). The fifteen year old girl who had the stick with the blade on it (ceremonial staff) was running up and down the bank trying to keep the men away from her sister, grandmother, and the three small children. Again to no avail because when the young boy was killed they also killed the grandmother and the mother with the baby on her back which was the young girl's sister.

The young boy about six years old who had just witnessed his family being slaughtered ran off on his own trying to avoid being killed. How terrifying it must have been thinking he would be shot to death like the rest. Jack Ferguson, on horse back, ran him down. Ferguson finally got him on his saddle and slammed his face onto the saddle horn to subdue him, later claiming that the boy tried to beat his brains out on the saddle horn. This story went around the country for years but it was a total fabrication. There was evidence to this effect in the statement of Frank Perry written years later.

"He (Ferguson) also told me afterwards that he slapped him in the face".

Bits and pieces of historical information would indicate the boy was biting, throwing rocks, kicking and fighting with everything he had to escape Ferguson. This desperate effort to escape is understandable and was most likely what led to his being slapped or more likely, his face banged onto the saddle horn. The mentality of the posse, especially by Ferguson was that the family was more akin to animals than humans.

It appears that most, if not all, eight of the Indians including women and children were shot numerous times. More evidence that they were shot numerous times was the fact

252

that none were wounded they all died immediately or within a very short time of being shot.

An article in the Humboldt Star newspaper February 22, 1911 stated: *"Indians are very likely to surrender when run down and find escape impossible, rather than make a fight and be shot to pieces by the posse".* Being shot to pieces was exactly what occurred. These kinds of statements were not atypical in any of the newspapers covering this tragic event.

They seemed to think it weird that the fifteen year old would run and cry and scream and hold her mother after the mother had been shot to death. Frank Perry called it wailing. Their lack of regard for human life and suffering is somewhat hard to understand even for those times. Had this family been white or related to one of those men, I ponder what their reaction would have been.

As most testified the horses of the Indians were in such poor condition they could hardly travel. The Indians were on foot, they had small children, babies, and there was no way they could have gotten away. There was no excuse for killing the whole family, especially the women and children.

By the time they had killed Mike and one son, near the Indian camp, they were in a killing frenzy each one wanting to make sure he got to shoot an Indian. Pushing ahead of the others is how Ed Hogle was killed.

After the family members were killed a wagon was retrieved from the Kelly Creek Ranch. This wagon, along with the wagon Captain Donnelley had, was used to transport the four children and Ed Hogle's body to the Kelly Creek Ranch which is located about six miles to the northeast from the site. They remained there until February 28th.

Imagine the scene! The roar of 10 rifles, each time they killed an Indian, the children clutching to their mothers, shot down all around them, the horror, fear, trauma, stress and any other adjective that you can think of to describe what is taking place with ten men hovering over them with rifles, they could only think that they too were going to be killed. Then they were pulled away from their dead mothers by these strangers, monsters in their eyes and loaded into wagons to be hauled away, leaving the only family they knew behind. What kind of a barbaric mentality did these men have anyway?

When the smoke settled, it had to have been obvious to the members of the posse, at the site where the women and children were killed, that Ed had been killed by one of their own. There were no weapons there that could have done it. At first it appeared that Cambron's 32 automatic pistol was at this site but further review and analysis of the inquest testimony, concludes that this pistol was found at the make-shift camp, about one mile up the draw from the site where the women and children were killed.

The testimony was so convoluted and contradictory that it leaves doubt as to the possibility of this pistol having not been fired at all or there may not have been any ammunition available for its firing. Several posse members mentioned the possibility of the Indians being out of ammunition.

Testimony before the Inquest Jury - March 1 and March 3, through March 5,1911, Part III Chapter V

There are stories floating around the the Indians had poor quality weapons, old blunderbuss and the such. It wasn't the quality of their weapons that had them out gunned, it was they only had two high powered rifles against eighteen of the posse.

There are two interesting possibilities that can be brought to the surface in this fiasco,

1 -the weapons at the camp were out of ammunition and no shots were fired from there

2 - the two adult males killed down the wash may have thought that if they were not carrying weapons they may not be shot.

Whoever shot Ed Hogle knew he had touched off a round unintentionally, but with all the confusion and the firing of rifles at that moment may not have realized that he had shot Hogle. This would have become evident afterward when there was no other explanation.

As for the women and children, what is the explanation for killing them? It appears to be, each of the eleven posse members at the lower site, has in his mind [if we are into killing Indians then I am going to get one too] or maybe they were thinking leave no witnesses.

Those involved in the posse Feb. 25 and Feb. 26.

1--Capt. Donnelley, J. P. - age 51 - Carson City Nev. - Supt. of Nev. State Police

2--Newgard P. M. - age 32 - Carson City Nev. - Sergeant Nev. State Police **

3--Stone, Charles H. - age 35 - Carson City Nev. - Sergeant, Nev. State Police **

4--Buck, - Private, State police (first name and age of Private Buck not known he
   had gone to Elko with Washoe County Sheriff to cut off escape of the Daggett family)

5--Smith, A. E. - age 45 - Alturas, Calif., - Sheriff of Modoc County, Calif.

6--Ferrell, Charles P. - age ? - Reno, Nev. - Sheriff Washoe County, Nev.
   (Went to Elko with Private Buck to cut off escape of the Indian family)

7 --Skinny Pascal - age 42 - Winn., Nev. - Indian tracker -
   Humboldt County Sheriffs Office (did not testify at inquest)

8--Byrnes, Charles T. - age - 36 - Paradise Valley, Nev. - Constable

9--Prussia, Mearl W. - age 21 - Paradise Valley, Nev. - Butcher (** ?)

10--Cambron, Ben F. - age 40 - Constantia, Calif. - Stockman

11--Ferguson, Jack - 34 - Eagleville, Cal. - Stockman **

12--Perry, Frank - age - 22 - Eagleville, Calif. - Teamster **

13-Parsons, Wm. M. - age - 27 - Eagleville, Calif. - Buckaroo

14--Fruit, Warren - age - 21 - Eagleville, Calif. - Buckaroo **

15-- Van Norman, Otto - age - 28 - Grass Valley, Nev. - Farming **

16--Reeder, Joseph - age - 33 - Gerlach, Nev. - Miner **

17--Hughes, Henry - age - 33 - Eagleville, Calif. - Rancher**

18--Holmes, George - age - 46 - Eagleville, Calif. - Carpenter **

19--West, Mort - age - 24 - Eagleville, Calif. - Buckaroo **

20--Hogle, Edward - age - 31 - Eagleville, Calif. - Buckaroo**
   (killed at the very end, shooting stopped within minutes of his death) (mother lived in
Anderson, Calif)

Note: Pascal joined the posse at the north end of Jackson Mt.
   Ferrill and Buck left for Elko and Tuscarora on Feb. 23rd
   Byrnes and Prussia did not join posse until after the posse reached Winnemucca.
**Posse members present at the lower site, where the women and children were killed,
   which was about 1 mile down from the camp where shooting started.

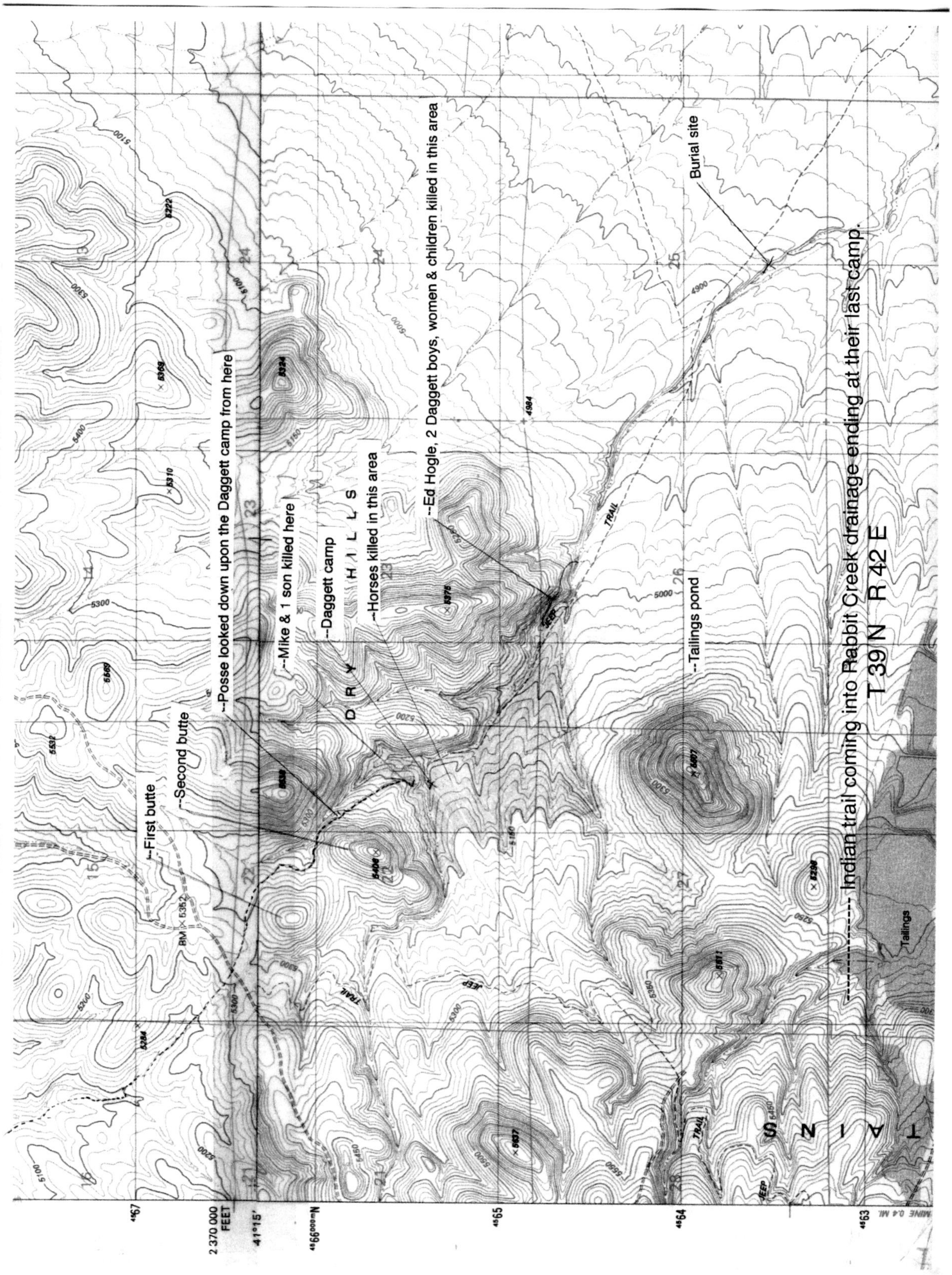
--Posse looked down upon the Daggett camp from here
--Mike & 1 son killed here
--Daggett camp
D R Y H I L L S
--Horses killed in this area
--Ed Hogle, 2 Daggett boys, women & children killed in this area
Burial site
--First butte
--Second butte
--Tailings pond
-------- Indian trail coming into Rabbit Creek drainage ending at their last camp.
T 39 N R 42 E
Tailings
TRAIL
JEEP

DAGGETT'S SHOTGUN

This is one of the many items looted by the Donnelley posse, from the possessions of the (Shoshone) Mike Daggett family, after their killing at Rabbit Creek.
It was in evidence at the inquest for the Indians killed but disappeared into the hands of one of the posse members.
All of the possessions of the family, legally, belonged to the four surviving Daggett children, however they were all stolen/looted and or doled out to the different ones involved in the killing, while the children languished in jail.

INDIAN WEAPONS

Humboldt County Museum

WEAPONS of the MIKE DAGGETT FAMILY

Items identified: top left appears to be the ceremonial staff wielded by Henny (a willow about five feet long) wrapped in red flannel, blade attached to bottom and feathers on the top; to the right, two bows; then left to right, double barreled shot gun; cartridge belt with cartridges; then item not identified, appears to be a broken stick and one other item; above that, arrows; then the two rifles (left to right:38-55 Winchester model 1894 and 40-82 Winchester model 1886) and the drum.

The bows and arrows were used by the grandmother and the mother of Baby Mosho, in their defense against the eleven posse members, each carrying repeating rifles. The spear was used by the young girl to fend off the posse from getting to her mother, sister and the children.

These are the weapons (except for one, that being the 32 caliber Savage automatic pistol) and drum, that were submitted in evidence at the inquest for the eight that were killed at Rabbit Creek. The pistol was taken, by the Indians, from Harry Cambron when he was killed at Little High Rock and therefore probably taken back to Eagleville by Harry's brother Ben Cambron, when Ben returned there about the 7th of May 1911. These items were gathered up at the site near Rabbit Creek where the Indians and Ed Hogle were killed.

If one is to believe the testimony that the so called posse members gave, under oath, at the inquest, the grandmother and mother with the infant on her back, were each shooting arrows, the 32 caliber pistol and beating on the drum, all at the same time. With the ferocity of these two women, it is any wonder that the killing of the Daggetts was labeled as the last Indian battle in the United States.

WEAPON of the FIFTEEN YEAR OLD GIRL

Two young Indian boys holding the ceremonial staff (spear as described by posse members) and the drum. This picture was most likely taken right after the Daggetts were killed, early March. Boys have heavy coats and there are no leaves on the trees.

WEAPON OF THE TWO INDIAN LADIES

The small arrow, being compared to a modern hunting arrow, was taken from the site
near Rabbit Creek where eight of the Daggett family were killed Feb. 26, 1911.
Bow hunters of today work to get within forty to fifty yards of their target to make a clean
kill. The bows and arrows the Daggett women were using would not have
been lethal to a person beyond forty or fifty feet and not then against men in heavy
winter coats. From the testimony of the posse members it appears the two women, the
grandmother and the mother with the infant on here back, defending themselves with
bows and arrows, were at a distance of approximately thirty or forty yards.

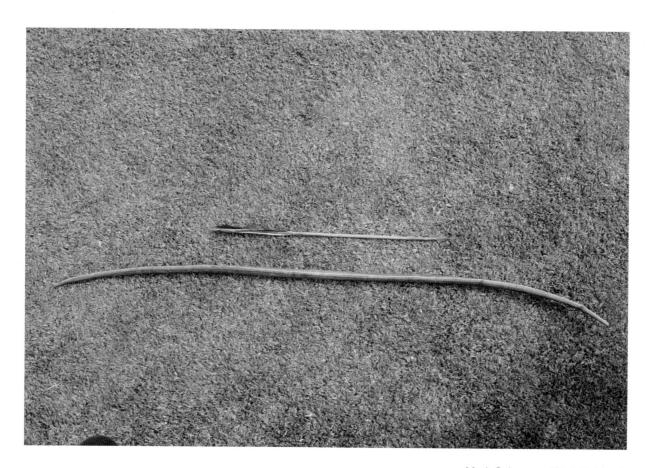

Mark Schopper / Dick Caldwell

BOW & ARROW

One of the bows and one of the arrows the Daggett women were trying to
defend themselves with.

HARRY CAMBRON'S PISTOL

(Silver dollar is for scale)

Cambron's pistol was identical to the one shown above (Savage - Model 1907 - 32 caliber semi-automatic, pocket size, three and three quarter inch barrel, ten shot magazine, manufactured by Savage Arms Co. Utica, N. Y. in 1910).

It was taken from Harry Cambron, by the Indians, when he was killed at Little High Rock Canyon January 19, 1911.

Right after the bodies of the sheepmen were found at Little High Rock, property of the sheepmen was listed in several newspapers, Cambron's pistol included. The serial No. of the pistol was listed as 14160 or 13911.

These numbers do not come near matching the numbers in the testimony of Stone and Parsons. At the inquest they identified this pistol as having Serial No. 26474.

To be noted, these are the only two posse members that clearly testified that the pistol was found at the Indian camp.

Henry Hughs testified that he recognized the pistol and that he had sold it to Cambron.

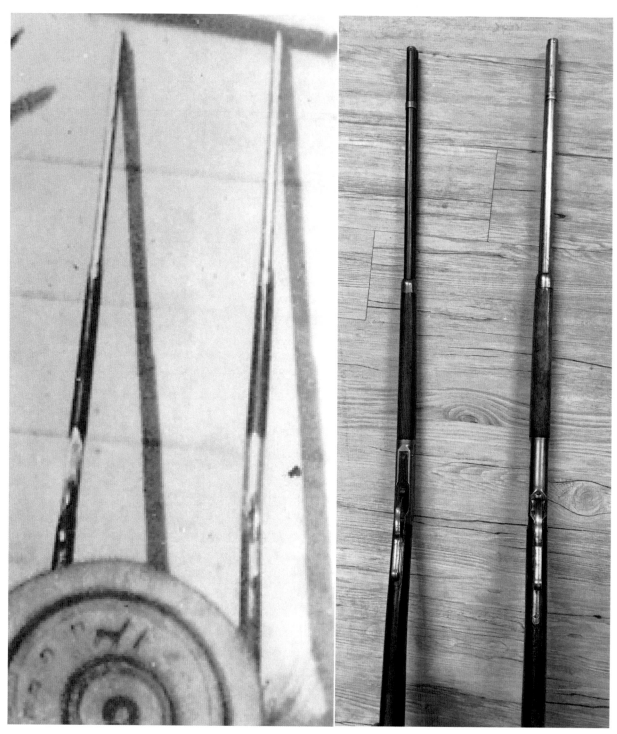

WINCHESTER RIFLES
Left: The Daggett rifles (38-55 & 40-82) February 1911
Right: Similar rifles (38-55 & 40-82) October 2018

WINHESTER RIFLES

38-55 & 40-82

Left: (38-55) Model 1894
Right: (40-82) Model 1886

These rifles are similar to
the rifles the Daggetts had
when they were killed at
Rabbit Creek.
The 1886 rifle is identical to
the one Mike had with him
when he was killed.

Photo courtesyJeff Williams
Elko, Nevada

3 p.m. Sunday, February 26, 1911

Kelly. Creek, Camp showing Buildings

KELLY CREEK RANCH

ca 1890

Kelley Creek Ranch, located twenty five miles northeast of Golconda, Nevada, was established in the late 1870s by T. D. Parkinson. It later became part of the Nevada Land and Cattle Co. holdings, headquartered at Fairlawn, in Squaw Valley.

Ed Hogle's body and the four surviving children from the killing at Rabbit Creek were brought here February 26, 1911. Two days later, on the 28th the children were taken from the Kelly Creek Ranch to Golconda and locked in jail.

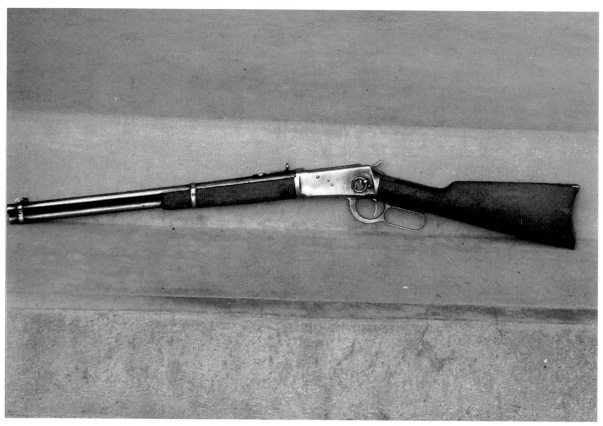

JOHN (Skinny) PASCAL'S RIFLE

Skinny Pascal, Sheriff Lamb and Lamb's brother Kise, met up with Frank Perry, Sgt. P. M. Newgard, Jim Tahem and Jack Ferguson, at the Lay Ranch on the west side of Jackson Mt., on Feb. 20, 1911. Perry, Newgard, Tahem and Ferguson had split from the Donnelley posse, at Piaute Meadows, on the morning of the 19th. These seven joined the Donnelley posse at the north end of Jackson Mt., the next day, Feb. 21st. Sheriff Lamb and Kise, left the posse at Winnemucca, on the 23rd, Pascal remained with the posse until the end, Feb. 27, 1911.

Humboldt County Museum / Hist. Society

HORSES SHOT NEAR RABBIT CREEK
Feb. 27 or 28, 1911

When the Mike Daggett family killed the four sheepmen in Little High Rock Canyon, Jan. 19, 1911, they took the sheepmen's horses. Those horses were described as follows:

1-Sorrel horse, light main & tail, white face, Wt. 1100 lbs. LT on right thigh.

1-Bay horse, white stripe on face, white feet, wight 1100 lbs. 5 years old and branded HP on left shoulder, 76 on left side.

1-Bay horse, white star on forehead, stripe on nose, quarter circle on left shoulder, JA on left side.

1-Black Oregon horse 7 or 8 years old no brand known. (I believe Oregon was mistaken for Morgan since "Oregon horse" is not a description but a Morgan horse has identifiable characteristics. This would be Indiano's horse as only the Denios had seen the horse and would not have been looking for brands, already difficult to see due to long winter hair). Horses are not usually branded on the side therefore side was probably mistaken for thigh on the two bay horses.

At Rabbit Creek the posse shot and killed two and possibly three horses that were in the possession of the Indians. Two of the horses killed belonged to the sheepmen killed at Little High Rock.

On the 3rd of March Jack Ferguson testified that one of the horses killed at Rabbit Creek, the horse branded with the HP on the left shoulder and a 76 on the left side belonged to Harry Cambron. Since the horse branded with the HP & 76 belonged to Cambron and the black horse belonged to Indiano it is concluded the horse shown in this photo, with the white face, was ridden into Little High Rock by Erramouspe or Laxague on January 19, 1911. .

269

By Captain J. P. Donnelley

Part of the report includes the following:

In January, 1911, four stockmen operating in northern Washoe County were reported missing. Search was instituted for the missing men and on February 11 news was received that their bodies had been found and that the men undoubtedly had been murdered. The department was called upon to assist in the pursuit of the murderers. A posse was formed, composed of members of this department, peace officers and stockmen. I assumed command of the posse. We found the bodies, stripped of the greater part of their clothing, concealed from view by willows, in Little High Rock Canyon. Carcasses of cattle and horses and a deserted Indian camp were found near the murdered stockmen. The bodies of the men were taken to Camp Denio, where an inquest was held over the remains and a verdict found to the effect that the four men had come their deaths from gunshot wounds inflicted by persons unknown but believed to be Indians. We picked up the trail of the Indians where they had left the deserted camp. Later it developed that the trail was about a month old. Under very unfavorable conditions during the coldest month of one of the most severe winters known to Nevada we followed the trail about 450 miles before the Indians were over taken. At several points along the trail conclusive evidence was obtained that the posse was following the same band of Indians that had camped near the scene of the murder.

Fifteen days from the time the bodies of the stockmen were found the Indians were over taken 35 miles northeast of Golconda. The Indians evinced considerable concern at the approach of the posse and they were commanded to surrender. They immediately fired upon our force. Through an interpreter they were again told to submit to arrest. Their only reply was another volley from their rifles. A sharp engagement, lasting about three hours, resulted. One member of the posse, Ed Hogle, four buck Indians, two squaws and two Indian boys were killed during the engagement. "Shoshone Mike," the leader of the hand, had eight bullet wounds in his body. One squaw, one boy and two small children were captured. None of the band escaped. The killing of the squaws and boys was unavoidable, as they fought as fiercely as the bucks, using firearms, arrows and spears. Also the squaws, realizing that we were endeavoring to avoid injuring them tried to protect the bucks from our fire. The Indians proved to be a band of outlaws known as "Shoshone Mike's" band, who had been committing depredations in eastern and northern Nevada and northern California for period of eighteen months. They were suspected of having committed several murders prior to the killing of the stockmen. The captured squaw confessed that the band had killed seventeen human beings. The coroner's jury returned a verdict "That the Indians came to their death by gunshot wounds inflicted by Captain J. P. Donnelley's posse; that their deaths were unavoidable, and further, the Captain J. P. Donnelley and posse were justified in their actions."

I wish to highly commend the individual members of my posse for the courage, endurance and perseverance displayed during the pursuit and engagement that resulted in the extermination of "Shoshone Mike's" band. I also wish to thank the ranchers and stockmen along the route gravel, who invariably supplied the posse with food, shelter and fresh mounts.

Rewards aggregating $9,143.50 were offered for the arrest and conviction of the murderers. Of this amount $2,143.50, offered by the citizens of Surprise Valley, and $1,000 offered by the H. C. Cattle Company, have been collected and distributed to the eighteen members of the posses who were present at the engagement. The $5,000 offered by the State of Nevada, and $1,000 offered by the State of California have not as yet been paid.

A detailed history of this case is on file at this office and can be referred to should further details be required.

CHAPTER II

RETURNING TO THE SCENE OF THE KILLING - February 27,1911

There is not a lot of reliable information about what occurred on the 27th of February. What we do know is:- 1) some of the posse, we are not sure who, returned to the sight of the carnage, or killing, if you will- 2) the body of Ed Hogle and the four Daggett children remained at the Kelly Creek Ranch that whole day, until the next morning, February 28,1911 when they made the thirty five mile journey to Golconda, Nevada- 3) the bodies of the Indians were brought down about a mile below from where they were killed and stacked in a pile in preparation for burial. (When I say preparation for burial I mean tossed into a pile like so many animal carcasses). The removal of the bodies before the coroner arrived could also distort the scene where the Indian boy was killed and supposedly the women were killed by accident.- 4) Baby Mosho would have been breast fed up until now as she could not survive at her age on dried beef and jack rabbits [the Daggetts certainly did not have milk or baby formula on hand]. 5) a messenger was sent ten or twelve miles (depending upon whether he left from the site of the killing or from the Kelly Creek Ranch) to the North's Ranch (later known as the Lower Clover Ranch) to report by telephone, probably to Sheriff Lamb in Winnemucca. According to the Humboldt Star newspaper dated February 27, 1911 a messenger from the posse arrived at North's Ranch (Lower Clover Ranch) last evening to report from the battle site. However the telephone office was closed so no information was transmitted to Winnemucca until the following morning February 27.

This information came from the Humboldt Star newspaper and is probably true, it's consistent with other reports and to send a messenger to the North's Ranch is a logical thing for Captain Donnelley to have done.

A writeup in THE SILVER STATE newspaper and other historical information indicates John S. "Skinny" Pascal was sent on to Golconda on the morning of the 27th to report the killing of the Indians and the capture of the four Indian children and ask that the coroner be sent out to the site where the Indians were killed. This may not have been the case, the information as written in the newspaper article does not read like it came from the Indian trailer, Pascal. Perry in his writings does not mention dispatching Pascal to Golconda. Some of the information may have been passed on to the news paper via telephone from North's Ranch as claimed by the Humboldt Star. Due to the inaccuracies of the newspapers it is very difficult to ascertain what the true facts are. On February 28, 1911 THE SILVER STATE newspaper printed in this column, under the headline:

BAND OF MURDEROUS SHOSHONES WIPED OUT BY POSSE,

the latest information from the Donnelley posse.

The first detailed account of the battle Sunday between Captain Donnelly's posse and the Shoshone Indians was brought to Winnemucca last evening by "Skinny" Pascal, the Indian tracker, who left the Bliss Kelly Creek Ranch yesterday morning , arriving in town last evening at about 7 o'clock.

"Indian Mike" Fires First Shot

Riding over a ridge the posse came in full view of the entire band of Indians, evidently on the lookout, stationed at a point a few rods from the entrance to a canyon, where their camp stood. "Skinny" Pascal rode out to talk to the Indians who, when they saw him coming, started on the run for their camp, with the exception of old Mike, who run in an opposite direction and disappeared from view. When Pascal had arrived within about a quarter of a mile from the point where he was lost to view, Mike suddenly rose and fired a shot at him, but missed, dropping to the ground again. Pascal slipped from his horse to the ground, bringing his rifle to his shoulder, ready for action. Mike raised again, exposing the upper half of his body, when Pascal fired twice. Captain Donnelley, who was in the vicinity, fired at the old savage at the same time. Mike fell and started to crawl off in the brush. Members of the posse rushed in on the old man, whom they found dying, and took his gun away.

Indians Run Down Canyon

The balance of the party, who had run for camp, then started down the canyon, the squaws and children driving the horses and the men dodging and firing at the posse, who kept up on incessant fire in return. In this manner one of the young bucks was shot dead, at a point about half a mile from the entrance to the canyon.

Indians Rounded Up

The indians proceeded on the run down the canyon for about two miles, when they turned to the left, passing over the ridge into another canyon, half a mile distant. When the posse came up they saw the fugitives executing a war dance, one of the squaws beating a drum, made of a sheepskin stretched over a hoop, several of the party having their faces decorated with war paint.

Battle Begins in Earnest

As soon as they ascertained that they had been followed the Indians put up a terrific battle, the men using rifles and the women and children bows and arrows. Hundreds of shots were exchanged and when the fire from the Indians had quieted the posse rushed in finding that the remaining two bucks, with two squaws and two children, were dead. A young squaw with an infant in her arms, sat huddled up on the ground but the remaining two children, boys aged about eight and ten years respectively, run away, and when taken offered to continue the fighting with rocks and stones. One of the boys was placed astride a horse, when he attempted to butt out his brains against the horn of the saddle.

Battle Lasts for Three Hours

From the time "Indian Mike" fired the first shot until the two boys were taken is estimated at about three hours.

After all was over, a messenger was despatched to the Bliss Ranch, some six miles away, for a team and wagon, when the body of Hogle and the young captives were taken to the ranch. Another messenger was sent to North's ranch, 13 miles away, to summon Coroner Buckley from Golconda.

Beginning with the first paragraph in the news article above, Pascal bringing news from the site where the Indians and Hogle were killed, I guess I have to accept that he was the messenger.

Under the heading **Indian Mike Fires First Shot,** the only parts that may be true could be that, a. Skinny Pascal brought the news from Kelly Creek and he may also have ridden out to talk to the Indians. Each posse member testified that Pascal was asked to communicate to the Indians that they should surrender. All of the remainder of that part is untrue.

Frank Perry in his writings about the incident stated *"With all due respect to Sheriff Lamb and his brother Kise, I would like to state that Skinny Pascal never took the lead at any time on the trail, nor took any participation in the battle that ensued. He was asked by Captain Donnelly, and later by Newguard to act as interpreter to ask the Indians to surrender, but as the battle started at about four hundred yards, with a blizzard blowing snow and sleet, conversation was void.*

Under the heading **Indians Run Down Canyon,** the only part that is true is the women and children started down the canyon/wash.

Under the heading **Indians Rounded Up,** none of that part of the story is true.

Under the heading **Battle Begins in Earnest,** the only part that is true "the women were fighting with bows and arrows. The remainder untrue.

Under the heading **Battle Lasts for Three Hours,** other than there is some question as to whether Mike fired the first shot, I have to accept the remainder of that part is true.

Pascal may not have had a very good command of the English language so if he truly was the messenger from Kelly Creek it may explain why the article is so inaccurate.

However in the book KARNEE by Lalla Scott which is a biography of a lady (Annie Lowry) who's father was white and who's mother was Indian, there are two statements that indicate Pascal was quite literate, one *"John S. Pascal an English speaking Paiute"* and the other *"visiting with his many friends in the village, and he* (Pascal) *read a lot".*
Annie was married to Pascal for many years until he died in 1930.

The other possibility being the newspaper decided to make up a story to help sell papers.

Now, back up again to the article in the Humboldt Star dated February 27, 1911, under the headline:

DESPERATE BATTLE IN CLOVER VALLEY
BETWEEN POSSE AND HUNTED INDIANS

All of the Band Except Three Pappooses and One Young Girl Are Killed
Ed Hogle of Eagleville Also Slain

The two-hundred mile chase of the posse headed by Captain Donnelly of the State police after a band of renegade Shoshone Indians who so fouley murdered the four French sheepmen, Harry Cambron, Pete Erramauspe, John Laxague and B. Indiano, in Little High Rock canyon, in northwestern Washoe county, came to a bloody ending yesterday afternoon in the extreme eastern part of this county, when the Indians were overtaken and eight of them shot to death, one member of the posse, Ed Hogle of Eagleville, Cal. being killed in the battle which took place.

Fitting and fearfully was the fiendish crime of the Indian renegades avenged. Of its twelve members only four escaped, one young mahala about sixteen years old, and three papooses. The leader of the band, the old warrior "Indian Mike" three young bucks, two squaws and two children were killed, eight in all two lives for each one taken by the Indians.

The pursuers, a detachment of State police under command of Captain Donnelley, and the posse from Eagelville, headed by Sheriff Smith of Modoc County, Calif. and Ben Cambron, brother of one of the murdered sheepmen, after following the Indians on a hot trail since early morning, over-took them shortly afternoon at a point in Clover Valley, about eight miles west of what in known as the Kelley Creek Ranch. The Indians were hurrying across the valley when over-taken, trying to reach the mountains on the east side. Being practically without cover they had to battle in the open or surrender. Contrary to the Indian nature they chose to exchange shot for shot with the avengers, who were all too willing for such a climax, and the bloody battle commenced.

Only very meager details of the battle, in which the Indians were practically annihilated, can be obtained, all the news available having been telephoned to

275

Winnemucca from North's ranch, early this morning. The messenger from the battlefield arrived at North's ranch last night, but owing to the telephone office at Golconda being closed the news would not be transmitted to the outside world last night.

From the details that can be obtained it is described as having been a running fight lasting three hours and covering over a mile of country. When the Indians saw the approaching posse the four braves astonished their pursuers by stopping and engaging in their tribal war dance. This continued until the advance guard of the posse had ridden up to within hailing distance, when the summons to surrender was answered by cries of derision and defiance and the Indian braves, squaws and children scattered into the brush and opened the battle which was to terminate in what was little short of a massacre.

"Indian Mike" fell fatally wounded early in the fight, but the loss of their leader only spurred his followers to more desperate efforts. Realizing that it was a battle to the death, none intimated by voice or gesture the slightest desire to surrender. Answering shot with shot, the Indians fell back slowly, falling one by one before the withering fusillade from the rifles of the posse. The Indians fought like veritable demons, the squaws taking part and selling their lives no less dearly than their men folk. In their last stand they used every available weapon of offense, bows and arrows and tomahawks being resorted to when the ammunition from their rifles and revolvers was exhausted. Thus the bloody battle continued until none of the Indians remained alive but three pappooses and the young Indian girl, who were found in the brush near where the fight was begun. The squaws were shot down with as little compunction as the braves, as the women fought throughout no less fiercely than the men, but killing of the two children was accidental and could not be avoided.

The only details of the battle known at this hour are those given by the messenger who brought the new last night to North's Ranch, the remainder of the posse remaining at the scene to gather up the bodies and make arrangements to convey them to Golconda, the nearest railroad point, and about fifty miles distant. This morning the posse started for Golconda, the bodies being carried in wagons secured from ranches in the neighborhood. They will probably reach Golconda some time this evening and there the inquest will be held by Justice of the Peace Buckley. The bodies of the Indians will be

276

buried there, while the remains of young Hogle, the only white victim of the bloody conflict, will be shipped back to his home in Eagleville.

It is interesting as to who the messenger that was sent to the North's ranch might have been because this is where the story takes on a personality of its own, setting the stage for what is to follow, in the newspapers and in the testimony at the inquest for Ed Hogle and the family members that were killed.

The first part of this article reflects the mind set of most of those in Surprise Valley, Calif. and northwestern Nevada. It was perfectly ok to kill women and children with no thought as to whether they were guilty of anything. The Indians were thought of as so many vermin, reflecting bigotry, racism and ignorance on the part of the citizens and more specifically the members of the posse.

Then the article begins to dramatize the viciousness of the Indians and the bloody battle that ensued. The Indians, including the women, are made out to be dangerous warriors, the squaws fought as fiercely as the bucks but the children were killed accidentally.

If the messenger left anything out, the newspaper seemed willing to fill it in.

This article and the many many others that followed reflect the not so accurate reports and dramatized mind set of most of those who were ever so anxious to immortalize the posse as the great heroic Indian fighters. The body of one posse member, Ed Hogle, killed in battle, was proof enough that there had been a fierce Indian battle in which the brave men of the Donnelley posse courageously battled the very dangerous Indian warriors.

In analyzing the information coming from the Rabbit Creek-Kelly Creek battle/killing/ massacre as reported by the HUMBOLDT STAR and THE SILVER STATE newspapers, it can be seen that a lot of effort is put into portraying the confrontation as a battle between a fierce band of outlaw Indians and the bravery of a courageous posse that successfully stamped out this terrible band of renegade Indians. However if you back away a bit so you can see the whole picture and analyze the facts it becomes clear what is motivating the posse members to distort the facts and sensationalize the fight with the Indians.

To begin with, in the posse there were seventeen young men armed with repeating high powered rifles. There are only four adult males in the band of Indians, one being a grandfather of about sixty five years of age and the remainder being women and children. Their arms with which to do battle consisted of two high powered repeating rifles, one shot gun, one small 32 caliber pistol, two small bows with arrows (used for killing small game) and one ceremonial staff used as a spear. The posse had no burdens of responsibility other than themselves. On the flip side the Daggett family had the grandmother and a mother with a baby in a cradle board on her back and five small children to try to protect. Those children ranged from one boy, twelve years of age at the very most, to one boy eight to ten years old, one boy about six years of age, one toddler about four years of age and baby Mosho, a little over ten months of age. Secondly, when the slaughter was over the posse realized the last six members of the Daggett family had no weapons other than the two bows and arrows and the one spear at the location where these six were killed.

Thirdly, the posse members suddenly realize when they looked down into that wash, saw six bodies, of the the Daggett family riddled with bullets and the only Indians alive are three very small children and a teen age girl, that they had made a huge mistake. Later on at the inquest for Ed Hogle and the Indians, the testimony of the posse members becomes contradictory and self serving.

Inquest testimony March 1 and March 3 and 4

With the confusion and racket from ten rifles blazing away, it is understandable how different stories could come of this happening. On the flip side when all was quiet again and weapons inventory taken, there could be no question as to what had really taken place at Rabbit Creek. Thank God for Ed Hogle!

On the 28th a group came out from Golconda and buried the Indians. A shallow grave was blown in the ground with dynamite and the bodies all dumped in together.

A piece of canvas was placed over the bodies then boards on top of the canvas and then about two feet of soil on top of the boards. By December of 1911 animals had dug into the grave and scattered body parts about.

It is interesting that the photos taken of the dead Indians in a pile and one photo showing a blanket pulled back to reveal the face of the young boy would indicate some one had an inkling that all was not as told of this horrific event.

Back to February 27, there were seventeen members of the posse at the Kelly Creek Ranch, not including Ed Hogle, so why did Capt. Donnelley not dispatch several members of the posse to escort the children and the body of Ed Hogle to Golconda on the 27th? They did not need seventeen men to bring the bodies of eight dead Indians down to the site where they were buried and toss them into a pile, half a dozen men could have easily done that and remained with the bodies until the coroner arrived. Eight or ten men could have easily transported Ed Hogle's body and the captive children from Kelly Creek to Golconda. Some had to remain with the children anyway, while others returned to the site where the bodies lay. In addition there were one or more men residing at the Kelly Creek Ranch and there would have been several wagons at the Kelly Creek Ranch so that would not have been a limiting factor.

It seems the most logical thing to do would be to get the children to a place where they could be properly cared for. The youngest baby Mosho was a mere ten months old, another little girl was only four years old. There were no facilities nor other means for properly caring for the children at Kelley Creek.

Who cared for the children? What did they feed them for three days? Baby Mosho breast-fed up until this time wasn't living on dried beef! Who changed her diapers? Or did they? Who stayed with the body of Hogle & the children while the others cleaned up the carnage and piled up the bodies?

It seems quite clear that these men had no concern for the children.

The answer could have been it would spread Donnelley's forces to thin and he did not trust the Surprise Valley bunch. There were only three state police there including Donnelley.

Another part to that answer could be, this day did offer the posse members the opportunity to conjure up a story to be told, in justifying the killing of the women and children and to explain the killing of Ed Hogle.

The most reliable documented information available was written in February 1949 by Frank V. Perry, one of the posse members who was there. The story was published in the Nevada Historical Society Quarterly Volume 15, Issue #4, Winter, 1972.

Perry's writings have so many inaccuracies that it makes suspect the whole document. The document has to be judged on what makes sense and other information.

We do not know for sure whether Perry stayed at Kelly Creek with the children and Hogle's body or went with others to retrieve the bodies. Mort West also wrote about the incident but his version is much less reliable.

Perry's version is as follows:

"It all happened in a flash. Ed happened to be the first one to come in sight of the Indian. He was shot with the last shell from the 32 automatic the Indians had taken from Harry Cambron. The instant the buck shot Ed, he jumped up and started to run down the wash. We were all ready and it looked as though the force of the bullets lifted him off his feet and slammed him face down. In the volley that was fired at the Indian, also killed the two squaws. The battle was now over. The young squaw Snake, threw herself on the ground with the little girl and the papoose. Wailing and sounded like she was crying, but we didn't see any tears. A kind of death song we guessed. The little boy had run down the wash trying to get away, but was soon overtaken by Jack Ferguson. He fought like a little demon. Jack put him in the saddle, and got on behind. He scratched and bit Jack's hands trying to hold him. When Jack returned with the kid this face was all bloody. When I asked what he had been doing to the poor little fellow, Jack said that the kid tried to beat his brains out on the horn of the saddle, but he also told me afterwards that he slapped him in the face.

A messenger was dispatched to Kelly Creek Ranch about six miles from where we were, to get a team and spring wagon to haul Ed Hogle and our captive youngsters in for the night. We all felt so bad about Ed getting killed after it was practically over.

The morning leaving Golconda, Ed was riding a little buckskin horse, we were trotting along when Ed's saddle turned. He got skinned up a little and he remarked "I guess I'll get mine today, I'm getting a damed good start."

The team and wagon arrived just about dark. We loaded up and started for the ranch. We were riding along behind the wagon, 'twas a mournful ride. Snake and the kids wailing their monotonous tune. After arriving at the ranch we placed Ed Hogle's body in one of the rooms at the ranch house. There was a large room with a fireplace. We placed some bedding down on the floor by the fire for the squaw and children.

As the telephone was closed for the night at Golconda, we could not telephone any news of the battle to the outside. Ed Hogle's death, or the capture of the young Indians until next morning.

There was a shoshone buckaroo at Kelly Creek Ranch. Captain Donnelly asked him to try and talk to the young squaw, Snake. Some one had just brought her in a tin plate to eat, some milk for the young children. This buckaroo started to talk to her, she threw the plate, food and all at him. She thought him a traitor, that he was probably in the battle against them. The next day she confessed to several crimes her band had committed. Probably more before her time. Mike and his band killed a young fellow near Tuscarora a year or so before. This boy was killed and Mike got away with the horses. A small posse was organized and a running skirmish, but no justice was done".

It is almost certain that the Indian boy that broke from cover when Hogle was killed was shot in the back, unarmed and was no more than ten years old. One photo of the Indians in a pile illustrates a child with a portion of his head missing as result of a rifle bullet.

The ten posse members there were indiscriminately firing away at every Indian regardless of age or gender.

Perry didn't think the young girl was truly crying and shedding tears. How callous is that? Her family shot to pieces all around her, only three very small children left alive and she wasn't crying!

The little boy trying to escape down the wash and biting and kicking is truly understandable. What else is there to do but fight for your life? If the boy was fighting and biting Ferguson, in Ferguson's way of thinking the boy was more akin to being an animal than a human being, he would not have hesitated to slam the boy's face into the saddle horn.

Perry states: *riding behind the wagon with the children crying was a mournful site.*

That was probably true and could be expected under these horrific circumstances?

The claim, by the posse, that a Shoshone buckaroo at the Kelly Creek Ranch got a confession from the fifteen year old Indian girl in her state of mind is absurd and a total fabrication.

C. H. Asbury from the Carson Indian School at Stewart, Nevada reported no such response from the young girl when he interviewed her April 27, 1911 at the jail in Reno, Nevada. He had sent in an Indian lady to get acquainted with the girl before he went in to interview her through the interpreter. Asbury spent a good part of the day there in the interview with Henny, the Indian girl. Her name was not Snake.

Report to Commissioner of Indian Affairs from C. H. Asbury April 27, 1911 - National Archives W. D. C.

I will discuss this supposed confession, the purpose of this story, and it's ramifications later.

Perry's understanding of what took place when a young man was killed by Indians near Tuscarora, Nevada was totally wrong. The same as the rest of the confession reported by the Donnelley posse.

This statement was made for the same purpose as the story of the confession, to help justify the killing of unarmed Indians including women and children.

After reading and analyzing every document I could find which included numerous newspaper articles, short stories and books, I can actually say, without reservation that Perry was speaking for and reflecting the mind set of the the Surprise Valley members of the posse. The state police and the men from Paradise Valley, Byrnes and Prussia, were taken in by the Surprise Valley bunch. Even though they did show a little more professionalism, however very little.

Removal and stacking of the bodies before the coroner arrived certainly compromised the scene of the killing, destroying evidence that might have told what actually took place there the day before.

Photographs were taken of the bodies when the coroner arrived.

This may not have been by accident but a necessary thing to do in order to set the stage for the explanation as to why the women and children were killed and no fire arms were actually in the hands of the Indians at the lower site.

The whole day there allowed time for the development of the story that they were all supposed to remember. However they had evidently forgotten the script as the

282

testimony at the inquest of Hogle on March 1st and the Indians on March 3rd and 4th was so distorted and contradictory that facts were left out or changed to fit the story they wanted told.

Inquests - Hogle March 1 and Indians March 3 & 4

By December of 1911 animals had gotten into the common grave of the Daggett family and scattered body parts around the area.

For many years afterwards different ones dug into the site collecting bones and basically grave robbing. From historical records available it appears most of the remains were removed around 1919. Much of that material was sent to the National Museum of Natural History by William Kent who as part of the Kent family, who owned ranches in the area known as the Golconda Cattle Co.

[In 1992 an Inventory and Assessment of Native American Remains was made by the National Museum of Natural History. This assessment and inventory identified the remains of ten individuals from the Shoshone Mike burial site.

The partial remains of two of the individuals, supposedly from the Shoshone Mike site, were identified as being from children ages four to six years old. There were no children of this age group killed at Rabbit Creek. In addition none of the remains included the remains of a sixty five year old male (Shoshone) Mike Daggett.

Inventory and assessment of Native American Human Remains - Western Great Basin, Nevada Sector July 1, 1992
Repatriation Office - National Museum of Natural History - NHB MRC 138 - Smithsonian Institution - WDC - 20560

The Shoshone Mike material had to have been contaminated with remains from other sites.

These remains were a part of a large collection of remains from the Great Basin.

It appears those remains were released to Corbin Harney, (a Shoshone traditional healer and spiritual leader), from the Duck Valley Indian Reservation. (maybe)

THE NATURE WAY By Corbin Harney as told to and edited by Alex Goldtooth 2009

In criticizing Mort West and Frank Perry, I am fully aware that had they not written their versions of this tragic incident we would all know less about what actually took place at Rabbit Creek.

Mike had made it through 1900 to 1910 and should now be safe from the predatory white man but that was not be, he now lay dead at the hands of the white man.

Humboldt County Museum

THE DAGGETTS in DEATH

Feb. 28, 1911

Eight members of the Daggett family piled up as so many animal carcasses, no respect given them as human beings.

The Nevada State Police and their Surprise Valley Posse, piled these bodies here on Feb 27, 1911.

The pile of bodies included women and children.

They were the grandfather, Mike, the grandmother Maggie, three adult sons, two adolescent sons, and their daughter, (mother of three of the small children, who were taken as "captives"). She may have also been the mother of the ten year old boy, also killed and in this pile of humanity. The grandfather can be seen on top of the pile. In the foreground is the face of one of the adult sons and parts of various others protruding from under the pile.

284

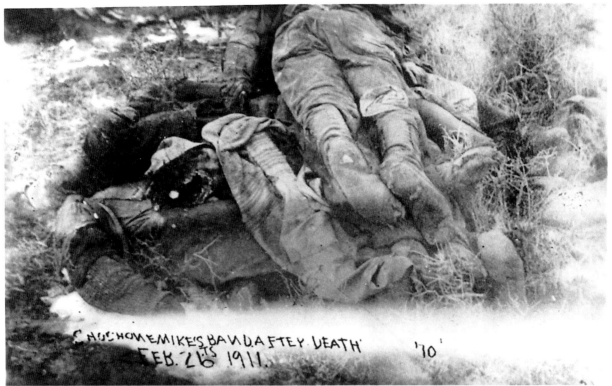

THE DAGGETTS in DEATH - II

Feb. 28, 1911

The Daggett family gathered in a pile for burial in a common, shallow grave, blown in the frozen earth with dynamite.

Mike on top of the pile then to the left of center, probably the ten year old boy and under him can be seen the mother of the smaller children, with a strap over her shoulder that supported the cradle board.

On Feb. 28th, James Buckley, Humboldt County Coroner and E. J. Lying, Constable at Golconda, Nevada, were on the scene and either took these pictures or knew who did

It appears that whoever took this picture pulled the blanket back to show the face of young boy with part of his head shot away. This kind of damage to the head of a young boy / girl would be typical of a gunshot from behind. The posse members at the scene, stated in testimony and in other interviews that they shot the one Indian in the back as he ran down the wash. They shot this Indian believing he had shot Ed Hogle.

Posse members testified that they heard a shot but no one actually saw the Indian shoot Ed Hogle, only at that moment he broke from cover and ran down the wash.

285

Golconda, Nev.
Dec. 20, 1911

(file)

Dept. of Indian Affairs
Washington, D.C.

I wish to protest
against the manner in which
Indian Mike and his family
were buried, when they were killed
near Kelly Creek last February.
The bodies eight in number were
placed in a shallow grave, covered
with a piece of canvas, a few loose
boards, and a couple of feet of
dirt.

Visiting the said grave a few
days ago I met with a ghastly
sight. Coyotes had entered the
grave; and strewn around the
mouth of the hole were human
bones, hair and pieces of clothing

FILED BY H. M/V.

Should such conditions be allowed
to exist in a civilized country?
Trusting that the proper authorities
will be notified, and that something
will be done to overcome this
condition of affairs, I am,

Very truly yours,
Geo. Paul Kettlewell
Calistoga,
Napa, Co.
Calif.

287

Photo by George Paul Kettlewell

COMMON GRAVE OF THE DAGGETT FAMILY

December 1911

On February 28, 1911 a large, common, grave was excavated with dynamite at this site and eight members of the Daggett family piled in together. Besides being a barbaric attempt at burial the grave was too shallow for adequate burial. The bodies were (covered with a piece of canvas, a few boards and a couple feet of dirt). Animals dug into the grave, scattered about the area body parts and other material from the site. The site was dug into by human-beings many times over the years until very few bones or other material remained. A number of bone fragments were sent to the Smithsonian Institute of National History in Washington D. C. Those bones represented ten individuals. Since only eight individuals were buried there the collection was contaminated with other body parts. In addition none of the bones were from an individual near sixty five years of age therefore (Shoshone) Mike Daggett's remains were not part of the collection.

SHOSHONE MIKE
and his
BAND OF MARAUDERS

This grave marker was placed at the common grave site of eight members of the Daggett family some time after December 1911.

The marker speaks for itself, showing the disrespect and inaccuracy expressed by those who erected it.

Mike's band were not marauders they had gotten into trouble when three of his sons returned to Cow Creek to avenge the killing of their brother by the Tranmer gang.

They were not marauding when they were cornered in Little High Rock Canyon and the Daggett boys ended up killing the four sheepmen. They knew no other way out.

This marker was placed with Humboldt County Museum by Les Sweeney in May of 2011.

JACK MURDOCK & ROBERT AMESBURY

June 24, 1978

Jack Murdock & Robert Amesbury, with the help of others, replaced the old grave marker of (Shoshone) Mike Daggett and seven of his family with wording they thought more appropriate, on a new marker, June 24, 1978.

The original marker,lower left, weathered and barely legible, read:

SHOSHONE MIKE and his BAND of MARAUDERS

The grave site is located on mining property 3 miles northeast of the Getchell Mine. Situated on the ridge, a few yards above, lies a one ton stone marker placed there in Nov. 2006, by boy scouts from Sparks, Nev. On this stone is attached a brass plate listing the names of those killed here, February 26, 1911. The original marker was placed with the Humboldt County Museum / Historical Society by Les & Cheri Sweeney in May of 2011.

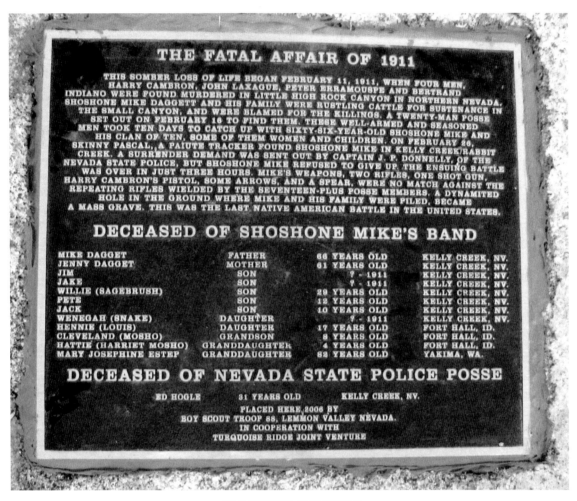

THE FATAL AFFAIR OF 1911

THIS SOMBER LOSS OF LIFE BEGAN FEBRUARY 11, 1911, WHEN FOUR MEN, HARRY CAMBRON, JOHN LAXAGUE, PETER ERRAMOUSPE AND BERTRAND INDIANO WERE FOUND MURDERED IN LITTLE HIGH ROCK CANYON IN NORTHERN NEVADA. SHOSHONE MIKE DAGGETT AND HIS FAMILY WERE RUSTLING CATTLE FOR SUSTENANCE IN THE SMALL CANYON, AND WERE BLAMED FOR THE KILLINGS. A TWENTY-MAN POSSE SET OUT ON FEBRUARY 16 TO FIND THEM. THESE WELL-ARMED AND SEASONED MEN TOOK TEN DAYS TO CATCH UP WITH SIXTY-SIX-YEAR-OLD SHOSHONE MIKE AND HIS CLAN OF TEN, SOME OF THEM WOMEN AND CHILDREN. ON FEBRUARY 26, SKINNY PASCAL, A PAIUTE TRACKER FOUND SHOSHONE MIKE IN KELLY CREEK/RABBIT CREEK. A SURRENDER DEMAND WAS SENT OUT BY CAPTAIN J. P. DONNELLY, OF THE NEVADA STATE POLICE, BUT SHOSHONE MIKE REFUSED TO GIVE UP. THE ENSUING BATTLE WAS OVER IN JUST THREE HOURS. MIKE'S WEAPONS, TWO RIFLES, ONE SHOT GUN, HARRY CAMBRON'S PISTOL, SOME ARROWS, AND A SPEAR, WERE NO MATCH AGAINST THE REPEATING RIFLES WIELDED BY THE SEVENTEEN-PLUS POSSE MEMBERS. A DYNAMITED HOLE IN THE GROUND WHERE MIKE AND HIS FAMILY WERE PILED, BECAME A MASS GRAVE. THIS WAS THE LAST NATIVE AMERICAN BATTLE IN THE UNITED STATES.

DECEASED OF SHOSHONE MIKE'S BAND

MIKE DAGGET	FATHER	66 YEARS OLD	KELLY CREEK, NV.
JENNY DAGGET	MOTHER	61 YEARS OLD	KELLY CREEK, NV.
JIM	SON	? - 1911	KELLY CREEK, NV.
JAKE	SON	? - 1911	KELLY CREEK, NV.
WILLIE (SAGEBRUSH)	SON	29 YEARS OLD	KELLY CREEK, NV.
PETE	SON	12 YEARS OLD	KELLY CREEK, NV.
JACK	SON	10 YEARS OLD	KELLY CREEK, NV.
WENEGAH (SNAKE)	DAUGHTER	? - 1911	KELLY CREEK, NV.
HENNIE (LOUIS)	DAUGHTER	17 YEARS OLD	FORT HALL, ID.
CLEVELAND (MOSHO)	GRANDSON	8 YEARS OLD	FORT HALL, ID.
HATTIE (HARRIET MOSHO)	GRANDDAUGHTER	4 YEARS OLD	FORT HALL, ID.
MARY JOSEPHINE ESTEP	GRANDDAUGHTER	82 YEARS OLD	YAKIMA, WA.

DECEASED OF NEVADA STATE POLICE POSSE

ED HOGLE	31 YEARS OLD	KELLY CREEK, NV.

PLACED HERE, 2006 BY
BOY SCOUT TROOP 88, LEMMON VALLEY NEVADA.
IN COOPERATION WITH
TURQUOISE RIDGE JOINT VENTURE

RABBIT CREEK

November 18, 2006

Plaque placed here November 18, 2006

Further research after plaque was installed discovered that Jenny Daggett's name was not Jenny but Maggie.

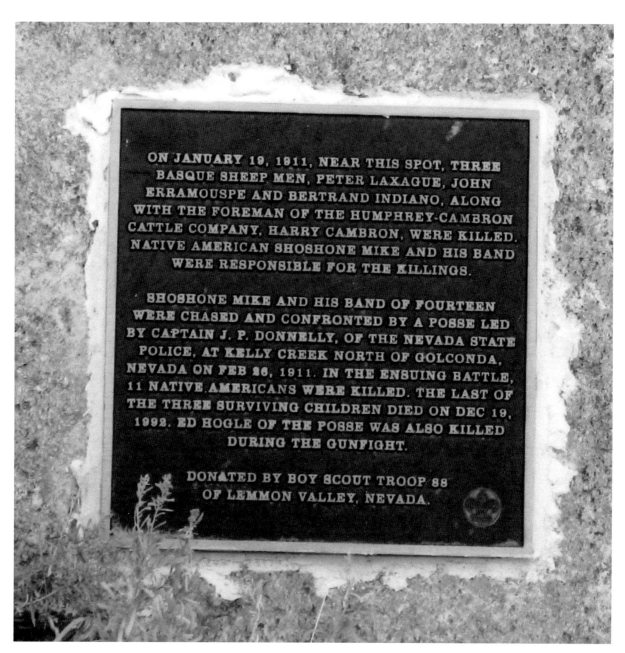

ON JANUARY 19, 1911, NEAR THIS SPOT, THREE BASQUE SHEEP MEN, PETER LAXAGUE, JOHN ERRAMOUSPE AND BERTRAND INDIANO, ALONG WITH THE FOREMAN OF THE HUMPHREY-CAMBRON CATTLE COMPANY, HARRY CAMBRON, WERE KILLED. NATIVE AMERICAN SHOSHONE MIKE AND HIS BAND WERE RESPONSIBLE FOR THE KILLINGS.

SHOSHONE MIKE AND HIS BAND OF FOURTEEN WERE CHASED AND CONFRONTED BY A POSSE LED BY CAPTAIN J. P. DONNELLY, OF THE NEVADA STATE POLICE, AT KELLY CREEK NORTH OF GOLCONDA, NEVADA ON FEB 26, 1911. IN THE ENSUING BATTLE, 11 NATIVE AMERICANS WERE KILLED. THE LAST OF THE THREE SURVIVING CHILDREN DIED ON DEC 19, 1992. ED HOGLE OF THE POSSE WAS ALSO KILLED DURING THE GUNFIGHT.

DONATED BY BOY SCOUT TROOP 88 OF LEMMON VALLEY, NEVADA.

LITTLE HIGH ROCK CANYON
September 2008

Plaque placed here April 16, 2005.

INFORMATION SIGN

Photo date unknown ?

This information sign was attached to the rock face here in Little High Rock Canyon by troop #53 in 1970. Removed in 2002 or before.

Another information sign (same subject) placed here (same location) by Troop # 48, from Cederville, California, in 2002.

It is unclear as to why the 2002 sign was placed here. Was it to replace the 1970 sign because it was torn down at some earlier date or in deteriorated condition and needed replacing The 2002 sign was here in May of 2004 however gone April 16, 2005.

Amesbury

MIKE'S HEADDRESS

ca 1975

Looted by members of Donnelley's posse.

CHAPTER III

KELLY CREEK TO GOLCONDA

February 28, 1911

What transpired on February the 28th is no less confusing.

On the morning of the 28th Capt. Donnelley's posse loaded the body of Ed Hogle in one wagon, the four children in another and began the journey to Golconda, Nevada. The posse escorted these two spring wagons to Golconda where upon their arrival the children, referred to as Indian captives, were caged in the Golconda jail.

However, the best information available indicates that the coroner Buckley and Constable Lying came out to inspect the carnage and at their direction had men proceed with the burial of eight members of the Daggett family that are now deceased and stacked in a pile.

The two photos of the Daggett family, bodies unceremoniously stacked one on top of the other, were probably taken by either Golconda Constable E. J. Lying or Humboldt County Coroner James Buckley.

There is little reliable information regarding who or how the men (Coroner Buckley, Constable Lying and whoever was sent out to bury the bodies) from Golconda arrived at Kelly Creek and/or the site where the Indians were killed. As stated above the best information and speculation indicates Coroner Buckley and Constable Lying arrived there in a spring wagon and returned to Golconda with the body of Ed Hogle along with Capt. Donnelley who was transporting the four children in the same wagon he had started out with from Golconda or Willow Point. It is not clear whether he had acquired the wagon,at Willow Point, on the 26th or the day before at Golconda.

One of the wagons is believed to be at Midas, Nevada today as part of their antique collection and had at one time belonged to the Hammonds. This may have been a wagon that they retrieved from Kelly Creek.

How can you hold your head up with any kind of pride or dignity, when arriving in Golconda with three small children and a teenage girl as captives? It would seem to be an embarrassment to come marching into town with their small subjects while the many onlookers, gathered along the street, are expecting to witness brave Indian fighters to have strong brave warriors as captives. It is obvious these so called brave Indian fighters have killed mothers of children in order to have children as captives.

They have left eight dead behind that included women and children. Six of the eight were unarmed when killed but to save face they had reported the story, a day earlier, that told of a three hour running battle with fierce Indians. They had also reported that the young squaw had confessed to many crimes and they had the body of Ed Hogle so how could they not be brave Indian fighters? (Thank God for Ed Hogle)

#4 Posse entering Golconda Page 12

Hogle saves the day not only saves the day from total embarrassment, but now he is their ticket to justifiable homicide rather than murder. (Thank God for Ed Hogle)

Relating the story must now go forward with this dangerous mission they had to accomplish as the focus for justification for their actions.

#1 & 2 Citizens of Golconda waiting on the posse to arrive with Indian captives - Page 13

Lying, however distasteful, has to be the order of the day and carried through testimony at inquest.

It is hard to believe the posse members had to resort to lying and distorting of the facts, but they did playing the role of heroic Indians fighters to the hilt. The justification, it saves their dignity and possible prosecution for murder, at all cost.

After arriving at Golconda members of the posse repeated the story that had been passed on, by wire, from the Norths Ranch on the 27th of fifteen year old Henny confessing to several killings and robberies that her family had committed over the past year.

No one who testified at the inquest hearings, testified nor mentioned such a confession at those hearings. The story was picked up by the newspapers from posse members unofficially relating the story to help in their defense for killing Indians. It worked with the help of the body of Hogle and years later repeated in the writings of Perry and West stating that the fifteen year old confessed to those crimes and many others. This was a total fabrication by the so called posse!

This fabricated confession helped to justify the killing of the women and children.

296

If her confession was so accurate and compelling then why was it that the Shoshone buckaroo who was alleged to be the interpreter for the young girl at the Kelly Creek Ranch was not asked to testify at the inquest hearings?

Answer, because there was no reliable confession by the young girl!!

The fact that the eight members of the family did not live to tell the story and neither Pascal nor the young girl were asked to testify made it convenient for posse members. They can now dream up, fabricate, lie and tell all kinds of stories.

Everyone bought their story. The newspapers exaggerated and embellished the story and they sold the story that the fifteen year old girl had confessed to all kinds of killings. The stories worked so well that the posse members soon began to believe it themselves.

While the children were caged like animals in the Golconda jail the brave heroes of the Last Indian Battle proceeded to loot and steal all the family possessions.

The HUMBOLDT STAR March 1, 1911, reported the event of Feb. 28 as follows:

POSSE BRINGS IN INDIAN PRISONERS
THE BODY OF COMRADE AND TROPHIES

Bringing with them their dead and the prisoners captured in Sunday's bloody battle, which resulted in the practical extermination of Shoshone Mike's band of renegades and murderers, the victorious posse arrived in Golconda shortly after 3 o'clock yesterday afternoon after traveling since early morning from the Kelley Creek ranch, six miles from the scene of the fight.

Golconda was crowded with throngs of the curious, its own population being largely augmented by people from Winnemucca and neighboring places, most of whom expected that the bodies of the Indians were to be brought into Golconda for the inquest. But in this they were disappointed, as Coroner Buckley, who went out with Constable Lying to the battlefield Monday, decided to have the Indian bodies buried there. Accordingly the bodies were all piled in a heap at the place where the last stand was made and Coroner Buckley arranged with two men to go out from Golconda and dig one large grave in which to bury all the bodies. The ground being frozen to considerable depth, the men took along a case of dynamite to use in making the excavation.

The four prisoners, in charge of two members of the State Police and the Eagleville posse, were first to arrive in Golconda. The Indian girl , her baby sister in arms and two brothers, one about seven and the other nine years of age, were placed in Golconda's little box like jail, where the girl shrank into a corner, covering her face with a blanket to evade the gazing of the curios crowd. Indian women were permitted to enter the jail to care for the little prisoners, and of one of the women the girl asked for a pair of scissors in order that she might cut off her long jet-black hair, saying that she must do this to carry out the tribal custom of morning for her dead. This request was refused, for fear that the girl might try to kill herself and possibly her brothers and sisters as well.

Shortly after the posse and prisoners arrived, Captain Donnelly, Corner Buckley and Constable Lying reached Golconda in a spring wagon with the body of Ed Hogle, the only white victim of the battle. The body was wrapped in a bed canvas, clothed as when he fell, chaps and all, and beside the remains lay one of the Indian war drums whose staccato sound had encouraged the two Shoshone bucks to fanatical desperation in Sunday's battle and the long spear with which the young girl fought desperately before she was finally captured and disarmed. The drum and spear are part of the trophies of the battle which the Eagleville boys will take back with them.

Indian Girl Confesses

For several hours after being taken to the Kelley Creek ranch Sunday evening, the girl prisoner refused to talk even to a Shoshone Indian who was used as an interpreter in trying to get her to tell her story. She berated this Indian for not having come to the aid of her people, so they could have killed more of the white men. The next morning the efforts to induce the girl to talk were renewed and she finally made a complete confession of the crimes that had been laid at the door of her father's band as well as other murders committed by them of which nothing has been known. She admitted that they had killed Frank Dopp in Elko county last May and murdered the four sheepmen in Little High Rock Canyon. She said that one of the men (Indiana) had seen them butchering cattle the day before and that when he came back to the place with three other men the next day they believed that a party of officers was coming to arrest them and her father and older brothers hid in the rocks and shot the four white men to death. The girl also told of the killing of a Chinaman somewhere near the California line and before they killed the sheepmen. She said they killed the Chinaman for money, but they found only four dollars on him. The murder of the Chinaman is verified by finding of his queue among the effects of the Indians in their camp where Sunday's battle commenced.

The Indian girl's confession is important because it removes any possible doubt that might have existed of Shoshone Mike's band being the ones who killed the sheepmen and for which crime they were being hunted down. The evidence of their guilt was practically conclusive from the finding of three of the murdered men's horses at the camp where the battle was fought, the identification of the automatic pistol as one which taken from Cambron's body and clinching fact that Cambron's watch and check books were found on Shoshone Mike's body.

The first two paragraphs of the above newspaper article pretty well articulate the mind set of the citizens of Humboldt County, their mood, prejudices and willingness, without any scrutiny, to accept the story the posse members are putting forth.

In the third paragraph the age of the children and who they are is incorrect, they are the fifteen year old girl, six year old boy, four year old girl and Baby Mosho, ten months of age. These children are not the girl's sister and brothers but nephew and nieces. This is one of many inaccuracies printed in the newspapers which puts into question the reliability of the reporting of other parts of the story where the facts are not known.

The fourth paragraph of the article reads in one place *"Indian war drum's staccato sound had encouraged the two Shoshone bucks to fanatical desperation in Sunday's battle".*

The Indians were in desperation mode. They were traveling in silence and hiding out so why would they cause the echo of a drum to vibrate through the mountains? They were trying to avoid being killed and did not have time to drum up the good spirits and drive away the bad nor did they have time or the opportunity to beat on a drum, shoot guns and bows and arrows all at the same time. The drum was not a **war** drum and it is highly unlikely the Indians were beating on a drum at any time, during their trip from Little High Rock.

In addition if any one of the Indians was beating on the drum then he or she weren't armed with any kind of a weapon. So again, why were they killed?

Under that part of the article labeled ***"Indian Girl Confesses"*** is the extended text that is nothing short of preposterous. This fifteen year old girl has been on the run with her family for nearly a year, living and surviving in extremely harsh conditions to avoid capture and being killed. Then her mother, father, sister and brothers are shot to pieces all around her. Then she is taken to a strange place by seventeen men armed with rifles and where she does not know whether she and the other three small children may also be killed. She has no friends or relatives, no one, to turn to. And now she confesses to all that is laid out in this news article and it is supposed to prove all the atrocities that have been laid on her family?

Two of Mike's boys did kill Frank Dopp on Gollaher Mountain back in April of 1910 but there were extenuating circumstances that few people understood. The horse runners on Gollaher Mountain had first killed their brother.

The family had two rifles and the Indians did kill the sheepmen at Little High Rock.

Two of Mike's boys shot down the the sheepmen and a third picked up Cambron's pistol shooting two of the sheepmen in the head. There is little doubt that these three were the same Indians that killed the Dopp boy back at Gohllar Mountain. The women and children that died at Rabbit Creek did not kill anyone.

When this confession is coupled with the story put forth by the posse, that Ed Hogle was killed by the Indians, which also was believed by most every one then and now, it illustrates how the Donnelley posse got away with murdering the Daggett family with no consequences. In fact they became the last heroes of the Indian wars and very few people ever suspected or knew the difference.

At the time of Ed Hogle's death, Ed had a mother, now widowed in Anderson, California, a younger brother, Robert, working in the mines in that part of California and an older brother, Charles, in San Quentin Prison for armed robbery. Later however, Charles Hogle wound up attending Stanford University, possibly graduating from there and became a contractor in southern California in the Monterey area where he finally passed away, and at the time of his death was thought to be very well to do.

The inquests into the killing of Ed Hogle and the Indians began on the 1st day of March and concluded on March 5, 1911.

The one factor that may have entered into the equation that caused the posse members to act so brutally and callously was the possibility they were so dramatized and desensitized after retrieving the bodies from Little High Rock Canyon that it played a major part in their senseless action at Rabbit Creek.

Photographs that are numbered and include the numbers 1 through 16 were donated to the National Guard Armory of Winnemucca, Nevada August 19, 1938.

They were donated and narrated by Mrs. J. R. Starkey. Mrs. Starkey is the sister of Mrs. J. B. Fayant who along with her husband J. R. Fayant owned the Fayant Hotel in Golconda, Nevada in 1911.

301

At the Pinson Ranch near Golconda, Nevada
Feburary 28, 1911

PINSON RANCH - (near Golconda, Nevada)
July 7, 2018

The lift wheel left center, used to lift a beef when butchering, still stands after over one hundred years.

The famous Humboldt County, Nevada sheriff, Silah G. Lamb, was killed here at this ranch on October 6, 1933. Lamb was responding to a domestic violence situation, when he was shot by Glen Hibbs, ex-husband of Camy Pinson.
(This lift wheel has seen a lot of history.)
Sheriff Lamb had joined the Donnelley posse at Jackson Mountain February 21,1911.

#9

From Lft. to Rt. - Cannot recall parties, only Mr. J. A. Langwith of Winn., Nev. with his back turned on right of the horse's head. Bldg. Golconda jail. Captured Indians being placed in Jail. Wagon with men, is wagon that had the Indian boy tied up with ropes as he fought like a demon and would not go into the jail. Coat on this Indian was a coat belonging to one of the murdered sheepmen.

By Mrs J. R. Starkey

The spring wagon appears to be the wagon that brought in the body of Ed Hogle. The Humboldt Star newspaper, March 1, 1911 identified the three men that brought in Hogle's body in a spring wagon as: Captain Donnelly, Coroner Buckley and Constable Lying. I believe they are Donnelley, Modoc County Sheriff Smith and Coroner Buckley.

Text on this photo, taken in Golconda, Nev. Feb, 28, 1911, reads:

"Captured Indians - Feb. 26, 1911"

This wagon brought the four Indian children who survived the killing at Rabbit Creek on February 26th to Golconda from the Kelly Creek Ranch on February 28, 1911.

The men from left. to right are believed to be Jack Ferguson a member of Captain Donnelley's posse, E. J. Lying Constable Golconda, Nevada and unknown.

92 YEARS AGO

in February of 1911, a band of Indians were surprised and massacred by a posse west of Midas where Kelly Creek and Rabbit Creek come together. After the skirmish had ended, this buggy was brought from the Kelly Creek Ranch to transport three surviving female Indians and one fatally wounded posse member to the ranch. For many years, this wagon was at the Jake Creek Ranch before being moved to Midas.

#4 - Posse on horseback waiting and watching for captured Indians (Note riderless horse) on end or right. This riderless horse was Ed Hogle's who was the only white man killed on the posse.

Donnelley Posse Entering Golconda

February 28, 1911

L. to R. - Ben Cambron, Sergeant Charles H. Stone, Mort West, Jack Ferguson, George Holmes, Warren Fruit, Frank Perry, Sergeant P. M. Newgard, (empty saddle possibly Ed Hogle's)

1 & # 2

Humboldt County, Nevada

Museum

#1

On porch roof are:

Left - Mrs. C. C. Wilson,

Right - Mrs. Rosa Ruiz,

Below left - J. B. Fayant,

Bldg. - Fayant Hotel

All were waiting to see posse come in after the battle.

By Mrs. J. R. Starkey

#2

On porch (Fayants Cottage) opposite Golconda jail, residents of Golconda, Nev. watching for the posse to deliver captured indians to jail.

From left to right on railing (who could be recalled):

1st - Mamie Manning (half breed Indian) who is sister to Guy Manning of Duck Valley Indian Reservation.

2n- Mrs. Rosa Ruiz

3rd - Jim Carter

4th - Mrs C. C. Wilson

5th - Mrs J. B. Fayant

6th - Mr Sherman Berlin,

Others I am unable to recall.

By Mrs. J. R. Starkey

#10

Mr Carrigan (formally of Rineharts store at Golconda, Nev.) with face forward. Next Captain Mc Donald of the posse dragging Indian boy into jail. This Indian boy was Indian Mike's son.

By Mrs. J. R. Starkey

This is Sergeant Stone of the Nev. State Police not (Mc Donald) Captain Donnelley of the State Police. The boy is not Mike's son. He is Mike's grandson.

309

#7

Constable, Mr. Lying of Golconda, Nev. in 1911 taking captured squaw back to jail

after she was given a bath. Small bldg. in foreground is the Golconda jail.

By Mrs. J. R. Starkey

310

#8

Front of jail (open door) man in front is Mr Fergerson (posse man).
Next Mrs C. C. Wilson
Man in back is Mr. Ed Dame of Golconda, Nev.
Next Mrs. J. B. Fayant with back turned examining the filthy cloths of captured Indians.

By Mrs. J. R. Starkey

#11

Indian woman with papoose on her back and little Indian girl 2 and one half years old being taken out for a walk by Constable Lying who can be seen in front of the Indian woman.

By Mrs. J. R. Starkey

The age of these three children: Henny - fifteen years Hattie, four years, Baby Mosh 10months.They were headed to the out house. No toilet facilities in the jail.

#12

Mamie Manning (half breed Indian) with back turned and Indian boy (Indian Mike's son) being taken into cottage for a bath. All these captured Indians were filthy and loaded with vermin. This Indian boy is the boy who was tied with ropes and wearing the coat of one of the murdered sheepmen.

By Mrs. J.R. Starkey

The Indian boy is Mike's grandson.

312

#13

This is Mr. Fergerson (posse man) carrying Indian baby about one year old. Squaw in back of Mr. Fergerson is mother of baby, hiding as she did not want her picture taken. They were being taken for a walk after their baths.

By Mrs. J. R. Starkey

This child is Hattie four year old niece of the girl in back of Ferguson. This may not be Ferguson.

#14

This is Mr. Fergerson (posse man) carrying Indian baby back to jail. Squaw in back of Mr. Fergerson, Ed Lying (Constable of Golconda, Nev.) in back ground.

By Mrs. J. R. Starkey

Indian baby is four year old Hattie. Squaw is fifteen year old Henie. This man may not be Ferguson.

CHAPTER IV
ALONE NOW

Following the carnage at Rabbit Creek the children found themselves alone and orphaned, first among the bodies of there family then where ever they were taken and incarcerated.

As the last of the family, two adult sons, two adolescent sons, mother and grandmother were slaughtered and, literally, shot down around them, the children found themselves alone now among the bodies of the family all shot to pieces by the northern California and Nevada <u>vigilante</u> posse. The oldest being a 15 year old girl clinging to her dying mother, the six year old boy in shear terror knowing he was to be next, the 4 year old frightened to death, standing among the carnage, totally confused and Baby Mosho face down, in the bottom of the wash, under the weight of her dead mother. According to one news article one of the posse rolled the mother over so the baby could breathe. Baby Mosho pulled from her dead mother's back, the four year old frightened and confused, the six year old boy bloodied from Ferguson slamming his face into the saddled horn and the young girl hog tied, are loaded into a wagon and hauled from the killing scene to the Kelly Creek Ranch.

Baby Mosho, breast fed until now will undergo huge changes in her life all because of the senseless killing of her mother on that bloody Sunday of February 26, 1911.

What these defenseless children must endure now no human being should have to experience let alone children.

The four surviving children are alone now and are caged like animals in the Golconda jail, all the family they have ever known lay dead back there at Rabbit Creek. There are no other relatives that can be found, no friends no one they even know.

Locked behind bars in the Golconda jail they are subject to the gaze of the curious who can stare at them like visiting a zoo where strange animals are kept in captivity.

Though the children may have been a little dirty and infested with a few bugs the likes of which might be identified as fleas or lice, they were otherwise in good condition and healthy. It was quite a feat in itself for the family to have kept the children in good health during the past ten months as this family of Indians trekked across the barren, dissolute and uninhabited back country of Idaho, Nevada, into California and then back into Nevada. They had made this journey through all kinds of weather conditions, winter and summer, good weather and bad without shelter other than a few blankets and a canvas tarp.

Through all the extreme hardships and stress the Daggett family experienced, they never wavered in their support of each other. They stuck it out together from April 1910, at Cow Creek until February 26, 1911, at Rabbit Creek, nearly 1,000 mile journey, over an extreme land scape in extreme summer and winter conditions, even in death.

The revenge killing of the sixteen year old horse wrangler back on Gollaher Mountain last April by two of Mike's sons was that death sentence, no matter that the Tranmer gang had killed another of Mikes sons earlier that day. That did not matter in the white man's world.

The Daggetts had to have known that the killing of the Dopp boy at Gollaher Mountain spelled a death sentence to the family. Though only three sons, at most, were involved in the killing of Dopp, one now dead, the family faced what lie ahead, together. The fear and hate of the white man can only be imagined, as they struggled on for ten months, knowing what the end would be.

In the months and years that followed the killing of the Indian boy, Jake or Charlie we were never quite sure which, was never an issue that came up nor was there any attempt to investigate that killing, after all he was only an Indian.

CHAPTER V

INQUESTS-ED HOGLE & THE EIGHT INDIANS KILLED AT RABBIT CREEK

FEBRUARY 26, 1911

[MARCH 1 THROUGH MARCH 5, 1911]

Held by James Buckley, Coroner of the County of Humboldt, State of Nevada

Oblique words are as they appear in the inquest testimony.

In **BOLD** letters are my comments and analysis on the testimony of each posse member.

Posse members did not want to be held long in Golconda for inquests. Me either if I had just murdered defenseless women and children.

Frank Perry's and Mort West's writings (Perry in 1949 West in 1934)

INQUEST MARCH 1, 1911 - ED HOGLE

Fifteen of the eighteen posse members there testified at the inquest of Ed Hogle. Hogle did not, he was dead; Pascal did not, he was an Indian and may not have testified that he made all those requests for the Daggett family to submit as claimed by the posse members who testified; Prussia from Paradise Valley did not, which would indicate he was not at the scene where Hogle and the women and children were killed. In the case of Ed Hogle the inquest jury that were called on to appear before James Buckley, corner for the County of Humboldt, State of Nevada included the following Jurors:

Wm Polkinghorne, Edward Davie, James G. Stewart, Adrien Bernard, John Chuetuc and Barney Gill.

O. D. VAN NORMAN -

Q. *State all the circumstances surrounding his (Hogle's) death.*

A. *I was within about 100 ft. from him when he was shot. I went up to him and he tried to speak to me but he could not.*

Q. *Was the young squaw captured at that time present when he was killed?*

A. *Yes she was present and in the ditch close by.*

Q. *Go on and state what she did and whether in your opinion she conspired to induce him to get within range of the Indian who killed him?*

Where did this juror, Buckley, get the idea that the 15 year old Indian girl was trying to get Hogle within range to be shot? Ans. He heard it (gossip) or was told this before the hearing. The attempted cover-up begins and the young girl blamed for Ed's death.

A. *She kept getting out of the ditch and kept running up towards our men all the time. My opinion is she conspired to induce Hogle to get within range of the Indian as she kept advancing out of the ditch with an Indian spear so as to attract their attention.*

She kept running up towards our men, not him. She was facing 11 rifles with a four and one half foot staff with a blade on the end to keep them away from her mother, sister and children. Every member of that group had a heavy winter coat, that could have been thrown over the end of that blade and the young girl taken down. She had absolutely nothing to do with the killing of Ed Hogle.

68 years later, in an interview by Jeff Rabin of the Sacramento Bee, Oct. 11, 1979,

O. D. stated: *"killed the whole works except for one squaw and little kids" "We'd a killed them too, but old Capt. Donnelley (of the State Police) he says not to kill that there squaw cause he wants to find out everything"*

Remember, Donnelley was not at the location where the women and children were when they were killed.

O. D. must have thought this one up on his own unless, they were thinking about killing the 15 yr. old girl after she was captured.

He says nothing about hearing a shot. Although being one of the posse members the most distant from Hogle he goes directly up to Hogle when he was shot. If

you accidentally fired a shot and you saw some one go down, what would you do? Go directly to that person hoping you were not the one who shot him?

C. H. STONE -

Q. State all circumstances surrounding the death of Ed Hogle.

A. *Well he was acting with us and attempting to take the Indians that were in this ditch and there was one squaw kept running up out of the ditch with a spear towards the posse and then in back in to the ditch, it is my opinion that she was advising the other Indians in the ditch of our whereabouts. Hogle advanced forward to edge of the ditch, I heard a shot from the ditch then and Hogle put his hand up to his left (breast) ditch and explained something to the effect "My god boys I have been shot"*

Again young girl running up and out of the ditch with a spear. Stone trying to blame her. Note: "he heard a shot from the ditch," also hand up to his left breast. Hogle advancing ahead to the edge of the ditch.

Q. *In your opinion was the squaw using her sex as a shield to protect the buck or bucks so as to enable them to get a clear shot at Hogle by taking up the attention of the posse.*

A. *I think she was not using herself as a mark but carried the idea she could expose herself with impunity and that she was encouraging and advising the men with the guns in the creek.*

Again trying to lay blame on the 15 year old girl. Can you imagine a fifteen year old girl watching her family being slaughtered all around her, using her sex to shield others in her family who are all dead by now except for; one young boy eight to twelve years of age, the grand mother, the mother with the baby in a cradle board on her back, one boy six or seven years old and a toddler about four years old.

What a sick accusation, she was scared to death. There are no guns at that location so Stone has not seen one however he does not know that at this point.

Q. *How old you think that squaw was?*

A. *15 years*

319

Q. *What did she do after the death of Ed Hogle and where did she go.?*

A. *Immediately after the death of Hogle I do not know what became of her.*

Q. *Did you see the Indian that killed Ed Hogle?*

A. *Saw him immediately after.*

Stone did not see the Indian shoot Hogle.

Q. *Was he killed or is he alive still if you know.*

A. *He was killed.*

Q. *How far from the ditch was Hogle when he was shot?*

A. *Within a few feet of the bank of the ditch.*

Q. *Do you think Ed exposed himself unnecessarily?*

A. *I think he was deceived by the Squaws firing arrows into the belief that the occupants of the ditch was out of ammunition.*

Stone saw squaws firing arrows! They would not be firing arrows if they had guns! The Indians were out of ammunition they didn't even have a gun at this location.

Hogle within a few feet of bank of the ditch.

Note: Sergeant Stone was only one at the scene that did not state how far he was from Hogle when Hogle was shot. Could it be Stone shot Hogle and not Van Norman?

P. M. NEWGARD -

Q. *Did you see Ed Hogle killed?*

A. *Yes sir.*

Q. *How far were you from Hogle when he was killed?*

A. *About 20 feet.*

Q. *Did you see the Indian fire the shot that killed him?*

A. *I saw an indistinct person fire the shot.*

What kind of answer is that? He suspected the shot was not from the Indian.

This way he couldn't be caught lying, but insinuating it was an Indian.

Q. *What place was it that Hogle was killed?*

A. *Rabbit Cr. Humboldt County, Nevada*

Q. *State what you know regarding his death.*

A. *We were advancing towards the Indians in a sort of semi-circle and some of the boys told the Indians in the ditch to come out they would not be hurt, they paid no attention to that, there was a young squaw kept running back and forth with a spear in her hand, and some of the boys would try to get hold of her, finally Ed Hogle advanced about 10 feet ahead of the balance and there was a shot from the ditch and he put his hand to his breast and started back.*

If the semicircle ends were pointed toward the ditch and OD Van Norman was 30 or 40 yards beyond Hogle on the end of the semi-circle he would be looking back on Hogle, who had advanced ahead, 10 feet. O. D's rifle would be pointed at Hogle. He was also in a position to cut off any means of escape, down the draw, by the Indians. If Hogle was turned slightly towards OD and OD unintentionally, touched off a round Hogle would be in the line of fire and easily shot by OD. They were all very close to the edge of the wash.

Note: Boys told Indians in the ditch to come out and they would not be hurt. Squaw running back and forth with a spear. Boys tried to get hold of her. Didn't try very hard but then again that would put them out in front of 10 rifles.

Also "there was a shot from the ditch" Newgard did not say he saw an Indian shoot from the ditch!

Q. *Did you see the young squaw retreat from him and lead him on to where the Indian was who killed him?*

A. *I do not think she led Ed on in particular or single him out but think her main object was to lead anyone of the posse in that vicinity on towards the ditch where the Indians were.*

This juror can't get over trying to implicate the 15 year old girl in the killing of Hogle. And Newgard is having a hard time helping in that effort.

Q. *Was the Indian who killed him afterwards killed by your men or is he still alive as far as you know?*

A. *He was killed.*

Q. *Was the Squaw that was captured the one that was acting conspicuously before Ed?*

A. *Yes.*

321

JOE REEDER -

Q. *Did you see Ed Hogle killed?*

A. *I did*

Q. *How far from him was you when he was killed?*

A. *About 50 feet.*

Q. *Did you see the Indian fire the shot that killed him?*

A. *I heard the shot fired but did not see the shot fired.*

Note: heard the shot did not see it fired.

Q. *State what the circumstances were regarding his death.*

A. *We were crowding in on those Indians they being in the sage brush in the wash there were 2 squaws in the wash shooting at us with bows and arrows, Ed Hogle fired 2 shots in to the brush where the bucks were and he was dodging arrows from these squaws I heard a shot fired and Hogle put up his hand to his left breast and started back saying "for gods sake boys get back" Henry I am shot and there was some shots fired into that brush and that buck started down the creek and was killed right there, the old squaw was also killed in that shooting.*

"Two squaws in the wash shooting arrows. Ed fired 2 shots into the brush while dodging arrows. Buck started running _down_ the creek and was killed right there. Old squaw killed in this shooting".

The two adult Indians were dead in the wash 30 to 40 yards up the wash from the women and the two young boys were dead in between. Therefore if they were shooting at a buck in the wash and killed the woman, they were shooting at the young boy running down the wash. In fact they shot him in the back of the head. Is this how the boys told the Indians to come out and they would not be hurt? Firing into the brush?

Ed put his hand up to his left breast.

Q. *Did you see the young squaw retreat from Hogle and lead him on to where he was killed by the Indian?*

A. *No the old squaw was the one that was conspicuous before Hogle, the young squaw was front of me shooting arrows at me at time Hogle was shot.*

322

Posse members are getting confused, hard time remembering what the story was. Young squaw, old squaw, there were three; grandmother, mother with the baby on her back, fifteen year old girl. Who is he talking about, grandmother & mother with baby on here back, shooting arrows? The young girl had a spear.

Q. *Do you think Hogle exposed himself unnecessarily in this fight.*

A. *No don't think so, but think he exposed his body more than the others did in that vicinity.*

HENRY HUGHES -

Q. *In what capacity were you acting*

A. *With the posse hunting Indians*

Q. *State all the circumstances you can surrounding the death of Hogle.*

A. *I was some 20 feet from Hogle just preceding his death, the Indians were in the wash we advanced up Hogle was in the lead a little there was an old squaw in the wash shooting arrows at him and he dodged some of them and fired a couple of shot at them with his rifle and there was a shot from the wash and he says " my god Henry I am shot" get back boys and then walked back a few steps and fell.*

Hogle was in the lead and the old squaw (grandmother?) in the wash was shooting arrows at him (not shooting a pistol). He fired a couple shots at them. A shot came from the wash? Then, my god Henry I'm shot?

Q. *What part did this young squaw that was taken prisoner play as to enticing Hogle or any of the posse in towards the wash where the Indians lay concealed.*

A. *She did not single out any particular one of the posse, nor Hogle in particular but am satisfied her object was to get any of the posse to advance closer in to the wash so as to enable the Indians concealed to have better chance of a shot.*

Juror obsessed with placing blame on young girl. Henry helping best he can.

Q. *What did she do after the death of Hogle and where did she go?*

A. *I did not see her for 5 minutes after the death of Hogle but there was a volley fired into the wash and she was found with her arms around an old squaw.*

Volley fired at who, the young Indian running down the wash and/or the grandmother and the mother, with the baby on her back, as they were huddled with the small children?

Q. *Did you see the Indian that killed Hogle?*

A. *Saw him a few seconds after the shot but did not at time shot that killed Hogle was fired.*

Henry did not see an Indian kill Hogle.

Q. *Did Hogle advance using any precaution as to keeping under cover while advancing.*

A. *Yes he advanced in a crouching position.*

This position puts Hogle in line with a shot from OD or other posse member, that would cause the bullet to enter the upper left shoulder and exit under the right arm as stated in the news paper articles, (Humboldt Star March 1, 1911 and ?)

Quote: "He was shot in the left breast the bullet passing through his body and coming out under his right arm, probably touching the heart"

All newspapers that addressed this incident got 95% of the story wrong. Did they get this one right?

Also note: Hughes and Hogle both worked for Demick (Miller & Lux). Hogle most likely knew Hughes better than any of the others which would explain why he called out " My god Henry I'm shot".

MORT WEST -

Q. *Where you on Feb 26, 1911*

A. *On Rabbit Cr. with the posse that were hunting renegade Indians.*

Q - *Under whose authority?*

A. *Under the authority of Captain Donnelley*

Q. *Did you know Ed Hogle personally?*

A. *I did*

Q. *Were you present when he came to his death?*

A. *I was*

Q. *How far from him?*

A. *About 10 feet from him.*

Q. *At the wash who was in front of him, an old squaw or a young squaw?*

A. *An old squaw.*

Q. *What was she doing?*

A. *Shooting arrows at men as they advance particularly at Ed Hogle.*

Q. *Where was the young squaw at the time?*

A. *She was a little farther south brandishing a spear to attract their attention, but was not attracting the attention of Hogle at all that I saw.*

Old squaw shooting arrows, young squaw with spear, further south would be to the _right_ of Hogle

Q. *By Juror Dame - Was the young squaw attracting the attention of the posse so as to cover up the hiding place of the bucks in the wash so as to give them a chance to get a line to make a shot at Hogle?*

A. *At no time during the engagement, I am positive was the young squaw that was captured alive within from 30 to 50 feet of south of the direct firing line and the same distance south of the point where the Indian lay that shot Hogle.*

The jurors won't give up on the 15 year old girl! The adults are dead so lets convict her of something. If there is going to be a cover up some one has to pay for the death of Hogle.

Again, south would be to the _right_ of Hogle. The jury is struggling with this one, trying to lay blame on the young girl and the posse members keep pushing back.

Q. *State all the circumstances surrounding the death of Hogle.*

A. *We were advancing upon the Indians in a washout to drive them from their position, Ed Hogle was slightly on the lead and made himself probably a little more conspicuous than the rest. I heard the shot and saw Hogle stagger backwards, he said "My god Henry I am shot keep back boys" He then walked past us to the rear, I thought he was wounded in the arm and seeing him continuall walking went forward with the rest to locate who shot him.*

Note: Ed in the lead and West did not see the Indian shoot Hogle.

FRANK PERRY -

Q. *Were you a member of Donnelley's command?*

A. *I was with his party.*

Note: He was with them, but not deputized? It was never clear if any member of the posse was ever deputized. Different ones had different answers.

Q. *How far from him (Ed).*

A. *Probably 100 feet.*

Q. *In the wash who was in front of him an old squaw or a young squaw?*

A. *Am not positive but think it was an old squaw.*

Q. *What was she doing?*

A. *Shooting arrows.*

Q. *At any one in particular?*

A. *No shooting at the nearest ones of the posse that came toward the wash.*

Perry 100 feet away which would indicate he was on the northwest end of the semi-circle and in a position to have accidentally killed Hogle, but being right handed, his rifle would be pointing away from Hogle. When asked specifically who was in front of Hogle, answered "I think old squaw". Old squaw shooting arrows at who ever came nearest, no mention of the other Indian women nor other weapons.

Q. *Give us all the information you can regarding the death of Hogle.*

A. *We were advancing toward the gulch where the Indians were and they were concealed in this gulch and whenever we could see a buck we would shoot trying to take the squaws and children captive and Ed was a little ways ahead of the rest of us when he was shot. I saw him when he was shot and throwed up his hands and walked backwards probably 25 feet and then dropped, the buck that shot him started down the creek and I and the others opened fire on him.*

"Whenever we could see a buck we would shoot trying to take the squaws and children captive". Hell this should have worked, if they just hadn't shot them before they had a chance to surrender. "We opened fire on the buck that ran down the wash". Since he fell dead next to a young boy, already dead in the wash, both lying between the 2 adult males and the 2 women, you have to

conclude they all shot the young boy, 10 or 12 years old, in the back. He didn't run up the wash and he wasn't dead with the women. Which brings up another point, how could they have shot the women accidentally?

Q. *Could you say what part the young squaw that was captured alive had as to enticing Hogle to advance toward the wash?*

A. *Am unable to say positively, as I was 100 feet away and did not notice in that regard.*

Q. *Did you see the Indian that killed him?*

A. *Yes sir.*

Buckley can't let go of incriminating the young girl. Perry said he saw the Indian that killed Hogle but was careful not to say he saw the Indian kill Hogle.

Again Perry states he is 100 feet away. He would be at the upper end of the line and O. D. 100 feet from Hogle at the lower or southeast end of the line.

Perry and O. D. were 75 or 80 yards apart and every one else in between.

In Perry's writings years later he said he was coming down the wash.

GEORGE HOLMES -

Q. *Were you under the command of Capt. Donnelley*

A. *Yes*

Q. *How far off were you at the time he was shot?*

A. *About 30 or 40 feet.*

Q. *State all the circumstances surrounding the death of Hogle.*

A. *We were crowding on the Indians when he made some remark that he was shot and then dropped dead.. I had heard a shot from the washout and he put up his hand to his breast.*

Q. *Was the young squaw named Indian Maggie who was captured at that place any time in any way instrumental in causing the death of Hogle so far as you know*

A. *Don't think I noticed her very close up to Hogle, was dancing up and down up to close where we were.*

He was under the command of Capt. Donnelley. He heard a shot from the wash. Again trying to pin Hogle's death on the young girl and the jury begins to use the fictitious name "Maggie" for the young girl.

"Close to where we were", Holmes must have also been at the right of Hogle, by 30 or 40 feet.

Q. *Did you see the Indian that killed Ed Hogle?*

A. *Not in life no.*

Q. *You saw him after he was dead?*

A. *Yes*

Q. *Was it the old squaw that was facing Hogle?*

A. *Could not say there was so many of them.*

Did not see Indian shoot Ed.

Was the old squaw facing Ed? He couldn't say "there was so many of them",

(all of 3) including the 15 year girl, who was off to the right and not mixed up with the other 2 women, (mother with baby on her back, the grandmother and 2 small children huddled with them), and also not in front of Ferguson as Ferguson claimed.

JACK FERGUSON -

He stated he was with Donnelley's posse.

Q. *How far off were you when he was shot?*

A. *About 30 feet to the left.*

Q. *In advancing was he ahead of the posse and how far?*

Well he was ahead of some of them and probably the closest man to the buck that shot him.

Q. *Which one of the squaws the young or old one was facing him?*

A. *At the time he was shot there was no squaw in front of him.*

Q. *State all you know leading up to and including the death of Hogle.*

A. *This young squaw named Maggie danced out in front of me just a short time before Ed was killed shaking this war staff with both hands up and I thought she wanted to give up it was a sign of peace. I had both of my hands up with the gun in my left hand to show her I would not hurt her if she would come on up to me and told her if she would come up to me I wouldn't shoot her and she got up within sixty or one hundred feet and fell over into a little ditch right quick the buck raised up that was*

sitting behind her and fired 2 shots at me one of them just grazing my thumb.

Note: Ferguson did not say the Indian shot Ed only that the Indian raised up and shot at him twice, one bullet grazing his thumb. According to testimony, only one buck was alive at this point. Ferguson saw this buck shoot at him but not at Hogle?

Q. *Do you believe by your observation that this young squaw named Maggie was in any way directly responsible for the death of Hogle?*

A. I do it is my belief that if she had been killed previously Ed would have been alive *today.*

Q. *Did you see her doing anything to entice Ed forward?*

A. *Could not say that I did to see her enticing any one man to come forward in this fight. Just a minute or two previously I had started forwarded to knock her down but could not get to her.*

Buckley tries again to implicate the 15 year old girl, instead of asking Ferguson which Indian shot at him and with what weapon.

And finally Buckley got someone to state it was the girl's fault Ed was killed.

He was 30 ft. to the left and behind Ed. He saw all kinds of things no one else saw, the buck shot at him twice the bullet grazing his thumb. In Perry's recollection, written years later, he stated the six year old boy tried to run away and when captured by Ferguson bit Ferguson's hand. Maybe that six year old boy wounded Ferguson in the thumb.

The wash varied from about 30 feet wide to about 100 feet wide. She kept running up towards him, therefore she was in front of him, at a distance of about 35 or 40 feet.

He was holding his hands up with rifle in left hand while everyone is advancing on the wash where the Indians are located. Not likely, everyone is on the alert with rifles at the ready, they do not know but what there may be someone in that wash with a rifle.

WARREN FRUIT -

Q. *How far away were you to Ed prior to his death?*

A. *About 30 or 40 feet.*

Q. *Did you see him at time he was shot?*

A. *Yes sir.*

Q. *Was he ahead of you?*

A. *Yes*

Q. *Did you see this young squaw named Maggie prior to the death of Ed?*

A. *Yes*

Q. *Where was she?*

A. *Well she was running toward the boys with that magic stick she had.*

Q. *Was she directly in front of Ed when he was shot?*

A. *She was not.*

Q. *Which squaw was in front to him?*

A. *Couldn't say if there was any squaw in front of him.*

Q. *To the best of your knowledge was the young squaw Maggie that was captured in any way instrumental for the death of Ed?*

A. *Could not say that she was.*

Q. *State all you know in regard to the death of Ed.*

A. *Well we were all crowding in on the Indians and Ed was the closest and then he fell making a remark & walked back & fell. I heard the shot from the wash that killed him.*

Q. *Was the young squaw that was captured at that time present when Ed was killed?*

A. *Yes*

Again no luck incriminating the young girl & he only heard a shot from the wash. Some testified "old squaw in front of Hogle, others young squaw, others did not identify any one in front of Hogle" as did Fruit.

INQUEST March 3, 4 and 5, 1911 - INDIANS KILLED at RABBIT CREEK

The inquest for the eight members of the Daggett family began on the 3rd of March 1911.

The inquest for Ed Hogle had taken place two days earlier on March 1, 1911.

The inquest jury that were called on to appear before James Buckley, corner for the County of Humboldt, State of Nevada included the following Jurors:

E. H. Winters, A. L. Dela Vega, Barney Gill, Nelson Pitts, Leon Hammond, Felic Configliacco, James G. Stewart.

Buckley decided to lump all the Indians together rather than holding an inquest on each individual. It is much easier that way and facilitates a cover up. After all they were only Indians.

The Surprise Valley bunch were incensed that there was going to be a hearing or inquest into the killings. They thought that the killing of the Indian family was justified and that there should have been no legal ramifications. As it turned out there were no legal ramifications for any of the posse members.

News paper accounts, Writings of Frank Perry and Mort West

John (Skinny) Pascal was never called on to testify at the inquest hearings even though he was right in the middle of the whole fiasco and each member of the posse testified that Pascal was called on numerous times to ask the Indians to surrender.

The young fifteen year old Indian girl was also right in the middle of the whole fiasco and she also was not asked to testify.

I wonder if her and Skinny's testimony would have been in conflict with those trying to cover up what they had done like killing of women and children. Except for the three small children, all of the others are dead so who needs another side of the story.

If they were lying about what they had done, they would not want the testimony of her nor Skinny Pascal to be heard. It isn't as if Pascal could not testify he was called to testify at the trial of Nimrod Urie on April 18, 1911, just forty seven days later. Urie was being tried for the killing of the Quilicies, at Imlay, Nevada.

Before arriving in Golconda from Kelly Creek Ranch posse members and the newspapers put out the word that the young girl, while at Kelly Creek confessed to killing the sheepmen, Dopp and many other crimes. This confession was supposedly made to a Shoshone Indian that was present at Kelly Creek while the fifteen year old girl and the other children were held captive there.

After reviewing the testimony and many other documents I have concluded she never made any such confession. Under the stress and duress she was being subjected to, any statement she might have made under those circumstances had no legitimacy. This confession, as portrayed by the posse, of the young girl's confession would have had no credibility it was ludicrous and exaggerated. They were trying to distance themselves from the killing of unarmed Indians. If such a confession was made to that individual then why was he not asked to testify?

INQUEST MARCH 3rd 1911 - INDIANS KILLED

Wording in **bold** letters are my comments on the testimony of each posse member.

CAPTAIN DONNELLEY - *(Captain Nevada State Police)*

Q- Tell what happened on that day while you were acting in your official capacity.

A- I left Willow Point in the morning of that day took up the trail of the Indians my party had preceded me as they had stopped at the Stewart Ranch as that was 2 miles nearer and arrived at Rabbit Creek after the fight had started and continued there until the end of the fight. My party was in charge of my Sergeant P M Newgard.

Q- What were the circumstances which led up to that fight with the Indians? why were you following them?

A- For the murder of the 4 men in Washoe County. I received a fone from the Stockmen at Reno to come to Reno I was at Carson City at that time and on the arrival at Reno they informed that the 4 bodies of the stockmen had been found murdered and asked me if I would take full charge of the hunt for the white men not knowing at that time if they were Indians or white men, I saw Sheriff Ferrel and cooperated with him in his county went to the place where the men were found and were murdered by Indians. I went to Washoe County with Sheriff Ferrel and then took command of the party or posse. We followed their trail until we came up to the Indians.

Donnelley was not on the scene when the shooting started!

He may have taken command of the posse but he was not up to the task and the consequences were fatal.

Q- Go on and tell all that occurred on the scene of the fight with the Indians.

A- When I arrived there the Indians were firing from ambush they were hidden some of them and others were working down from the canon to where they made their final stand and I had the horses gathered up prior to this 2 of the horses had been killed by my instructions and also had our horses taken back further so they would not apt to get hit and kept some of the men there to prevent the Indians from slipping back and getting to the horses the men who were holding the Indians in the canon at first I sent 2 or three men down as soon as I could to help them at that time, afterwards sent men down as they came in Ed Hogle was one the men I sent to gather in the Indian horses and after the horses were taken care of he asked me what he had better do so I asked him if had plenty of ammunition and he replied that he had so I told him to go down and help the boys hold the Indians in the canon and be careful and not expose himself in going down and after arriving there. He said he would not or try not do not remember which it was.

He had Indian's horses gathered up and 2 shot. Covering his butt on telling Ed not to expose himself.

No medical examiners report found, detailing Hogle's bullet wounds.

Q- Did you know Shoshone Mike during his lifetime?

A- I saw him just before he died.

Q- By whom was he shot if you know?

A- I don't know

Q- Did you search the body of SS Mike before the arrival of the Coroner?

A- I did not

Q- What property was found on the body?

A- I don't know

Q- When you came up to the Indians did you make an effort to arrest them without killing them?

A- My Sergeant was in charge and I believe he called on an Indian trailer to ask them to submit.

Q- Who fired the first shot if you know?

A- I don't know

He did not know who fired 1st shot.

Q- Did the other Indians also resist arrest?

A- Yes all of them

They sure as hell did. There were at least 15 of the 18 rifles shooting at them. What else could they do?

Q- Were they all killed at same place?

A- No there was 2 of them killed close by the camp and rest of them in the canyon where they made the last stand I should judge about a mile away from there the first were killed.

Q- After Mike was shot was it necessary to also shoot the other Indians?

A- It was

Q- Why was it necessary to kill the squaws?

A- Because they were in hiding with the bucks and the bucks were firing and we could not ascertain which were firing. Could not tell whether whey were bucks or squaws when we fired at the objects. Our men could have shot the women at most anytime as they were conspicuous objects and my orders were not to shoot the women or children during the engagement.

How about this for a grandiose statement? First off he wasn't even down where the women and children were killed. 2nd They were shooting at objects and they knew there were women and children present? 3rd Then he says our men could have shot the squaws at any time. 4th Was this how the Indians were resisting arrest, by not coming out to be shot?

Q- Did any of them attempt to escape and avoid arrest?

A- All of them yes

They sure as hell did attempt to escape and avoid arrest if 11 men were shooting at them as objects in the brush. They were running for their lives.

Q- Why did you kill the horses?

A- To keep the Indians from mounting them.

Q- When you killed the horses did you try to avoid killing the squaws?

A- I did

Q- Was the squaw who was attempting to get the horses killed at the same time?

A- She was not

Q- Do you know who killed the different Indians and Squaws?

A- I do not

Q- Describe the position of the different Indians and squaws when the fight was over.

A- There was two of them old Mike and a young Buck lying within about 30 or 40 yards of each other at where the their camp was, Mike had crawled thirty of forty yards to that place after he had been shot. The other indians were lying in the wash two squaws close together, two bucks nearly together but a few yards further east of the squaws and two children close together between these two bucks and two squaws.

How did he know Mike crawled 30 or 40 yards after being shot he wasn't there and what is meant by "that place"? Did he mean the camp?

Two bucks actually west of the squaws, every member would be asked that question. All answered the same, two, two and two lying in the bottom of the wash.

Note: he states two children!

Q- Had they been killed by members of your party?

A- They had

Q- Did you know that the band of Indians which you came on at Rabbit Cr. were the ones you had started out to follow from Little High Rock Canyon in Washoe County?

A- Yes sir. at least it was the band whose trail we had been following.

Q- How many Indians and squaws were there in the band when you caught up with them?

A- There were four large bucks and two young boys, three squaws and three children.

Q- How did you identify them as the band of Indians you were following?

A- By articles they left in their 1st camp such as pieces of oil cloth articles of clothing that were taken from bodies of the dead men and their general way making up their camp.

Q- Describe all the property by which you make the identification?

A- I was not acquainted with what property they had.

He was in charge and he doesn't talk about the weapons the Indians had! Inventorying weapons and identifying who had them is rule number one in law enforcement even in those days.

No sense in putting himself in a position of admitting there only two rifles, one pistol, a shotgun and the rest bows and arrows and one spear. And he doesn't have to describe where the weapons were found.

Q- Is there anything else you can add to your testimony at this time that will show the necessity for killing the Indians and squaws.

A- Yes by articles later found which identified them as the right parties who were wanted and also the fact that they resisted arrest.

By articles later found? You kill them then decide if they are the right ones?

Yes they were the right ones to kill even if they were not the actual ones who did the killing at Little High Rock and they resisted being killed, I mean arrested.

Q- Will your testimony be the same as given here in the case of Shoshone Mike be the same as all the other cases (old squaw Jennie, squaw Indian Mary, Buck Cupena, Buck Disenda, Buck Kinnan, and one buck and two boys names unknown?

A- It will be the same

Note: This question "Will your testimony be the same" listing the Indians by there fictitious names was asked of each witness & the answer of each witness was the same, "in the affirmative".

No one seamed to notice they killed more Indian <u>bucks</u> than were there!!

Also note: this is the first time the name Jennie shows up on official records. It latter shows up when there is an attempt to to identify family members when trying to ascertain who the family members were in dispersing of Mary Jo's estate as Jennie Daggett, Mike Daggett's wife. I believe the name Jennie was gotten from the book the LAST FREE MAN by Dayton Hyde whom I believe got it from the inquest jury as shown above. Further research leads me to conclude that Mike's wife was not Jennie but Maggie. This information comes from the book BUCKSKIN & SMOKE by Anna Hansen Hays and a letter from Carrie Hansen Crockett to Mary Jo dated Nov. 5, 1975. Anna and Carrie are sisters and knew the Daggetts from the time their father acquired the Hansen store at Rock Creek, Idaho in 1900.

ELSEY SLMITH - *(Sheriff, Modoc County, California)*

Q- Were you under the command of Capt. Donnelley?

A- After leaving Washoe County I was.

When asked the same question at the inquest of Hogle, he stated "not under the command of anyone". He made that statement on March 1st, 2 days earlier.

Q- Where were you on that day?

A- I left Willow Creek Ranch in the morning kept on the trail of the Indians until we reached their camp on Rabbit Creek Humboldt County, Nevada.

He also left Willow Creek Ranch Maybe no one stayed at the Stewart Ranch. No testimony nor evidence found that placed any one of the posse members staying at the Stewart Ranch.

Q- What were the circumstances which led up to that fight with the Indians why were you following them?

A- We were following them for the murder of Harry Cambron, John Laxague, Peter Arramouspe and B. Indiana.

Q- Go on and tell all that occurred on the scene of the fight with the Indians. Where was the fight?

A- We came up around a little point coming down the canyon & some of the boys says "there they are now" & we all came along down the open country and the order was given to fall in line and we advanced towards the Indians who were about 450 yards and the word was passed to Skinney Pascoe to ask the Indians to submit. Skinney did and he reported that the Indians would not submit and then a shot was fired by some one but don't know who and fight was on. This fight was at place called Rabbit Creek, Humboldt County, Nevada.

Communications not too good at a distance over 4 lengths of a football field. Note: he did not know who fired 1st shot.

Q- Did you know Shoshone Mike during his life time?

A- I did not

Q- Did you search the body of Shoshone Mike before the arrival of the coroner?

A- No sir I dild not.

Q- Do you know what property was found on his body?

A- Only a gun that I know of also a belt of cartridges.

Q- What was done with them?

A- Last time I saw the gun and belt, Mr Cambron had them.

Why would Cambron have them? Modoc County Sheriff Smith and Captain Donnelley were both at that location for two hours. Some one from the State Police should have been responsible for the weapons of the Indians.

Q- *When you came up to the Indians did you make an effort to arrest them without killing them?*

A- *I shouted them to throw up their hands, Skinney Pascoe did also but they wouldn't.*

At 450 yards or approximately one quarter of a mile?

Q- *Who fired the first shot?*

A- *The first shot came from either Shoshone Mike or one other Indian, the first shot came from that side.*

Earlier in his testimony he said he didn't know who fired the 1st shot.

Q- *Did the other Indians also resist arrest?*

A- *Yes they did resist arrest.*

Q- *Were they all killed at same place?*

A- *No sir*

Q- *After Mike was shot was it necessary to also shoot the other Indians?*

A- *Yes sir it was at that particular place.*

Q- *Why was it necessary kill the squaws?*

A- *Could not say I was not down where they were.*

Q- *Did any of them attempt to escape & avoid arrest?*

A- *Yes sir*

Q- *Do you know who killed the different Indians and squaws?*

A- *No sir I do not.*

Q- *Describe the different position of the different Indians & squaws when the fight was over.*

A- *Old Mike & another buck lying about 30 yards from each other the others down the wash were in different places some close & others a few yards apart.*

Q- *Had they all been killed by members of your party?*

A- *Yes sir*

Q- *Did you know that the band of Indians which you came on at Rabbet Cr. were the ones you had started out to follow from Little High Rock Canyon in Washoe County?*

339

A- Only by the way they acted when we came on to them.

Q- How many Indians were in the band when you came up to them?

A- There were twelve.

Q- How do you Identify them as the band of Indians you were following?

A- By the stuff that was left along the trail.

Q- Describe all the property by which you make the identification

A- Mr Cambron picked up two check books in camp which I describe as follows: Check book property of Peter Erramouspe on Surprise Valley Bank of Cedarville Calif., Check book on Nixon National Bank of Reno, Nev. no name to tell who was the owner. A gun that was laying on the brush by old Mike description of gun as follows, Winchester 40-82 Caliber Model 1886.

Q- Is there anything else you can add to your testimony at this time that will show the necessity for killing the Indians and squaws?

A- Only thing I know the boys gave them chance to surrender and they would not take advantage of it.

Will your testimony be the same ----------------------- ?

The rifle with Mike - 40-82 Model 1886. Finally some one identifies and inventories a weapon. He doesn't know that the boys gave the six including women and children, a chance to surrender, he wasn't down where they were killed.

Ben F. CAMBRON - (brother of Harry Cambron killed at Little High Rock Canyon)
A- I was with the posse.

Q- Go on and tell all that happened on that day while you were acting in your official capacity.

A- We started out from the Stewart Ranch on the morning of the 26th on the trail of the murderers and we traced the track the night before, the 25th, over the summit of the mountains and on the morning of the 26th we took up the tracks from the summit of the mountains and we followed their tracks in a southeasterly course we came up on them at 12 o'clock noon when we came around a butte as we was coming round the boys says the tracks are getting fresh and we must be careful and keep together as we were

340

coming around the butte leaving the butte to our left we noticed a rim rock and heard some the boys better look out as we are lible to come on them right here, had not gone but short distance some of the boys said there are some of the horses we had not gone but a short distance when some of the boys said see their smoke looking down the ravine we noticed a squaw running down a ravine and we saw her run into a camp where we saw it was made up with sage brush as she ran into the camp there were four or five Indians ran out and then turned and ran back into camp and then came out on a run the boys said "hurry up they have got their guns" and there were three running from the camp in northerly course running as though they were getting in position for a battle. Heard some of the boys say "throw up your hands and Indian Pascal crawled off to our left we jumped off our horses at that time and one of the posse said tell them to throw up their hands and come out and then I heard a shot from the direction of where the Indians were. Some of our posse began firing, as they began firing heard some of our boys say "get down get down" or you will get shot when our posse began firing there were three Indians started back for their camp headed them off from where they were making for noticed one of them to fall shortly after noticed another one fall saw the third Indian run down the draw and get out of sight few moments after noticed a squaw running down towards the horses some of our boys said she is running those horses down so that the bucks can get away, the boys said don't shoot the squaws but shoot the horses so they can't get away.

Did he start from the Stewart Ranch or did he start at Golconda and meet others from Willow Point at the Stewart Ranch and then start out? Other bits of information indicate some of the posse left Golconda very early and joined Donnelley party at the Stewart Ranch and started from there.

Note: butte to their left. The butte being to their left makes no sense, does not fit with the lay of the land nor other testimony, and stories. If the butte was to their right it all fits and makes sense.

Shot from the Indian side then posse began firing, 3 Indians started back for their camp, two fell one got back to their camp. For the 3 Indians to run out and take a shot at 18 armed men and then run back to camp doesn't make sense. Bad decision could get you killed. Did the posse shoot them in the back?

341

Q- What were the circumstances which led up to that fight and why were you following them?

A- I volunteered to go with the posse to capture those that were responsible for the death of my brother and others in Little High Rock Canyon.

Q- Did you know Shoshone Mike during his lifetime?

A- No sir I did not.

Q- By whom was he shot if you know?

A- I do not know.

Q- Did you search the body of Shoshone Mike before the arrival of the coroner?

A- Took a cartridge belt off his body as he was alive and did not want to use also took the gun from him so as not to let him have any weapon. The gun was a few feet from him against a bush.

Q- What was done with the gun and belt?

A- Brought in to Golconda and is now here in evidence.

Q- When you came up to the Indians did you make an effort to arrest them without killing them?

A- Yes sir I did.

Q- Did the other Indians also resist arrest?

A- Yes sir.

He didn't know if they resisted or not he wasn't down where others were killed.

Q- Were they all killed at same place?

A- No sir they were not.

Q- After Mike was shot was it necessary to also shoot the other Indians?

A- Yes sir it was.

Q- Why was it necessary to kill the squaws?

A- Because they were shooting at us with arrows and guns.

Again he wasn't there he had no knowledge of what went on at that place.

Q- Did any of them attempt to escape and avoid arrest?

A- Yes sir.

The Indians tried to escape to avoid being killed.

Q- Was the squaw who was attempting to get the horses killed at same time ?

A- No sir

Q- Do you know who killed the different Indians and squaws/

A- No I do not.

Q- Describe the position of the different Indians and squaws when the fight was over.

A- The Chief was about 100 yards from the camp in a northerly course one within about 35 or 40 yards from the camp. That is all Indians I saw.

"That is all Indians I saw" noting he was not down where the women and children were killed.

Q- Had they all been killed by members of your party?

A- Yes sir

Q- Did you know that the band of Indians which you came on to at Rabbit Cr. were the ones you had started out to follow?

A- Yes sir

Q- How many Indians & squaws were there in the band of Indians you were following?

A- 12 of them

No one seemed to notice the jury, led by Buckley, listed 9 killed.

Q- How did you identify them as the band of Indians you were following?

A- By the different they dropped at their camps as we came along their trail and by horse tracks.

Q- Describe all the property by which you make the identification.

A- By the Chief's rifle, cartridge belt, my brother's chapereus, brothers boots, coat watch and revolver and Peter Arramousepe's check book. My brothers gun is a savage Automatic 32 caliber, Watch is a Waltham silver case & has my brothers name engraved on back of it.

The jury is working hard to exonerate the posse from killing the women and children.

Cambron's list by which he made identification includes, chief's rifle, cartridge belt and his brothers pistol, Savage automatic 32 caliber pistol, only, no other weapon. He could not have identified the Indians by Mike's rifle and cartridge belt, he had no way of knowing if those two items were at Little High Rock.

Q- Is there anything else you can add to your testimony at this time that will show the necessity for killing the Indians and squaws?

A- No sir

Q- A Juror. On their trail from the time they left the place where they were camped did they put them in a conspicuous place? Did it look like a fortification?

A- Yes they always camped in a hole so as to leave us that were following come on them in an exposed position.

It would be stupid to camp on top of ridge where they could be seen from a distance and with out any natural protection from the elements. The Indians had very little in the way blankets and clothing to protect themselves from January and February weather in northern Nevada. The family camped in a hole or low place more for protection from the elements than anything else. They had no other shelter.

Q- Juror. On the way did you find anything on the trail that would show that this band had anything along with them to show it came from the murdered cattle men.

A- A piece of Chaperareau that had been cut off that belonged to my brother who had been killed.

Q- Will it be same ---------------------------------- ?

Again only 8 total killed & using fictitious names.

Q- How much money did you find on the bodies of the Indians?

A- Did not find any but a pocket book containing $30.00 in currency was picked up in camp and same has been turned over to you. (coroner)

Later Frank Perry testified that he took $20 dollars from the camp and had spent it but would make it good before adjournment. Did the Indians have $50 dollars in cash? $20 or $30 was a lot of money in those days.

Did the sheepmen have that much cash on them? There was no where to spend it where they were going. However they had check books in the event they had to go 30 or 40 miles (depending on where they started from) to Gerlach for supplies. He indicated the pocket book belonged to the Indians. In fact none of the posse members gave any indication that the money belonged to the sheepmen which is quite interesting.

P. M. NEWGARD - *(Sergeant with the Nev. State Police)*

Q- Where you on that day? Feb. 26, 1911

A- On the trail of what I believed to be the murderers of the four men in Little High Rock Canyon.

Q- Go on and tell all that happened on that day while you were acting in your official capacity.

A- We arrived within sight of the Indians about 12 noon on Rabbit Cr. Humboldt County Nevada. We demanded their surrender and they responded by shots and we opened fire on them, we continued to shoot until three o'clock stopping every few minutes to ask them to surrender, we probably asked them to surrender seven or eight times and I called up the Indian trailer Pasquel twice to ask them to surrender in his Shoshone language, they responded each time with shots.

They did not stop every few minutes to ask the Indians to surrender, some members of the posse testified they were shooting into the brush where they believed an Indian to be and at objects. They continued to shoot for 3 hours? What at? When the Indians were cornered down where the women and children were killed they were unarmed. There is little evidence that the 32 pistol was found at that location or that it was fired.

Q- Did you know Shoshone Mike during his life time?

A- No

Q- By whom was he shot if you know?

A- By our posse, individual not known.

Q- Did you search the body of Shoshone Mike before the arrival of the coroner?

A- No

Q- What property was found on the body?

A- I don't know.

Q- When you come up to the Indians did you make an effort to arrest them without killing them?

A- Yes

Not much effort. The Indians were surrounded, there horses about done in and the posse knew it and the Indians were all on foot with small children, and the posse also knew that.

Q- Who fired the first shot if you know?

A- I don't know.

Q- Did the other Indians also resist arrest?

A- Yes

He didn't know who fired the first shot! How could they have resisted arrest? The women were huddled together with the children but were shot down anyway. Maybe on purpose.

Q- Were they all killed at same place?

A- No

Q- After Mike was shot was it necessary to also shoot the other Indians?

A- Yes sir

No not necessary. They were unarmed.

Q- Why was it necessary to kill the squaws?

A- I believe they were killed in a volley that was fired at the bucks as near as I can figure out.

The "bucks" were all dead except for the, young boy who was shot down, in the back, in the final volley.

Q- Did any of them attempt to escape and avoid arrest?

A- Yes

The squaws could not attempt escape. They had small children to care for.

Q- Did you kill the horses?

A- No sir.

Q- Was this squaw who was attempting to get the horse killed?

A- No

Q- Do you know who killed the different Indians and squaws?

A- I do not.

Q- Describe the position of the different Indians and squaws when the fight was over.

A- Two bucks laying close together and about 15 feet below them was the two boys further east was the two squaws all in the bottom of the creek.

Q- Had they all been killed by members of your party?

A- Yes

Q- Did you know that the band of Indians which you came on at Rabbit Cr. were the ones you had started out to follow from Little High Rock Canyon?

A- I did

Q- How many Indians & squaws were there in the band when you caught up with them?

A- 12 of them.

Q- How do you identify them as the band of Indians you were following?

A- By articles found in each camp corresponding to what was found in first camp.

Q- Describe all the property by which you make the identification.

A- By a watch that has the name of "H. H. Cambron" engraved on back of it, now in possession of you (coroner)

Q- Is there anything else you can add to your testimony at this time that will show the necessity for killing the Indians and squaws?

A- No it is all covered.

Q- Is there anything else that will add to the identification of the Indians as the right parties?

A- Not that I could testify to myself.

Q- will your testimony be same ----------------------------- ?

Q- A Jr - Did you personally hear Capt. Donnelley tell his men the posse to come along?

A- Yes the posse was asked at Camp Denio to follow & they would be members of the State Police.

No mention of weapons, even when asked about property of the Indians.

C. H. STONE - *(Sergeant Nev. State Police)*

Q- Where were you on that day? (Feb. 26,1911)

A- I was with Capt. Donnelley's posse following a party of Indians with the intention of arresting them if possible for the murder of four men in Little High Rock Canyon,

Washoe County Nev., at 12 o'clock noon we overtook these Indians at Rabbit Cr. Humboldt County Nev. We demanded their surrender in English and in the Shoshone Language, they replied with a shot, our posse then commenced firing and continued to fire until 3 o'clock in the afternoon.

Mike & one grown son were killed in first volley. How could it take almost another 3 hours to kill 6 unarmed indians, 2 adults, 2 children & 2 women?

How could the posse members, continually demanded the Indians surrender, if the posse commenced firing at noon and continued until 3 PM and were shooting into the brush and at objects?

Q- Go on and tell all that occurred on the scene of the fight with the Indians.

A- The Indians were encamped in a ravine on our approach three bucks ran from the camp in a northerly direction with their guns as though hunting a position to fire upon us in a few minutes two of them were knocked down with bullets from our posse, the other ran back toward the camp and in an easterly direction down the gulch and was soon out of our sight around the bend in the gulch. It was at this point that a squaw came out and tried to drive the horses toward where the buck had disappeared command was given to be careful and not shoot the squaw but to shoot the horses three of the horses were shot.

Now there are only 4 horses left standing for 10 remaining Indians to escape on!! Donnelley stated 2 horses were shot.

Q- Did you know Shoshone Mike during his lifetime?

A- I did not.

Q- By whom was he shot if you know?

A- I do not know the individual that shot him.

Q- Did you search the body of Shoshone Mike before the arrival of the Coroner?

A- I did not.

Q- What property was found on the body?

A- When I saw him he had a cartridge belt on him and a rifle near him on a bush he was not yet dead.

Q- What was done with it?

A- I don't know haven't seen it since but saw it in court.

Note: Rifle & cartridge belt by Mike, both in court as evidence.

Q- When you came up with Indians did you make an effort to arrest them without killing them.

A- Yes sir

Q- Who fired the first shot if you know?

A- One of the Indians.

Q- Did the other Indians also resist arrest?

A- They did

Not true the women and children were surrounded they had small children with them the posse made no effort to arrest them!

Q- Were they all killed at the same place?

A- No sir

Q- After Mike was shot was it necessary to also shoot the other Indians?

A- It was

Q- Why was it necessary to kill the squaws?

A- Well the squaws were acting as combatants and it was impossible to avoid killing them as I believe the squaws were killed by bullets intended for the bucks, they were mixed up so.

Mixed up so! Two adult males dead in the bottom of the wash, the rest were women & children another 20 or 30 yds. down the wash. The women and children were mixed up, but not with the adult males.

The last volley fired killed the 10 year old child, running down the wash. He was shot in the back and died 40 or 50 feet from the women. It was not possible, for the posse members, to not know they were shooting at the women.

Q- Did any of them attempt to escape and avoid arrest?

A- They did

Q- Did you kill the horses?

A- I killed one of them.

Q- When you killed the horse did you try to avoid killing the the squaw/

A- I did

Q- Do you know who killed the different Indians and squaws?

A- I do not know the individuals that were killed nor who killed them but know they were killed by the posse.

Q- Describe the positions of the different Indians & squaws when the fight was over.

A- Two Bucks old Mike & big young buck was near the camp & the other 6 bodies, 2 squaws, 2 bucks & 2 boys were about a mile east of there in a bed of dry creek or gulch all of these in gulch were not separated more than a hundred feet in the gulch.

Q- Had they all been killed by members of your party?

A- They had

Q- Did you know that the band of Indians which you came on at Rabbit Cr. Humboldt County, was the one you had started out to follow from Little High Rock Canyon in Washoe County?

A- I did

Q- How many Indians & squaws were there in the band when you caught up with them?

A- There were twelve.

Q- How do you identify them as the band of Indians you were following ?

A- In the first camp at Little High Rock Canyon numerous articles they had left behind and in the various of their camps along the trail we found articles that corresponded with those that were at first camp in Little High Rock Canyon & also by their horses tracks.

Q- Describe all the property by which you make the identification.

A- I identify the Savage revolver now in court by the number taken at the Indian camp, number 26474.

Note: pistol taken at the Indian camp and specially identified by serial number. Also number not close to matching number listed on the missing pistol, back around the 10th of Feb. (14160 or 13711).

Q- Is there any thing else you can add to your testimony at this time that will show the necessity for killing the Indians and squaws?

A- Their continued resistance to arrest and their refusal to surrender and their continual firing upon us, but as I stated before I believe the squaws were killed by bullets intended for the bucks.

Their continual firing on us! With what? Bows and arrows? The last 6 Indians, killed, had no guns. Harry Cambron probably shoved this pistol into his chap pocket with 10 rounds in the clip. Since he had no plans to use it, he may or may not have had any more ammunition for it and if so very few rounds.

Q- Is there anything else that will add to the identification of the Indians as the right party.

A- Nothing that I know of.

Q- Will your testimony be same ----------------------------- ?

C. T. BYRNES - *(Constable at Paradise Valley, Nevada)*

Q- Were you a member of Capt. Donnelley's command on 2-26-1911?

A- Yes I left Willow Point the the morning of the 26th at Capt. Donnelley's request.

Q- Where were you at that day?

A- At Rabbit Cr. just over Ward Summit towards Kelly Cr., Humboldt County. Nev.

Q- What were the circumstances which led up to that fight with the Indians & why were you following them?

A- I received poster from the State Police to watch out for certain men & certain horses & I learned through fone a message to Paradise that the same horses had been seen in Lying Canyon so Saturday morning I left Paradise with 4 men to investigate & we came up to where they had been camped in Lying Canyon at what I judged to be about 2 PM in the afternoon of the 25th 1911 & came around on a little high bluff just below a ridge we saw this camp below in a ravine & we rode up in to where the camp was & one of the boys with me wanted to know where the fire had been did not see where they had cooked any & I got off my horse and went into the center of the camp & I saw there had been loose dirt piled up there and dug down & had glove on & in digging down found a hot cinder which showed they had their fire there & while we were there we see a bunch of men advancing from the west coming up the canyon & we took our horses & rode down to meet these men & that is where I had met Capt. Donnelley the first time I had ever met him & we went back to Willow Point with Ferguson. Capt. Donnelley asked me where I was going & I told him did not know & he said you go with us & we went with him next morning to the scene of the battle following along the trail of the Indians. The next morning I left with Capt. Donnelley from Willow Point he with rig & myself with horseback & I overtook him as he was leaving the Stewart Ranch, rode along with Capt. Donnelley thereon, the rest of posse were all ahead of us.

Where did Byrnes's 4 men go? No mention of these men after the 25th.

He was looking over the camp site recently occupied by the Indians when he saw men coming up the canyon from the west. Here he met Captain Donnelley for the first time and no mention of wagon or rig. He rode back to Willow Point with Ferguson on the 25th.

Donnelley evidently acquired the wagon at the Willow Point Ranch on the 25th to continue on the trail of the Indians. He knew by this time they were going to overtake the Indians very soon, most likely on the following day the 26th. He also knew that there were women and small children with the band of Indians and that these women and children were going to have to be transported to some place which would be very hard to do on horseback.

This was probably the best decision he had made during the entire episode.

Next morning Byrnes and Donnelley left Willow Point (Donnelley) with a rig (wagon) Byrnes on horseback.

Traveling across country in a wagon is much slower than those on horseback and the reason Donnelley was not there when the shooting started.

Q- Go on & state all that occurred at the scene of the fight with the Indians.

A- On the morning of the 26th we Meril Prussia and Warren Fruit and Frank Perry went around the hill at south side of the first camp they were in as we got around there there was a shot came from the brush where Indian Mike was laying shot towards the posse on the west side and the four of us then shot in to that brush and we stayed there probably ten minutes on the side of the hill and two of the boys said they were going in to see if there were any more Indians there as only two had fell & some had gone upon to the hill, and Prussia and Frank rode their horses through and circled the camp and the posse on the hill moved toward the boys and led right in to the camp we crossed over by the camp and it was there we found this Indian Mike there in a dying position. The rifle in court was laying in front of Mike and the rifle had a cartridge in the barrel and some one took the cartridge out and laid it against the sage brush.

352

This answer is hard to follow. It almost sounds as if he was there from the beginning. Byrnes and Donnelley must have arrived shortly after the shooting began which was much sooner than I would have expected. His statement indicates he along with other members of the posse was one of the first to arrived on the scene where Indian Mike was down.

Q- Did you know Indian Mike during his lifetime?

A- I did not

Q- By whom was he shot if you know?

A- I do not know.

Q- Did you search the body of Shoshone Mike before the arrival of the Coroner?

A- I did not.

Q- When you came up to the Indians did you make an effort to arrest them with out killing them?

A- Was not there at first fire was back with Capt. Donnelley.

Q- Who fired the first shot?

A- I do not know was not there then.

Q- How do you identify them as the right parties you had been following?

A- By their camp which was placed in a fortified position in Lying Canyon & by their fire that had been buried up.

Finding a camp site in low place with a camp fire buried was not evidence they were the right parties. It was his 1st day on the trail. He had nothing to compare it with.

Fortified position? No mostly for protection from the weather and not to be in plain sight of some one in the area.

Q- Is there anything else that you can add to your testimony at this time that will show the necessity for the killing of the Indians?

A- No sir

Q- Will your testimony be same ---------------------------- ?

JACK FERGUSON

Q- Where were you on that day?

A- I was with Capt. Donnelley's posse on the trail of the Indians.

Q- Go on and tell all that happened on that day while you were acting in your official capacity with Capt. Donnelley.

A- On Feb. 26th we left Willow Point about 7 AM taking up the trail of the Indians at Lyng Springs where we had left it the day before. We trailed them until about 12 noon I was out in the lead trailing at the time I see two horses, I said boys here they are the boys all came forward and they rode about two hundred yards when some of them said there is the smoke there is the camp. Sergeant Newgard commanded the boys to fall in line we advanced forwarded about two hundred yards to best of my knowledge, horseback and we see the three Indian Bucks run out and then run back and some of the boys said they got their guns. They came on in a northerly direction for about two hundred yards the boys commanded them to throw up their hands spoke to them in English then Newgard told the Indian trailer Pasquale to tell them to throw up their hands and give up & they replied with a shot at us at that the firing commenced all along the line, finally there was three bucks in all fell, that is to the best of my memory and the Indians split and a bunch of them started down the canyon Ben Cambron said for gods sake boys someone go down there and head them off. Sergeant Newgard & myself crossed over the canyon and went down the ridge under fire of the Indians all the time and headed them off about three quarters of a mile below the camp & held them there for some little bit finally Sergeant Newgard got this Indian trailer to come to us and had him to holler to them to come out and give up and they came out shooting.

How could <u>they</u> have come out shooting? Close scrutiny and analysis of testimonies at the inquest puts in great doubt that there were any guns down where the women and children were killed. The only weapons the Indians had were bow & arrows & one ceremonial staff. The 32 pistol was every where depending upon who who was asked.

There is no evidence Pascal was down at the lower site asking the Indians to surrender other than this statement by Ferguson.

Also above, Skinny Pascal, ask the Indians to "throw up their hands," at 2 to 400 yards? Then "firing commenced all along the line." How could any one have repeated a demand to surrender, with 15 to 18 rifles firing on the Indians, at that range? He said he was in the lead when they came upon the Indians. Why was he in the lead? Was he in charge?

Q- *Did you know Shoshone Mike during his lifetime?*

A- *I did not*

Q- *By whom was he shot if you know?*

A- *I do not know.*

Q- *What property was found on the body?*

A- *I do not know was not there.*

Q- *When you came up with the Indians did you make an effort to arrest them without killing them?*

A- *Yes sir*

Q- *Who fired the first shot if you know.*

A- *The Indians*

Q- *Did the other Indians also resist arrest?*

A- *Yes sir*

Q- *Were they all killed at same place?*

A- *No sir*

Q- *After Mike was shot was it necessary to also shoot the other Indians?*

A- *It was*

Q- *Why was it necessary to kill the squaws?*

A- *The squaws were fighting with bows and arrows some with pistols but I don't believe any man ever shot at a squaw to kill her but they were bunched up and the squaws were bound to come in range if you shot at the bucks .*

Some kind of women, shooting bow and arrows, (which takes two hands) and with pistols. Where are the pistols? You have to conclude the women were shooting bows & arrows, nearly every posse member stated that. But where are the pistols? They are trying to justify killing the women & children, they can specifically identify bows & arrows but not a pistols! Ferguson is lying, the

women had no pistols! And besides there were no, bucks, as the adult males were referred to, near the squaws they were children. One boy was running in the direction of the women and he was shot in the back.

Q- Did any of them attempt to escape and avoid arrest?

A- Yes sir

Q- Did you know who killed the different Indians and squaws?

A- I do not

Q- Describe the positions of the different Indians and squaws after the fight was over.

A- There were two children and two bucks and two squaws within a radius of a hundred feet scattered along the wash.

Q- Had they all been killed by members of your party?

A- Yes sir

Q- Did you know that the band of Indians which you came on at Rabbit Cr. were the ones you had started out to follow from Little High Rock Canyon in Washoe County Nevada?

A- To the best of my knowledge and belief it was.

Q- Why do you think so?

A- By stuff that I had picked up at the different camps that correspond with stuff that we found at Little High Rock Canyon the first camp of the Indians.

Q- How many Indians & squaws were there in the band when you caught up with them?

A- 12 of them

Q- How do you identify them as the band of Indians you were following?

A- By the articles found on them that were identified as taken from the bodies of the men murdered at Little High Rock Canyon.

Q- Describe all the property by which you make the identification.

A- By one of the dead horses at battle ground which was branded HP on left thigh and 76 on left side property of Harry Cambron. Also his saddle and boots.

Q- Is there anything else you can add to your testimony at this time that will show the necessity for killing the Indians and squaws?

A- Nothing more than I received a gunshot from them and asked them repeatedly to surrender.

Again he is lying, repeatedly asked them to surrender, with all that shooting that is supposedly going on and shooting into the brush where they believe Indians were hiding? The 10 year old boy is running away towards his mother and he is shot in the back by maybe as many as 10 rifles? Teaches him not to surrender!

Q- *Will your testimony be same ----------------------------- ?*

Q- *Did you search any of the Indians bodies?*

A- *No did not search any of them.*

Q- *If you do not know the names of the Indians describe their ages as near as you can.*

A- *Old Indian Mike was 55 or 60, one of the other bucks probably 25 or 26, one of the others 23 or 24, one of the others about 18, two of the boys 12 or 13, one boy captured 7 or 8, young girl captured about 14 or 16 & the young papooses one about 4 & the other about 18 months. One squaw about 40 years & the other squaw about 17.*

Note: he listed 12 Indians total and squaws shooting with pistols and with bows and arrows.

It is interesting that of all those who testified Ferguson was the only one Buckley asked to estimate the ages of each Indian.

INQUEST MARCH 4th, 1911 - INDIANS KILLED

Wording in **bold** letters are my comments on the testimony of each posse member.

FRANK PERRY

Q- Where were you on that day (26th)?

A- At Rabbit Creek, Nevada engaged with the Indians.

Q- What were the circumstances which led up to that fight with the Indians why were you following them?

A- For the murder of the four men in Little High Rock Canyon.

Q- Did you take up their trail from Little High Rock Canyon?

A- Yes sir

Q- Go on and state all that occurred on the scene of the fight with the Indians.

A- We came on to the Indians about noon on the 26th day of Feb. and asked them to surrender in our language and in the Shoshone language and they responded by shooting at us, we commenced shooting and kept firing until about 2 PM.

They asked the Indians to surrender in our language & the Shoshone language. The Indians responded with a shot so they commenced shooting and kept firing until 2 PM! That should make the Indians want to surrender, if you could work it in with the firing for 2 hours. No one testified that they were any closer to the Indians than 2 to 4 hundred yards. Communicating over 2 lengths of a football field? Years later Perry wrote: "*I would like to state that Skinny Pascal never took the lead at any time on the trail, nor took any participation in the battle that ensued. He was asked by Capt. Donnelley, and later by Newgard to act as interpreter to ask the Indians to surrender but as the battle started at about four hundred yards with a blizzard blowing snow and sleet a conversation was void*". I believe this to be true and there was never any real effort to communicate with the Indians,

Q- Did you know Shoshone Mike during his lifetime?

A- I did not

Q- By whom was he shot if you know?

A- I do not know.

Q- Did you search the body of Shoshone Mike before the arrival of the Coroner?

A- I helped to

Q- Who assisted you to search him.

A- I do not remember who it was .

Q- Why did you search the body before the Coroner arrived?

A- He was still alive and we searched him for weapons.

Q- What property was found on the body?

A- Cartridge belt and few matches in his pockets.

Q- Did you search any other bodies?

A- No

Q- Was there any money found by you on the bodies or camp or near the bodies by you

A- I found $20.00 in camp of old Mike.

In those days $20 dollars could have bought them weeks worth of groceries.

Q- Please produce it.

A- I lost it but will make it good before adjournment.

Q- When you came up to the indians did you make an effort to arrest them without killing them?

A- We did.

What effort? The continual firing until 2 PM?

Q- Who fired the first shot if you know?

A- To the best of my knowledge they did.

Note - "to the best of my knowledge"

Q- Did the other Indians also resist arrest?

A- Yes sir

Q- Were they all killed at same place?

A- No, Indian Mike and a young buck was killed at the camp and the rest were killed probably a mile below.

Q- After Mike was killed was it necessary also to shoot the other Indians?

A- It was

Q- Why was it necessary to kill the squaws and little boys?

A- Well they were in the line of fire & they were shot by accident in shooting at the bucks.

Not true, proven by testimony, identifying the location of the dead Indians and their being in plain sight of the posse. How could they have been shot accidentally! The only buck standing was the young boy running down the wash, they shot him in the back on purpose. The women <u>may</u> have been in the line of fire, to some of the posse members, depending upon where they were in the line, when firing on the boy began.

Q- Did any of them attempt to escape and avoid arrest?

A- They did

Not true the Indians were unarmed trying to avoid being killed.

Q- How many horses did the Indians have in their band when you came up with them.

A- Six I believe

Q- In what condition were the horses?

A- They were pretty poor and in bad condition & could hardly get them in to Kelly Cr.

Q- Did you kill any of the horses?

A- Don't know but was shooting at them.

Q- When you shot at the horses did you try to avoid killing the squaws?

A- I did

Q- Do you know who killed the different Indians squaws and children?

A- I do not

Q- Had they all been killed by members of you party?

A- They had

Q- Did you know that the band of Indians you were following were the same band that you had been following from Little High Rock Canyon?

A- Yes sir

Q- How did you know this?

A- By the evidence we found in their camps along the trail.

Q- How many Indians were in the band when you came up with them?

A- There were twelve

360

Note: twelve

Q- *Describe all the property by which you make the identification as the same band killed at Rabbit Creek with the band that had killed the four men at Little High Rock Canyon*

A- *Two of the horses we found one of them belonged to Harry Cambron this one was killed at Rabbit Creek, one of the horses now at Kelly Cr. the Savage Revolver property of Harry Cambron now in court.*

One of the horses killed belonged to Cambron the other made it to Kelly Creek.

Q- *Is there anything else that you can add to your testimony at this time that will show the necessity for killing the Indians and squaws.?*

A- *Nothing that I can think of.*

Q- *Will your testimony be the same as given here in the case of Shoshone Mike be the same in all the other cases (Old Indian squaw Jennie, Squaw Indian Mary, Buck Big Cupena, Buck Disenda, Buck Kinnan, and one buck and two boys name unknown)*

A- *Virtually the same.*

The only weapons mentioned are arrows and the pistol, in this testimony.

His testimony on March 1st (regarding the death ofEd Hogel) mentioned bows and arrows no mention of other weapons or their location only that he was shot.

W. M. PARSONS

Q- *Where were you on that day?*

A- *On the trail of the Indians.*

Q- *Where did the fight commence?*

A- *On Rabbit Cr. Nev.*

Q- *What were the circumstances which led up to that fight with the Indians why were you following them?*

A- *For the murder of four men in Little High Rock Canyon, Nevada.*

Q- *Go on and state all that occurred on the scene of the fight with the Indians.*

A- *We took the trail in the morning of Feb. 26th overtaking them about noon they were asked by the Indian trailer in shoshone language and also in English to surrender. They refused and commenced to fire. When they commenced shooting at us we returned it under the direction of the sergeant.*

Q- Did you know Shoshone Mike during his lifetime?

A- Saw him shortly before he died after he had been shot.

Q- By whom was he shot if you know?

A- I don't know

Q- Did you search the body of Shoshone Mike before the Coroner arrived?

A- No sir

Q- Did you talk to Shoshone Mike after he was wounded and before he died?

A- Yes sir

Q- What did he say?

A- Said me Shoshone.

Q- When you came up with the Indians did you make an effort to arrest them without killing them?

A- Yes sir

Q- Who fired the first shot if you know?

A- I don't know but it was one of the Indians.

Q- Did the other Indians also resist arrest?

A- Yes sir

Q- Were they all killed at same place?

A- No sir

Q- After Mike was shot was it necessary to also shoot the other Indians?

A- Yes it was.

Q- Why was it necessary to kill the squaws and children?

A- Well they were in the line of fire as we shot at the bucks.

Q- Did any of them attempt to escape and avoid arrest?

A- All of them.

Note: He did not know the answer to four of the last five questions above. He wasn't down where the other indians were killed, he was one mile away.

Q- How many horses were there in the band when you came up with them?

A- Six or seven

362

Q- In what condition were they?

A- Poor, could not have traveled much further.

Q- Did you shoot any of them?

A- No sir

Q- Do you know who killed the different Indians and squaws and children?

A- No sir

Q- Describe the position of the different Indians, squaws and children after the fight was over.

A- Old Mike & young buck was about sixty yards from the camp in the brush & the others were some fifteen hundred yards below, two bucks on the north side, two children in the middle and two squaws on the south all nearly close together.

Q- Had they all been killed by members of your party?

A- Yes sir

Q- Did you know that the band of Indians which you came on at Rabbit Cr. were the same ones that you had been following from Little High Rock Canyon?

A- Yes sir

Q- How did you know?

A- By articles or pieces of articles that we found in Little High Rock Canyon were identical with what we found in nearly all their camps along the trail.

Q- In what kind of positions did you find their camps along the trail?

A- Looked as if they had always picked out a sheltered place so as to have good defense in case they were followed.

Q- How many indians were there in the band when you came up with them?

A- Twelve

Q- How do you identify them as the band you had been following?

A- We found check book belonging to Erramouspe and also watch and automatic pistol. I identify the watch of Harry Cambron now in court as the property of Harry Cambron found in Indian camp and also his Savage Revolver Number 26474.

Note: pistol found in camp! Parsons spent a good amount of time at the camp and should have known where the pistol was found. What else would he have been doing for the two hours he was there?

363

Q- Is there anything else that you can add to your testimony at this time that will show the necessity for killing the Indians squaws and children?

A- Not any more than they resisted arrest and trying to kill us.

Q- How many guns did the Indian party have during the battle?

A- Four of them.

Four was the number of guns in evidence!

Q- Did any of the squaws or children have guns and did they use them?

A- One squaw had the Savage revolver and was using it.

First off he just testified the pistol was found in camp 2nd he wasn't present when and where the women and children were killed, he arrived there after they were dead.

Q- What weapons did the other squaws and children have?

A- Bows and arrows and a spear.

He had just testified above, that one squaw had a pistol and was using it. Then he says all the weapons they had were "Bows and arrows and a spear".

Q- Will your testimony be same ---------------------------- ?

WARREN FRUIT

Q- Where you on that day?

A- At Rabbit Creek Humboldt County Nevada

Q- What were the circumstances which led up to that fight with the Indians why were you following them?

A- For the murder of the men at Little High Rock Canyon. was asked by Sheriff Ferrel to join the posse being formed and I started from Denios camp and was with the posse all the way up to the scene of the fight.

Q- Go & state all that occurred on the scene of the fight at Rabbit Creek Nevada.

A- Well we came on to them at 12 noon & the first battle lasted about 2 hours at the upper camp & some of the boys went down to head off the Indians that were trying to get away & Capt. Donnelley sent me down & we fought there for about an hour.

Q- Did you know Shoshone Mike during his lifetime?

A- Only at time I saw him just before he died.

Q- By whom was he shot if you know?

A- I don't know.

Q- Did you search the body of Shoshone Mike before the arrival of the Coroner?

A- No sir

Q- Search any of the other Indians?

A- No sir

Q- Do you know what property was found on the body of Shoshone Mike?

A- Gun and cartridge belt also some matches.

Q- Can you identify this gun?

A- Yes the one now in court is the gun. Also the Cartridge belt.

Q- When you came up with the Indians did you make any effort to arrest them without killing them?

A- Yes sir

Q- Who made the demand for their surrender?

A- Sergeant Newgard ordered the Indian trailer Pasquale to ask them in shoshone language to surrender.

Q- What was their answer?

A- A shot from the Indians.

Q- Did the other indians also resist arrest?

A- Yes sir

Q- Were they all killed at same place?

A- No sir

Q- After Mike was shot was it necessary to also shoot the other Indians?

A- Yes sir

Q- Why was it necessary to kill the squaws and children?

A- Well they were under fire & stuck their heads up & they were killed in firing at the bucks.

Not true one child was shot in the back as he ran down the wash, the 2 women were standing with smaller children in plain sight shooting arrows.

Q- Did any of them attempt to escape and avoid arrest?

A- Yes sir

365

What else could they do? They were being shot when they stuck their heads up, according to testimony.

Q- How many horses were in the band when you came up with them?

A- There were 7

Q- In what condition were they?

A- Very poor, could not have travelled much further.

Q- Do you know who killed the different Indians squaws & children?

A- No sir

Q- Describe the position of the different Indians squaws & children after the fight was over.

A- At or near the camp there were Old Mike & Indian Jim & further down the wash the other six killed were there.

Where did he get the name Indian Jim? The jury had other fictitious names.

Q- Had they all been killed by members of your party?

A- Yes sir

Q- Did you know that the band of Indians which you came on at Rabbit Creek were the same ones that you had been following from Little High Rock Canyon

A- Yes sir

Q- How did you know?

A- By the evidence of things we found in their camps such as clothing etc in their camps along the trail that were identical with the same things we found at Little High Rock Canyon such as pieces of oil cloth hair from Chapereaus.

Q- In what kind of positions did you find their camps along the trail?

A- Camped in a fortified position and pitched their camps in out of the way places that looked as if they wanted to hide.

Yes and down out of the wind in what ever shelter they could find.

Q- How many Indians were there in the band when you came up with them?

A- Twelve

Q- How do you identify them as the band you had been following?

A- We found Harry Cambron's watch, Savage revolver & on the Indian boy a pair of pants that had been made out of a coat worn by John Laxague one of the murdered men.

Q- Is there anything else you can add to your testimony at this time that will show the necessity for killing the Indians squaws and children?

A- No only they were trying to kill us.

With what bows & arrows & a ceremonial staff?

Q- How many guns did the Indian party have during the fight?

A- Four I believe.

Note: four

Q- Did any of the squaws use guns on your party?

A- Yes sir one of them.

What?, shooting arrows and guns at the same time? Scary women

Q- Will your testimony be same ---------------------- ?

Q- Did you find a gun near the young buck in the wash?

A- Yes found Savage revolver.

He testified earlier that one of the squaws was using a gun, now Savage revolver (Cambron's) found near young buck. Which buck, the child shot in the back or one of the adults, 30 or 40 feet up the wash?

Q- Do you think the Indians understood the posse & Indian trailer when they were asked to surrender?

A- Yes I do as they stood up & listened to what was said.

He testified earlier that they were shot when they stuck their heads up!

How could they stand up and listen when they were shot when they stuck their heads up?

The Indians were shot when ever the posse saw one and they did not stand up and listen, that part makes absolutely no sense, especially under those circumstances!!

The only weapons Fruit identifies in this testimony and his testimony on March 1st is; arrows, spear, pistol and rifle found with Mike.

MEARL PRUSSIA - *(accompanied Constable Byrnes from Paradise Valley)*

Q- Where did you join their command?

A- At Stewart Ranch, Nevada on the 26th day of Feb.

Q- What part did you take in the fight?

A- Fought at upper camp & then was ordered down to the lower camp by Capt. Donly.

He states he was ordered down to lower camp. I don't believe he arrived at the lower site (not camp there was no lower camp) where the women & children were killed. He did not testify at the Ed Hogle inquest, therefore probably not there in addition he was not asked about the killing of the women & children.

Again, he may have been ordered down to the lower site but wasn't there when the last six of the Daggett family were killed.

Q- Did you know Shoshone Mike during his lifetime?

A- Not until the last few minutes of his life.

Q- Did you search his body or any of the other Indians?

A- No sir

Q- Who fired the first shot if you know?

A- Well it came from the Indians I do not know which one of them.

Q- Was any demand made on the Indians to surrender?

A- Yes sir

Q- By whom?

A- By Skinny Pasqualle the Indian trailer in Shoshone language & also by some of the posse who made motions by their hands & also asked them to give up.

Q- Did you find any money or property of the Indians?

A- No sir

Q- Will you testimony be the same ------------------------- ?

OTTO VAN NORMAN -

Q- Where were you on that day?

A- At Rabbit Cr. Nevada

Q- Where did the fight commence?

A- At place known as Rabbit Creek Humboldt County Nevada.

Q- What were the circumstances which led up to that fight why were you following them

A- For the murder of four stockmen at Little High Rock Canyon.

Q- Go on and state all that occurred on the scene of the fight with the Indians.

A- We rode up to them about 12 o'clock noon on 26th Feb. Sergeant Newgard hollered to them to surrender & also Indian Pasquale hollered in his own language & they answered us back with a shot fired by one of the Indians.

"Hollered to them to surrender" This was made clear to each posse member, in testimony they must say the Indians were offered a chance to surrender!

Q- Where was your location during this fight?

A- North of west where their camp was located.

Q- Did you do any shooting at the lower end of the wash where the majority of the bodies were found?

A- I did

Q- How far off were your party from the bed of the creek where the Indians squaws and children were killed?

A- About 35 yards

Van Norman's answer to: *"did you do any shooting at lower site?", "I did".* This distance fits perfectly with where I judge they were from the women and children.

Q- What kind of firearms did they use at the lower camp?

The inquest jury is now starting to use the term "lower camp". There was no lower camp. It is only the location where the last 6 Indians were killed.

A- Bows and arrows and also one pistol.

Q- Did these bucks at the lower camp have at any time any rifles in their possession?

A- They had one shot gun that was afterwards picked up on their trail in going from the higher camp to the lower.

Note: He was asked twice about fire arms and all he came up with was bow and arrows & one pistol, at the lower site, where 6 were killed. The Shot-gun was found up the wash some where.

369

He was asked specifically about rifles in the hands of the bucks, at lower site. He came up with a shot gun, found in the wash, *"on their trail leading from higher camp to the lower".*

Q- Did you know Shoshone Mike during his lifetime?

A- I did not.

Q- By whom was he shot if you know?

A- I don't know.

Q- Did you search the body of Shoshone Mike before the arrival of the Coroner or any of the other Indians?

A- I did not

Q- Did you talk to Shoshone Mike after he was wounded?

A- I did not.

Q- When you came up with the Indians did make effort to arrest them without killing them?

A- I did

Q- Did the other Indians resist arrest?

A- They did

Q- When you were at the lower camp did the Indians show any sign of understanding English?

A- They seemed to understand by the way they acted the squaws did not seem to be fraid as the boys hollered to one another not to shoot them.

More evidence the women were in plain view of the posse the entire time. They were not killed while shooting into the brush at the bucks.

Q- Was there any answers in English made to your demand to surrender?

A- Not to me. Only answer we got was firing back.

With what?

Q- Was there any squaws shot or hurt before they got to this lower camp?

A- Not that I know of.

Q- Why was it necessary to shoot the squaws and children?

A- They resisted arrest and they were shooting bows and arrows at our posse and also they shot with a pistol so I was told.

370

"They shot with a pistol so I was told"! **All he saw them shoot was arrows! He stated** *"they were shooting bows and arrows".*

Q- Did any of the squaws & children attempt to escape and avoid arrest?

A- They did

The squaws did not ! The 10 year old boy and the 7 year old boy did. They shot the ten year old in the back!

Q- How many horses were there in the band of Indians?

A- There were seven.

Q- In what condition were they?

A- Very poor could not have traveled much further.

Q- Do you know who killed the different Indians bucks squaws and children?

A- I do not

Q- Describe the position of the different Indians & squaws & children after the fight was over.

A- Mike & a younger buck was laying I should judge about thirty yards from the camp the younger one was closer to the camp than the old Indian Mike about twenty yards apart, the others at lower camp I did not pay much attention to they were in the bottom of the wash.

Q- Had they all been killed by members of your party?

A- They had

Q- Did you know that the band of Indians which you came on at Rabbit Cr. were the same ones that you had been following form Little High Rock Canyon?

A- yes I did by seeing dead horses along the trail & also by the tracks of three shod horses which were the property of the murdered stockmen at Little High Rock Canyon.

Q- How many Indians were there in the band when you came up with them?

A- Twelve

Q- How do you identify them as the band you had been following?

A- By saddles belonging to the murdered men also horses a watch & pistol property of Harry Cambron.

Q- Will your testimony be the same ---

JOSEPH REEDER

Q- Where were you on the 26th of Feb. 1911?

A- About Rabbit Creek Nevada. in engagement with the Indians.

Q- Where did the fight commence?

A- At Rabbit Creek Nevada.

Q- What were the circumstances which led up to that fight & why were you following them?

A- We were following them for the murder of 4 men in Little High Rock Canyon.

Q- Go on & state all that occurred on the scene of the fight with the Indians.

A- We were coming down hill & saw their camp we were ordered by Sergeant Newgard to form a line which we did & advanced forward about 2 hundred yards there we took positions & the Indians were ordered to surrender by Sergeant Newgard instead of surrendering some of them fired a shot from their camp at that Sergeant Newgard ordered us to fire & 2 of the indians dropped & they quit firing the rest sneaked down the canyon we stayed & held our positions there awhile & then advanced down to the camp & found 1 buck dead & old Mike in a dying condition taking his gun from under his head & laying it on a bush about 6 feet away. From there we were ordered by Capt. Donnelley to the other place where the rest of the Indians were, we fought there at tolerable long range and was not doing much good & we advance right on to them close up to the creek the fight soon ended after we got to close range.

"Two Indians dropped & they quit firing the rest sneaked down the canyon", was their no firing from the camp? I believe there was firing from the camp. Hard to say how much firing. I think they soon ran out of ammunition. Reeder must have forgotten the script, getting confused again.

"We fought there at tolerable long range then advanced on to them close up to the creek the fight soon ended after we got to close range"

If they were fighting at long range, how were they communicating to the Indians to surrender? How could they be fighting when the Indians had no weapons? Only the posse members would have been shooting. And they were asking the Indians to surrender? Hard to follow what he was saying.

Q- Did you know Shoshone Mike during his lifetime?

A- I saw him when he was in a dying condition.

Q- By whom was he shot if you know?

A- I do not know.

Q- Did you search the body before the Coroner arrived?

A- Searched him to see if he had any deadly weapons. Found no property on him.

Q- Did you search any of the other bodies?

A- Searched the young squaw that was captured & the old squaw that was dying to see if they had any deadly weapons. Young squaw was hugging the old squaw who was in a dying condition.

Searching old squaw for deadly weapons while she is dying? She was shooting arrows. He found no guns or he would have stated so.

Q- Did you talk to Shoshone Mike after he was wounded & before he died?

A- I did

Q- What did he say?

A- Me Shoshone Indian.

Q- When you came up with the Indians did you make efforts to arrest them without killing them?

A- Yes sir

Q- Who fired the first shot in the engagement?

A- The Indians

Q- Did the other Indians also resist arrest?

A- Yes sir

Q- After Mike was shot was it necessary to shoot the other Indians?

Q- Why was it necessary to kill the squaws and children?

A- They were in the brush with the bucks & don't think the squaws or children were killed intentionally, there would be shots from the bushes and we would answer the fire in the bushes and think in this manner the squaws & children were killed.

The women were not in the brush, they were in plain sight firing arrows as nearly every posse member testified, including Reeder at the Hogle inquest. There is no evidence that the Indians had weapons to fire from the brush.

Q- Did any of them try to escape and avoid arrest.

A- Yes they ran down the creek & part of the posse headed them off.

They did try to escape from being killed. What else could they do when the posse was shooting into the brush trying to kill Indians? All six Indians were dead in the wash. Were they shot in the brush then run out and die in the wash?

Q- How many horses were in the band when you came up with them?

A- Seven

Q- In what condition were these horses?

A- Very poor

Q- Had the Indians got to their horses after the arrival of the posse could they have gotten away from the posse?

A- Did not know at the time that they could we had the better horses.

True the posse did not know for sure, but they had a pretty good idea that the Indians could not have gone far with the horses they had and in the poor condition the horses were in.

Q- Do you know who killed the different Indians squaws and children?

A- I do not.

Q- Did you know that the band of Indians which you came on to at Rabbit Creek were the ones you had ben following from Little High Rock Canyon?

A- I did by seeing a dead horse at Little High Rock Canyon with a "B" brand on it & also saw a dead horse which they had shot about 12 miles from Rabbit Cr. which had the same "B" brand on it.

What I have not been able to determine, up to this point, is whether this brand was one the Indians used or belonged to some one else who ran horses on Gollaher Mt. in Northeast Elko County, Nev. One possibility of ownership is Buck Rice who ran horses on Gollaher Mt. His cattle brand "frying pan over the hip bone" was identified but no horse brand was ever found, of record. In October of 2013 Alex Kunkle, of Hollister, Idaho was interviewed, he believes the horse brand of Buck Rice was a pot hook (upside down J). I believe the Indians were branding their horses with the "B" brand and when the Indians found the Tranmer gang altering this brand to a back wards, (B E) is when the altercation took place back

on Gollaher Mt., April 25th 1910. In 1916 the backwards (BE) brand was registered to Ed Diffendarfer, one of the horse runners of the Tranmer outfit. The two brands were located on the same place on the horses, "left thigh".

Q- In what kind of positions did you find their several camps along the trail?

A- Did not follow the trail much was with the pack horses most of the time.

Q- How many Indians were there in the band when you came up with them?

A- Twelve

Q- After the fight did you find any more evidence that the band you had fought were the same band that had started from Little High Rock Canyon?

A- Yes sir saw a pair of chaps that had been picked up in their camp as Rabbit Creek that had belonged to Harry Cambron also a pair of boots that had belonged to same party.

Q- Is there anything else that you can add to your testimony at this time that will show the necessity for killing the Indians?

A- Could not take them alive and they would not surrender.

Q- How many guns did the Indian party have during the fight?

A- Three rifles and two pistols.

Per his earlier and later testimony, only one of these 5 weapons were found down where the last 6 Indians were killed, including the women & children.

Q- Can you identify and other paraphernalia the Indians had during the engagement.

A- Saw shot gun now in court down at the was after fight was over, Winchester rifle 40-82 gauge now in court, this gun was taken from under old Mikes head, also Savage revolver now in court also spear now in court this spear the young squaw chased me with, also the war drum now in court as picked up in the wash.

Q- by juror - Do you think the spear now in court is a dangerous weapon?

A- I do yes if she had gotten close enough to me to use it.

Q- Was the war drum beaten during the fight?

A- It was yes.

Some very dangerous and tough squaws, shooting arrows, shooting a pistol and beating on a drum, all at the same time, how scary!!!

The fact is they were running, for their lives, down the wash carrying bows & arrows and small children, not beating on drums. I would agree the drum was found in the wash however up by the make shift camp. Reeder was a large man, 6 foot tall or more, weighing around 190 lbs. The 15 year old girl, nearly a foot shorter and 80 lbs. lighter wielding a spear was of no danger to Reeder. He could have thrown his jacket over the end of the spear, wrapped her up and carried her off.

Q- Was this feathered end spear carried as if it was to be used?

A- Yes it was carried in a position to be thrown at first opportunity.

Again very scary! How far could a 15 year old girl throw a 5 ft. stick with a blade on it? Each posse member was wearing a heavy winter coat. Any one of them could have thrown a coat over the end of the so called spear and taken that 15 year old girl down with ease. But justifying the killing of unarmed women and children requires some creative testimony!

Q- Have you any knowledge of the 38-55 rifle being used?

A- There was a lot of rifle fire from where this gun was afterwards found.

Q- Have you any knowledge where this 38-55 rifle was found?

A- It was found at the camp.

This rifle did exist but no evidence that it was found any where else other than at the camp. His answer is true. Why was it found at the camp? Because it was out of ammunition. If Mike, in his haste, picked up the wrong rifle for the cartridges in the cartridge belt, the cartridges left behind were 40-82, they would not fit in the 38-50.

Further research & information from a gun collector who examined the cartridge belt stated that the cartridges in the belt were 40-82s.

Later stories eluded to the possibility of the Indians getting the rifles mixed up. (Mort West)

Q- Have you any knowledge what has become of the 30-US and the 38-55 rifle?

A- Last I saw of them they was in the wagon.

376

Out of the blue, Buckley asked about the 30-US rifle. No one had testified that it existed, even when asked specifically about firearms, weapons or guns. Hughs testified that the Indians had a box magazine Winchester but no mention of a 30-US rifle. It appears that Hughs testified after Reeder, at least that is the order the documents are in. Hughes left Eagleville 12 days earlier with a 30-US box magazine Winchester rifle. He had checked it out at Johnson's store in Eagleville.

Q- Was there a gun found by this young buck that was killed by old Mike?

A- Yes there was a long pistol.

Sixteen posse members testified and only Reeder saw a long pistol, after each was specifically asked about weapons. Six or seven members of the posse remained at the site, for about two hours, where this Indian with the supposedly long pistol was killed but not one mentioned it. Reeder was not one of those who remained at that site.

Q- Do you know where it now is?

A- I do not.

Q- Have you any knowledge where this shot gun was picked up?

A- I first saw this shot gun where the lower fight took place.

Q- Was there a tomahawk found in the wash.

A- No it was found at the camp.

The camp, meaning at the upper site, where Mike and one of his sons were killed.

Q- How many firearms were they at the lower camp where they were fighting?

A- Only one pistol.

NOTE: only one firearm found at lower camp, a pistol.

Q- What weapons did the squaws and children have?

A- Had spear now in court and bows and arrows.

One pistol found at the lower sight where women & children and 2 adult males were killed. Women & children had bows & arrows and a spear. I think the tomahawk was the ax the Indians had in camp. He placed no weapons in hands of women. And no one mentions weapons at or near the 2 adult male Indians lying dead in the wash. If there were weapons available why weren't they found

with the two adult males? Ans; there were no weapons available except for the bows & arrows and ceremonial staff.

Q- Will your testimony be the same ------------------------------ ?

Q- Did Capt Donnelley or any of the officers order you to take these or any of the Indians alive if possible?

A- Capt. Donnelley told us to take them alive if we could.

Q- At any time did the Indians seem to understand English when they were asked to give up?

A- Yes the young squaw we caught did and at times said would surrender but did not.

Pure fabrication she was scared to death trying to keep the posse members away from her mother, sister and children, with a ceremonial staff.

Q- Why was this shot fired after this Indian said she would quit?

A- We fired into the brush where the buck was.

Fired into the brush! And what shot is he talking about?

Q- This squaw ran back to cover and continued fighting then?

A- Yes

Buckley or other juror testifying for Reeder, putting words in his mouth.

What cover? She remained in plain sight trying to keep posse members off of her family with a spear. All testified to her having a spear and running back and forth towards and away from the posse.

Q- Is that the only time any of them showed any inclination to surrender?

A- The only time.

How did he know this if they were all hidden in the brush?

Q- Did you tell this squaw to come out and surrender and no harm would be done?

A- Yes I made a motion for her to come out and I would not hurt her.

Q- This spear now in court is the only weapon she had when you asked?

A- Yes sir

He never asked her to surrender. The circumstances being what it was, she wouldn't have understood. She was trying to protect the family. A confusing and traumatic time for a girl 15 years old trying to protect the family with a spear while the posse was killing her family all around her.

378

The spear was the only weapon she had. Reeder placed no other weapons in the hands of the young girl.

HENRY HUGHES -

Q- Where were you on that day?

A- Rabbit Creek Nevada

Q- What called you to Rabbit Creek on that day?

A- We were following some Indians that murdered 4 men in Little High Rock Canyon.

Q- Where did the fight commence?

A- Commenced shortly afterwards over the ridge as we came into Rabbit Creek.

Q- What were the circumstances which led up to that fight with the Indians why were you following them?

A- I started with the posse from Little High Rock Canyon & we followed them to Rabbit Creek demanded their surrender & was answered by a shot we formed in a skirmish line & Sergeant Newgard he hollered them to surrender & the Indian trailer hollered to them in Indian language & they opened the fire first shot. I think it was Newgard who said fire on them & we all opened fire there were three Indians who had ran out in front of us & exchanged several shots with us. I saw two of them drop that did not get up any more & I saw that there were some getting away below the camp. Six of us took after those & rounded them up in the wash out about a mile below where the first fight started they shot at us from the washout some little time we saw that we could not get them out of there without killing the women so we took stands around this washout so they could not escape. The Indian trailer went back for more men we thinking that if quite a lot of us around there they might surrender. The men did not come right away I took my horse went back & reported the way they were in the wash out where we could not get at them & several of the boys came down with me at lower camp about forty yards to where the Indians were in the wash. We shouted to them to surrender & a squaw answered back at us " go back you sons of bitches" & she fired arrows at us & we held them in the washout from our stations around one squaw came out with a pistol fired point blank twice at a couple of us. We did not shoot her because we did not want to shoot the squaws if we could keep from it. Another thing that makes me know that they

379

could understand english we would holler from one to the other not to shoot the squaws and they took no precaution to protect themselves from our fire. The squaws & papooses that were killed in the washout I think was killed with bullets intended for the bucks.

Take a hard look at this story! Need to sort out facts from fiction!

Sorting out fact from fiction has proven difficult due to contradicting testimony of the posse members and contradicting testimony of Hughes himself.

When specifically asked *"what were the circumstances leading up to the fight with the Indians"* Hughes goes off on a long dissertation to justify their killing. After the Hogle inquest the posse and or others recognized there was not enough evidence to justify the killing of women and children. Not enough guns and they needed testimony that the Indians were asked to surrender. So Hughes begins to improvise.

"They hollered & shouted for them to surrender and the Indian trailer hollered to them to surrender".

Not likely under those circumstances. Perry years later wrote that Skinny took no part in the fight and communication was void due to distance and weather conditions.

"3 Indians ran out, we all opened fire, 2 dropped".

This is true, coincides with other testimony and evidence.

"I saw some getting away below camp".

True.

"We rounded them up about a mile below camp. They shot at us from the wash, we shouted for them to surrender a squaw answered, go back you sons a bitches"

Pure fabrication! Can you imagine one of the women who likely spoke little english watching her family slaughtered all around her and in fear for the life of the other children, huddled around her, making such a statement. This was a family not a bunch of animals.

"She fired arrows at us".

True coincides with other testimony and evidence.

"One squaw came out with a pistol and fired point blank, twice, at us".

Did not happen the women had no pistol only bows and arrows. But they needed this testimony to justify the killing of women & children.

"Another thing that makes me know that they could understand english we would holler from one to the other not to shoot the squaws and they took no precaution to protect themselves from our fire".

"They took no precaution to protect themselves" if true the women remained in plane sight the whole time and were not killed in shooting at the bucks in the brush.

If he and Skinny were going back and forth to get others to come to lower site, there was no shooting and the Indians were held at bay in plain sight.

The posse did not know how many Indians might be hidden in the wash nor if they were armed, which probably led to their killing. The hair was standing up on the back of their necks, rifles loaded and hammers back. Any sighting or movement of an Indian resulted in their being fired on, no asking them to surrender.

"The squaws & papooses that were killed in the washout I think was killed with bullets intended for the bucks".

At the time the women were killed there was an Indian, one of the boys, running down the wash. They shot him in the back. The women were in plane sight with small children huddled around them and a baby in a cradle board on the back of one of the women. He says squaws and papooses were killed in the washout. The youngest Indian killed was a nine or ten year old boy.

When Hogle was shot they immediately thought an Indian had shot him so they opened fire on the boy and all Indians killing the boy and the two women.

Q- The rifles you were using could it have been possible for the bullets to have passed through their bodies and then killed the children and squaws?

A- Yes very easily.

The 2 adult males were 30 or 40 yards up the wash. No way the bullets could have gone through their bodies and killed the women & children!!

Cover up question and answer!

Q- How many horses were there in the band when you came up with them?

A- Seven

Q- What condition were they in?

A- Very poor condition.

Q- Do you know who killed the Indians squaws and children?

A- No sis [was] only the posse.

Q- How many weapons were in the hands of the Indians?

A- I think I saw 4 guns and 3 pistols.

What kind of an answer was this? "I think". Why didn't the jury ask where each was found and with which Indian?

Ans. - Because the jury suspected there was something wrong here with the number of weapons & did not want to jeopardize the justification for killing women and children.

Q- How did you know that the band of indians you were following were the band that had started from Little High Rock Canyon?

A- When we started from Little High Rock Canyon there were some dead horses in their camp branded "B" & the day we overtook them we found a horse on the trail with the same brand & by the hostility shown when we demanded their surrender.

Note a horse (1) found on the trail.

Q- Can you describe the kind of guns the Indians had in their possession?

A- They had a 40-82 Winchester, a shot gun, box magazine Winchester, a 38-55 Winchester, 2 revolvers & an automatic pistol. I sold Cambron the automatic pistol that is now in court myself. This pistol was found near the body of the dead bucks in the wash.

Hughs had in his possession a 30-US, box magazine, Winchester rifle, that he had checked out of the Johnson Store in Eagleville, at the beginning of the chase. There is no evidence that the Indians had a box magazine Winchester. If they did why didn't someone, when asked, describe where it was found and which Indian had it? Same goes for the 2 revolvers.

Buckley asked Hughes to describe the weapons but did not ask where the Box Magazine Winchester was found nor which Indian had which weapon.

The automatic pistol was found every where, depending who you asked. It was there but it is a mystery as to where it was found and which Indian had it. The posse members did not know which Indian had it and in putting their story together couldn't keep it straight as to where it was found.

If it was found by the dead bucks how could the squaws have been shooting it and arrows?

Q- Can you identify the guns now in court as part of the weapons in the hands of the Indians?

A- Yes sir

Q- Will your testimony be the same as ----------------------- ?

GEORGE HOLMES -

Q- Where were you on that day?

A- After a bunch of Indians and caught up to them at Rabbit Creek.

Q- Where did the fight commence?

A- I believe they called it Rabbit Creek.

Q- What were the circumstances which led up to that fight with the Indians & why were you following them?

A- For the murder of four men in Little High Rock Canyon, Nevada.

Q- Go on and state all that occurred on the scene of the fight with the Indians.

A- I was in the fight at the upper camp with the rest of them.

Q- How did you know this band you fought with was the same band that had camped at Little High Rock Canyon?

A- I did not know.

Q- Who ordered you to fire on them?

A- Sergeant Newgard

Q- Did you see Shoshone Mike before or after the engagement?

A- Yes both before and after.

Q- Did you search the body of Mike or any of the other Indians?

A- No sir

Q- Have you any of these Indians property.

A- I found a watch in an old coat down the wash (watch Waltham 15 jewels No. 10973688) produced in court.

Q- Who fired the first shot if you know?

A- The Indians did.

Q- Have you any doubt that this band you was following was the ones that started out from Little Rock Canyon?

A- I was not on the trail very much.

Why was he not on the trail very much?

Q- You could then have mistaken this band of Indians for a peaceable one?

A- They could not have been or they would not have commenced shooting.

Q- Can you identify the watch you turned in as the property of 1 of the murdered men?

A- No sir I could not.

Q- Where was this shot gun now in court picked up?

A- About 2 hundred yards south of the wash?

I would suggest he meant south of the camp, in the wash. South of the wash makes no sense, it puts the shot gun clear out of the picture.

Q- Will your testimony be the same ----------------------- ?

Holmes is never asked about weapons nor does he offer to discuss the issue of weapons, including his testimony on March 1st at the Hogle inquest.

He was quite reserved and did not go off on a long dissertation on what happened when asked to: *"go on and state all that occurred on the scene of the fight with the Indians".* **Each posse member was asked to state what occurred at the scene, however Holmes was reluctant to get into a discussion about what occurred and was able to get out without having to lie about what he saw. I believe Buckley sensed this and did not push the issue. Holmes was 10 to 20 years older than any of the other posse members. He was probably more reluctant than the younger guys to lie.**

MORT WEST -

Q- Was you a member of Capt. J. P. Donnelleys command on the 26th of Feb.?

A- I was deputized by Sheriff Ferrel at Denios Ranch Nev. & I was a member of the Eagleville Posse & supposed I was under J. P. Donnelleys command.

If he was deputized by Washoe County Sheriff Ferrel, did he have any authority in Humboldt County?

Q- Did Capt. Donnelley make any request that you accompany him on the trail?

A- It was understood that we were to accompany him on the trail, Sheriff Ferrel deputized us.

Q- Why were you on the trail and for what purpose?

A- We were on the trail of the murders of the 4 men that had been murdered in Little High Rock Canyon, Nevada.

Q- Where did this fight take place at?

A- About 6 miles from Kelley Creek Ranch on what is known as Rabbit Creek.

Q- How did you know that the band you found at Rabbit Creek were the band that had started from Little High Rock Canyon?

A- They had taken some of the clothing from the murdered men at Little High Rock Canyon & on the trail in their camps we found pieces of their clothing hairs from & pieces of yellow chaps in nearly every camp of the band. Also found horses tracks that had shoes on. Also found piece of oil cloth in Little High Rock Canyon & we took a piece of this along for comparison, finding pieces of this oil cloth in several of the camps as we followed the trail. We always found their camps hidden or in secluded spots from the beginning as we also found the High Rock camp all made up in same way & built a brush wood break around the camp as they evidently had no bedding & most of their traveling was done at night in the beginning of the night & they travelled within a mile of a sheep camp about 12 miles from Little High Rock Canyon. Sheepmen saw their trail next morning but did not get to see them in the night. Little Indian boy at Kelly creek after the fight that they had intended to leave their camp at Rabbit Creek that night.

Why would you take oil cloth along for comparison? They did not know what they would find to compare it to.

I think he is right the Indians didn't have much bedding. They would naturally camp in a protected spot for all the shelter they could get. It was in the middle of the winter.

The little Indian boy said *"they intended to leave their camp at Rabbit Creek that night"*. First he likely did not speak English and he was in such a state of mind, due to the killing of his mother and rest of the family, that he did not tell them anything. Pure fabrication!

Q- Did you know Mike during his lifetime?

A- I did not.

Q- Did you search his body or any of the other Indians?

A- I did not.

Q- Did you find or get any of their property?

A- No

Q- By whom was he shot if you know?

A- I do not know.

Q- When you came up with the Indians did you make any effort to arrest them without killing them?

A- Yes sir I heard Newgard & a number of the men ask them to throw up their hands we shouted to them in English to throw up their hands then I heard Sheriff Smith to tell Skinny Pasquale to tell them to give up in the Indian language. I heard Skinny shout to them a half dozen times and he put his own hands up then I think they shot at him & during a lull in the firing Skinny shouted the same thing to them. They answered back by warwhoops.

Warwhoops were made by Indians in movies and earlier by young braves attacking wagon trains or groups of settlers where the Indians had the upper hand, not a family being shot at and running for their lives.

It does not fit with other testimony or the turmoil that was going on, firing, weather conditions and distance. Plus Smith was not down where the Women and children were killed.

Q- Can you identify any of the guns now in court as part of the weapons in the hands of the Indians?

A- I recognize this 40-82 as a gun in the hands of the Indians after the fight also the shot gun also the 38-55.

Note: he did not mention the pistol which was their somewhere, and no other weapon. Because there were none!

Q- Did you think it unavoidable that the squaws and children were shot?

A- Yes I do.

They all had to stand by this statement or it was murder, which it was.

Q- Will you testimony be the same ---------------------------- ?

MARCH 5th 1911 - INDIANS KILLED

E. J. LYING - *(Constable at Golconda, Nevada)*

Q- What is your name, age residence & occupation?

A- E. J. Lying, 27 years, Golconda, Nev., occupation Constable.

Q- Did you inspect the bodies at Rabbit Creek, Humboldt County Nevada, February 28th 1911, of the Indians Shoshone Mike, aged about 55 years, Indian squaw Jennie aged about 40 years buck Cupena aged about 25, Buck Kinnan aged about 23, buck Disenda aged about 18 years, one young squaw name unknown aged about 17 years and two boys unknown, aged about 10 or 12 years?

A- Yes

Q- Do you identify them from this description?

A- Yes

Lying went to the scene of the killing on Feb. 28th. He and Buckley must have gone there together. Their purpose inspect the scene, the bodies and to bury them. Did he take the pictures of the dead Indians in a pile?

Coroner Buckley, finally got the number of Indians killed right after questioning every posse member except Skinny Pascal, which he failed to question. They did not need Skinny's testimony, it might not match up with the other posse members. Interesting that Pascal was not questioned since he was the main one that was supposed to have asked the Indians to surrender in the Indian language!!

CHAPTER VI

TESTIMONY MARCH 1st, 3rd & 4th - IN REVIEW

Coroner Buckley evidently deemed it necessary to give the Indians names for the inquest so they just gave the deceased Indians fictitious names. Names given during testimony were: Shoshone Mike, Old Indian squaw Jennie, young squaw Indian Mary, Buck Cupena, Buck Disenda, Buck Kinnan, one Buck and two boys names unknown a total of <u>nine</u>. The inquest jury also concluded that the Indians killed, died of gunshot wound inflicted by Captain Donnelley's posse.

" And we further find that Captain Donnelley and posse were justified in their action".
The inquisition upon each Indian explained why each was killed and listed them by name and age as follows:

"Shoshone Mike, age about 55, died while resisting arrest when called upon; Indian squaw Jennie, age about 40, died of gunshot wound which was unavoidable; Buck Cupena about 25 died while resisting arrest when called upon; Buck Kinnan about 23 died while resisting arrest when called upon; Buck Disenda about 18 died while resisting arrest when called upon; young squaw unknown about 17 died of gunshot wound which was unavoidable and two boys names unknown, one age about 12 years, the other unknown about 10 both died of gunshot wounds which was unavoidable. A total of <u>8.</u>
The ages of the Indians killed were taken from the testimony of Jack Ferguson.

In the findings of the jury the killing of the women and children was unavoidable. The two adult males were lying dead up the wash. The posse members were shooting directly at the women and children they were not in the line of fire. It wasn't unavoidable all the posse members had to do was not shoot directly at women and children.

The jury finally got the number of Indians killed correct, eight.

Had they not been Indians they would have done a proper inquest on each body, identifying the number of bullet wounds and the entrance and exit of those wounds.

The inquest on the sheepmen at Little High Rock offered those details.

With eleven men shooting at the women and children there would have been numerous bullet wounds in each individual Indian.

How they could justify or why they attached the fictitious names is hard to understand but further illustrates the lack of concern to see the Daggett family as human.

An interesting point as to the name "Indian squaw Jennie," is that there is no formal record of that name anywhere. It was picked up from the news papers, inquest jury and Dayton Hyde. However in the book "BUCKSKIN AND SMOKE" by Anna Hansen Hays she refers to Mike Daggett's wife as Maggie. Anna new and visited with the Indians at Rock Creek, Idaho. In additions Carrie Hansen Crockett, sister of Anna refers to Mike's wife as Maggie in a letter to Mary Jo Estep November 5, 1975. Carrie also knew the Daggetts and Carrie's husband knew the Indians and had played with the Daggett children when they all were little kids. In short Mike's wife's first name is Maggie not Jennie.

Also note, during the inquest testimony of each posse member Buckley listed nine Indians killed including those with fictitious names however only eight killed, another example of sloppiness and being inconsiderate on the part of the inquest jury after all they were only Indians.

In Frank Perry's account, years later he stated, *"Skinny Pasco never took the lead at any time on the trail, nor took any participation in the battle that ensued".*

Not a lot of Perry's account was accurate, but I believe this one could very well be true.

March 1st Testimony   (Ed Hogle)

Ten of the eleven posse members who were at the lower site, where the women, children and Hogle were killed, testified at the inquest for Ed Hogle. Eight stated: "the women and fifteen year old girl had and were using bows & arrows and a spear/war staff/magic stick".

None of the ten described nor testified they saw a firearm. Ferguson stated: "buck fired 2 shots, at him". Hughes stated: "the squaws fired 2 shots at us".

No weapons were identified nor mentioned by Newgard or Holmes.

On March 3rd & 4th there was conflicting testimony as to where the Savage automatic pistol that belonged to Harry Cambron was found and who might have been using it. Testimony given during the three days of the inquest revealed that the posse members were within 30 yards or less of the women and children that were killed. All but 2 posse members testified that they were within a few feet of Hogle and that he was out in front

390

at the edge of the wash. At no place is the wash/creek more than 30 yards wide. The young girl was running up at them from the bottom of the wash and when it was all over the women lay dead in the bottom of the wash. At lest eight of the posse members were no further than 50 or 60 feet from the women when the women were killed.

If any of the six Indians killed, at that site, had or were using fire arms how could eight posse members specifically see and identify bows & arrows and a spear, in the possession of the women and children and not specifically see nor identify a firearm? Because there were **no** operable firearms at the sight where the last six Indians were killed!

Not one of the posse members testified they saw an Indian shoot Ed Hogle, only that they heard a shot!

Coroner Buckley did everything he could to get each posse member to incriminate the 15 year old girl. Buckley asked every posse member if she had anything to do with the killing of Ed Hogle. Only Ferguson cooperated!

In a cowardly effort, the inquest jury tried to coach posse members into testifying that the young girl lifted her skirt to distract and draw the posse members within range of the bucks with fire arms so that they could be shot.

When Hogle was killed there were only eleven posse members at the lower site where he and the last six of the eight Indians were killed. The Indians killed included two adult males, two women and two children.

The posse members at that site included Ed Hogle, Sergeant Newgard, Sergeant Stone, Jack Ferguson, O. D. Van Norman, Henry Hughes, Frank Perry, Joe Reeder, Warren Fruit, George Holmes and Mort West.

Nearly all saw the grandmother & the mother shooting arrows and the young Indian girl, with a spear, running back and forth up and out of the wash.

What she was actually doing was trying to keep the posse members away from her mother, sister and small children huddling together in the bottom of the wash. Ferguson saw all kinds of things no one else saw, only he saw a weapon fired. He said a buck fired at him twice and a bullet grazed his thumb.

No weapons identified except bows and arrows in the hands of the women and a spear in the hands of the fifteen year old girl.

NO ONE, saw the grandmother, the mother with the baby on her back nor the fifteen year old girl, with or use a weapon other than bows and arrows and a spear, not even Ferguson! The Indians were not armed except for bows & arrows and the ceremonial staff.

It was a cover up, the 15 year old girl had absolutely nothing to do with the killing of Ed Hogle.

COVER UP ? Donnelley's posse with the help of Buckley's jury covered up the facts in this tragic event.

They did not ask the Indians to surrender they were shooting Indians wherever and whenever they saw one.

One of the Posse members accidentally killed Ed Hogle. Two members of the posse testified they were about 100 feet from Ed when he was killed, O. D. Van Norman and Frank Perry. Perry claimed to be to the left of Hogle which would put him up the wash from Hogle (he also indicated this in his writings years later). Frank Perry was in a position to shoot Hogle but the young Indian boy was running away from him down the wash, he would have had to shoot Ed in the back.

If in one of those rare occasions the newspaper (Humboldt Star dated March 1, 1911) was correct, Ed Hogle was shot from the front. The bullet entering his left breast and exiting under his right arm. Two posse members also testified that he put his hand up to his "left breast" and said he was shot. One said "breast". Another thought he was wounded in the arm.

From testimony it appears to be O. D. Van Norman was down below the others looking back and in a position to accidentally shoot Hogle.

The jury asked no specific questions regarding guns, as to where they were found nor who was shooting guns. Was this part of a cover up or were they too dumb to ask?

If the Indians had all those weapons, as was claimed at the inquest why were the women using bows and arrows?

Why would the posse members keep talking about spears and bows & arrows if there were guns involved and why would the jury keep asking over and over again, of each posse member, what role the 15 year old girl played in the killing of Hogle and not ask specifics about guns involved?

392

BECAUSE THE INDIANS AT THIS SITE HAD NO GUNS!!

Although each posse member who testified stated they were with in a few feet of Hogle when he was shot, NOT ONE stated he saw an Indian shoot Hogle!

Later, on March 3rd and 4th, nearly every one of them stated they were near the wash and could easily see the women and children in the wash, so how could they not see an Indian shoot Hogle?

BECAUSE AN INDIAN DID NOT SHOOT HOGLE!!

If any one had seen an Indian kill Ed Hogle they would not have hesitated to say so. They needed that kind of testimony to justify the killing of women and children.

Fifteen of the eighteen posse members there, testified at the inquest of Ed Hogle. Hogle did not, he was dead; Pascal did not, he was an Indian and may not have testified that he made all those requests for the Daggett family to submit as claimed by the posse members who testified; Prussia from Paradise Valley did not testify which would indicate he was not at the scene where Hogle and the women and children were killed.

The inquest on the body of Ed Hogle was conducted by Coroner James Buckley on the March 1, 1911 at Golconda, Nevada.

The most cowardly action of all was when the inquest jury signed the document stating that the fifteen year old girl, (Maggie) fictitious name, was instrumental in the cause of Ed Hogle's death!

Inquisition by Coroner's Jury dated March 2, 1911 Page 24

March 3rd, 4th and 5th Testimony (Eight members of the DAGGETT FAMILY)

Three things that those who testified at the inquest made clear was: a)- they offered the Indians a chance to surrender, b)- the Indians tried to escape, c)- the Indians resisted arrest. To justify the killing of the women and children these three items are a must in there testimony and all answers were the same from each posse member, in the affirmative. The answers were short, concise and to the point. They had been coached. This was their justification for killing the women and children. Answers to other questions, for the most part, were lengthy, in-concise and contradictory.

In order to have a true fight/battle with the Indians there needed to be more guns (fire arms) in the hands of the Indians. They were a little short so they began to improvise, however not as well orchestrated as their testimony on the three items above. So testimony was all over the place, fabrication, contradictions and sometimes with their own testimony.

The Indians who had been killed were within 20 or 30 yards of each other. First up the wash were the two adult males, then the two adolescent boys ten and twelve, next the two women, grandmother & mother with baby in cradle board on her back.

The posse members were all within a few yards of the Indians, had them surrounded and shooting down on them from the bank above, kinda like shooting guppies in a fish tank.

The two women were not shot accidentally, nor were any of the other Indians. Miraculously, the fifteen year old was not shot and killed, on purpose, and none of the three small children were killed accidentally. All of the Indians were shot numerous times none were wounded. They were shot until dead.

Except for Donnelley and Pascal every posse member tried to get one or more rifle bullets into an Indian. From all available information, it appears that neither Captain Donnelley nor Skinny Pascal fired at any Indians and they shot no horses.

In the case of Newgard it is not clear if he shot any Indians.

Weapons of the Indians where Hogle and women & children were killed

NEWGARD - March 1st - *no mention of weapons.
             March 3rd - no mention of weapons.

STONE - March 1st - squaws firing arrows, *no mention of other weapons.
             March 3rd - saw a rifle by Mike, saw the pistol (Cambron's) taken at
             camp.
             No mention of other weapons.

FERGUSON - March 1st - saw war staff. Buck fired 2 shots, *no mention of a weapon.
             March 3rd - squaws were fighting with bows & arrows, some with pistols.

REEDER - March 1st - 2 squaws shooting arrows. *no mention of other weapons.
             March 4th - Indians had 3 rifles- 40-82 Winchester, found by Mike;-
             38-55 found in camp;- 30-US, **(30-US not in evidence and not
             placed at any site)**; 1 shot gun; 2 pistols,- Savage revolver at lower
             sight,- long pistol at the camp **(but not in evidence)**; 1 spear and bows
             & arrows.

HUGHES - March 1st - saw squaw firing arrows, *no other weapon noted.
             March 4th - one squaw fired arrows, one squaw fired pistol at us. Think I
             saw 4 guns: 1- 40-82; 2- 38-55; 3- box magazine Winchester, 4- shot gun
             and 3 pistols: 1- two revolvers; 2- automatic pistol (Pistol found near body
             of dead bucks) **(box magazine Winchester and the two revolvers
             were not in evidence nor placed at any site)**.

WEST - March 1st - old squaw shooting arrows; 1 spear *no other weapons noted.
             March 4th - 40-82; shot gun; & 38-55 all in evidence, no mention of
             pistols.

PERRY - March 1st - 1 squaw shooting arrows *no other weapons mentioned.
             March 4th - Identified Savage revolver but did not say where it was found.

HOLMES - March 1st - *no weapons mentioned.
             March 4th - shot gun 200 yards south in wash. *no other weapons noted.

FRUIT - March 1st - magic stick, *no other weapons mentioned.
             March 4th - gun in court found on Mike; Savage revolver; 4 guns;
             one squaw used a gun; Savage pistol found near young buck.

O. D. - March 1st - Indian spear *no other weapons mentioned.
             March 4th - fire arms used, bows & arrows and one pistol. When asked
             specifically "did bucks have rifles at lower camp?" he answered "one
             shot gun" Cambron's pistol.

* Eight of the ten posse members saw a war staff/magic stick/ spear and or bows and
arrows. No one stated they saw a fire arm. Ferguson stated "there were 2 shots fired".

CAMBRON'S Auto SAVAGE Pistol

Newgard - I D'd no weapons, although 2nd in command.

Stone - Pistol taken at **Indian camp**

Ferguson - Did not I D pistol

Reeder - I D'd 2 pistols - long pistol by camp & Savage pistol at **lower camp**

     There was no lower camp only the place where the last Indians were killed.

Hughes - This pistol found near body of this dead buck **in the wash.**

West - No mention of pistol, although asked to I D guns.

Perry - I D'd pistol, did not say where found.

Holmes - No mention of pistol

Fruit - Found pistol near young buck **in wash.**

O. D. - Pistol **at lower camp**, Squaws shot with pistol, <u>so I was told</u>.

     ID'd Cambron's pistol. There was no lower camp.

Parsons - Watch & pistol found **in camp.** He was at that camp for two hours.

     He was not at the lower site until after those last six Indians were killed.

Donnelley Did not know about weapons, although he was in charge.

Smith - I D'd rifle by Mike only.

Cambron - I D'd brother's pistol, did not say where found.

Of the 10 posse members at the lower site, who testified; Ferguson, Hughes, Fruit & VanNorman testified the women fired or used firearms. They also said the women were shooting arrows, which takes both hands, also firing a pistol and as Reeder testified, "beating on a drum" all at the same time . Quite a feat!!

Not one of those ten testified they found or saw a firearm of any kind by the women that were killed! The shot gun was found some where farther up the wash.

Only Reeder, Hughes, Fruit & O D testified Cambron's pistol was found in the wash at the lower site. Reeder and O. D. said "lower camp" there was no lower camp.

Only Hughes & Fruit testified where the pistol was found, that being by the bucks. No other firearm of any kind was placed at the lower sight where the six Indians, including women and children were killed!

Reeder was asked specifically about the 30-US. It had not been mentioned before or after Reeder testified. It was something Buckley had picked up outside the jury room.

Q- Have you any knowledge what has become of the 30-US and the 38-55 rifle?

A- Last I saw of them they was in the wagon.

Only Reeder, when specifically asked, identified a long pistol and stated that it was found near the young Indian. Most of Reeder's time was spent at the lower site.

Q- Was there a gun found by this young buck that was killed by old Mike?

A- Yes there was a long pistol.

Seven posse members (Donnelley, Smith, Byrnes, Prussia, Pascal, Cambron and Parsons) <u>not</u> including Reeder, remained at the camp sight for two and half to three hours where the young Indian and Mike were killed. None of those seven testified that they saw a gun by the young Indian that was killed near the camp. Neither the Long Pistol, the US- 30, identified by Reeder nor the Box Magazine Winchester & the two pistols, identified by Hughes, were in evidence in court nor in the photo taken of the Weapons of the Indians. Of the seven who testified, only Reeder & Hughes spoke of these 4 weapons.

No posse member stated where these four weapons were found not even Hughes. They needed the 32 automatic pistol to be found where Hogle was killed to explain his killing. Posse members testified differently as to it's use and where it was found. It most likely was empty and was found at the Indian's camp.

Stone & Parsons testified that they identified Harry Cambron's pistol by the serial No. Stone 26474., Parsons 26474. <u>T</u>hey would not have known the serial No. of that pistol, until they saw it and did not match the Nos. identified as listed on Cambron's pistol to watch out for back around the 10th of Feb. *(14160 or 13711).*

Women were Not Hidden in the Brush/Bushes

NEWGARD ----STONE ---- WEST-----FERGUSON ---- HOLMES -- These five posse members, in there testimony, did not say the squaws were hidden it the brush.

REEDER -

Q - Why was it necessary to kill the squaws and children?

Ans.--They were in the bush with the bucks & don't think the squaws or children were killed intentionally, there would be shots from the bushes & we would answer the fire in the bushes & think in this manner the squaws & children were killed.

They were shooting into the bushes and didn't know what was in the bushes! The squaws were not in the bushes, they were together, huddled with three very small children, in the bottom of the wash, in plain sight, shooting arrows. Later in his testimony:

Q - "Why was this shot fired after this Indian said she would quit"?

A - "We fired into the brush where the buck was"

What shot fired? There was no mention of a shot fired after the young girl supposedly said she would quit or give up.

Q - "This squaw ran back to cover & continued fighting then"?

A -" Yes"

A - "Yes"? None of this makes sense. *"Fired into the brush where the buck was." "Squaw ran back to cover & continued fighting?"* This Indian girl was never in the brush nor ran back to cover, she remained in plain sight the whole time!!

HUGHES -

Another thing that makes me know that they could understand english we would holler from one to the other not to shoot the squaws and they took no precaution to protect themselves from our fire.

He saw that they took no precaution to protect themselves from our fire. If this was true he had the squaws in plain sight the whole time, they were not in the brush.

398

PERRY -

Q--Why was it necessary to kill the squaws and little boys?

A--Well they were in the line of fire & they were shot by accident in shooting at the bucks.

The buck they were shooting at, when the squaws were killed was one of the little boys and they shot him in the back. The two bucks (adult males) were laying dead in the wash above where the women and boys were killed and shooting at them would have been away from the women and children. They were not in the line of fire.

FRUIT -

Q--Why was it necessary to kill the squaws and children?

A--Well they were under fire & stuck their heads up & they were killed in firing at the bucks.

Later testimony:

Q--Do you think they understood the posse & Indian trailer when they were asked to surrender?

A--Yes I do they stood up & listened to what was said.

Just a few minutes earlier Fruit said: "Well they were under fire & stuck their heads up & they were killed in firing at the bucks".

If they were killed when they stuck their heads up how could they have stood up and listened?

VAN NORMAN -

Q--When you were at the lower camp did the Indians show any sign of understanding English?

A--They seemed to understand by the way they acted the squaws did not seem to be fraid as the boys hollered to one another not to shoot them.

If O. D. could see the women reacting to understanding English, then they were not hiding in the brush. And he saw them shooting bows & arrows.

In trying to lay blame on the young Indian girl for the death of Hogle, Buckley asks each posse member where she was when Ed was killed and he got these answers.

In attempting to give the answer Buckley wanted they begin to improvise instead of sticking with the facts, and when they did that they couldn't keep their stories straight. Very hard to do when one tries to state what they think they are supposed to say instead of how it actually happened.

NEWGARD - *"squaw acting conspicuously before Ed".*

HUGHES - *"old squaw in the wash shooting arrows at him [Ed].*

FERGUSON - *stated "no squaw" conspicuously before Ed.*

REEDER, PERRY, WEST - *stated "old squaw" before Ed.*

WEST - *stated, squaw "30 to 50 feet south of Ed" not in front of him.*

FRUIT - *"young aquaw] was not in front of Ed, couldn't say if any were".*

HOLMES - *"could not say there were so many of them" but dancing up close to where we were.*

VAN NORMAN & STONE - *young squaw not in front of Ed but running at all of them.*

1st Two Indians Killed

Each posse member testified some one asked the Indians to surrender, most said "in English & Shoshone". Most indicated Pasco was ordered to call for them to surrender in Shoshone. Some said they were ordered to surrender, by no one in particular. Donnelley and Byrnes - were not there when firing began.

Smith - *word was passed to Pasco to ask Indians to surrender*
  Shot fired by someone but don't know who.

Cambron - *Heard some of the boys say throw up your hands. Instructed Pasco to*
  tell the Indians same thing. Heard shot from the direction where the Indians
  were. Some of the posse began firing.

Newgard - *We demanded their surrender - asked Paso to demand also.*
  They responded by shots and we opened fire on them.

Stone - *We demanded their surrender and in Shoshone language.*
  They replied with a shot. Our posse then commenced firing.

Ferguson - *Boys commanded them to throw up their hands. Newgard told them same*
  thing. They replied with a shot at us and firing commenced along the line.

Perry - *Asked them to surrender and in Shoshone language.*
  They responded by shooting at us. We commenced firing.

Parsons - *They were asked to surrender in Shoshone and English.*
  They commenced to fire and we returned it under direction of the Sergeant.

Fruit - *Newgard asked Pasco to ask them to surrender. There was a shot from the*
  Indians.

Prussia - *Pasco asked them to surrender. 1st shot it came from the Indians*

O. D. - *Pasco asked them to surrender. Answered back with shot from the Indians.*

Reeder - *Ordered to surrender by Newgard. Fired a shot from their camp.*

Hughes - *Pasco ordered them to surrender. Was answered by a shot.*

Holmes - *Newgard ordered them to fire on the Indians. Posse commenced firing.*
  (He did not say as the others did that "the Indians were asked to surrender").

West - *Pasco ordered them to surrender. I think they shot at him (Pasco)*

Fifteen men setting on the hill side looking down on three Indians, close enough to communicate and they didn't specifically see one of them fire a shot! If the posse members were too far away to determine which Indian shot then they were too far away to communicate. The posse was all psyched up to start killing Indians and if one in the posse shot first then all hell broke loose. At that point firing started all along the line and no one was going to be left out from shooting an Indian.

Mike may have never fired a shot.

The spelling (Pasco) is how his name was spelled in the inquest testimony.

401

What Were They Thinking

First of all: eighteen posse members, armed with repeating rifles, all lined up, looking down on three Indians, heard a shot and as testified all commenced firing down at the three Indians. Eighteen posse members were not needed to face three Indians so why didn't they surround the Indians and then move in? This is another example of lack of leader ship and common sense. The state police and sheriff Smith should have been able to figure that out. Why not? Because of the lack of leadership and common sense in the form of the state police and Sheriff Smith.

Jack Ferguson blamed the fifteen year old girl for the death of Ed Hogle.

O.D. Van Norman, in interviews years latter stated "that they should have killed the young fifteen year old girl along with the rest".

(Elko Free Press - Oct. 19, 1979)

In Frank Perry's account, (1949), he states *that Sheriff Lamb's wife made a similar statement, (Rats breed lice, you should have killed them all).* He also stated *"her parents were massacred by Indians".*

This may not have been true as there were so many inaccurate statements being made by posse members, the newspapers and most anyone else who wanted to become a part of this event in history.

In Mort West's written account, he talks about running from bush to bush, rolling behind one then another bush and dodging arrows and shooting and Indian fighting. The problem with him in the first place he is what we would call a blow hard, and had read too many wild west novels or seen too many wild west shows and he envisioned himself as some kind of a hero Indian fighting machine, as I think he called himself.

Though second hand information, one elderly lady in Surprise Valley, who knew Mort, made reference to Mort's story published in the Modoc County Historical Society Journal in 2003, stating "he was kind of a joke and must have thought he was John Wayne".

Frank Perry took it upon himself to ransack Mike's pockets. In Perry's writings years later he stated when authorities told him it was against the law to take stuff from dead bodies and to turn those items in, George Holmes says, *"Hell, he wasn't dead"*, meaning it was still okay to ransack Mike's pockets because he wasn't dead yet.

I question whether Holmes made this statement this may be something Perry thought up thirty eight years after the incident.

Perry's 1949 written account.

The fifteen year old girl's actions consisted of attempting to ward off the posse with long willow having a blade attached to it, while eleven members of the posse poured rifle fire into the small band of Indians with repeating rifles killing every Indian that showed himself including; her two brothers, two adolescent boys, ages ten and twelve, her mother and her sister who was carrying baby Mosho.

She had absolutely nothing to do with death of Ed Hogle!

If one was to believe the testimony of each posse member, the two women (one being fifty five years of age and one with baby Mosho on her back) were shooting with a 32 caliber pistol, shooting arrows with bows and beating on an Indian war drum all at the same time. Is it any wonder the posse was so fearful of the grandmother and the mother with the baby on her back. What scary combatants they must have been!

Joe Reeder testified that he saw the 38-55 at the camp. There was no other testimony that specifically countered Joe's recollection. Testimony placed the shotgun in the wash, some distance above where the last six were killed (that no one testified it had been shot is some evidence of there being no shells for it). The 32 caliber pistol and the 38-55 were most likely also out of ammunition. The 38-55 may have been jammed. One can easily conclude that the only weapons the Indians had at the end, when the six were still standing, were; bow & arrows (flimsy bows and arrows that the kids used to hunt rabbits and other small game), a stick with a blade on it and hands full of rocks.

Reference testimony of the posse.

Each posse member testified that the Indians tried to escape. The last ten remaining family members alive who the posse members claimed, tried to escape, consisted of; two adult men, two young boys (ten to twelve years old), one lady (fifty plus years old), one lady about twenty five years old with a baby, (in a cradle board) on her back, a fifteen year old girl, one little girl four years old and one boy six or seven years old. With no horses in an area where there was very little cover, you can see for miles and with the posse members on horse back there was absolutely no way for Mikes' family to escape! Mike and one of his boys had already been killed about a mile up the draw. At least one gun was at that location and possibly two. Since there is little or no evidence that there were more than 4 guns in the possession of the Family, the two women, six children and two young men were basically unarmed.

In analyzing the testimony of the fifteen members of the posse who testified I find their statements were contradictory, erratic and self serving, even with in each man's own statement. In self serving I mean they were trying to rationalize and justify the killing of unarmed Indians.

In the previous month, January 1911, Humboldt County Sheriff S. Graham Lamb and Indian tracker John (Skinny) Pascal had done a much more detailed investigation of the Quilicy murders. One must remember however the Quilicys were not Indians.

The attitude of the posse and others is pretty well laid out in accounts that were written of the incident in almost each and every article numbering over two hundred articles in twenty or thirty newspapers, in over a dozen towns and cities.

The Daggett family was never referred to as a family or human beings by anyone including the inquest jury or the newspapers. The family members were always referred to as Bucks and Squaws to belittle them, to make them look as animalistic as they could. They were labeled as murderers, renegades and every other derogatory adjective that people could come up with. I don't know that the actions of the posse members and the inquest jury could be called a cover up but the Jury did everything they could to help justify the killing of the women and children and exonerate the posse of wrong doing. The newspapers and wagging tongues convicted the Daggetts of murder long before the the killing at Little High Rock Canyon.

If your going to be heroic Indian fighters you have to have fought vicious, mean, renegade, killer Indians so the posse members made out the Indians to be just that. Women and children hardly qualified, imagination and ingenuity were necessary to make that connection.

The Donnelley report re-emphasized the cowardice and deliberate cover up of what took place in the killing of Indians at Rabbit Creek.

Probably the most atrocious, self serving document ever written, containing lies, misinformation and false statements. The coverup of the killing of an Indian family

404

including unarmed women and children and he got away with it. If there ever was proof Donnelley was incompetent it is in this report. I could say bordering on criminal behavior but that would be sugar coating what they really did. Donnelley and his posse were criminals and got away with murder!!

Report of the Nevada State Police - 1913 - By Captain J. P. Donnelley

The Daggetts were not the killers they were made out to be. They could have killed O. D. Van Norman at Hog Ranch Creek and taken his horse, they didn't; they had the opportunity to kill and steal at Denio Camp, they didn't; they could have killed and stolen an entire sheep camp (horses, supplies, tents, bedding,etc.) at High Rock Lake, they didn't; they could have killed and stolen horses at Soldier Meadows, they didn't; they could have plundered and killed at the Lay Ranches on either side of Jackson Mountain, they didn't; they could have stolen at Paradise Valley, they didn't; scouting the area ahead would also provide them information on the availability of horses and supplies if they were so inclined to steal such items or do bodily harm to anyone in order to obtain horses, they didn't. However now they were more desperate than ever, they and their horses were tired and hungry, they had no place to hide and no safe place to go . Their next move may have been to steal or kill and steal but the posse killed that option [literally] and that option never presented itself.

Responsibility Shared

Hard to express the magnitude of the damage & influence the newspapers had on the outcome of this historical event.

Each time the story or parts thereof is told it becomes more embellished.

The media (newspapers) may have had nearly as much to do with the killing of the Daggetts as bullets from the posse. They followed this saga with journalistic sensationalism, innuendoes, false statements and labeled the Indians, guilty renegade murderers, which had the public believing the Indians were guilty of far more crimes than they could have committed.

Newspaper articles page 23

It is hard to believe the media at this late date, 1911, could be so insensitive and so ignorant of facts, so bigoted that they looked upon Indians especially the Daggett family as only animals including the children.

However there was the body of Ed Hogle. What else was needed to prove that they were in a fierce Indian battle? Thank god for Ed Hogle!

Two examples of shared responsibility were the Humboldt Star and the Reno Evening Gazzet.

To the Elko County Authorities they were renegade Indians.

To the public: "This is one of the most atrocious murders ever committed in Elko County and it is to be hoped that officers everywhere will keep this matter in mind as it seems to me that we certainly ought to land these Indians sooner or later".

September 20, 1910   *E. J. L. TABER*

District Attorney of Elko County, Nevada)

Elko Free Press Print

Only those in southern Idaho and northeastern Nevada who new the Daggetts stood by and voiced their opinion that the Indians were never troublesome or criminals as alleged. From a report of the Gollaher Mountain affair (killing of Frank Dopp) by G. A. Gutches dated February 6, 1911, he reports as follows:

"The ranchers about Rock Creek and the employees of the Cattle Co. all spoke highly of these Indians. They said the Indians were honest, industrious and to the best of their knowledge had never stolen any stock. The Indians worked for the Stockmen, were trusted at the company's store (San Jacinto) and always paid their bills".

Gutches report Feb. 6, 1911 National Archives W.D.C.

This was especially clear in statements by T. Baily Lee, the District Attorney of Cassia County, Idaho; Evan Estep, the Superintendent at the Fort Hall Indian Agency, Idaho and C. H. Asbury the Superintendent at the Carson Indian School at Stewart, Nevada.

a) T. Baily Lee, District Attorney, Cassia County, Idaho:

"The missing Indians were well-behaved , old residents of Rock Creek and had many friends among the whites". "They work for their neighbors and were generally respected and it is impossible that they would have made the attack Gay Tranmer said they did, killed the white boy, and gotten out of the country without leaving some sign or trace of their travel".

Letter to Hon. E. J. L. Taber, Elko, Nevada, February 14, 1911, National Archives W.D.C.

b) Evan W. Estep, Superintendent, Fort Hall Indian Agency:

"These Indians were not enrolled here and I understand were not on the rolls of any agency". "The clippings are forwarded for your information and for what they are worth.". I feel sure that the story is somewhat fanciful, for the drum-beating and war dance did not likely take place under the circumstances and if there are any Indians in this part of the country that have and can use bows and arrows I have failed to see any of them".

Letter to Commissioner of Indian Affairs, Washington. D. C. March 2, 1911, National Archives W.D.C.

c) C. H. Asbury Superintendent, Carson Indian School:

"I do not think it is necessary to look for a special institution for the girl as she is hardly more than 15 and she may be less and I can see no reason for the fear of her that has been expressed by the state officers and by the stockmen, that she would commit some crime or instigate further depredations if allowed among her own people". "It is not

unnatural that she would have been wild when arrested as she had just seen eight members of her family killed, including her father and mother".

Letter to Commissioner of Indian Affairs Washington D.C. April 27, 1911, National Archives W.D.C.

"The Office will recall the killing referred to which occurred Feb. 26, 1911 and the surviving children are here". The history of the case runs back more than a year to the killing of Frank Dopp in northeast Nev.".

"If time permitted I would still like to make a through investigation of that crime and the history of that party as there are some things about it that are not clear yet".

Letter to Commission of Indian Affairs Washington D.C., Aug. 3, 1911, National Archives W. D. C.

At this time in history this massacre had to be a most cowardly, barbarous and inconsiderate killing of Indians.

It was labeled as the last Indian battle in the United States, which was not true. It was actually the last slaughter of Indians in the United States.

In white mans writings, when they were killing Indians it was referred to as a battle when the Indians were killing white people it was referred to as a massacre.

The killing of the Daggett family at Rabbit Creek in 1911 is in parallel, or a copy of what happened in 1863 when the military annihilated a winter camp, at Bear River in south eastern Idaho and Wounded Knee December of 1890, only fewer Indians involved.

Band of Contact Indians Murder a Boy.

George B. Grim, deputy sheriff at Contact, came in from that place yesterday afternoon on horseback, arriving

TMENT OF THE INTER
ED STATES INDIAN SERVICE

5-8-10 62684

SHOSHONES SAID TO BE MURDERERS

Reservation Indians Are Blamed

ging the brands couple of men, not be learned the Indians we ne of their out to ma k. During came across ensued. During r of shots were en and th Indi ing in the injur-

(Special to the Gazette.)
WASHINGTON, D. C., Feb. 22—From a statement made by a Shoshone Indian now in Washington, the commissioner of Indian affairs here believes that he has a

Indians Murder Boy Who Caught Them in Crime

RECEIVED
AUG 1 - 1910
62684

uty sheriff at place yes- arriv-

the melee fired by tl ans, the b ing of believes

CATTLEMEN OUT FOR BAD INDIANS

Rock Creek Man Murdered By Marauders.

CAPTURED SQUAW CONFESSES MURDER OF THE STOCKMEN

Large Amount in Rewards to Be Divided Among the Captors.

RENO, Nev., March 1.—The feature of the news from the scene of Sunday's confession made by

INDIAN SQUAW TELLS OF SEVENTEEN DEATH SHE HAS WITNESS

CAPTAIN DAVE TALKS WITH SNAKE

Draws From the Girl the Story of Numerous Murders in Past 18 Months

ONE CHINAMAN IS KILLED

Crimes Cover Period of Year and Half Extend From Utah to Idaho

From the lips of a 13-year-old girl who in the short space of eighteen months had seen seventeen killings, who has seen father and mother, sisters and brothers, shot on the last big

JURY ACCUSES THE INDIAN GIRL

CHARGE HER WITH COMPLICITY IN THE DEATH OF ED HOGLE.

After a two days' session, the inquest in the case of Ed Hogle, the unfortunate victim of last Sunday's battle with Shoshone Mike's band of In-

FURTHER PARTICULARS OF THE MURDER OF A BOY BY INDIANS

From District Attorney Taber last night, we learned the following particulars regarding the killing of boy by the Indians in the northeastern part of the county on the 5th of April:

DONNELLEY POSSE

ca March 2, 1911

Standing: Lt. to Rt. - Chas T. Byrnes, constable Paradise Valley; *Sergeant C. H. Stone, Nev. Stare Police, Carson City,Nev.; *Otto D. Van Norman; *George Holmes; *Joe Reeder; *Jack Ferguson; *Frank Perry*; Capt. Donnelley, Superintendent Nev. State Police; *Sgt. P. M. Newgard, Nevada State Police

Kneeling: Lt. to Rt. - William Parsons; *Warren Fruit; Merl W. Prussia; *Henry Hughes; *Mort West; Ben Cambron, brother of Harry Cambron, killed at Little High Rock; Modoc County Sheriff, Elsey Smith

*Posse members at the lower site where the women and children were killed.

Not shown, Ed Hogle, killed at the lower site in the last volley. Also not shown John Skinny Pascal. Why?

410

EIGHT of the SURPRISE VALLEY POSSE with RIFLES

March 2, 1911

This photograph was most likely taken on the 2nd of March during the one day break between the inquest of Ed Hogle and the Daggett family.

Left to right - Warren Fruit, O. D. Van Norman, Jack Ferguson, Joe Reeder, George Holmes, Bill Parsons, Frank Perry, Henry Hughes? or possibly Peter Itziana, not a member of the posse. Not shown; Mort West, Sheriff Smith nor Ben Cambron.

Humboldt County Museum

FOUR POSSE MEMBERS
c March 2nd 1911

L to R Mort West, Frank Perry, Joe Reeder, Jack Ferguson -
It is interesting that these four characters are in the same picture. **West & Perry** were the only two of all the posse members who ever wrote of the incident. **Reeder** was the only one of all the posse members who stated, at the inquest, that he saw a weapon (long pistol) with the Indian that was killed near Mike Daggett. Joe was the only one of three of all the posse members (the other being Henry Hughes) that testified that the Indians had weapons (fire arms) other than those in evidence at the inquest.**Jack Ferguson** was the only one of all the posse members that was mentioned the most times by written accounts in new papers, West's & Perry's accounts and in testimony. He also had some kind of special influence on the entire posse.

SIX of the SURPRISE VALLEY POSSE

Photo taken at Golconda loading docks probably on the 5th or 6th of March 1911.

Posse members with their gear waiting for the train on which they will load and begin their journey back to Eagleville, California.

Left to Right:(believed to be Henry Hughs), Joe Reeder, Jack Ferguson, Frank Perry, George Holmes, Bill Parsons

Not shown are: Mort West, O. D. Van Norman, Warren Fruit Ben Cambron and Sheriff A. E. Smith.

Also not shown; Ed Hogle who was killed at Rabbit Creek.

Two boys to the right are unknown.

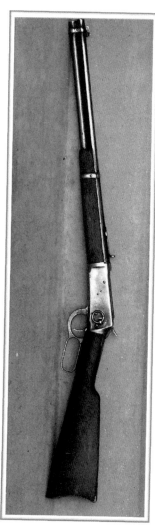

Harry & Nancy Summerfield

JOHN (Skinny) PASCAL

ca 1900

And the rifle he carried when part of the Donnelley posse.

There is no evidence he fired his rifle at Rabbit Creek. All testimony and other evidence (Perry & West writings) indicate he did not fire on the Daggett family at Rabbit Creek February 26,1911.

GRAVE MARKER of SKINNY PASCAL

April 2010

Indian tracker, John (Skinny) Pascal had accompanied Sheriff Lamb and Lamb's brother, from Sulphur Nevada where they had unloaded their horses from the train and rode north to intercept the Indians if the Indians turned south after crossing the east arm of the Black Rock.

These three joined Newgard, Perry, Ferguson and Taham, of the Donnelley Posse, at the Lay Ranch on Jackson Creek Feb. 20, 1910.

Pascal remained with the posse for the remainder of the pursuit, until Feb. 27, 1910. It is unclear what part he took in the killing of the Daggetts, if any.

State of Nevada   )
)
     County of Humboldt)

In the matter of the inquisition upon the body of __Edward Hogle__

before James Buckley, a Coroner of the County of Humboldt, State of

Nevada.

     We, the Jurors, summoned to appear before James Buckley, a

Coroner of the said County, at Golconda, Gold Run Township, in said

County and State, on the _____28th_____ day of __February__ 1911

having been sworn duly sworn according to law, and having made such

inquisition, after inspecting the body and hearing the testimony

adduced, upon our oaths each and all do say, that we find the deceased

was named ____Edward Hogle_____

_____ was a native of ___California_____ aged

about 27 years; that he came to his death in the County of Humboldt

at Rabbit Creek_____ on the__26th___

day of __February 1911_____By , Gunshot wound by the hand of

an Indian, one a member of the band of Old Mike outlaws--------------

And we further find that, that the young squaw known as Maggie, now

in captivity, one of Old Mikes' outlaws is instrumental in the cause

of Edward Hogles' death.

     All of which we duly certify by this inquisition in writing by us

this 2nd day of March A.D. 1911.

                          Wm Polkinghorne

                          Edward Dams

                          Jas G Stewart

                          Adrien Bernard.

                          John Mueton

                          Barney Gill

Appendix to Journals of Senate & Assembly
1913
Volume 2 - Pages 8 & 9
REPORT OF NEVADA STATE POLICE

By Captain J. P. Donnelley

Part of the report includes the following:

In January, 1911, four stockmen operating in northern Washoe County were reported missing. Search was instituted for the missing men and on February 11 news was received that their bodies had been found and that the men undoubtedly had been murdered. The department was called upon to assist in the pursuit of the murderers. A posse was formed, composed of members of this department, peace officers and stockmen. I assumed command of the posse. We found the bodies, stripped of the greater part of their clothing, concealed from view by willows, in Little High Rock Canyon. Carcasses of cattle and horses and a deserted Indian camp were found near the murdered stockmen. The bodies of the men were taken to Camp Denio, where an inquest was held over the remains and a verdict found to the effect that the four men had come their deaths from gunshot wounds inflicted by persons unknown but believed to be Indians. We picked up the trail of the Indians where they had left the deserted camp. Later it developed that the trail was about a month old. Under very unfavorable conditions during the coldest month of one of the most severe winters known to Nevada we followed the trail about 450 miles before the Indians were over taken. At several points along the trail conclusive evidence was obtained that the posse was following the same band of Indians that had camped near the scene of the murder.

Fifteen days from the time the bodies of the stockmen were found the Indians were over taken 35 miles northeast of Golconda. The Indians evinced considerable concern at the approach of the posse and they were commanded to surrender. They immediately fired upon our force. Through an interpreter they were again told to submit to arrest. Their only reply was another volley from their rifles. A sharp engagement, lasting about three hours, resulted. One member of the posse, Ed Hogle, four buck Indians, two squaws and two Indian boys were killed during the engagement. "Shoshone Mike," the leader of the band, had eight bullet wounds in his body. One squaw, one boy and two small children were captured. None of the band escaped. The killing of the squaws and boys was unavoidable, as they fought as fiercely as the bucks, using firearms, arrows and spears. Also the squaws, realizing that we were endeavoring to avoid injuring them tried to protect the bucks from our fire. The Indians proved to be a band of outlaws known as "Shoshone Mike's" band, who had been committing depredations in eastern and northern Nevada and northern California for period of eighteen months. They were suspected of having committed several murders prior to the killing of the stockmen. The capture squaw confessed that the band had killed seventeen human beings. The coroner's jury returned a verdict "That the Indians came to their death by gunshot wounds inflicted by Captain J. P. Donnelley's posse; that their deaths were unavoidable, and further, the Captain J. P. Donnelley and posse were justified in their actions."

I wish to highly commend the individual members of my posse for the courage, endurance and perseverance displayed during the pursuit and engagement that resulted in the extermination of "Shoshone Mike's" band. I also wish to thank the ranchers and stockmen along the route gravel, who invariably supplied the posse with food, shelter and fresh mounts.

Rewards aggregating $9,143.50 were offered for the arrest and conviction of the murderers. Of this amount $2,143.50, offered by the citizens of Surprise Valley, and $1,000 offered by the H. C. Cattle Company, have been collected and distributed to the eighteen members of the posses who were present at the engagement. The $5,000 offered by the State of Nevada, and $1,000 offered by the State of California have not as yet been paid.

A detailed history of this case is on file at this office and can be referred to should further details be required.

CAPT. JOHN P. DONNELLEY

Capt. Donnelley's experiences in life leading up to the tracking down and killing of he Indians should have better prepared him for the task and the situation in which he found himself. In summary they included: business dealings in mining, hotel management, real-estate, life insurance, mercantile , law enforcement in sheriffs offices (Humboldt County, Calif., and Goldfield, Nevada) and military (National Guard in Calif.) where he moved up in rank to Captain and then as Captain of the Nevada State Police. It appears he had been Captain of the Nevada State police for only about two months before he took up the trail of the Indians.

Latter he also served as a prohibition director in Nevada. It was as prohibition director that he ran into trouble. He was convicted of failing to report a violation of the prohibition law to the United States district attorney. He appealed his conviction all the way to the supreme court of the United States where his conviction was up held and he was fined $500.00. Donnelley died on Sept. 5, 1928. Washoe County Sheriff, Charles Ferrel, had died just one week earlier.

CHAPTER VII

LOOKING BACK to EAGLEVILLE

To back up a little, by the time Captain Donnelley arrived in Eagleville a ragtag posse had already been formed and had gone on ahead. That so called posse, maybe more appropriately referred to as a vigilante posse, was made up of buckaroos and farm hands and the last thing they were capable of was law enforcement. As members of a posse they rationalized that the killing of Indians was justified.

The so called posse was organized at Denio Camp but Captain Donnelley never was able to gain control of the posse. It appears that the closest thing to anybody being in charge was Modoc County Sheriff Smith and Ben Cameron or possibly Jack Ferguson. Smith was completely out of his jurisdiction, he shouldn't have even been on the posse. Ben was strictly bent on avenging the killing of his brother and probably should not have been on the posse. Ferguson is another matter altogether as will be illustrate later.

By the time they got to Soldier Meadows they were out of Washoe County Sheriff, Ferrel's jurisdiction. Should Sheriff Ferrel have remained with the posse beyond this point? The chase started in his county and proceeded into Humboldt County therefore it was probably appropriate for Sheriff Ferrel to pursue the Indians to the end. Sheriff Lamb was called on, appropriately, when the posse found they were following the Indian trail into his jurisdiction, Humboldt County. Lamb his brother Kies and Indian tracker John (Skinny) Pascal joined the Donnelley posse at Jackson Mountain. These three remained with the posse until the night of February 23rd when the main contingent of the posse arrived in Winnemucca, Nevada. For some reason only Pascal remained with the Donnelley posse the following day. By this time Washoe County Sheriff Ferrel and Nevada State Police Private Frank Buck had gone on to Elko, Nevada to intercept the Indians if they got into Elko County. A much different scenario may have played out at Rabbit Creek if Sheriff Ferrel and or Sheriff Lamb had been at Rabbit Creek on the 26th and had the renegade posse members from Surprise Valley been left in Golconda.

419

Looking back one hundred years, who ever made that decision could have easily cost the lives of the women and children at Rabbit Creek. Sergeant Stone or Sergeant Newgard should have gone on ahead with Private Buck and not Sheriff Ferrell. Had Donnelley been in charge and capable of the task, the attitude of the, posse would not have deteriorated to gang mentality, but he was totally inept and lost complete control and so they were just a gang out to avenge the killing of the stockmen and kill an Indian. In the minds of these men the Indians were little more than some kind of vermin needing extermination.

The psychology of the group as discussed above, could not be more emphasized than it was when they caught up with the Indians and began indiscriminately killing them. Dr. Morrison reported that the upper lip and mustache was removed from the body of Erramouspe but it was never mentioned again after Little High Rock except in the writings of Frank Perry the media and wild stories. There were stories floating around claiming one of the women had it at Rabbit Creek but it was never an item at the inquests. It is interesting that it's existence never came at the inquest. If the posse members wanted to show the savagery of the Indians this item would have been good to include as evidence. Maybe it was never removed from the body or did not exist. One possible explanation the body could have been dragged through the snow face down
and the lip rolled up then froze in that position and looked as though it had been removed. Another story floating around in history, describes a Chinese que being found with the Indians that the Indians had taken from a Chinaman they supposedly had killed. If it existed it was probably a braid cut from one of the Indians as is their custom when in morning from the death of a relative. In this case it would be the death of the Indian boy back at Cow Creek in April. A newspaper article stated the 15 year old girl asked for a pair of scissors to cut her hair. Maybe she did. The paper went on to say they didn't give her scissors because they thought she would attempt to harm herself or one of the children.

Ferguson

The interesting member of the posse was Jack Ferguson. At Denio Camp,February 15 he was one of eight selected from a posse of 30 men to act as a juror at the inquest for the four murdered sheepmen. One February 20, 1911 he was selected (or selected himself) to go back from Paiute Meadows with Newgard to pick up the trail of the Indians, where the posse had left it the day before. The trail headed across the east arm of the Black Rock Desert and Quinn River. He was noted by Perry here also. He was referred to by Perry as the one with him when they picked up the trail of the Indians where they left Jackson Mt. and entered the area of the sand dunes.

Ferguson was the only one mentioned by Byrnes as to who he rode back with to Willow Point, Feb. the 25th, "*& we went back to Willow Point with Ferguson*". Who was we? Probably the four men that left with him from Paradise that morning. If Ferguson went back to Willow Point then did he not go to Golconda, that night, with the main group of posse members? Also did Byrnes think Ferguson was in charge on the 25th? Ferguson testified *"we left Willow Point about 7 am on the 26th"*.

He was leading the posse when they came upon the Daggetts at Rabbit Creek.

Mort West mentioned Ferguson several times in his writings including, 1 - he was the only one Mort mentioned, by name, that could hit the bulls eye when they were sighting in their rifles at Soldier Meadows, 2 - he was one of only two who Mort said left Golconda early with Perry & others on February 26 the day they killed the Indians.

He was only one who identified the horse with HP on left thigh and 76 on left side as belonging to Harry Cambron. He also identified Cambron's boots and saddle, when asked to describe the property found at the Indian's camp. Why didn't Ben Cambron identify these items?

Of all the posse members who testified he was the only one who was asked to estimate the ages of each of the twelve Indians. Ferguson's estimates were used as the ages of the eight Indians killed in their finding, on the 5th day of March 1911, that the Donnelley posse were justified in their killing of the eight Indians. These ages were far from being correct.

He was the only one of those, who testified, that cooperated and helped Buckley incriminate the 15 year old Indian girl for causing the death of Ed Hogle. When asked by the jury if Maggie had any thing to do with Hogle's death? He said *"I do it is my belief that if she had been killed previously Ed would have been alive today"*.

He was the only one at the inquest other than Cambron who labeled himself as a stockman.

In the writings of E.M. Wilson (from Sheriff Smith story) he shows up again - Ben shouts *"they are getting away head them off"* Newgard & Ferguson mount horses & secure a position on a 60' bluff, ahead of the Indians. Ferguson also testified that : *"Ben Cambron said for gods sake boys someone go down there and head them off".*

When asked how he identified these as being the right Indians, his answer:*"By stuff that I had picked up at the different camps that correspond with stuff that we found at Little High Rock Canyon the first camp of the Indians".*

In the Alturas newspaper THE NEW ERA March 22, 1911, under the heading of **Outlaws Killed** *Story of the Pursuit and battle as told by - Elzie Smith and Ben Cambron;* Ferguson is mentioned again numerous times.

The article also describes Smith and Cambron as the main heroes of the Battle with the Indians and criticizes the State Police. The article goes on to portray the Surprise Valley members of the posse as rugged individuals that endured unbelievable hardships. The killing of unarmed women and children does not portray a lot of bravery.

Nearly two dozen snapshots were taken while the posse members were in Golconda, some of the posse were identified in two or three, Ferguson was identified in nearly half of them. Assuming that Ferguson was not the one identified in some of those pictures, for some reason his name was still out there more than the others and connected to this incident.

Ferguson is in the news again in the Nevada State Journal March 3,1911. Washoe County Sheriff Ferrel was interviewed by the Journal after he had arrived in Reno with the Indian children on March 2nd. The Journal reported that Ferguson was riding a white horse and had ran down the little Indian boy (Cleve) who tried to escape. It was also reported that the boy bit him on the wrist but was saved from a severe laceration by Ferguson glove. Newspapers were lacking in facts and credibility in reporting on the saga however research of old photos reveal that Ferguson was in fact riding a white horse and wore gloves with long gauntlets.

It appears he was an overbearing, pushy type person probably a bully. He evidently went around doing whatever he wanted, whenever he wanted and in his way, without any restraint from Captain Donnelley or Sheriff Smith nor questioning by other members of the posse.

It was Donnelley's posse but he had little control over anyone especially Ferguson. The posse in their pack mentality seemed to resemble a pack of dogs, whatever Ferguson flushed out everyone tried to kill.

The one time he was not mentioned as taking the lead or front and center was when the party of Sergeant Newgard, Jim Tahem, Frank Perry and Jack Ferguson made the dangerous crossing on Quinn River February 19th. He allowed others to do that. In Frank Perry's writings he mentioned only Tahem, Newgard and himself going into the river breaking ice and clearing the way.

The members of the posse were so captivated by their own fictitious stories that they soon believed the stories they told were actually true. Very easy to do, you do not want to believe you actually killed unarmed women and children, the populace believes you are a hero Indian fighter, you have Ed Hogle dead, shot to death (by one bullet), surely not one of them shot Ed, it had to be an Indian, after all didn't the Indians kill four sheepmen, you have four Indian children, proof there were real Indians killed, there were guns there they are in evidence surely there was a pitched battle look at the guns (maybe only two rifles but they truly are lethal weapons), all, including the newspapers believe these Indians are more akin to animals that humans. Then to top it off they (the Surprise Valley Boys) all go up to Cedarville to have their picture taken as hero Indian fighters. Every one else believes your are a hero Indian fighters so it has to be true. Who wants to go back to reality, it's too easy this way and too hard to go back and see yourself as killing unarmed women and children.

Easy to take on a fictitious identity when being rewarded for doing so. By way of illustration:

1) They were looked upon and told they were heroes by everyone.

2) Newspapers, especially the Alturas paper THE NEW ERA - March 22, 1911 raved about what heroes they were and how brave they were.

3) The inquest jury by blaming the young girl for Hogle's death absolved them of any wrong doing.

4) They were not indicted for murder which meant they were killing Indians in battle.

423

5) By telling each other they were courages and heroic Indian fighters they soon believed it themselves.

6) They were allowed to take on role of Indian fighters without question.

7) Everywhere they went they were honored with parties and drinks for all.

8) Allowing the children to be seen as animals justified their killing.

9) And the grand finale, dressed up & photo taken in Cedarville as Indian fighters.

The fact that the posse took on a personalty or life of its own is not necessarily a great mystery. In the right environment, right circumstances and often with a certain personality as a catalyst (maybe Jack Ferguson) a group of men (posse) can dehumanize others, such as the Indians. The human psyche of otherwise rational people can change to one of no empathy or recognition of others as being human. There was a study/experiment, at Stanford University, in August of 1971 that illustrates, although under far different circumstances, what the human mind can degenerate to.

EAGLEVILLE BOYS

Shortly after returning from Nevada

Top: Bill Parsons, *Otto. Van Norman, *George Holmes, *Joe Reeder, *Jack Ferguson

Bottom: *Mort West, *Henry Hughes, *Warren Fruit, Sheriff Smith, *Frank Perry

Not in attendance, *Ed Hogle, he was residing at the Anderson Cemetery in Anderson, California.

These ten plus *Ed Hogle accompanied the Nevada State Police from Eagleville to Rabbit Creek near Golconda, Nevada, where eight of the Daggett family were killed.

*
- Present at the site where the women and children were killed.

PART IV

CHAPTER I

GOLCONDA TO RENO, TO CARSON INDIAN SCHOOL, TO FORT HALL, IDAHO

On February 28, 1911 the four surviving children were taken from the Kelly Creek Ranch, as prisoners, hauled to Golconda, Nevada and like so many animals, they were locked in the jail at Golconda.

March 2, 1911 the children were transported from Golconda to the Washoe County jail in Reno, Nevada where they were again locked in jail and kept there in jail squalor for nearly two months while the authorities were trying to determine what to do with these orphaned children.

From the Nevada State Journal March 3, 1911:

"Captives were placed in a single steel cell in the basement of the jail. The cell was bare except for two hammock like couches strapped at either end to the walls"

"Efforts to get any talk out of the captives proved fruitless. As visitors started down the stairs the prisoners were engaged in an animated chatter. The older girl laughing and playing with the 7 year old but immediately the chatter stopped and they remained silent and almost motionless while strangers peered through the bars at them".

Evidently during their incarceration visitors had been allowed in to visit the children or I should say look at them through the bars of the jail cell not unlike an exhibit at a zoo.

Later in the article it describes the 7 year old as a boy and an older boy also being in the cell. There was only one boy about six years old among the four children. The seven year old described above was a four year old girl.

The children were not laughing and playing only five days after the fiasco at Rabbit Creek where they had watched their family members shot down all around them.

What to do with the children included the ludicrous idea that maybe they should be put in a vaudeville show or in a moving picture presentation of the scene of pursuit and capture of the Indians.

Letter to Commission of Indian Affairs from George Haggett Superintendent & Indian Agent at Owyhee, Nevada dated March 17, 1911 National Archives W. D. C. Reno Evening Gazette March 2, 1911.

The main concern of Captain Donnelley and other authorities was that the children may cause problems and they thought that the young girl, fifteen years old, should be kept locked up in that she might incite an Indian uprising.

National Archives W. D. C. letter dated March 6,1911

The newspapers of the day picked up on this thoughtless idea and quickly spread the word on how dangerous the children might be.

One example was printed in the Nevada State Journal March 6, 1911:

"The problem of the disposition of the captives remains. Yesterday Major Ingalls took the matter up with District Attorney Woodbury, but no definite solution was made. Major Ingalls says that these Indians are born in outlawry. Their fathers and brothers and uncles were outlaws and never were on any reservation. It is the duty of the reservation officials to gather in all the Indians, but this has not been done.

Major Ingalls who saw service in the Indian campaigns, says these Indians are regarded by the friendlies as outlaws just the same as some of the gangs such as the Hatfields in Kentucky and Jesse James' band are regarded as outlaws by white folks. He says these captives don't know any other life. They have lived as savages and have made first-rate savages, standing high in their profession, and he finds it hard to demand punishment for them any more than to demand imprisonment for wildcats".

Ingalls was totally and one hundred percent wrong about these Indians, if this is what he said. The paper is lacking creditability but this was the typical attitude of many of the people at that time and the newspapers were more than glad to print it.

It is also noted that the Nevada State Journal referred to the children as captives and not as children. Most everything printed in the newspapers has to be taken with a grain of salt. It is hard to determine what is true and what isn't.

The fact that children were incarcerated in jail so as to protect society from these vicious children as they might cause trouble or initiate this imaginary uprising is difficult to understand. The fifteen year old, oldest of the children had now taken the place of the mother of the three younger children. She was carrying the smallest of the children around on her back in a blanket. She must have been extremely dangerous at about 5 foot tall and weighing in at at least 100 pounds.

After all the brave Indian fighters had just killed eight members of her family, including women and children, none of which had a fire arm when killed.

What was the mentality of these men in that they saw these children as being dangerous to the white population?

I guess if you're afraid of little children, ages fifteen to eleven months, as dangerous then those in charge must have been living in mortal fear. The cowardice that existed among those people suggesting the children should be feared as they may cause an Indian uprising, is incomprehensible!

Except for Evan W. Estep, Superintendent, Fort Hall Indian Agency Ross Fork Idaho, all of the authorities who had been searching for the Indians since May of 1910 were taken in/duped by the findings of the Inquest jury newspaper reporting, posse members and Captain Donnelley.

None more so than T. Bailey Lee, Cassia County D. A., who had been so loud in condemning the Elko County authorities for doing nothing to get to the bottom of the killings at Gollaher Mountain. Not realizing the information coming from the Donnelley posse, the inquest jury and the newspapers was not true, he was evidently embarrassed. He is now thinking the Indians actually were renegade murderous Indians as nothing more was heard from him.

C. H. Asbury Superintendent of the Carson Indian School, at Stewart , Nevada was also taken in/duped as illustrated in his letter to the Commissioner of Indian Affairs Washington D. C. March 8, 1911.

Asbury had been believing all the false information that he was getting until he visited the children at the Washoe County jail on April 25, 1911 and saw for himself the children and the terrible conditions they were subjected to.

At that point he realized that most of the information he had been receiving in regards to the children was false. It was obvious to Asbury the children were not being properly cared for and that they were of no danger to society.

By the 27th, two days after he had visited the children at the Washoe County jail, C. H. Asbury, had made arrangements to have them brought to the the Carson Indian School at Stewart, Nevada and that they did, April 27, 1911.

429

In the words of C. H. Asbury:

"I found them so ragged and dirty and so like hunted creatures that I felt I must take them and care for them until some disposition is made".

"Two days ago, I had a very satisfactory interview with the young woman, who with the three children, is held in custody at Reno. I sent a Shoshone woman, who was formerly a pupil of this school, in to get acquainted with her and to pave the way somewhat for my later talk, then I spent a good part of the afternoon with her with no one else present except my interpreter, and she told me at length of their movements from the time they killed Frank Dopp, which killing was the subject of all this Elko County correspondence. She says that her brother Jack, a young man, was driving their horses to camp when he was shot by some white man, they did not know who, and his leg was broken by the bullet besides being lacerated, resulting in his death. Under the anger caused by this unwarranted attack, her other brothers went out and shot Frank Dopp, the boy from over in Idaho".

That same night, they left that section and on leaving stole several horses taking them out of the corral or pasture and riding some and driving some loose. They worked their way gradually westward keeping away from the settlers, stealing beef as it was need for their food, also taking provisions from sheep or cattle camps, in fact, any place they could get it. In this way, they went clear through into the central part of California, evidently to the Sacramento River where they found abundant fruit in the orchards and melons in the fields to which they helped themselves. Towards winter they started back east over the main range of the Sierra Nevada Mountains, and going over the mountains at this time, they lost most of their horses as they became poor and weak, and in the deep snow they could not travel. They had gotten back into the western part of Nevada where they were camping in an isolated place at the time they killed the four stock men which caused that pursuit and the wholesale killing already related.

As to the horses that were killed in Elko County and buried and which Attorney Lee thought had been done by the cattle rustlers and that the Indians were probably buried with them , she says she knows nothing about it, that they certainly did not kill those horses and in fact it would be impossible to conceive of any motive for such killing as the were leaving the country and were in more particular need of the horses just then than at any other time.

This girl insists that prior to the killing of Frank Dopp, which was aggravated by the unwarranted attack on her brother, they had never stolen cattle or horses, but had made their living by the father and sons working in the hay fields and by hunting fishing, etc. The Indians in the party were all of the same family sons and daughters of the same father and mother , as follows; Mike and his wife; a daughter grown who had been married but whose husband was not with them; three grown sons, Jim, Charley, and Pete, Heney the girl now in jail; two boys 10 to 13 years old; Cleve, the boy now in jail about 6 years old, Hattie, now in jail, and near 4 years old; and the girl baby about 18 months old.

These were all killed but Heney and the three youngest children.

The girl tells me that she has an aunt living at Tacoma, Nevada, which is a small station on the S. P. main line near the Utah line, a sister of her mother and that this aunt and here husband work right there all the time about the store and that if she were allowed to return to her people she would got to that aunt.

These children are not criminals and I am opposed to any action that would seem to regard them as such.

Asbury's letters and report April 27, 1911: National Archives W. D. C.

The young Indian girl's response to Asbury's questions, at the Washoe County jail April 25, were the most truthful and accurate of all the information gleaned from <u>any one</u> regarding the saga of Shoshone Mike, then or now including Buckley's inquest jury.

The girl spoke of her brothers and sisters and a sister of her mother. They may or may not have been brothers and sisters as Indians referred to close relatives as brothers and sisters, they made no distinction. Her mother would have been 45 to 50 years old when the 10 year old boy, that was killed, was born.

This is the first written account of the names of the family members including her own that were given by the fifteen year old girl (Heney) to Superintendent Asbury. These names were found listed in no other historical documents prior to this date.

Also I now believe it was Jack that was killed at Gollaher Mountain and not Charlie.

The very first name given Baby Mosho was Josephine Mike, at the Carson Indian School, Stewart, Nevada. There, also Hattie was given the last name Mike. These names were written/embroidered on to little dresses, made for them at the school.

The young fifteen year old Indian girl's name was spelled four different ways depending upon who wrote it.

No historical information could be found relating to the period that would list the children at the Stewart Indian school.

It is ironic that Congress had given the agency permission to destroy statistical reports including the years 1911 through 1919. The Annual Report for 1911 from the Carson Indian School at Stewart, Nevada included the narrative only.

"The file of statistical reports begins with 1920 because those for the years 1911 through 1919 inclusive were destroyed with congressional authorization in 1932".

National Archives Microfilm Publication - M1011   G. S. A. - 1975   Record Adm. 1000 Commodore Dr. San Bruno, CA.

Very little of the property looted and stolen, by the Donnelley posse, while the children were in jail, can be found today.

To this day descendants of those who murdered eight members of this small band of Indians believe they have some possessory right to the stolen and looted property of the children.

There are a few arrows in the Nevada State Museum and Mike's headdress at the Historical Society in Reno. But upon the author requesting permission to take a picture of said headdress, or even look at it, was denied by somebody by the name of Brown. Brown, who it seems owns the head-dress or at least he thinks he does, was contacted by Sheryln L. Hayes-Zorn of the Historical Society and asked if I could look at it. My request was denied. He has control over whether it can be photographed or seen.

This was property that was looted and stolen from the Indians, while the little ones languished in jail.

There was a recent report that Mr Brown had died and his son had the headdress.

From the Nevada State Journal March 3, 1911:

"Dave Staunton, who had gone to Golconda to take charge of the remains of Ed Hogle and who returned yesterday brought with him a number of trophies of the battle. He brought a brilliantly fashioned war headdress and a number of the arrows used as well

432

as a rudely fashioned tomahawk". "The headdress was made out of bright colored
flannel decorate with feathers of the eagle and other birds and the top part
had much bead work and feathers".

The credibility of newspapers is always in question however in this case the detailed
and accurate description of the headdress is a very creditable bit of evidence that it was
actually seen by the reporter.

Who was Dave Staunton and why did he have these trophies?

The Journal had gotten most of the information for the article from Sheriff Ferrel. Most
of what the Sheriff told the paper was incorrect and most of what they made up on their
own was incorrect. Ferrel had gotten most of his information from members of the
posse.

Immediately after the children arrived at the Carson Indian School, beginning with a
letter from Evan Estep, Superintendent at the Fort Hall Reservation (Ross Fork) to C. H.
Asbury, Superintendent at the Carson Indian School at Stewart Nevada dated May 9,
1911, evidently an enquiring as to who the four children were as they might have
relatives on the Indian Reservation at Fort Hall. [letter not found in the national
archives].

From the May 9th letter there grew a multitude of pieces of correspondence. The
correspondence included letters back and forth between the Fort Hall Indian School, the
Carson Indian School, the Commission of Indian Affairs,W.D.C. and the Department of
the Interior in Washington D. C.

A letter dated May 15, 1911, from the Superintendent at the Carson Indian School, C. H.
Asbury, in response to Estep's May 9th letter, clearly welcomed Estep's inquiry about
the children and he asked Estep if he could take them to Fort Hall to be taken care of by
relatives there. Asbury had been concerned for the children's welfare since he retrieved
them from the squalor of the Washoe County Jail on April 27th.

The correspondence went on for seven months ending with a telegram dated November
10, 1911. giving the final approval for Estep to move the children to Fort Hall and enroll
them at the Fort Hall Reservation.

Telegram dated Nov. 10, 1911 - (Telegram from F. H. Habbott, Assistant Indians Affairs Washington D. C. to C. H.
Asbury, Superintendent Indian School, Cason City, Nevada) National Archives W. D. C.

The Indian Agency had finally concluded that the children had relatives, in Idaho, at the Fort Hall Indian Reservation.

Mr. Estep traveled to the Carson Indian School at Stewart, Nevada, on or about the 15th of November 1911, picked up the children and returned with them to Fort Hall.

The children had been at the Carson Indian School since April 27, 1911.

Baby Mosho had turned one year old while incarcerated in the Washoe County jail.

CHILDREN LEAVING GOLCONDA JAIL

March 2, 1911

From the Golconda jail the children were taken by rail to the Washoe County jail in Reno, Nevada.

WASHOE COUNTY SHERIFF FERRIL & the INDIAN CHILDREN

ca March 2nd or 3rd, 1911

WASHOE COUNTY JAIL - RENO, NEVADA

The date on this photo is incorrect.

Lt. to Rt. Hattie,Henny with Baby Mosho on her back, Sheriff Ferril and Clev.
The children did not arrive at Golconda until February 28th. They were kept in the
Golconda jail until the 2nd of March before being taken to Reno.
This photo may have been taken when the children arrived at the Washoe County jail
from Golconda or just a photo op.

INDIAN CHILDREN and SHERIFF FERRIL

ca March 3, 1911

Turning to go back into the county jail.

Lft. to Rt.: Hattie (age 4), Henny with Baby Mosho on her back and Clev. (age 6 or 7)

Baby Mosho can be seen on the young girl's back with just the top of her head showing above the blanket.

The young fifteen year old Indian girl (Henny) carried Baby Mosho about everywhere they went as can be seen in the various photos, at least until they got to the Carson Indian School at Stewart, Nevada.

Henny kept in close contact with the three small children from the time the children were picked up out of the bloody carnage at Rabbit Creek on February the 26th until they arrived at Fort Hall in November of 1911.

JOSEPH STUBBS & TEDDY ROOSEVELT

APRIL 3, 1911

Joseph Stubbs, University President left foreground, welcoming former President Theodore Roosevelt right foreground, to the University of Nevada Campus at Reno, Nevada, April 3, 1911.

On this date the four Daggett children were languishing in the Washoe County jail in Reno, Nevada.

CHILDREN of the (SHOSHONE) MIKE DAGGETT FAMILY
April 27, 1911

HENNY, CLEVE, HATTIE & JOSEPHINE MIKE
These children were orphaned by Captain Donnelley's posse on February 26, 1911.
(There were 20 armed men in Donnelley's posse)
When Asbury visited the children in jail April 25, 1911, he reported they were dirty & caged like animals. When they were taken from the Washoe County jail Sheriff Ferrell had them dressed up for show as if they had been kept this way all along which was not true.

DRESSES OF MARY JO ESTEP

Photo taken February 26, 1995

In the photo, CHILDREN of the (SHOSHONE) MIKE Daggett Family , the four children in front of the jail, are all dressed up in their fineries, to present to the newspaper (photo op) when they were taken to the Carson Indian School at Stewart, Nevada. In that picture, Mary Jo is wearing the dress second from left..

The four dresses were kept by Mary Jo for over 80 years until her untimely death, December 1992. Louis and Ester Jarneke, her closest friends and executors of her estate, passed them on to Les & Cheri Sweeney to place in a venue of their choice. The dresses were donated to the textile museum in Carson, Nevada May 11, 2011. Two of the dresses were made for Josephine and her sister, Hattie, at the Carson Indian School. The dress on the far left had Mary Jo's name (Josephine Mike) written in it. The dress on the far right had, her sister's name (Hattie Mike) stitched in it.

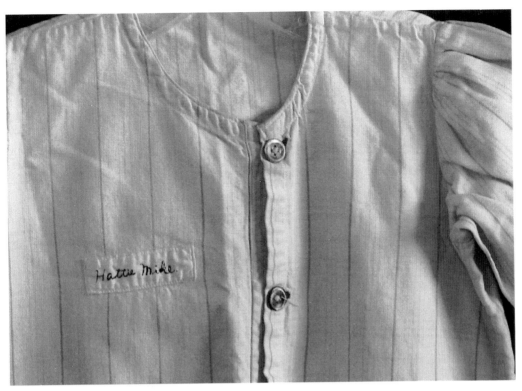

DRESSES of HATTIE and JOSEPHINE MIKE

CHAPTER II

CHILDREN AT FORT HALL

The nightmare the children were living did not end when they arrived at Fort Hall it only got worse.

They had traveled for 37 excruciating winter days, with their family, across some of the most barren and hostile lands in the west. Their only protection from the winter elements were blankets and possibly a canvas tarp.

They endured nearly two months in the Washoe County jail and spent another seven months at the Carson Indian School. The only survivors of this tragedy, up to this point, were: Baby Mosho just 10 months; her sister Hattie, four; her brother Cleave, six and her aunt Henie, fifteen.

But tragedy struck at Fort Hall and the children became sick. Only Josephine survived beyond January 19, 1913.

The arrival of the Daggett children at Fort Hall in November of 1911, began the final and short chapter for Hennie, Cleveland and Hattie for with in a short time all four had contacted one or more of white man's diseases. The family had lived their whole life away from exposure and with very little close contact with white man. They had no immunity to these deadly diseases, reported to be Spinal Meningitis and Tuberculosis.

The first bit of business Mr Estep took up when he arrived back at Fort Hall with the children was to make application to the Council (Indian governing body of the Fort Hall Reservation) for their enrollment as members of the tribe and select land for their Indian Allotments.

The Dawes Act or General Allotment Act of 1887 provided for the issuing of an allotment to each Indian enrolled at any reservation. That allotment was to total one hundred and eighty acres.

In a letter to Commissioner of Indian Affairs in Washington, D. C. dated July 8, 1911, which included an affidavit of Mosho Jack and the action of the Tribal Council, Evan Estep recommended that the children that were taken from the killing site at Rabbit Creek on February 26, 1911 be enrolled as:

Henie Mosho, female, aged 16 years

Cleveland Mosho, male, aged 6 years

Hattie Mosho, female, aged 4 years

Mary Mosho, female, aged 2 years

Note: Mary Mosho would have been less than one and a half years old. Also note that at the Carson Indian School the children had been given the names:

Heney Mike

Cleveland Mike

Hattie Mike

Josephine Mike

He did not get that fully accomplished before the four year old Hattie died on March 12, 1912 just four months after arriving at Fort Hall. She was enrolled but no allotment was awarded.

The following information comes from an affidavit dated March 21, 1917 signed by Evan Estep:

"(On March 31, 1912), less than 6 months after arriving at the Fort Hall Indian Reservation , Hattie died of Spinal Meningitis at the For Hall Hospital.

Shortly after, Louise (Henie) was pronounced tubercular by the physician and proceeded to the home of Jack Mosho on Bannock Creek. She died there in a very short time on July 26,1912 The allegation was that she was poorly taken care of by the Mosho family which hastened in her death".

Native Americans still alive after 300 years of genocide and slaughter were a broken people, consequently the Mosho family cannot be totally at fault for the poor care of the Daggett children. It was also a practice to send sick Indian children home from from the hospital to keep them from infecting other patients.

1911 annual report from the Carson Indian School, Section II

Within six months, January 19,1913, of Henie's death Cleveland died in the school hospital at the Fort Hall School. He supposedly also died of tuberculosis or possibly meningitis.

Estep also stated that, "Mary Josephine is a sister of Henie Louise and Cleveland and as such she is the sole heir of these deceased children".

In this affidavit Mr Estep also stated he retrieved the children from the Carson school in 1912. This is incorrect, either a typographical error or confusion with other 1912 dates. Mary Josephine was in their home and she appears to be quite healthy in July of 1912. A photograph of Josephine in the Estep home has a date of July 1912.

Mary Josephine being a sister to both Cleveland and Henie is not biological possible. She was a sister to Hattie and Cleveland but not Henie. However that relationship and information was accepted and she inherited their Indian Allotments.

Some time between March 12th and July 26th of 1912, Josephine Mike Mosho was also pronounced tubercular by the Agency Physician. Believing her to be contagious and at risk to other patients was ordered from the school.

(I thought sick children were supposed to be taken care of in a hospital,thinking that was what hospitals were for)

There being no place for her to go, Rita Estep, wife of Fort Hall School Superintendent Evan Estep, intervened and they took her into their home rather than to allow her to be sent elsewhere on the reservation to die.

Within fourteen months of their arriving at Fort Hall the three older children were dead. The only one of the four to survive was (Baby Mosho) (Josephine Mike) (Mary Mosho) the youngest which would not reach her 3rd birthday for another three months. They had died at Ft. Hall from white man's diseases, tuberculosis, spinal meningitis, poor care and stress from their long ordeal beginning on the 25th of April 1910 to the time of their death.

We also must be reminded that the first ten months of this ordeal was one of extreme hardship which included the crossing of a large portion of northern Nevada in the dead of winter in that harshest of conditions with little or no shelter. However at the end of that ten month ordeal, ending February 26, 1911, the children were in good health. They may have been a little dirty and infested with a few vermin such as lice but in good health.

Disease and sickness came to the children following the killing of their family and incarceration in cold jail cells without proper care. The point being "The Donnelley posse was responsible for their deaths as well"!

445

It could never be determined whether the children were infected at the Carson Indian School or if they had become infected after reaching Fort Hall.

Mary Josephine recovered fully from what ever she had which leaves in question, did she truly have tuberculosis? It also leaves in doubt the true cause of death of the other three children. The stress from what they had been through had to of been a significant factor. Had the Estep's not rescued Mary Josephine from the hospital she also would have died.

Sworn statement by Evan Estep, Superintendent at the Crow Agency Big Horn County, Montana March 21,1917.

To send sick children home was not an uncommon practice at the time, as illustrated in the 1911, annual report from the Carson Indian School, Section II -- **Health**.

"We have had a few cases of Tuberculosis which have been sent home as promptly as practicable."

Hospitals evidently were not for the very ill, especially children.

The Esteps who had no children of their own took Mary Josephine Mike Mosho into a very loving home in 1912. Although never formally adopted they nursed her back to health, raised her as their own and saw to it that she got an education.

They were never the legal parents nor step parents of the little girl let alone blood relatives yet no one could have possibly been more perfect parents than the Esteps. Shortly after she joined the Estep family they gave her (Josephine Mike) the name Mary Josephine Estep.

She quickly became known as Mary Jo, as a daughter and part of the Estep family for the rest of her life and they continued to be a very close family from the day they took her in.

From the Estep home and environment came the most loving, caring, honest and positive person in the name of Mary Jo Estep, that any one could possibly have imagined.

These were attributes she maintained for her entire 82 years of life.

Fortunately for Mary Jo, in those days the Esteps were able to keep her as part of their family without any formal documents or authorization. Who was going to object? The Indians had few legal rights. They were not yet citizens of there own country.

446

Although Mary Jo had some status as a citizen through her Indian Allotment, it was not until June 2, 1924 that Congress granted all Indians full citizenship of their own country. It was not until she started 8th grade at age 14 that she could enjoy full U. S. citizenship of the country of her birth and the birth of her ancestors that have resided here for the past 30,000 years..

It is not clear as to why they never formally adopted her. A couple reasons come to mind. One, they did not want the issue to raise it's ugly head and have, supposedly family come and try to take her back to Fort Hall, in other words, "leaving sleeping dogs lie". Secondly it may have had to do with getting her an Indian Allotment and to see that she would be an heir to the Indian Allotments of her aunt and brother.

Estep had gone to great lengths to get the children enrolled at the Fort Hall Indian Reservation as part of the tribe of that Reservation. He somehow managed to navigate the bureaucracy of the Bureau of Indian Affairs in the Department of the Interior in getting the children enrolled, getting them each (three) an allotment and when two of the children died he was able to show that Mary Josephine was the true heir of their estates. In addition he was also able to show that she was an heir to the estate of Mosho Jim when he died. She eventually ended up with 720 acres of Indian allotments on the Fort Hall Indian Reservation.

The fact that Estep had a law degree and had a practiced law for a time and was familiar with the workings of the Bureau of Indian Affairs that he was able to successfully navigate the system.

He may also have experienced some guilt having brought the children to Fort Hall and their dying so soon after.

Josephine (Baby Mosho) was less than three years old when the Esteps took her in and did not remember any part of the grueling episode that her Indian family had been subjected to.

Another point of interest; shortly after taking Mary Jo into their home they began to encourage her to talk and learn the english language. One of her 1st words was "Muddy" evidently from her interpretation of the words mother or mommy. Mrs Estep was known as Muddy to Mary Jo for the rest of her life.

Letter from the Esteps to Mary Jo Feb. 1, 1935

Chapter III
MARY JO EMBARKS ON A NEW LIFE

Baby Mosho/Josephine Mike/Mary Jo Estep settled in with her new family to start a life that is much much different than the past 2 years.

Mary Jo, now in the loving care of Rita and Evan Estep as of early summer 1912, has her bad days behind her, until December 1992.

In the Estep home she got a birthdate and her name "Mary Josephine Estep.

Henie, her aunt, told Mr Estep she was born when the flowers started to bloom so they gave her the birth date of Evan Estep, April 12th, 1910.

Mr Estep transferred from the Indian Reservation at Yankton, South Dakota to the Fort Hall Reservation in Idaho in November of 1910. Then two years after taking Mary Jo into their home Mr Estep was transferred to the Crow Agency (Crow Indian Reservation in Montana) in May of 1914.

Mary Jo began her schooling at the Crow Agency however due to sickness and other complications Mrs Estep did not start Mary Jo in 1st grade until she was 8 years old.

In those days it was not uncommon to find kids much older than their classmates.

By the time Mary Jo was ready for second grade, in 1917, Evan Estep was again transferred this time to the agency at Shiprock, New Mexico on the Navajo Reservation She completed 2nd grade through 6th grade at Shiprock.

In 1923 Mr Estep was again transferred, this time to the Yakima Indian Reservation in Washington. The agency headquarters was at Toppenish, Washington.

It was in the fall of 1923 that Mary Jo began 7th grade in Toppenish.

At the age of sixteen Mary Jo was on the agenda to speak at the 1926 National Indian Congress held in Spokane, Washington July 21 through July 27.

Agenda for Wednesday July 21st:

4 : p. m.   *"How a White Women Saved Me,"* by an Indian girl of the Shoshone tribe; *a story stranger and more thrilling than fiction.*

Mary Jo was very shy. We do not know if she ever spoke at this function.

She went on to finish her education through high school, graduating from Toppenish High School in the spring of 1929.

From there it was on to Ellensburg, Washington where she enrolled at Central Washington College of Education in the fall of 1929.

She earned a teaching certificate from Ellensburg Normal School at the end of her second year and had gone on to teach at Chemawa, Washington in the Music Department. Mary Jo worked through the end of the school year at Chemawa.

In June of 1932 she applied for loan at Fort Hall so she could continue her education. To help her attain the loan she received some very supportive and complimentary letters which included accolades telling of her past good standing and future potential in becoming an excellent teacher.

She evidently got that loan as she started back to school at Ellensburg at the beginning of the 1933 winter quarter and graduating from there June 6, 1934 earning her B. A. in Education.

Mary Jo had started piano lessons in Farmington, New Mexico before Mr Estep was transferred to the Yakima agency at Toppenish, Washington. After the family moved to Toppenish Mary Jo's piano lessons began in earnest. Music was her passion.

After enrolling at Ellensburg she took on sharping her skills in music in earnest, practically became a permanent fixture in the music department and she never let up. She became a very accomplished concert pianist. She played in the school orchestra and came back to Ellensburg to play in concerts long after she had graduated from college.

One of the highlights in her music career was when she was selected or chosen with a couple of violinist to appear on the Young Artist's program for Music Federation of the State of Washington.

In the mean time Estep began the arduous job of again navigating the system to see that Mary Jo was recognized as the true heir of Henie's, Cleveland's and Jim Mosho estates a process that lasted well past October 4, 1919 nearly seven years after the death of her brother Cleve.

Jim Mosho died October 10, 1912 -   Allotment No. 1513 -180 acres

Henie Louise Mosho died July 26, 1912 -   Allotment No. 1438 -180 acres

Cleveland Mosho died January 19, 1913 -   Allotment No. 1439 -180 acres

Mary Josephine Mosho died December 19, 1992 - Allotment No. 1440 -<u>180 acres</u>

Total - 720 acres

Testimony was taken from Ditchentomatse a 74 year old lady who lived on Bannock Creek on October 4, 1919 in trying to help determine the rightful heir of the estate of Jim Mosho. The name Crawfish comes up in her testimony as a grand daughter. Other documents indicate she (Crawfish) is also an heir to Jim Mosho's estate but she drops off the radar after 1919.

Then a letter to Mike Lynch, examiner of Inheritance, Probate District 3, Sorrento, Idaho from Evan Estep directly addresses the case of Crawfish Amelia Mosho. She has died and Mary Jo is the sole heir of the estate. There are most likely records at Fort Hall that bridge the gap.

An interesting note in this letter, Estep states "both children are of the Wildcat Family". Mary Jo ends up as the sole heir of the Mosho estate as shown in the letter below.

Evan W. Estep received a letter, dates December 17, 1930, from F. A. Gross, Superintendent at the Fort Hall Indian Agency, Fort Hall, Idaho giving Evan the status of Mary Jo's 4 allotments including those that she had inherited from her aunt, brother, Jim Mosho and Crawfish Mosho.

No. 1440 - "The irrigable portion is described as follows: W/2 SE/4 Sec. 11, T4S R34E, **something wrong** *this 80 acres should be 20 acres. This is not leased and still is in sage brush. The grazing portion of her allotment is described as NW/4 Sec. 8, T6S R33E, 160 acres. This land was leased for grazing purposes during the past year and the rental is $12.80. This land will be leased from year to year until the Michaud Project is completed. Of course, the development of the Michaud unit is not a certain thing. However there is legislation pending at the present time which if enacted into law will mean the construction of irrigation canals, structures, etc. covering the Michaud within the next few years. Whenever this work is done this portion of Mary's allotment will be valuable for agricultural purposes and can no doubt be leased to good advantage.*

451

No. 1438 - the W/2 SW/4 SW/4, Sec. 11, T4S R34E, 20 acres, irrigable, not leased, still in sage brush. SE/4 Sec. 8, T6S R33E, 160 acres, within the proposed Michaud Project. This tract lies near the road and is used for a sheep trail. Fees collected for this purpose this year amounted to $13.35 for this tract.

No. 1439 - E/2 SW/4 SW/4, Sec. 11, T4S R34E, 20 acres, irrigable , not leased, still in sage brush. The SW/4 Sec. 8, T6S, R33E, 160 acres, within the proposed Michaud Project. This, too, is being used for a sheep trail and the amount collected for crossing fees amounted to $15.35 this year.

No. 1513 - the S/2 NW/4 NW/4, Sec. 32, T6S R33E, 20 acres, irrigable, along Bannock Creek, within the proposed Michaud Project. Not leased at the present time. The E3/8 NE/4 Sec. 32 and the W5/8 NW/4 Sec. 33, T6S, R33E, 160 acres, grazing land leased for the next three years at $24 a year.

Mary Josephine Estep ....Seventh grade
Teacher ....Miss P . Thoma

Loyalty to my Home Community

Loyalty means to be faithful and true to any person or thing:
to be faithful is to trust, to believe, and to honor: to be true
is to live up to what we believe.

We, the pupils of this school, owe a great deal to some one
for this beautiful building so splendidly equipped, for our
efficient teachers and the many things we have furnished to give
us an education. We all know this comes from the taxes paid by
our home people and merchants and not from outside firms in distant towns and cities.

Should the peoples of this community send away for all the
things we need to buy, subscribe for newspapers in other towns,
ship our produce away, in fact quit doing business with our home
community, how soon our people would be looking for a new home,
our merchants would have to get out of business, our taxes
would be cut down, our schools have less money, we could not
build ra roads, or in any way improve our community

Then why should we not be loyal to the
town that does these things for us By patronizing
our home stores it helps them to grow. We should
induce other people to trade in our stores
for it is to these people we go for assistance
when we need money to help along some
good cause.

We should see we loyal to our town
for what they do for us in the same
way that we are to our parents who
provide homes, food, and clothing for
us.

Every dollar spent outside of our town
for goods takes a dollar out of our community
and when a large part of our population
buys goods in other places, we can see
all what a large sum of money is taken
away that should be used to better our home
community.

Let us resolve to patronize home & home
industries be boosters for J first last
and always.

(Long Live   )

453

Honolulu, Hawaiian Islands
June 23, 1891

Crow Agency, Montana
June 23, 1916

Yakima
Washington

June 23
1941

RITA & EVAN ESTEP

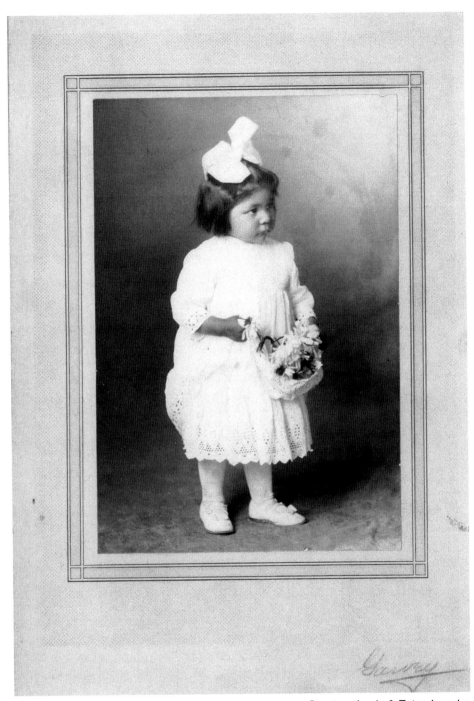

MARY JO ESTEP
July, 1912
After she was taken into the home of the Estep at Fort Hall, Idaho

MARY JO ESTEP
1915
Mary Jo at about five years old taken at the Crow Agency in Montana

MARY JO ESTEP
1917
Mary Jo at about seven years old probably taken at Ship Rock, N. M.

MARY JO ESTEP
ca 1926
Toppenish, Washington

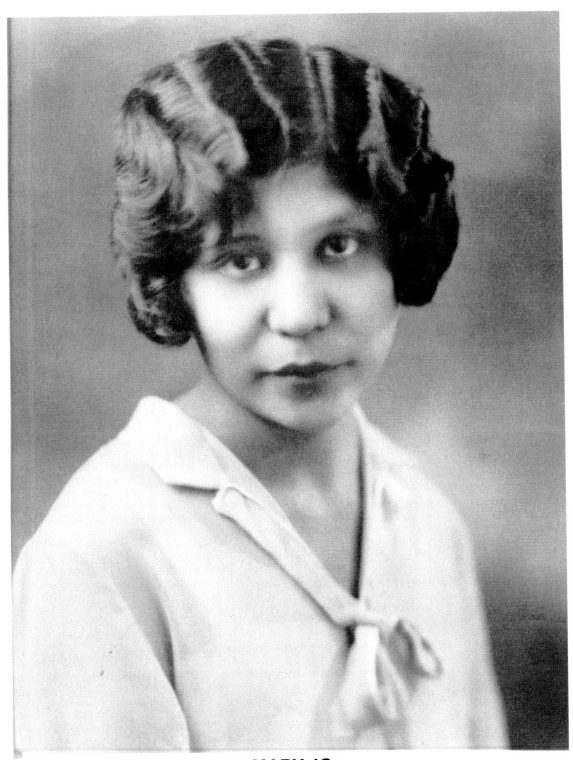

MARY JO
ca 1930

MARY JO ESTEP

June 1979

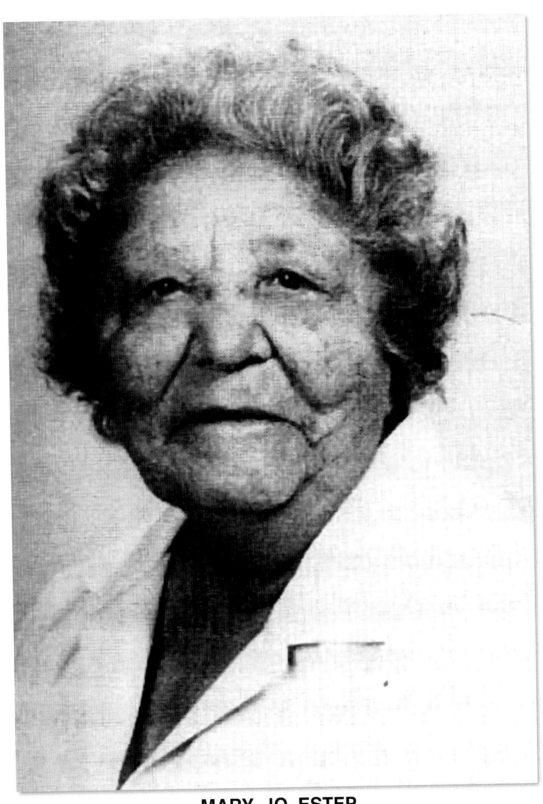

MARY JO ESTEP
1985

MARY JO ESTEP

c 1975

Mary Jo at her Steinway baby grand piano. For many years she had two pianos in
her home. Mary Jo and her very good friend Ruth Sweany would often play duets on
the two pianos entraining there many good friends and or themselves.

MARY JO'S HOME
May 2006

Yakima, Washington   98902

Top Row: Lasko Hellwig Champlin Moise Jacobs Barnes Barkuloo Hunter Tuttle Holm Bradford Matzen Cartmell Burge
Second Row: Wirt Desmond Jacobs Lockhart Rudd Bliss Dawson Collins Allison Clark DeVries Estep Brumback
Third Row: Laidler Wood Jacobs Murphy Sanders Goode Farrington Matzen Parker Pace Keech Bittle Williams
Fourth Row: Brayton Hiser Olsen Fear Martin Brown Yama Wright Brumback Waymire Shoemaker Ritchey Eagle

TOPPENISH HIGH SCHOOL
1927
From the top - 2nd row 2nd from right Mary Jo Estep

(sophomore and only Native American in the class)

MUSIC

The Music Department of the high school has had a prominent part in activities this year. The girls' glee club presented a cantata, "The Land of Heart's Desire," with a baritone obbligato sung by Mr. Clare Mendenhall, accompanied by Mary J. Estep at the piano. In the fall, the glee club was asked to sing at the Teachers' Institute in Yakima. At a later date they entertained the local Rotary Club with a few numbers.

Twenty girls and ten boys were chosen from the glee clubs to represent Toppenish in the Musical Ensemble in Yakima, May 3.

Mrs. Woodard believes that the choruses have done excellent work this year and she looks forward to an equally successful musical program for next year.

1st—Bourgaize, Wolfe, Hashimoto, Koboski, Young, Coach Freeman, Hunter, Phillips, Barnes, McCaslin, Donaldson, Barnes.
2d—Brown, Wernitsch, Moise, Lockhart, Jacobs, Riggins, Tucker, Hadley, Weiser, Matlock.
3d—Lyons, Nesby, Yama, Philips, Keech, Cartmell, Tucker, Anthony, Brackett, Myers, Yamamoto.
4 h—Marrow, Owens, Ward, Jacobs, Bell, Rentschler, Wyckoff, Asbury, Miller, Alexander, Estep.
5th—Faa, Wolfe, Layman, Matheson, Warrell, Barkuloo, Bernier, Williams, Russell.

TOPPENISH HIGH SCHOOL

1928

From top 4th row far right Mary Jo Estep

(Junior and only Native American in the class)

HELEN COPE—Classical

Operetta cho. 1, principal 3; S. O. S. 3; Cantata 3-4; Honor Society 3; Folk Dance Club 4; Carnival 3-4; Music Club 3; Tohiscan staff 4; Dramatic Club 3; Senior play.

EUGENE DAVIS—Scientific

Football 3-4; Debate 4; Track 4; Good will program 3; Operetta principal 3; Glee Club 3; Annual staff 3; Editor 4; Tohiscan staff 4; S. O. S. 3; Carnival 1-3-4; Class officer 2, president 4; Pep Club 3-4; Music Club 3, A. S. B. officer 3-4; Letterman's Club 3; Yell leader 3; Senior play.

ELLEN DESMOND—Classical

Pep Club 3-4; Annual staff 3; S. O. S. 2-3; Girls' League president 4; Carnival 2-3; College Club officer 4; Class officer; Dramatic Club 3.

PAUL DEES—English

Entered from Grandview 1928. Dramatic Club 4; Carnival 4; Senior play.

DELLA EAGLE—Home Economics

Girls' League officer 4; Glee Club 1-2; Kodak Club 4; Hiking Club 3; Operetta cho. 2; Honor Society 1-3-4; Carnival 3-4.

MARY J. ESTEP—Classical

Carnival 1-2-3-4; Operetta 1-3; Glee Club 3-4; Cantata 3-4; Music Club 3; Folk Dancing Club 4; S. O. S. 2; Orchestra 3-4.

JEAN FEAR—Scientific

Operetta principal 1-3; Cantata 3; Carnival 1-2-3-4; A. S. B. officer 4; Pep Club 2-3-4; Tohiscan staff 4; Journalism Club 4; Good will program 2-3-4; S. O. S. 1-2-3; Debate 4; Music Club 3; Honor Society 1; Orchestra 3-4; Senior play; Glee Club 1-2-3.

LENA GOODE—Scientific

Entered from Mabton 1926. Glee Club 1-4; S. O. S. 4; Art Club 3; Cookery Club 3; Carnival 3-4.

HAROLD HALL—English

Football 3-4; Operetta 3; Good will program 3-4; Pep Club 4; Carnival 3-4; Senior play.

OPAL HISER—Scientific

S. O. S. 3; Dramatic Club 3-4; Hiking Club 3; Operetta 3; Carnival 3-4; Senior play.

TOPPENISH HIGH SCHOOL SENIORS
1929

467

FRIENDS OF MARY JO (Fort Hall, Idaho)
Date - 1981 (give or take 10 years)
From left - Vivian Hardy, Jeanette Pocatello, Susie Yupe Lippi

On the back of this photo is written:

Dear Josephine
*   Should you happen at Fort Hall call on us.*
*   Your friend Jeanette Pocatello*
Vivian Hardy.   -   My daughter
Jeanette
Susie Yupe Lippi

Chapter IV

A TEACHING CARRIER BEGINS

Mary Jo had graduated from Central Washington College of Education in in 1934, right in the middle of the Great Depression. Being a Native American Indian girl made it extremely difficult to find a teaching job. She was only considered in Indian schools and not at all at public schools. Even at Indian schools she was not always accepted. White teachers were preferred for teaching at Indian schools.

More evidence of racial discrimination is detailed in two letters (dated May 14, 1934) written by Evan Estep to Mrs Ruth M. Brensen of Bernice,Oklahoma and Hon. John Collier, Commissioner of Indian Affairs in Washing, D. C.

Estep to Brensen: *"There was no vacancy at the White Swan schools or she would without a doubt have had it. I knew all the board down there and they told that the only question was that of a vacancy. But at Harrah they had two vacancies but evidently they do not want an Indian for teacher, though they have about 35 Indian pupils in that school. Any way two white teachers were selected for the vacancies. As there is but little likelihood that she could secure a place in a public school where there are no Indians it looks as if she will have to look to the Indian schools for a position the coming year and I hope that you can assist her in securing a reasonably desirable place".*

Estep to Collier: *"There was no vacancy at White Swan where nearly half of the pupils are Indian. Had their been a vacancy I am sure that she would have been given the place. At Harrah there were two vacancies but evidently they do not want an Indian teaching though some 35 pupils of that school are of Indian blood. There is not much likelihood that she will be able to secure a <u>public school</u> position where there are no Indian pupils on account of her being of Indian blood.*

If you can find any thing in your office with reference to my Indian service work that would seem to justify my asking some consideration from the Department I would like to ask it in behalf of this full blood Indian girl".

Evan Estep helped her navigate through the prejudices against Indians, especially Indian teachers until she finally landed at the Indian school on the Apache Indian Reservation at Whiteriver Arizona in the fall of 1934. Her 1st job after graduation was teaching first grade at Whiteriver.

At the end of that school year she applied for a public school position at White Swan, near Yakima, Washington. She was accepted and began her teaching carrier in the public school system in the fall of 1935 and never looked back.

That 1st year she taught at a one room school at Medicine Valley until the school closed. She started teaching 1st grade at White Swan in the fall of 1936 and continued teaching 1st grade there for the next nine years.

Mary Jo transferred to her next teaching assignment in Toppinesh, Washington, starting there in the fall of 1946, retiring from teaching at Toppenish in 1974.

Mary Jo had taught school for a total of forty one years.

For the most part of her teaching carrier she taught 1st grade however her main interest was in music and teaching piano. She taught music and piano in grades one through eight and it appears that was during her entire carrier.

She did not stop there, to improve her teaching skills she enrolled in summer school and extension classes, nearly every year during her entire teaching carrier.

Mary Jo became a teacher and a concert pianist. She taught school in Oregon, Arizona and Washington. Over the years, as a concert pianist, she played at churches, charities and other events around the Yakima area and southern Washington.

Mary Jo retired from teaching to her home in Yakima, Washington, in 1974.

After retirement she continued to play at concerts and write music with her many friends until her untimely death.

MARY JO ESTEP & HER 1ST GRADE CLASS at LINCOLN SCHOOL

TOPPINESH, WASHINGTON

ca 1947

TEACHERS AT LINCOLN SCHOOL - TOPPINESH, WASHINGTON

ca 1947

From left - Mrs Noble, Ms Thorup, Ms Lorain Tannamaker, Ms Sholtys, Ms Shell, Ms Whitti (principle), Mrs Francis Witte Leuning (cousin to the principle, Ms Witte), Ms Brese, Ms Davis, Miss Ruth Sweany and Miss Mary Jo Estep

TEACHERS at LINCOLN SCHOOL - TOPPINESH, WASH.

ca 1950

From left - back row - Mrs Noble, Ataberry,   ?   , Ms Dalmar, Ms Reiser, Ms Witte (principle),Mrs (Witte) Leuning

From left - front row -   ?   , Miss Swane (Sweany), Ms Sholtys, Ms Dutcher, Miss Estep, Ms Savis

TEACHERS AT LINCOLN SCHOOL TOPPENISH, WASHINGTON

ca 1970

Back row - #6 from left - Ms Tolafson ?, #7 Dixie (Walker) Elder? #10 Miss Estep

Front row - #1 from left Mr Temporaly (superintendent of schools) #3 Miss Sweany ?

far right Mr Ralph Mc Quin (principle)

LADIES MUSICAL **CLUB**

ca 1980s

Diana Chu, Ruth Sweany, Mary Jo Estep

From the Yakima paper - *"Ladies Musical Club will present its annual members Christmas concert Thursday, featuring its own musicians, in a 1:30 p.m. program in the sanctuary of Wesley United Methodist Church. The program will include Diana Chu playing her Chinese flute and a duet by pianist Mary Jo Estep and recorder artist Ruth Sweany".*

PART V

CHAPTER I

THE STORY of MARY JO in HER OWN WORDS

I refer the readers to Mary Jo's own story, in her own words, for more on the early years of her life.

After meeting Dayton Hyde the author of **THE LAST FREE MAN** and learning her story Mary Jo began to tell that story all around the country. She was invited to speak at church groups, educational organization, charity organizations and many others. She would some times change her presentation to what she felt may better fit the interests of the group to whom she was speaking however the story was basically the same.

She told the story as she knew it although there were many facets of her story that she did not know. Much of the story regarding killing at Rabbit Creek she had derived from the book THE LAST FREE MAN and her meetings with the author Dayton Hyde.

Dayton did not have all of the facts correct as to the happenings at Rabbit Creek.

By the late 1970s she had given over thirty five presentations and during the following decade she gave that many or more.

The goal here is to include all of the different versions into one and transcribe them exactly as she wrote them.

The organization may vary a little however the text and words are exactly as she wrote. Also note that what she wrote was not as much for publication as notes for her many presentations. In addition she often used the name Henie and Louise interchangeably.

The Esteps were so very proud of Mary Jo and all that she had accomplished and she gave them credit for it all.

I WAS THERE OR ONE AMONG US

By Mary Jo Estep

I always feel greatly honored when I am asked to speak. I enjoy telling people the little I know of the Massacre for I can hardly believe that this has all happened to me.

One title of my talk could be I WAS THERE since I am the sole Indian survivor of the Last Indian Massacre in the United States in the year 1911 in the state of Nevada. Another title could be ONE AMONG US as I was taken as a baby into a white household and raised among white people.

It has been a year ago this month that things began to change for me. I never dreamed that I would be making public appearances and speaking. At first I didn't think I could do it. In my younger years I was laughed at so many times because of the odd way I put words together in sentences. The teacher asked the class "Who has seen the wind? Of course, I had seen the wind. So I waved my hand vigorously in the air. "Yes, she said. "you have seen the wind? What did it look like? Just when did you see it. Why, no one has seen the wind." That really put me in my place and since that time I have been very careful about replying or talking for fear of making a dreadful mistake.

The story I have to tell you about to day only Mr Hyde , the author, and I know about. I have given my talk the name - - I WAS THERE.

My talk is divided into several different sections. First a glimpse into the lives of Mr. and Mrs. Estep - my childhood - my teaching career - and a word about the author Dayton O. Hyde, the man who researched my family's past, and the Massacre as told to the author by oldsters in Nevada.

Mr. Estep was a native of Indiana Mrs. Estep a native of Illinois. It was a college romance although they did not attend the same college. From Indiana Mr Estep went to the Hawaiian Islands where he was a clerk on a sugar plantation. Later he was head of a Boy's Training School. On the side he served as a judge for the Hawaiians and after hours he pulled teeth for the natives.

After much corresponding with Rita Garrison she follows him to the Islands. She often told me about her trip by train from Illinois to Seattle. As they passed through North Yakima she said she was so glad that she did not live there. As it was so desolate. Her first trip to the Islands was by sailing vessel. It took 27 days crossing the

Pacific. Sometimes they were becalmed and some days they lost knots. It seemed twice as long for she was a very poor sailor and was seasick most of the way. They were married the day she arrived in Honolulu at the Moana. Mrs Estep taught school for 17 years until her health failed and she was forced to return to the Mainland.

Mr Estep set up a law practice in Indiana. In a couple of years he decided against continuing law work. He applied for a Civil Service position and was accepted. He was assigned to clerkship in the Interior Department in Washington D. C. It was during Taft's administration. Mother told me about going to a park on Pennsylvania Avenue on Sunday morning and seeing President Taft strolling by on way to church. He would tip his hat and say, "Good morning, ladies."

In a few years Dad again had the urge for a change in jobs. He asked to be sent out into the field work. The first assignment he had was as Superintendent of an indian Reservation at Yankton, South Dakota in 1907 - 1908. The Indian people were still very primitive according to the white man's standards.

Imagine if you can Mother's feelings on coming out west to an Indian Reservation straight from Washington, D. C. Her first week there she was terrified of the Indians and then it rained, the roof leaked like a sieve. On Saturday night some of he Indian men got a little too much to drink and they came war whooping down the dirt road in front of their house. She was sure that at any moment they would appear over the transom. Later she became acquainted with one of these Indians and they had many a laugh over the experience.

From Yankton, they were transferred to Fort Hall, Idaho. This proved to be really out west. Mr. Estep helped in allotting the land to the Indians . He also had a government school to over see. At this reservation the indians were given rations of staples on Saturdays. They would flock in from the reservation in buggies, spring wagons, and on horse back to get staples of flour, sugar, coffee, potatoes also bedding.
It was here I joined the family.

The Interior Department never let a superintendent stay at one reservation many years. So they transferred him to the Crow Agency in Montana. This agency is located at the foot of Custer Battlefield. There are monuments and graves located on a knoll a few miles from the agency. I can remember driving out to the Battlefield with the folks in first Ford car they ever had.

The Indians on this reservation were starting to get into the cattle business and beginning to have some money. It was here I saw Indian graves above the ground. Some coffins were place on platforms and some placed high in the air on poles. It made quite an impression on me. The loneliness of it all. Dad was quite proud of the work he was doing there when the Interior Department decided to transfer him to the Navajo reservation at Shiprock, New Mexico. Shiprock was located right in the middle of a desert and the place was named after a rock formation which rose high into the air. It looked like a sail boat. In one direction it was 25 miles to Farmington, a small town, and in the other direction it was 100 miles to Gallup, New Mexico. In those days the roads were dirt roads full of ruts and chuck holes. Sometimes the roads were almost wiped out with the sand storms. Dad's favorite tribe of Indians were the Navajos. At that time they were so honest and wanted to work for everything they received.

Toppenish, Washington was the last reservation Mr. Estep was sent to. It was the first time we had lived in a small town. Before we were only around government employees and we made our own social life. These Indians were the most civilized ones we had been among. Money from renting their land created many a problem. It was from Toppenish that Mr Estep retired in 1930.

Now I would like to share with you a few memories of a long ago childhood. I was truly a primitive baby taken from a cradle board into the white man's world. The world that my grandfather was trying to escape.

Let us travel back to Fort Hall Idaho - back through the years to 1909 - 1910. On this reservation there were many Shoshone and Bannock Indians. Indians were being put on reservations, for the white people were making their way west. Some of the tribes fought back and some of the tribes didn't object to being segregated on reservations. My grandfather felt the push of the white man. He didn't want to fight and he didn't want to be put on the reservations where he would have to accept rations and hand outs to exist. He loved his freedom.

Many months of the year found his band on Rock Creek which is located near Twin Falls, Idaho. Here the water was fresh, clear and the fishing good. Not too far away were the camas fields and the wild grass from which they gathered the seeds to grind into flour. The wild onions were plentiful as was the wild game. Life was good for the small band of Indians. But this was soon to come to an end.

In those days the Indians had two names or maybe more. And so my grandfather had several names - Salmon River Mike; Idaho Mike; Indian Mike; Shoshone Mike, or Mike Daggett. It seems there happened to be a Superintendent by the name Daggett and it is thought Mike took that for his last name. Mike was the chief of his band of Indians which varied in numbers from time to time.

There was Mike (records prove he was a Bannock Indian and they were known as fighters); Jennie, his wife who was a Ute, two grown sons, Jack and Jim; three younger boys , Jake called Eat-Um-Up Jake; Charlie, or Catchum Charlie; and Cleve who I always had heard called Cleveland; three grown daughters - two were named after animals -Lizard and Snake - and Henie who I called Louise; two small girls, Hattie, who I knew as Harriet, and myself, a baby. It seems there was on older boy whose name was unknown and a girl who died. Mike said, "Girl him lay down and die."

Probably it was fall when Mike and his family suddenly broke camp on Rock Creek and headed for the hills. No one knows the reason for this move, but while he was on the trail word came that he had been charged with stealing horses a charge which was later proven to be unfounded. But he had no way of knowing that these charges had been dropped. Believing that they were being pursued , Mike and his band fled west, from Idaho into Nevada. The going was rough - the horses were wearing out. The little band was hungry and they were into the dead of winter. It seemed that at every turn there was evidence of white man. Records showed that this was the worst winter in Nevada history.

Mike prayed in his own way to his Creator. Praying and chanting and beating his drum, he prayed for the snow to cease and for some wild animal to come their way. And then one cold day they came upon a few cattle - an answer to his prayers. Never before had Mike killed something that didn't belong to him, but in desperation he and his sons killed a cow to feed his starving band. Before they were finished, they were discovered by a sheepherder. The sheepherder reported immediately his finding to the farmers. Then the battle was on - Indians and whites were killed in the skirmish. And

481

so the Indians were on the run again. Now anything that happened to the white settlers was blamed on Mike and his tribe. So it was decided something must be done to put a stop to this killing. Posses from Nevada and California joined the local police from Winnemucca and the chase was on. The posse traveled more than 300 miles after the family. They had a good incentive to hunt them for the reward money had grown to $15,000.

Mike and his tribe were now on their way into California and then they circled back and began to make their way back to Idaho. It has been said had they split up they could have melted into the rough terrain of Nevada but they chose to stay together.

During this time the posse were feeling the rugged winter, too and dissension broke out among them. The Nevada posse weren't pleased having Sheriff Lamb from Humboldt County, California join them and so they sent them in wrong directions. Some of the men went home, realizing that the reward money each would receive would be small.

It was during this time that Snake, one of Mike's daughters, had a baby; I was that baby. It was getting harder and harder to elude the posse. Several of their horses were wearing out and the feet of the Indians were wearing out too. Mike realized the end was close, but he knew this people must rest. So in a peaceful valley on the 26th of February he pitched camp and ordered everyone to rest except Louise and she was to watch the horses. The posse had about given up hope they would find them when they came over the crest of the hill and as they surveyed the landscape one of the men thought he saw smoke. He knew if it was smoke they had the band trapped. Louise saw the posse too and she rushed to round up the horses, but a shot was fired. There were many conflicting reports as to which side fired that first shot. My grandfather dashed away from the encampment. He was trying to get the posse to chase him and leave the women and children so they could escape into the sagebrush and grease wood. He was shot first but still he urged them to leave him. All stood their ground - the braves had guns with little ammunition; the women had bows and arrows and one primitive spear and the children used rocks and gravel. One of the white men said that every member of the posse fired a shot into Mike's body. But he did not immediately die. One man asked him as he lay dying, "What kind of an Indian are you?" To which

482

he replied, "Me Shoshone, Me Shoshone." It is thought the reason for that answer was that the Shoshones were friendly with the white man and were really not fighters.

Finally there was a sudden quiet over the valley. The war drums had ceased their throbbing, cries of the injured were no more and what had happened was history. Only one member of the posses was killed and it was thought the Indian band had been wiped out. The posse emerged from their hiding places and began taking account. They searched for souvenirs and it was during this time they came upon a young boy hiding in the sage brush. They then discovered Henie protecting Harriet. As they came near where my mother lay, they heard the crying of a baby. I always had known that I was found in a cradle board on my dead mother's back.

It was about that time that Sheriff Lamb and his posse came over the top of the hill and he couldn't imagine what had taken place. It is thought that none of this would have happened had he come upon the Indian Band first as he was a very fair man.

Eventually children and souvenirs were gathered up since night was coming on. They went to a farm house to spend the night. As is the custom among primitive people -- They wail for their dead. Louise who was close to 19 years old began her wailing for the dead. Since they were all housed in one large room, the posse could get little or no sleep. Every time anyone dozed she would begin her wailing. The next morning they all went into Winnemucca. Word had already filtered back that the posse had captured the wild Indians. The Townspeople were so relieved and overjoyed that they congregated on roof tops and balconies and upstairs windows to welcome the posse back with the Indians. They were greatly disappointed to see only four children being brought in.

We were put into jail until they could decide what to do with us. From there we went by train to the jail at Reno, Nevada. Louise was terrified of the train and they had a difficult time getting her on board, but after it started to move she settled down and enjoyed her train ride. At Carson City, Nevada there happened to be an Indian school and so we were sent there. My aunts and uncle were placed in the school and I was put in the school hospital. The children spoke a mixture of Paiute & Shoshone and no one could understand them. One day in the school laundry a girl working next to my aunt spoke to her in Shoshone and Louise replied. The girl told the women in charge,

483

she is a Shoshone. Serving as an interpreter for Henie (Louise) it was discovered the family had lived in Idaho. About this time the people in Carson City felt sorry for us and they decked us out in fine new cloths. I discovered that I possess the only picture in existence of the four of us in our finery.

The Interior Department wired Mr. Estep, who was the Superintendent of Fort Hall, about the orphan children since his reservation had a large majority of Shoshones on it. It was thought best to bring the children to that reservation. Now Mr. Estep loved children so he decided that he would go and bring them to Fort Hall.

He found I was being cared for by a Negro nurse. She was deeply attached to me and was really upset about his taking me. She wouldn't say goodbye. On the train I spied two black ladies. I kept poking Mr Estep and pointing to them; in fact, I was overjoyed upon seeing them, he had to go and explain to them why I kept pointing at them. In the dining car I wouldn't eat the food, but when piece of raisin bread was placed before me, I picked out the raisins. He had to order more raisin bread for me.

As soon as we arrived at Fort Hall Mr. Estep entered our names on the enrollment book as Shoshone Indians. Later he allowed each living child a certain amount of land.

They tried to find out what my name was. Nobody knew, or they would not give it if they did know. Mr. Estep had to have a name to enter on the enrollment form. So he decided Mary would be my name, and then later they found I did have the name Josephine. It was decided to use both names - Mary Josephine. One of the grade school teachers tried to shorten it to Mary J., but the folks did not approve of that at all. But when I went to college, a lot of things changed; I became Mary Jo and I learned to drink coffee.

After bringing us to Fort Hall, it was found that all the children had tuberculosis. Louise being around 19 could not be kept at the Indian school. They let her go out onto the reservation. She soon succumbed to the dreaded disease. Cleveland was out in the school hospital and Harriet, the five year old aunt, soon died.

I was too young to be put into the dormitory with the other children. The girls' matron being a real good friend of the folks said she would take me into her room and keep me which she did. I became very conscious of people and surroundings. It was there I remember Cleve my brother. Days when he seemed rather well they would bring him over to play with me. We spent many an hour playing in the warm sunshine. Often the ladies in the small community would come over to see the orphan baby. Other times the older girls would take me out on the stairway landing and we would all watch for Mr. Estep to come the mile from the Agency I knew he might take me home with him. When he did, the Matron would bundle me up an place me on Mr. Estep's shoulders, and away we would go the mile back to the Agency. This arrangement worked for awhile, but it soon became evident that I wasn't well. After Mrs. Estep saw me she wanted to take me into her home. Dad gave his consent. A neighbor loaned them a crib which her children had outgrown and they placed it by their bed. The first night I held Mother's hand all night. In fact I slept very little that night.

I thought you might be interested in the dress I wore the day they took me into their home.

[She holds up the dress and a gown that they had sent with her.]

Since I had been in a government school, each garment had to be labeled. On the inside is the name Josephine Mike. And this is the gown they sent with me. On the inside is the label Harriet Mike - my aunt.

It was the year 1911 that I came into the Estep's lives. They asked Louise how old I was. She had no way of telling them, but that I was born in the spring when the flowers started to bloom. Since Dad's birthday was in the spring, the 12th of April, it was decided to put my birthday on that day too. In my younger years we always had two cakes for I must have Angel Food cake and Dad the Devil's Food Cake.

After the Esteps took me, I became seriously ill. The doctor then told them not to expect me to live. Mother would not accept this verdict. She knew a little about medicine as her brother had been a doctor. She nursed me back to health and I have enjoyed unusually good health.

The Esteps had no children of their own but they had raised several children. For a few years they had a niece and a nephew in their home. Also a Sioux Indian girl who spent her summers with us. From the Islands they brought a Chinese boy to the states with them.

The members of the Estep family were Mr Estep, Mrs Estep, Mrs Estep's mother and her nephew, who was living with them and attending high school in Pocatello, Idaho.

485

He and I never got along very well as I was always all eyes watching him, especially when he practiced the trumpet. Many was the time he chased me down the steps away from his room. Grandma was a wonderful companion. She was a good listener and I could sit in her room and tell her amazing tales and she would tell me stories and read books to me that were far beyond my years. Grandma and I got along fine, although for some reason, she got tired of the little chatterbox. Our bedrooms were right next to each other and after my nap I would head right for her room. One afternoon I couldn't get into her room. I wonder why, so I peeked through the keyhole and there sat grandma playing solitaire. I bounced downstairs to find Mother. She asked, "Where is Grandma?" I said "She is in her room playing tads." She said, "How do you know?" I peeked through the key hole."

I remember meal time well. I wouldn't eat vegetables unless Dad did, and he was never very fond of them. I wouldn't talk either, but could poke and point at things. Finally Mother decided that must come to a stop Having been a school teacher, she knew how to handle children. So it was decided that I would have to ask for things. Well! I learned to talk real fast. In fact, I would rather talk than eat and that was frowned upon. Many was the time I have heard, "Little girls must be seen and not heard."

I'm afraid I was far from being an angel as I look back on my numerous escapades. One afternoon I was missed. I think as long as we lived at Fort Hall they were worried that the Indians might come and take me away. They searched high and low, running upstairs and downstairs, out into the yard and then into the chicken yard. On one of mother's numerous trips through the kitchen, she thought she heard a noise coming from the pantry. Thinking I couldn't be in there since there was no light in the closet, she opened the door, and there I sat, lighting matches and blowing them out. - the way Daddy let me blow them out after he lit his pipe. Each match was placed carefully on the hundred pound sack of sugar. Some were still smoking. That was the end of my blowing out of matches.

Another time when I went missing, [SIC] Mother of the nervous type went all to pieces when she couldn't locate me. She was packing in preparation for leaving and everything must be washed and ironed. What a bed full of ironed clothes. Since

486

everyone was tired that evening we went to bed early. During the night she arose to check on me. Imagine her feelings on opening my bedroom door and there was no one there. She dashed into Grandma's room thinking I might have crawled in bed with her. But I was not there. Then everybody was aroused and the search was on. She said she flashed the light on in the spare bedroom but didn't see anything. But when Dad looked he found me all curled up on the beautifully ironed clothes.

I always loved to go out to the chicken yard with Daddy. Well, one delightful autumn afternoon, dressed in my favorite red coat, trailing behind Dad, he heard quite a commotion and turned just in time to see the Turkey gobbler - feathers ruffled, dashing right at me. He had to kick at it repeatedly to get it away from me.

Another time on our way back to the house, pigeon-toed me had to cross a small irrigation ditch over a narrow board and down I went into the murky water. There I sat, screaming at the top of my lungs. Mother came flying from the house to see what had happened. There stood Dad laughing at the spectacle I made. Was she ever angry with him.

Christmas came early that year as Mother was so thrilled to have a little one in the house, she couldn't keep the new doll buggy a secret. The afternoon I found it setting on the fireplace hearth, I danced for joy. --"My Buddy! My Buddy!

One incident marred that first christmas season for Mother. I was so intrigued with the beautiful blossoms on the Christmas cactus, which was Mother's pride and joy. One afternoon after my nap, I proceeded to pick all the flowers off it and take them to Mother. That really left her speechless.

Everything wasn't all roses. Well do I remember my first sewing experience. Little friends would come over to play - and such fun. Crawling and crawling from room to room and when they went home, large gaping holes appeared in the knees of my long black stockings. Mother warned me but I didn't take too much stock in her warnings. So the next afternoon found us crawling again. Nothing happened after they went home but the next morning after breakfast she got my damaged stocking a darning ball, needle and thread and sat me down for my first darning lesson. Tears streamed down my face, but that ended my crawling.

One day an Indian man came to the front door and said he was my uncle. He would like to see me. Mother brought me in to see him. He looked me over and said, "I want to give her something." To which Mother replied, "That would be alright." Into his pocket went his hand and out came a handful of money. "Oh no," said mother, "one piece is enough." That was the last time I ever saw my uncle.

Mother discouraged people from bringing me candy. Instead she told them they might bring me fruit or nabiscos. So I acquired quite a taste for those delicious crunchy wafers. One spring afternoon Mother gave me some money and let me go through the park to the store. I told the storekeeper I wanted, "Bittoes." Finally I had to go home without the Bittoes. I told Mother, "Mr. Scalley doesn't know anything." I asked him as plain as I could for Bittoes and he didn't know what they were.

Once in awhile we would take the train into Pocatello. This particular time Mother dressed me in beautiful white clothes for a picture taking expedition. My trade mark, a gorgeous ribbon bow was placed upon my hair. After being photographed standing this way and that way, we still had plenty of time before train time. Mother thought we could go to a movie. It was a Fatty Arbuckle film. I became greatly excited over the furniture which was being tossed out of the house. I bounce up and announced at the top of my voice,"they are having a whoop la time, aren't they?" Of course everyone turned to see who had made such a statement.

We must have lived at Fort Hall about a year and a half after they took me. From there we went to Crow Agency, Montana. And it was here I started my schooling. I had to walk a mile to the public school, but like all Mothers, Mother worried over my being so far from home. So she took me out of the public school and place me in the government school which was within a block of my home I had both white children and Indian children as playmates.

From Crow Agency Mr. Estep was transferred to Shiprock, New Mexico. They had a public school, but it was a small room in the teacher's cottage, so they let me again attend the government school until the fourth grade. The employees decided to build a new public school building and make it a little larger, which they did. This was constructed of logs and so I can say I went to a log cabin school. I recall it as being a long narrow room with a stove in the middle of he room. They had all grades from first through the eighth. The boys and girls played on separate playgrounds.

At the different Indian Agencies the employees made their own social life. Every other Saturday they had dances. Everyone brought their children. I was place on a chair to watch them whirling and gliding to the waltzes when I caught sight of Mr. Estep with a baby in his arms. I climbed down from my chair and hurried over to him. Climbing and pushing the baby I made the statement, "One baby enough! One baby enough!"

1924, the year I was ready for the 7th grade, Dad was again transferred, to Toppenish, Washington. We were surprised to find such a nice town and such a fine school for me to attend. Coming from a one room school to a room that had five times as many pupils in it was quite an experience for me. At that time there were very few Indian children in the High School. Two Indian girls I remember were fine musicians and I really envied them. I had had a few lessons from a lady in Farmington and I seemed to have some ability. Mother had heard of the Ida B. McLagan School of Piano Playing in Yakima. She took me for an audition. Miss McLagan seemed pleased with my playing but such hand positions. She placed me with one of her teachers and said she would take me later, which she did.

In 8th grade the Toppenish community were sponsoring essay contests. I really became interested in them and tried my hand at writing. Imagine competing with seniors. I did that and got honorable mention. Another time I received five dollars for my essay on Loyalty to My Home Community. There were other contests and my teachers thought I should try for a writing career but I had long ago decided on a teaching career. I graduated from Toppenish High School in 1929. I enrolled at Ellensburg Normal and found dormitory life great. So many people to have for friends and they were friendly. Being of the Indian race didn't seem to make the least difference. School work wasn't to difficult. Then I enrolled in the piano department and found I was very popular. I played in the Spring and Winter Concerts at the college. The highlight of my college experience was when I was chosen with a couple of violinists to appear in the Young Artist's program for the Music Federation of the State of Washington.

I graduated from Ellensburg Normal with a B. A. in Education. Then there was the problem of trying to find a job. This was during the Depression and jobs were few and far between. Through Dad's influence I obtained a government job at Chemawa, Oregon in the piano department. Chemawa at that time was a government school with close to a thousand pupils. I received the wage of $50 a month. The reason I didn't qualify for more was that I had no Anthropology course in college. I wasn't especially pleased with the job. The children could have free piano lessons, but unless they were really interested, they failed to practice although practice rooms were provide for them. One year of that and I was ready to try for something else. Another job came my way in Whiteriver, Arizona. It was a first grade position. That was something else! The first day I faced a class of 25 Indian children straight off the reservation who spoke no English, only their native tongue, Apache. They were cute even if a bit grimy. At the noon hour all the children went to the dining room and were given a real good meal. I don't remember the children wasting food; all were so busy eating. After dinner the little ones were taken to the dormitories, given a shower and put to bed for an hour, and then, when they came back to the classroom one could hardly believe their eyes for everyone sparkled so. An hour of school, and then the buses came and took them home. At the end of the year the little ones were speaking English, but I had learned very little Apache. I could only take one year of this for I missed the folks and the Yakima Valley

It was thought I might try to get a public school position, so I applied at White Swan and was accepted right away. I was placed at Medicine Valley in a one room school. This was a most enjoyable experience. The next year this school was closed and I went into White Swan. There I stayed nine years. I taught first grade and public school music in grades one through eight. From White Swan I was asked to come to Toppenish and it was from there I retired in 1974.

Teaching little ones was filled with many an amusing experiences. One of my favorite stories. One day the children were telling about what they wanted to be when they grew up. Mose Dick, an Indian child said, "I want to be a cowboy." "And why do you want to be a cowboy?" I asked to which he replied -----"So I can shoot Indians."

Retirement has been great. My first year found me busy enjoying my garden and music and club activities and then a few years ago -- the phone rang and this little incident opened many a door for me.

It happened to be a college classmate who lives in Antioch, Calif. We had never been close. That was why I was so surprised. She said she had just finished reading a book that she knew was about my family. She had even corresponded with the author, Dayton O. Hyde. He seemed greatly excited upon hearing there might be a survivor of the last Indian massacre. A story he had worked on for 15 years. But he wanted her to call me and find out if it would be alright to phone me. Even after we had corresponded, he was hesitant about meeting me feeling he had intruded into a very private part of my life.

Yes, I had known there had been a massacre, but as to the details , I knew nothing. Why this interest in an event that had happened some sixty years ago.? I think you must know something of the background of the author.

Dayton O. Hyde came from the State of Michigan as young boy. He had always had a deep interest in the Indian people. Reading and playing he was an Indian, some of his activities got him and his friends in deep trouble. They tried coloring their skin, but for some reason it never turned out the right shade. Once they were playing cowboys and Indians, shooting arrows, but one of the arrows injured one of the cows so that put a stop to such activity.

The summer he was twelve , his uncle wrote and told him about his Oregon ranch. The tales were so luring that he just had to go -- promising his uncle he would help with the work if only he could come. Permission was granted and he arrived on the train with bow and arrows. And then, when his uncle said he was to have on Indian playmate, he was overjoyed although a bit hesitant about meeting him. Imagine his feeling on meeting the boy to find him as white in color as he was himself.

In later years he was to own his uncle's ranch. It is located thirty miles from Chiloquin, Oregon and 58 miles from Klamath Falls, Oregon The name of the cattle ranch is Yamsi which is a Klamath Indian word meaning "Home of the North Wind." Mr Hyde said it is six thousand acres of hard work. There he built his home and raised five children on the ranch he loved so well. But there had always been that urge to write.

491

He spent many an evening with the cowhands, listening to the stories of the early days. There was one story that really intrigued him about an Indian family that had been almost wiped out. This had occurred in Nevada near Winnemucca. Traveling into Nevada, he found that being a stranger in the different towns, he had only to mention the name of Shoshone Mike and the old timers had many a tale to tell of the event. And when they found he was a writer, they warmed to their subject. The more he heard about the Massacre, the more he felt there had been an injustice done.

For fifteen years he spent researching the life and habits of Shoshone Mike or Mike Daggett - my grandfather - a grandfather I had never known. In fact, all these years I thought Mike was my father and Henie, Hattie (Harriett), and Cleve were my brother an sisters. Instead I find that they were My aunts and uncle. The Esteps talked very little about my past. I have a feeling they knew little about the events of the massacre, communication being such as it was in those days.

Mr. Hyde visited with individuals who had known Mike. One was Carrie Crockett. At the time the book was written, Carrie Crockett was living in Rock Creek. It was here Mike's band made their winter home. Her father had the store where Mike took his leather gloves and lariats which he made and traded them for his staples. Since the book was published I have corresponded with Carrie Crockett; she is quite an elderly lady now, but she remembers Mike and his family. She said he was kind to his family and had a fine sense of humor; that he always paid his debts and was very honest. She still has one of his bowls which was used to grind seeds into edible food.

The author spent hours in the Twin Falls Public Library examining old records an periodicals of the time. He examined records in the Congressional Library in Washington, D. C. and 60 year old newspapers He talked to lawmen, sheep men, posse, and anyone who could help him unravel the story of Mike. The more he delved into the tragic incident, the more he became interested in it.

Many were the times he followed Shoshone Mike's trail - trying to live as the little band lived - eating the same food as they ate, making camp in the same campsites high in the mountains. He said he couldn't understand the hold Mike had on him, but he felt when he was far from civilization as if the indian family were there with him. He would return to this Oregon ranch, thinking that he would forget the story and write something else, only to find his thoughts turning again to Indian's plight and so he wrote the story, half hoping a surviver would be found. And when he did the survivor, it did upset him, thinking about what she would be thinking of the story and had he done justice to Mike. In a way, I had the feeling he was a bit disappointed to find me so civilized, but then again he was proud to hear of all I had done.

Mike's headdress is now in the Museum at Reno, Nevada. From one of the campsites Mr. Hyde found a lodgepole of Mike's. It is at his home in Oregon.

I had the privilege of being a guest in Mr. Hyde's home. He wanted me to see the lodge pole which he had discovered at one of Mike's camps sites. He brought it in for me to see. As I held it in my hands my thoughts raced back through the years. This weather beaten pole helped to make a shelter away from the howling winds and the driving snow for my family. It showed clearly the passing of time. It was gray in color. At one end it had been sharpened to point by some primitive instrument.

Most of Mike's things were taken by the posse and are now lost. Carrie Crockett has the one stone bowl. The Museum at Elko, Nevada has some arrow heads and other artifacts. Mike's headdress is in the Nevada State Museum at Reno, Nevada. The last day we were there he took us to his cabin where he does his writing. I was impressed with the amount of research material which he has accumulated. Stacks of photo static copies of newspaper articles about the Massacre and many, many pictures on the Nevada country around Golconda and Winnemucca, Nevada.

I think that Mr. Hyde did a beautiful piece of writing and if you haven't read The Last Free Man, I'm sure you would enjoy it.

As one report stated - I have had a life of peace and understanding. That is really so true. Each phase of it has been more rewarding than the preceding years. I owe all this to the wonderful life Mr. and Mrs. Estep gave me in their home. They were always interested and proud of all my achievements. I would never have been able to have accomplished this with out their guidance and help.

I always like to remind everyone that Mr Hyde is speaking of the very, very primitive Indian, Shoshone Mike, my grandfather.

In closing I would like to give you a glimpse into Mr. Hyde's style of writing by reading the last paragraph from his book the LAST FREE MAN.

493

"I am left alone with memories fragile as a waking dream. Mike lives on now in memory alone, but as I wander the lonely wastelands of northern Nevada and southern Idaho, I feel his presence still as though he rides the wind and guides my way over his lost domain to tell his story. From somewhere in the sage, a vesper sparrow lisps its silver song , and from the weathering rimrocks, Mike's friend the canyon wren pipes plaintively as though to ask where all the Indians have gone".

HYDE

CHAPTER II

AFTER HER PASSING

While at a nursing home, recovering from an injury, Mary Jo was accidentally given the wrong medication which resulted in her death, Saturday December 19, 1992, at age 82.

In the late fall of 1991 nearly eighty years after Mary Jo's close encounter with death, as a baby, followed by what she referred to as a wonderful life, tragedy had struck again. Upon returning home one afternoon she fell into the basement of her home through the cold air return for the furnace. Carpet layers, who were installing new carpeting had not expected her back and had removed the cold air vent screen/grate in order to allow them to install the carpet. She fell through the large vent hole in the floor resulting an extremely bad fall. She had hit the basement floor and was hospitalized for a extended period of time, nearly one year. Then on November 24,1992 she was transferred to the Good Samaritan Nursing Home where she died December 19, 1992.

She did not die of her injuries she died from heart failure due to three medications she was mistakenly given that was prescribed for another patient.

The doctor who was treating her refused to take any action to save her life nor would he allow any one else to take such action. When she died he failed to include, on her death certificate, dated December 21, 1992, that she had been given the wrong medication and noted that her death was age related. The coroner did however, in his report, dated December 23, 1992, include the fact that she had been given the wrong medication and *died of heart failure due to the accidental ingestion of prescription drugs meant for another patient.*

The error was discovered thirty minutes after the error was made.

The Jarnecke family, Louis, Esther, their two sons Chuck and Rich who were her closest and dearest friends, immediately asked that disciplinary action be taken against the doctor.

An investigation was launched December 23, 1992. However since the victim was a NO CODE the attending physician, who was contacted twice, "denied any medical intervention of any kind". Thus no action was taken to reverse the error because Mary Jo had signed the NO CODE form (HEALTH CARE DIRECTIVE) on November 25,

495

1992 which indicated that cardiopulmonary resuscitation should not be initiated. It did not however, address treating reversible conditions.

The error was reversible by either pumping her stomach or administering drugs that would reverse the action of the incorrect drugs.

On January 29, 1993 the Jarneckes sent a letter to Dr. Cornellius Brandt and the Good Samaritan Nursing Home outlining their complaint of the non-caring mistreatment Mary Jo received from Dr. Brandt and the Good Samaritan Nursing Home.

They answered February 17, 1993 saying an investigation was ongoing.

On March 4, 1993 the Yakima County Medical Society also answered the Jarneke's informing them that the circumstances would be reviewed and that they would be informed of the conclusions.

The Jarneckes were relentless in there pursuit of justice for Mary Jo. On September 10, 1993 they sent out a second letter, this one to the Yakima County Medical Society. Asking why Dr. Brandt was still practicing medicine when he was responsible for the death of their friend Mary Jo Estep. They went on to relate how Mary Jo had been a very close friend of family since 1946. They also went on to say: *"Dr. Brandt had also threatened the nursing home nurses that they would be sued if they did anything to save her life".*

The Yakima County Medical Society and the Washington State Medical Association (WSMA) did little to help them wade through the red tape and hurdles to get justice for Mary Jo. The State of Washington Department of Health dragged their feet, evidently hoping the issue would go away.

The letter dated September 20, 1993 from the WSMA to the Jarneckes is like asking the fox if he has been raiding the chicken house and when he said no, that was good enough.

Quote from that letter: *"They contacted Dr. Brandt and felt that the physician responded satisfactorily to their inquiry".*

October 8, 1993 the Jarneckes received a letter from the Yakima County Medical Society informing them that their complaint was being investigated by the State of Washington Medical Disciplinary Board.

For the first time there seemed to be some action taken in regard to the medial practice of Dr. Brandt.

In early November 1993 the Jarneckes received a copy of Statement of Charges brought against Dr. Brandt.

Finally on January 11, 1995 Dr. Cornelis D. Brandt sent out a letter:

"To whom it may concern stating as of February 1, 1995 he would be unable to attend to nursing home patients including in Emergency Rooms".

Mary Jo had willed her estate in the State of Washington, of nearly $600,000, to: Yakima Community College; Central Washington University at Ellensberg, Washington, where she earned her teaching degree; Yakima School District; Salvation Army; her Church and to two young men, whom, as toddlers, she helped care for when they lost their mother, Ruth (Beckam) Jarnecke. Mary Jo had taught with Ruth and was her best friend. She helped look after the two children until Louis Jarnecke was remarried to Ester in 1966.

Each year the Music Department at Central Washington University, gives out $11,000 in scholarships, from the endowment Mary Jo had left to the school.

Louis Jarnecke was the executer of Mary Jo Estep's estate.

In the words of the Jarneckes, Ester & Louis, *"the Esteps were very fond of Mary Jo and she of them".*

Interview with Ester Jarnecke - April 2009

"Mary Jo was as fine a person as anyone I have known. She was generous and kind. She was always there when we needed her. I can't say enough good things about her - she was wonderful".

Remembering Mary Jo Estep by Esther I Jarnecke July 2009

The following is a letter, transcribed word for word, from the Esteps to Mary Jo dated February 1 1935 showing what a close and loving family they were.

Yakima, Friday, Feb., 1, 35

Dear Josephine:

Not much news at this end of the line but I expect
It is time to drop you a line or two to let you know that we still
are able to write and do a few other things. We have been rather on
the quite this week as there was not lodge meeting so far though I
am to go out tonight to rehearse some of the stuff I learned several
months ago. I have had to relearn some of it and then there are some
new men on the team now who have to learn where and when it is time
for them to come in on their part of it. Guess I can get mine all right
before we are to put it on in March some time.

I was out day before yesterday to make some calls and to get a
little exercise. Called on Mrs McGuffie; he is in one of Ragan's
sheep camps down east of White Swan; the kids are all right; and she
has her boarders yet and inquired much about you. Then pulled on
and saw Mr. and Mrs. Watt for a little while. He was in getting a truck
fixed up. They are as well as usual and also inquired about you. He
and his partner will have about 3600 lambs this year. From there I
went over to Throssel's and had a very nice visit of more than an hour.
They also inquired rather extensively about you and your work
down there and I told them a lot about it; may be more than you have
told us but I did not want it to go begging for want of a good talk.
Guess there is no one there that they knew of have known.
Muddy was out to a do <u>lecture </u>Wednesday night at the nurses
home at St. Elizabeth's hospital. Guess she got by with it all right
as there was none who knew more about the subject than she did.
Any way she got a nice notice in the paper which is enclosed herewith.
She is at circle meeting this afternoon and about half an hour of this
FORE noon as she left about half past 11. And she did not get out of
bed until 9 this morning and then made a lemon pie to take with her. I
washed the dishes and cleaned up after I had my dinner. Did a pretty
good job I think but she may not think so when she gets home. Any
way I had the kind of a dinner I wanted today for I got it all myself--hot
dogs being a leading part of it. Muddy has not been sleeping any too
good most of this week and last night about the meanest she has had
as she did not sleep until after 4 this morning. That is the reason she
did not get up until 9. I got up and warmed a glass of milk for at 4 and
she went to sleep soon after that. I stayed in bed until 8 so as not to
wake her but did not sleep any after about 7.

498

Had a rather long letter from Dr. Wheeler this week. Says he is getting so he can kill time pretty well now. He gave us a list of your relatives on the reservation, both living dead. I set it out here:

Living	**Dead**
Oscar Wildcat.	Mrs. Sam Mosho (Wildcat)
Sparks Wildcat	Waren Wildcat
Levi Wildcat	Earl Wildcat
	Laura Warren (Wildcat)

It seems that Mrs. Mosho was a sister of the other Wildcat. I did not know that until now and no doubt accounts for the interest Sam took in you. Mrs. Warren was a very fine women and Earl was a good man. I am not sure if Sparks is an uncle or a cousin; if he is an uncle he is only a young man now. Oscar and Levi are uncles--I do not know which is the best man--both fairly good at any rate, but some times take on a little too much tanglefoot when he got in Pocatello with some of the other Bannock Creek fellows. I do not now remember which one that was.

Will mail you the Toppenish paper in the morning. Muddy has not read it yet.

We are having about the finest weather you ever saw in these parts; warm and some sunshine every day but not all day as there is a lot of fog at night and up until nearly noon. Am afraid it is too nice and that buds will be starting too soon and will get caught with a cold snap along the last of March or the first of April and kill the fruit. So far as the apples are concerned that might be good thing as they can not sell the ones they grew last year.

Best regards from both of us to you and to the Donners and any other old friends down there.

Very truly your

Dad

499

My dear Mary Jo:

Just a few lines with Daddy's letter. He has gone to lodge and I am so sleepy I can scarcely hold my eyes open. I've been having a true-four nights this week. I have not been able to get to sleep till about 3 o'clock and this morning it was nearly 5. Can't stay in bed-get up and sit in the back(?) room. I read and play cards. It's getting on my nerves. Have a pain in the back of my head so much so(?) If I don't get better I will go to Dr. soon.

Before I forget- I was talking to Mrs. Forsemann the other day and she said Miss Kennedy went back to Ellensburg the beginning of this New Quarter. Said M. McConnell asked her to come and take charge of Kamola (?) Hall. She has 17 girls in there and the work not so hard, yet she was not feeling too good. They thot it was just as well for her to go as to stay here and worry about it. Hope she does not break down again.

I see by the Toppenish paper that Ruth has been sick and out of school so much ??? ??. Lots of flu. Over 700 children out of school here last week at one time.

Did you get your tooth fixed. If you let it go you will likely lose it. Daddy had one pulled last Saturday.

I never have found the piano scarf. Have looked every place I can think of- yet I think I remember that I put it away.

Mrs Conrad's brother from Canada is here for a visit.

Did you get your music and are you practicing any? Do you give the Donner? children any help! Hope you can!

I owe so many letters. I just don't feel like writing now. I so much hope you have your Christmas "Thank-You" letters written.
Don't delay (?).
With heaps of love and hope you keep well. Use that medicine in your nose for its dry down there and that place will get dry quickly. Don't neglect.

Ever yours
Muddy

THE JARNECKE FAMILY
ca 1980

From left: Richard,Ester (step mother), Louis (adoptive father),Chuck

Mary Jo Estep

Keith & Keith Funeral Home

YAKIMA - Mary Jo Estep , 82,of Yakima, WA died Saturday December 19, 1992 at the Good Samaritan Health Care Center.

She was born April 12, 1910 and was one of only four survivors of the 1911 massacre of Shoshone Mike and his band near Winnemucca, Nevada. The other three survivors, her aunt and uncles, died of illness within a year of the massacre. Mary Jo was adopted by an Indian Agent and his wife, Evan & Rita Estep, who were sent to take charge of the survivors.

Mary Jo moved with her parents when they were transferred by the Department of the Interior to Montana and New Mexico before settling in Toppenish, WA in 1924. She graduated from Toppenish High School in 1929 and later graduated from Ellensburg Normal School with a B.A. in education in 1934. While in college, Mary Jo played the piano in spring and winter concerts and was chosen to appear in the Young Artists' program for the Music Federation of the State of Washington.

Mary Jo's first teaching assignment was in the piano department of the Chemawa Indian School in Chemawa, OR. She then taught first grade at Whiteriver, AZ where her class only spoke their native tongue, Apache. Seeking a position with public schools, she applied for and was accepted in White Swan, WA. Mary Jo was placed in a one room school at Medicine Valley.
The next year the school closed and she went to White Swan where she taught first grade and music for grades one through eight for the next nine years.

She was requested to come to the Toppenish School District and retired from there in1974.

After her retirement, Mary Jo was able to meet Dayton O. Hyde, author of the "Last Free Man". The book is an account of the Shoshone Mike Massacre and Mr. Hyde was able to provide Mary Jo with some of the missing pieces of her life. The massacre was unique in the fact that this was the last known band of Indians in North America living the old life, in the ancient way. Mary Jo was an active member of the First Christian Church of Yakima and the Ladies Musical Club. She was known as a concert pianist and had played in many concerts and recitals in the Yakima Valley. By request, she would travel to different school districts and give a presentation on her life story. She also loved to garden.

She is survived by many friends including Ken, Margaret & Bev Jones, Louis & Ester Jarnecke, Chuck, Nida & Christopher Jarneke and Rick & Dana Jarneke. Besides her friends she was proceeded in death by her good friend, Ruth Sweany.

Funeral services will be held Wednesday, December 23rd, at 1:00 P.M. in the First Christian Church (N. 3rd St. & B St.). Interment will be in Terrace Heights Memorial Park. Memorials may be made to the First Church and/or the Congressional Christian Church.

May 12, 2006

503

May 12, 2006

CHAPTER III
DO NOT HATE

As stated before the many stories, newspaper articles, magazine articles and books written about this incident are so lacking in facts and integrity that they lend themselves of little or questionable value as a historical record.

The facts of what happened or did not happen at Rabbit Creek continue to direct what has carried on to this day.

By killing unarmed women and children muzzled the facts and bred more inaccuracies that has guided the settlement of Mary Jo's estate.

Lawyers and judges are still trying to unravel her complicated estate at Fort Hall, Idaho, comprised of four Indian allotments, totaling 720 acres.

All of the affidavits and conclusions from interviews and research of documents are a mess and are of questionable accuracy. I wrote a letter to Judge Linscheid, Board of Indian Appeals, on March 1, 2007, explaining my skepticism. That letter generated a flurry of letters, 39 to be exact, "to interested parties", what ever that means. As of this date April 15, 2016, I have heard nothing back since the letters went out.

Evan Estep also, believed some of the the stories and rhetoric coming out of the Rabbit Creek incident. It is interesting that he had talked to Henie, maybe at great length, but did not reveal to Mary Jo any information that he had gotten from Henie regarding Rabbit Creek. Maybe he thought it too dramatic for either one.

To shield Mary Jo from the agony of thinking her family were these terrible people, the Esteps never passed on to her what they thought to be the true story of what took place at Rabbit Creek.

The Esteps had cared for, educated Mary Jo and got her started in life which was no easy task due to the prejudices of those times.

One of the best illustrations of their close family ties may be illustrated in the letter to Mary Jo February. 1, 1935. Same with District Att. T. Baily Lee and Superintendent C. H. Asbury they also believed the rhetoric coming from the Donnelley posse and Buckley's inquest jury was factual thinking they had the true story.

This false information, made out the whole Daggett Family, including the women and children, as murderous savages.

Mary Jo traveled to many places around the world which include Alaska, Hawaii, Europe and the Philippines.

Several people said she bought the Baby Grand Piano, she had in her home, in Europe and had it shipped to her home in Yakima. That may not be true. No concrete evidence of that was ever found.

She also took the two boys, she helped take care of, to Hawaii as a High School graduation present.

The smallest of the little "animals", Mary Jo, became a better person and more accomplished than any of those in the posse who pursued the family & all those who thought of them as "animals"!

The ironic part of this is, had all this drama and suffering not occurred Mary Jo would not have had the great life she had. She was so fortunate to have had the Esteps take her in. The right people at the right time. She was so fortunate to have Asbury recognize the plight of the children and the barbaric attitude of the general population involved in this horrific incident.

Had the tragic event not happened, ending her life at age 82, involving wrong medication who knows how many more years she could have enjoyed.

And so Mary Jo Estep who was taken from her dead mother's back in the blood, the mud and the gore at Rabbit Creek near Golconda, Nevada February 26, 1911, should be an inspiration to all peoples especially the Native American Indian who surrendered their homeland in a trail of blood and tears to white Europeans during the last half of the 2nd Millennium. For those young Native American Indians who might read this story, do not let it cause you to hate. Hate would only destroy your life over something you can do nothing about. I will however never ask you to forgive.

507

R E F E R E N C E S

THE LAST FREE MAN
by Dayton O. Hyde

500 NATIONS
bY ALIVEN M. Joshephy Jr.

THUNDER OVER THE OCHOCO
Volume I
by Gale Ontko

DESERT CHALLENGE
by Richard G. Lillard
Ch. III   1941

THE AMERICAN INDIAN HOLOCAUST
& SURVIVAL
by Russell Thorton (demographer)

EXTERMINATION
by Trafzer

THE INDIANS
Time Life Book Series
by Benjamin Capps

FROM THE DEEP WOODS TO
CIVILIZATION
by Charles Eastman

THE SOULE OF THE INDIAN
by Eastman- published 1911

LIFE AMONG THE PIAUTES
by Sarah Winnemucca Hopkins
aided by Mrs Horace Mann

The Last Indian Uprising In
The United States
Little High Rock Canyon, Nevada
By Frank V. Perry - 1949

TIME BOOKS
THE OLD WEST (Indians)

OWYHEE TRAILS
by Mike Hanley & Ellis Lucia

THROUGH INDIAN EYES
Readers Digest

BOISE MASSACRE on the OREGON
TRAIL
by Don H. Sannon

OH WHAT A SLAUGHTER
by Larry Mc Muertry

MASSACRES of the MOUNTAINS
History of Indian Wars of the Far West
1815 to-1875
by J. P. Dunn, LLB

THE BANNOCK of IDAHO
by Brigham D. Madsen
1958

DAUGHTERS OF THE PIONEERS
History of the Development of Southeast
Idaho   1930

AMERICAS FASCINATING INDIAN
HERITAGE

LIFE IN THE SADDLE
Stories of Thomas Gray
by Karen Quintin

THE BANNOCK INDIAN WAR OF 1878
by George Brimlow

NEVADA
copyright 1976 by Thomas C. Elgas & others

GOLD FEVER
by Helen Wilson

AMERICAN INDIAN HOLOCAUST &
SURVIVAL A POPULATION HISTORY
SINCE 1492
by Russell Thorton

Nimrod Urie Trial Testimony
November 1911

THE SHOSHONE FRONTIER and the
BEAR RIVER MASSACRE
by Brigham Madsen

THE ROAD ON WHICH WE CAME
by Steve Crumb

THE SHOSHONE of the DUCK VALLEY
INDIANS RESERVATION
by Whitney Mc Kinney

DISPOSSESSING THE WILDERNESS
INDIANS REMOVED
by Mark David Spence

NEW
A Western Shoshone History
published by ITC-N

OFF THE WALL
Death in Yosemite
by Grighim & Farlee Jr.

THE NEGRO COWBOYS
by Philip Durham & Everett Jones
1965

THE FOX AND THE WHIRLWIND
by Peter Aleshire

I S H I
IN TWO WORLDS
A BIOGRAPHY of the LAST WILD INDIAN in
NORTH AMERICA
by Theodora Kroeber
published in 1961

The TRAIL DRIVERS
of TEXAS
By Marvin Hunter & George W. Saunders
1924

DIAMOND FIELD JACK
by David H. Grovear
1968

RAILROADS of NEVADA & EASTERN
CALIFORNIA
by David Myriek
Vol II 1963

CAMP LIFE ON A GREAT RANGE IN
NORTHERN NEVADA
Sunset Magazine July 1910
by R. L. Fulton

NEVADA
A HISTORY
by Robert Laxalt
1977

MASSACRE FOR GOLD
by Gregory Nokes
2009

NEVADA MILITARY PLACE NAMES
INDIAN WARS and CIVIL WAR
By Dan C. Rathbun
2002

The ECOLOGICAL INDIAN
By Shepard Krech III
1999

The DEADLIEST INDIAN WAR
In The WEST
The Snake Conflict, 1864 - 1868
By Gregory Michno
2007

Land of Bunch Grass
Sage and Sun
By Ralph G. Parman
1990

THE NEVADA DESERT
By Sessions S. Wheeler
1971

THE SAGEBRUSH SOLDIERS
Nevada Historical Society Quarterly
Fall - Winter   1962

A FATE WORSE THAN DEATH
Indian Captivities in the West 1830-1885
By Gregory & Susan Mincho
2007

Steamboats,Shoshone, Scoundrels
and the such
By James Varley
2001

Buckskin and Smoke
By Anna Hansen Hayes
1971

Six Decades Back
By Charles S Walgamott
1926 &1928

ATLAS of
Indian Nations
By Anton Treuer 2013
[National Geographic]

VINA'S HISTORY IN
PHOTOS AND STORIES
By Frances V. Leininger
2010

The Jourlnal of the
MODOC COUNTY
HISTORICAL SOCIETY
No. 25 -- 2003

RG 75
Box 265
CARSON INDIAN SCHOOL
Admin. Files 1909-1923
Annual Report 1911
National Archives
San Bruno, California

KARNEE
A Paiute Narrative
By Lalla Scott
1966

The Various Writings of
Mort West
1934

The Journal of the
MODOC COUNTY
HISTORICAL SOCIETY
No. 25 - 2003
Letter by Mort West
April 16, 1934

HUNDREDS OF WOMEN AND
CHILDREN WERE COMING
TOWARDS US AND GETTING ON
THEIR KNEES FOR MERCY
Novembe 29, 1864
SMITHSONIAN MAGAZINE
December 2014
By Tony Horwitz

"THE GREATEST EVEL"
INTERPRETATIONS of INDIAN
PROHIBITION LAWS
1832 - 1953
Jill E. Martin

NEVADA'S BLOODY
INDIAN MASSACRE
1911
By Barbara Hegne
2006

EMPIRE of theSUMMER MOON
Quanah Parker & Rise & Fall of the Comanches
By S. C. Gwynne
2010

MO-CHI
FEMALE CHEYENNE WARRIOR
By Lynda Wormmack
Wild West -History Ass.-Journal
June 20, 2015 - Vol. VIII No. 3

THE CATTLE KING
By Edward Treadwell
1931

INDUSTRIAL COWBOYS
MILLER & LUX AND THE
TRANSFORMATION OF THE FAR WEST
1850-1920
By David Igler
1964

Oral History Interview with John Sipes

NATIVE UNIVERSE
National Geographic

THE NATIVE AMERICANS
An Illustrated History
By several authors
Edited by Betty & Ian Ballantine
Turner Publishing, Inc.
Atlanta
1992

NATIVE AMERICAN TESTIMONY
1492 - 1992
Edited By Peter Nabokov
1992

CRAZY HORSE
JOKA HEY
[It is a good time to die]
1971
By Vinson Brown

NEVADA
OFFICIAL BICENTENNIAL BOOK
Edited by Stanley W.Paher
1976

The Nature Way
By Corbin Harney 2009

INDIAN WARS of IDAHO
By Arnold

FEARFUL CROSSING
By Harold Curran

THE WEISER INDIANS
SHOSHONI PEACE MAKERS
By Hank Corless

TIME MAG.
Feb. 8, 2016
The Science of Mob Aggression
By Mina Cikara & Adrianna Jenkins

Letter to Mary Jo Estep
from Carrie Crockett
Nov. 5, 1975

Smithsonian Magazine
November 2016
GRANNT'S UNCIVIL WAR
By Peter Cozzens

NATIONAL GEOGRAPHIC
THE INDAN WARS
By Anton Treuer
2016

BLACK LIKE ME
By John Howard Griffin
1962

THE LAST STAND OF SHOSHONE
MIKE
(NATIONAL GEOGRAPH)
A true Indian story of 1911
By F. M. Wilson

Transcripts of the trials of Nimrod Urie &
Frank Tranmer for the murder of the
Quilcies in Emaly, Nevada, in Jan. 1911.
Urie - 4/17-20/1911
Trammer - ??/??/1911

KILLERS OF
THE FLOWER MOON
2017
By David Grann

OLDER THAN
AMERICA
2010
A Georgina Lighting Film

STANDING BEAR'S
FOOTSTEPS
Documentary by Christine Lesiak

A CITY in the SKY
Magazine Article -COWBOYS & INDIANS
July 2017 Page 134
By Clay Swartz

The **Bear River Massacre**
1982
By Newell Hart

WILD WEST
Magazine
June 2014

THE HEART OF EVERYTHING
THAT IS
2013
By Bob Drury & Tom Clavin

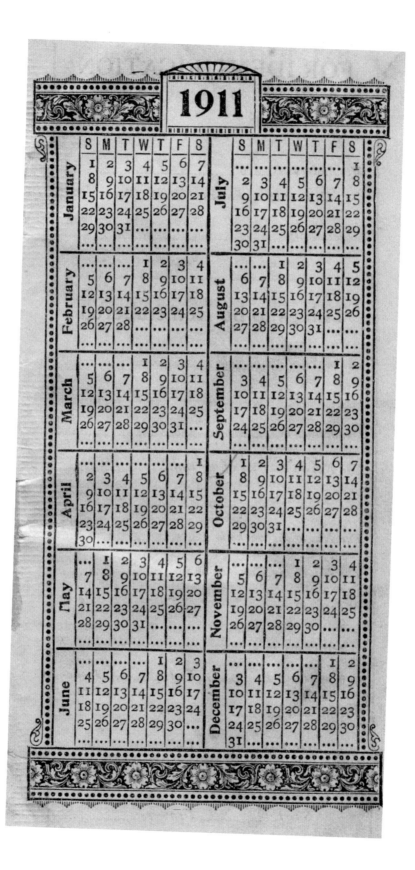

1911

	S	M	T	W	T	F	S		S	M	T	W	T	F	S
January	1	2	3	4	5	6	7	**July**	…	…	…	…	…	…	1
	8	9	10	11	12	13	14		2	3	4	5	6	7	8
	15	16	17	18	19	20	21		9	10	11	12	13	14	15
	22	23	24	25	26	27	28		16	17	18	19	20	21	22
	29	30	31	…	…	…	…		23	24	25	26	27	28	29
	…	…	…	…	…	…	…		30	31	…	…	…	…	…
February	…	…	…	1	2	3	4	**August**	…	…	1	2	3	4	5
	5	6	7	8	9	10	11		6	7	8	9	10	11	12
	12	13	14	15	16	17	18		13	14	15	16	17	18	19
	19	20	21	22	23	24	25		20	21	22	23	24	25	26
	26	27	28	…	…	…	…		27	28	29	30	31	…	…
March	…	…	…	1	2	3	4	**September**	…	…	…	…	…	1	2
	5	6	7	8	9	10	11		3	4	5	6	7	8	9
	12	13	14	15	16	17	18		10	11	12	13	14	15	16
	19	20	21	22	23	24	25		17	18	19	20	21	22	23
	26	27	28	29	30	31	…		24	25	26	27	28	29	30
	…	…	…	…	…	…	…		…	…	…	…	…	…	…
April	…	…	…	…	…	…	1	**October**	1	2	3	4	5	6	7
	2	3	4	5	6	7	8		8	9	10	11	12	13	14
	9	10	11	12	13	14	15		15	16	17	18	19	20	21
	16	17	18	19	20	21	22		22	23	24	25	26	27	28
	23	24	25	26	27	28	29		29	30	31	…	…	…	…
	30	…													
May	…	1	2	3	4	5	6	**November**	…	…	…	1	2	3	4
	7	8	9	10	11	12	13		5	6	7	8	9	10	11
	14	15	16	17	18	19	20		12	13	14	15	16	17	18
	21	22	23	24	25	26	27		19	20	21	22	23	24	25
	28	29	30	31	…	…	…		26	27	28	29	30	…	…
	…	…	…	…	…	…	…								
June	…	…	…	…	1	2	3	**December**	…	…	…	…	…	1	2
	4	5	6	7	8	9	10		3	4	5	6	7	8	9
	11	12	13	14	15	16	17		10	11	12	13	14	15	16
	18	19	20	21	22	23	24		17	18	19	20	21	22	23
	25	26	27	28	29	30	…		24	25	26	27	28	29	30
	…	…	…	…	…	…	…		31						

WHAT ELSE WENT ON IN 1911

BESIDES KILLING EIGHT INDIANS INCLUDING WOMEN AND CHILDREN?

- Marie Curie won a second Nobel Prize, this time for discovering the elements radium and polonium and opening the door to the age of nuclear chemistry.
- The 1st landing of an aircraft on a ship took place as pilot Eugene B Ely brought his Curtiss airplane in for a safe landing on the deck of the armored cruiser USS Pensilvania in San Francisco Harbor.
- Titanic launched May, 31 1911
- February 6, 1911 Ronald Wilson Reagan, 40th president of the US was born in Tampico, Illinois.
- Jack Johnson became 1st African American heavy weight boxing champion in 1908.
In 1910, in what was dubbed the "Fight of the Century" Johnson defeated Jim Jeffries in Reno, Nevada. He was married 3 times all to white women, the first marriage being 1911.
- The 1st Indi. 500 was run. Ray Morman was the winner at 75 MPH. It was the beginning of the Indy type cars built for long distance racing.
- The ballet "Petrunshka," with music by Igor Stravinsky and choreograph by Michel Fokine, was first performed in Paris by the Ballets Russes, with Vaslav Nijindky in the title role.
- Midget City on Cony Island burned to the ground.
- In the summer of 1911 the Great fire burned in Idaho & Montana
- Base ball great Eddie Grant married 2-28-1911
- One million patents issued by 1911, starting in 1836. In June of 2018 the 10 millionth patent will be issued.
- On October 11, 1911 California became the 6th state to grant women the right to vote, although they could finally vote in California it was not until 1920 that they could vote in national elections.
- The Nevada legislature in 1911 proposed amending the sate's constitution so as to permit women to vote. It finally passed in November 1914. Women first voted in Nevada in the election of 1916
- August-1, 1911,Harriet Quimby became the 1st women to receive a U. S. pilots certificate from the Aero Club of America. (Quimby's accomplishments included being the 1st woman to to fly across the English Channel; She was killed in an accident in July 1912 at age 37.)
- August-21, 1911 - Leonardo Davinc's Mona Lisa was stolen from the Lauvre Museum in Paris. (the Painting was recovered 2 years later in Italy)
- The British liner RMS Olympic collided with the Royal Navy Cruiser HMS Hawke off the the Isle of Wight ; although severally damaged the Olympic was able to return to Southampton under its own power.
- Copyright 1911 EIGHTH READER by Baldwin & Bender, American Book Co. -
- Pitcher Cy Young, 44, gained his 511th and final career victory as he hurled a 1-0 shutout for the Boston Rustlers against the Pittsburg Pirates at Forbs Field.

- Anita Hill's mother was born Oct. 16, 1911.
- March 12, 1911 William Patrick Hitler - Houston Stuart Patrick (son of Alois Hitler and great nephew of Adoph Hitler) was born in England. He changed his last name to Houston and moved to America. He had four sons. One died in an auto accident the other three made a pact not to have children and pass on the Adolf Hitler paternal blood line and so it ended.
- China abolished the requirement that men wear their hair in a bun or ponytail.

1-26-11 Silver State News Paper - Winn., Nev.
OLD-TIME RESIDENT
NOW IN LONDON

The Silver State is in receipt of the following letter from a former. resident of Humboldt Cnty.
"23 Hilton Road, Muswell Hill, London N., England, Jan. 13, 1911

Editor Silver State, Winnemucca, Nevada

As an old resident in Humboldt County, Nevada, to be exact, at Parkinson's
ranch, on Kelly Creek, some 20 years ago. I should like to see a current copy of your paper if it would not be troubling you too much to send one.

I was going through some old papers of mine the other day and came across a copy of the Silver State dated June, 1886.

My time in Humboldt County was in the days Frank and Joe Germain, Doc. Hanson Paul Neth, Levy Bros. and Reinhart, who had the stores in your town.

Louis Lay kept the Hot Springs Hotel at Golconda and Shallenberger the store there; Henry Pratt the cattle man, lived at Paradise' Silva, the sheep man near Iron Point, Pick Anderson and the rest.

   Yours Truly - Ernest G. Weth

("At this moment, 1-26-11, Mike Daggett and his family were crossing the Black Rock Desert and the Jackson Mts. in the dead of winter with out shelters other than a few blankets and a tarp").

- Ground was broken for Boston's Fenway Park
- Automobiling, less than 1% of the US population owned a car, when the Boy Scouts learned to drive. (Oct. 2018 Smithsonian page 20)
- The Chevrolet Motor Car Co. was founded in Detroit by Louis Chevrolet and William C. Durant. (The Company was acquired by General Motors in 1918)
- November 5, 1911, Aviator Calbraith P. Rodgers arrived in Pasadena, Calif., completing the first transcontinental airplane trip in 49 days.
- December 14, 1911, Norwegian explorer Roald Amandsen and his team became the 1st men to reach the South Pole, beating out a British expedition led by British Capt. Robert Falcom Scott. Scott had set out for the South Pole in October of 1911. Scott's team all perished. He and two others of his expedition were found dead in their last camp the last entry in his journal was March 29. They were on their way back and a mere 11 miles from their their base camp and cache of supplies.

516

- One of the buildings included in Boise Idaho's Historic Preservation District on the east side of downtown was the Peter Sonna House, a Colonial Revival built in 1911 at 121 W. Main St. Sonna was Boise's Mayor from 1893 to 1895.
- Boise,Idaho once had a Chinatown core. Thats where this Chinese New Years parade happened in February 13 1911.
- Twenty five people were killed and two hundred and eighty four injured in railroad accidents, Nation wide.
- Composer Gustav Mahler, despite a fever, conducted the New York philharmonic at the Carnegie Hall in what turned out to be his final concert (He died the following may)
- Inventor Charles F. Kettering demonstrated his electric automobile starter in Detroit by starting a cadillac's motor with the press of a switch instead of a hand-crank. (1st installed on the 1912 Cadillacs)
February 28, 1911,President William Howard Taft nominated William H. Lewis to be the first black Assistant Attorney General of the United States.
- President William Taft ordered 20,000 troops to patrol US-Mexican border in response to the Mexican Revolution.
- 146 people, mostly female immigrants, were killed when fire broke out at the Triangle Shirtwaist Co. in New York.
- Major National Parks had been established by 1911.
- 1st Tournament of Roses was held 20 yrs. before Mike was killed.
- 1st Pendleton Roundup
- Roy Rogers born November 5, 1911
- IBM had it's first beginnings as the Computing-Tabulation-Recording Co. which was incorporated in New York State.
- The Post Office at North's Ranch (Lower Clover Ranch, east of Golconda) closed February 28, 1911 the day the Donnelley posse transported the Daggett children from the Kelley Creek Ranch to Golconda. The North's Ranch post office, located on the county line between Elko and Humboldt County line, was established November 5, 1887. It was supposedly from the North's Ranch that the 1st bit of information on the incident at Rabbit Creek arrived, (via telegram) in Winnemucca, Nevada.
- Two other interesting events, regarding Indians, took place in 1911. One, just 3 days before the Dagger family was killed,Quanah Parker the last chief of the Comanches died February 23, 1911 in Cache, Oklahoma. His mother, Cynthia Ann Parker, was white and had been captured by the Comanches in 1836. She was 9 years old. Except for her color she became a Comanche. She was recaptured by the whites in 1860. Quanah was 12 years old when she was recaptured and he never saw his mother again. She died in 1870. Both Quanah and his mother Cynthia were famous in American History.

It is ironic that the other event occurred in the early morning hours of August the 29th, 1911 when the last wild Indian in America, (ISHI), was found searching for food. at a slaughter house near Oroville, California. He had reached there alone hungry, gaunt and nearly without clothes. He was the last survivor of the Yahi family band from the Yana Tribe. He was taken to the Museum of Anthropology September 4, 1911 where he spent the rest of his life. He died there March 15, 1916. ISHI In Two Worlds - by Theodora Kroeber - 1961

In the case of the Mike Daggett band white man had also brought them to near extinction. Neither Mary Jo nor Ishi, the lone surviver of their tribe, ever had children

From the best records available the Daggett family had been camped near Oroville during the summer of 1910. They may have been within shouting distance. They certainly heard the same train whistle at the same time as it traveled along the Rail Road from Oroville to Sacramento, California. The Daggetts could have looked him up for a spot of tea. The last free man was not Mike after all it was Ishi.

In 1911, a Peace Monument was set at Atlanta's Piedmont Park, in Georgia, Commemorating Post Cicil War Reconciliation. .

Dating back to 1911

Even though it has been 100 years ago, there are people alive today, February 26, 2011, that were old enough to have recalled the incident had they been there. It was not like it was in the "Dark Ages".

Some are saying no one knew any better and thats how they did it in the old days. Well "what ever" they were who they were and they did what they did.

"A great nation does not hide its history. It faces its flaws and corrects them".George W. Bush

- A lady by the name of Gertrude Bains died 9-12-2009, at age 115, in Los Angles California not long ago. She would have been seventeen years old on February 26, 1911.

- Henry Allingham celebrated his 112th birthday 6-7-2008. Henry would have been fourteen on the 26th of February 1911.

- Claude Choules died May 5, 2011 at age 110. He would have been eleven years old on the 26th of February 1911.

- Lela Pulney died 4-8-2011 at age 107.. She would have been seven years old on the 26th of February 1911.

- Emma Didlake at age 110 traveled to Washington D. C. July 18, 2015 to meet the president. An honorary trip in which she was recognize by President Obama as a veteran of the Women's Army Auxiliary Corps during World War II. She was 6 years old on the 26th of February 1911.

- Oldest federal judge in US dies at age 104 IDAHO STATESMAN 1-25-2012

- Frank Woodruff Buckles the last remaining WWI veteran died at age 110, February, 2011. He would have been nine years old on February 26, 1911.

- Emma Morano of Verbania, Italy celebrated her 117 birthday IDAHO STATESMAN 11-30-16. She was twelve years old in February 1911.

-As fugitive, Poncho Villa had come down out of the hills, accumulated an army of volunteers and in1911 had joined the Mexican revolution and was fighting the Mexican army.

MY GRANDMOTHER

May 1962

She was 35 years old in 1911. This incident did not happen back in the Dark Ages.
She holds my two oldest on her lap (two on the left) (The two on the right are my
nephew and niece). I was 25 when my oldest was born. Grandma lived another ten
years after this photo was taken.

THIS TRAGIC EVENT in SUMMARY and CONCLUSION

1 - The Daggett family had been moving ahead on the trail rather slowly since leaving their camp site in Little High Rock Canyon probably spending 3 to 5 days at a stop or camp site. The time at each site allowed for scouting ahead to find the next camp site and traveling in this manner also was necessary to avoid running into others that might be in their line of travel. Sheepherders were the most likely soles the Indians might encounter in this desolate land scape.

They had traveled in this manner the spring before on their way west and explains why there were only a couple of reported sitings of the family during their 600 + miles trek from northeast Nevada to the Sacramento River and back into Nevada.

The Daggett family were moving even slower the last few days, before they were finally run down by the posse.

2 - They were in their final camp on Feb. 26, 1911 and were planning to rest up as best they could. This camp was going to be more than just an over night or three or four day camp, their horses being exhausted and week from lack of feed since they left Little High Rock Canyon on January 19, 1911 They had to have also been contemplating about where and how they were going to get fresh horses. They could not have traveled far or at all with the weak and exhausted horses that were still alive.

3 - There were a total of 12 Indians, four adult males, (the grand father about 65 years of age the other three adult males ranged from their teens to late 30s); two adult women, (the grandmother in her mid to late 50s the other in her mid to late 20s); two adolescent males (ten to twelve years old); one teen age girl (about 15 years of age); one boy (about 5 or 6 years of age; one little girl (4 years) and one baby (10 months) all members of the Daggett family.

4 - When the posse encountered the Indians and shooting began two of the family were shot down at first volley (Mike and one of his boys).

No posse member stated that they were closer than two hundred yards when firing began some said four hundred yards. Communication was nonexistent at that distance as Frank Perry stated in recount of the incident years later. Weather records showed it snowed in the Winnemucca area that day. Most likely a cold front was moving through the area at the time they encountered the Indians.

5 - The teen age girl tried to get the horses in to camp with an attempt to allow their escape. Had she gotten the horses into their camp the horses were too fatigued to carry them far. It would have been a futile attempt at escape.

Soon after Henie's attempt to gather up the horses at least two horses were shot and killed, possibly three, at the orders of Captain Donnelley.

6 - Mike had a rifle (40-82 Winchester) and a cartridge belt in his possession where he was killed. When the Indians ran from their make shift camp, Mike grabbed the handiest rifle (40-82 Winchester) and a cartridge belt of shells. The 40-82 and the 38-55 would, at first glance, look identical. He could have easily gotten the wrong rifle with the 38-55 shells. Probably no big deal because it is quite probable that rifle was fully loaded with nine cartridges and Mike was shot down before he had a need to reload.

Maybe no big deal as far as Mike was concerned however back at the camp, if Mike got the rifles and the cartridges mixed up, those trying to protect the women and children would have been out of ammunition when the 38-55 magazine became empty. At that point the 38-55 rifle would have been totally useless.

No investigation was made or cartridges counted. Mike may not have fired one shot.

7 - Neither Capt. Donnelley nor Skinny Pascal did any shooting of horses or Indians. There is some question as to whether Newgard did any shooting of Indians and didn't likely shoot any horses.

8 - The women & children grabbed what ever article for defense they could and proceeded down the wash moving as fast as moving the children allowed. The women with bows and arrows, the young girl with a ceremonial staff, the children with nothing. It appears the two adult males stayed behind and fired at the posse from the camp (upper site) to allow the women and children time to escape down the wash as far as possible, before also following down the dry creek bed. The fire arms these two had were; 38-55 Winchester rifle, a shot gun and the 32 Savage pistol. Had these three weapons not been out of ammunition, the two brothers would have taken these guns with them when the followed the women and children down the wash. Had those weapons been at the lower site where the women and children were killed they would have been clearly identified. The posse needed firearms at the lower site to justify the killing of the women and children. Had the pistol been found at the lower site the testimony would have been more consistent and clearly detailed as to its location.

Nine of the ten posse members who testified, where women were killed, stated that the women were shooting with bows and arrows and 15 year old girl was threatening them with a spear, all in great detail. Other than the 40-82 found near Mike no rifles nor pistols were specifically nor consistently described as to use nor location. The "spear" as the posse members described it was a ceremonial staff. The blade allowed it to be stuck into the ground and religious rituals practiced around it.

9 - No "war drum" was carried down the wash and beaten, as stated by Reeder.
In the 1st place, Indians of this era had no war drums, only ceremonial. The use of drums as war drums had ended decades earlier.

The women and children had all they could do to get themselves and the smaller children a mile down the wash, let alone carrying along anything as useless as a drum.

10 - Ten members of the family made it down the wash about a mile.
The women could not have escaped with those children. How far could a 4 year old walk and how far could they pack a 4 year old and a 10 month old baby?
The women where shooting with bows and arrows. The 15 year old girl was trying to protect the family as best she could with a ceremonial staff with a blade on it.

11 - They were shooting at every Indian when they saw them and into brush where they suspected an Indian to be. At least most of the posse testified thusly and none contradicted it. Were they shooting into the bushes? Who the hell knows they didn't kill any Indians in the brush, they all died in the bottom of the wash.

12 - They were lying when each stated multiple efforts were made to get the Indians to surrender! The posse members were shooting into the brush, they were shooting at Indians when ever they saw one. The women were standing in plain sight and unarmed except for bows & arrows. When Hogle was killed the ten year old boy was flushed from cover and ran down the wash away from the posse. They shot him in the back. He died with the other young boy in the wash between the two adult males and the two women. The next day, Feb. 27th, the posse transported the dead indians down about a mile from where the last six were killed and stacked them in a pile. A small child was stacked on top of that pile. Part of his head was shot away from behind.

13 - Three questions were ask of each posse member. 1)- Did they make an effort to arrest the Indians without killing them? 2)- Did the Indians try to escape?
3) did the Indians resist arrest?
The pat answer to each of these questions was "Yes sir". Those answers reek of coaching and is so absurd when matched up with other testimony that it makes absolutely no sense. Those answers did not match with reality with the environment if the posse was shooting into the brush not knowing who they were shooting at. That answer to those three questions was necessary to justify the killing of eight members of the Daggett family including the women and children.
Close scrutiny of the testimony of the posse, shows neither to be true. It was their story and no one left alive to counter the posse's testimony, except for Pascal and Henny whom they did not ask.

14 - Each posse member was asked, "do you know who killed the different Indians"? .
All who testified, testified they did not know who shot which Indians. That is understandable with sixteen or seventeen rifles firing away and at least eleven rifles firing away down where the women and children were killed, how could you know?
With this kind of mayhem, it would be easy to be confused as to who shot who.
They were all shooting at every Indian they saw and did not know who killed any specific Indian, another reason to know that little or no effort was made to ask the Indians to

surrender! Also in this manner no one person could be identified as to have killed any specific Indian.

15 - The jury kept harping on fortifications where ever the Indians camped. The general answer to "what kind of position did you find their camps along the trail?" was, in a fortified position, and down in a low place. It was winter time and the Indians were trying to get into a spot that best protected them from the elements as well as hiding the best they could. They did not have the protection from the elements, every night as the posse members did.

16 - The posse members were all within a few feet of the bank of the wash when the ten year old and the women were killed. Nine posse members testified the young squaw kept running up at them from down in the wash/ditch and brandishing a spear. She and the two women were in plain view & had been for some time, probably from the time the posse headed them off from going any further down the wash.

17 -The posse members did not know but what there might be armed Indians hidden in the wash. They were all on hair trigger alert, reason Hogle was accidentally shot by O. D. Van Norman or Frank Perry.

18 - Only four guns (fire arms) can be accounted for; (1) Winchester 40-82,
(2) Winchester 38-55, (3) Shotgun and (4) Savage 32 pistol (semiautomatic).
The pistol was found at the camp as was the 38-55 because they were out of ammunition and or jammed. The 38-55 may have had a 40-82 cartridge jammed in it. The shot gun was carried part way down the wash and dropped, either because the Indian that had it was wounded or it was out of shells or both.
At the inquest no one was asked about cartridges for the 38 - 55, the 32 pistol nor shells for the shotgun.
NO FIREARMS WERE FOUND AT THE SITE WHERE THE SIX INDIANS WERE KILLED!
By the time the 10 members of the Daggett family had reached the lower site there were no operable fire arms available to the Indians except for the 40-82. However it was up where Mike lay dying and not available to those in the wash.

19 - The ten remaining members of the Daggett family, two adult males, two adult females, one fifteen year old girl and five small children were all together when the women and children were killed. The adults were trying to get the children out of harms way but no chance, against eleven armed and crazed posse members on horse back.

20 - The bodies of the last six Indians killed were all located in the bottom of the wash, all within a distance of 20 or 30 yards.

21 - The big question is; did some one or ones shoot the women to get themselves an Indian or did they realize what they had done and decide to leave no witnesses and shoot them down in cold blood?

Or maybe they were in a killing frenzy and shooting at any thing standing. If so it is a wonder they didn't kill one or more of the smaller children, they were all huddled together. The women and children could not have been killed accidentally! The women were shot down on purpose. They could leave no witnesses to this mess! All eight Indians were shot dead none were left wounded to tell their side of the story. Mike lived for a short time.

22 - The mind set of the Surprise Valley posse members enslaved the rational thinking of the Nevada State Police. Donnelley's posse became a vigilante posse.

23 - When it came to justification for killing women & children, their testimony conflicted with each other and often with their own testimony. When you falsify the facts it is hard to remember what you said the 1st time let alone he 2nd or 3rd time.

24 - There had been discussions between jury and posse members, after the inquest of Ed Hogle. More guns were needed to illustrate an Indian battle.

25 - The posse looked upon the Indians more as animals than as human beings!! HAD THESE INDIANS BEEN WHITE PEOPLE, THE WOMEN AND CHILDREN WOULD NOT HAVE BEEN KILLED!!

The two adult males killed with the women and children may not have been killed either since there is no evidence they were armed.

26 - In the coroners report of James Buckley, each of the Indians killed were given a fictitious name. The grandmother was given the name "Jennie" further research tells us her name was Maggie. The name Jennie has stuck in history, since her death. It was not her name nor ever spoken of as such before her death, as in the case of Shoshone Mike. Mike was known as Indian Mike or Mike Daggett, up until the day he was killed.

Also in the coroners report of Buckley, the Indian lady that was killed with the cradle board and baby on her back was listed as unknown, yet in the testimony of each of the posse members she is referred to, by Buckley, as Indian Squaw Mary. The three adult males, sons of Mike Daggett, were listed as Cupena, Disenda and Kinnan. These three names appear no where else, neither in historical records, testimony nor written documents.

Why did they give the Indians fictitious names? Did it some how make their sham of an inquest more authentic? Who dreamed up these names, the inquest jury, the state police or the renegade posse?

Also note Coroner Buckley identified more Indians killed than actually died there. Only at the end after questioning every posse member except Skinny Pascal did he get it straight, eight killed.

27 - One gets the feeling that much of the posse testimony was a macho thing in front of their buddies, i.e. calling the staff a "war staff, magic stick, shot at point blank, bullet grazed my thumb.

28 - No one mentioned finding the mustache, of Erramouspe. A good thing to have in evidence when depicting how savage the Indians were supposed to be.
One may have to accept that it had been removed, based on inquest testimony at the the Denio camp. But hard to believe since these were 20th century Indians not 19th century Indians, however, at this point the older sons of Mike were harboring a great deal of hate and resentment towards the white man.

29 - There are stories going around that the Indians had a Chinese que taken from a Chinaman that the Indians had killed however there was no mention of such an item in any of the testimony. The Indians did not have a que from a Chinese person they had killed. It did not happen. Explanation, Indians customarily cut their hair, braids, when a family member is lost/dies. If the posse found a braid at the site of the killing it would have been from one of the family members, in morning from the loss of the son at Gollaher Mountain.

30 - When the members of the posse realized what they had done, they began fabricating stories to justify the killing. At this point conflicting and fabricating stories began even though they now knew Hogle had not been killed by the Indians. The story to be told was agreed upon on the 27th of February.

31 - Pascal was never asked to testify he was a member of and key witness to this so called "fight", each said, "Pascal asked the Indians to surrender in the Indian language". So why was it that he was not asked to testify?
The answer could be, Donnelley and the others did not trust that Pascal's testimony would coincide with theirs. He may have had a different story to tell and they could not take a chance on that. He could have testified, he testified in the Nimrod Urie murder trial in April of 1911.

32 - E. J. Lying, Constable at Golconda, went to the scene of the killing on Feb. 28th. He and Buckley had gone there together. Their purpose inspect the scene, the bodies and to bury them. However by the time they had arrived at the site Donnelley's posse had already compromised the scene the day before, the 26th, by removing all evidence

including the bodies of the dead Indians. The bodies were transported down the wash about one mile from where the women and children were killed and stacked in a pile. It would be interesting to know who took the pictures of the dead Indians in the pile. It appears to have been either coroner Buckley or Constable Lying.

33 - The Jury and the posse members kept referring to the incident as a fight or battle. There being seventeen or eighteen rifles against two older rifles, shot gun, 32 caliber pistol, bows & arrows and one ceremonial staff brandished by a fifteen year old girl. There were only four adult males, the rest (8) were women and children. It was not a fight or battle it was murder.

34 - The posse put out the word on the day before they arrived in Golconda that the 15 year old girl confessed to the killing of the Dopp boy on Gollaher Mountain the four sheepmen at Little High Rock and other killings. All fabricated, there was no confession. If true why wasn't she asked to testify and if there was an Indian buckaroo at Kelly Creek Ranch who was the interpreter for the Indian girl, in her confession then why wasn't he asked to testify? The last thing the posse wanted was another side to the story. The Indian's side of this story was never told!
The only surviving Indians that could have told the story were Skinny Pascal and the young girl the other three survivors were small children. They were the only Indians there that knew the story. All of the others were killed and these two were never asked to testify! Why not? They were both there. In a cover up that side of the story was not needed.

OTHER ATTRACTIONS

FORT REDSKIN

On May 7, 1865 First Lieutenant Littlefield, while out scouting for Indians east from Camp Scott in Paradise Valley, encountered a large contingent of well armed and fortified Indians east of Paradise Valley. It was reported that they were secured behind some 15 to 25 rifle pits (rock protective structures) in a small box canyon. Some of those structures were large enough to protect as many as 25 defenders. Littlefield and 35 men were facing about 200 Indians looking down on them from their fortified structures, decided to withdraw.

In studying and reviewing military records and maps it is believed that site is located between Midas, Nevada and Spring Creek, just 3 miles west of Midas, on the south face of Snow Storm Mountain.

Captain Wells visited the site later with Littlefield and they followed what they believed to be the same Indians to Table Mountain.

Lieutenant Colonel Mc Dermit decided he wanted to visit the site of the Littlefield encounter of May 7th and the Wells/Littlefield encounter of May 20, on Table Mountain. After leaving the south end of Eden Valley on June 13 and marching northeast 25 miles and then on the 14th he marched another 14 miles to the site of the Littlefield encounter. He named the site "Fort Redskin".

This site is about 25 miles east of where eight members of the Daggett family were killed, on Rabbit Creek, Feruary 26, 1911. There was some speculation that the Daggetts were headed south of here going towards Squaw Valley if they could have made it this far. It was pure speculation and very unlikely. The Daggetts would have gone north of the Snow Storm Mountains in an attempt to reach the Owyhee Desert and the Owyhee River.

TABLE / GODFREY / TOE JAM MOUNTAIN

Captain Wells and Lieutenant Littlefield pursued the large Indian force, estimated at around 500 and engaged them on May 20, 1865. The soldiers numbered 46. The pursuit did not turn out well. As the soldiers approached near the top of Table Mountain they ran into rifle fire from the Indians fortified in rifle pits. One soldier, Godfrey, was killed and another wounded.

The Indians tried to surround the soldiers as they were greater in number resulting in the soldiers retreating. The wounded soldier was still alive and abandoned when the soldiers retreated.

This site, found in the early 40s remained a mystery as to its meaning for over 80 years.
Nevada Military Place Names Indian Wars and Civil War by Daniel S. B. Rathbun and The Deadliest Indian War in the West by Gregory Michno

They retreated to a site they called camp #16 and there they abandoned much of their equipment. In studying military records and maps that site appears to be on Trout Creek in or near the Trout Creek field just above its confluence with Rock Creek.

My dad found what he called an abandoned camp near where we camped on Trout Creek. He specifically mentioned pack saddles. I am 90% sure he had found camp #16. At the time and for nearly 80 years the site also remained a mystery.

When Mike Daggett and his family traveled west from Gollaher Mountain in, late April, they would have passed with in 15 or 20 miles of Godfrey Mountain. Had Mike ever been to Godfrey Mountain? Not very likely. Captain Wells reported that there were Bannock Indians mixed in with Shoshones and Paiutes. However Wells could not have determined with what tribe they were engaged. I have been there and identifying Indians by tribe would have been impossible.

At the time the mountain was referred to as Table Mountain. The top, from which the Indians defended them selves, is flat and is about thirty acres in size.

When Godfrey lost his life there it became known as Godfrey Mountain. Some time in latter years for some unknown reason it became Toe Jam Mountain.

Soldier Cap
V

RIFLE PIT

FALL 1988

Looking northwest, a prominent land mark (Soldier Cap) in the Tuscarora Mountains,
can be seen upper left.

Les Sweeney at a rifle pit, one of many, on Godfrey Mountain as described by Captain
Wells when he and Lieutenant Littlefield encountered the Indians there May 20, 1865.
I had known about this for many years but had no idea of its significance nor how it
came to be. My dad had had come across it in the early 1940s.

Gregory Michno, author of **"The DEADLIEST INDIAN WAR In The WEST"** and Dan
Rathbun, author of **"Nevada Military Place Names Indian Wars and Civil War"**, had
written about this event but neither knew the exact location of the site until 2005 when
I got in touch with Rathbun. He said it had to be somewhere on Toe Jam Mountain. I
explained to him, I know where that site is. I took he and others there in 2006.

Spring Cr.
V

Fort Redskin
V

Midas >

FORT REDSKIN

Looking north at the south face of Snow Storm Mountain. Three miles west of Midas, Nevada.

This is believed to be the site where Lieutenant Littlefield encountered an estimated 200 Indians on May 7, 1865. They were fortified behind 20 or more rock rifle pits/ defensive structures, some large enough to shield and protect as many as 25 men. He withdrew rather than face certain death of some of his men. Colonel Mc Dermit visited this site with Littlefield and Wells on June 14, 1865 and named the site Fort Redskin.

Nevada Military Place Names Indian Wars and Civll War By Daniel C. B. Rathbun

About the Author

Les was raised on a large cattle ranch in north central Nevada, near Midas, Nevada during the 1940s & 50s. He has a degree from the College of Agriculture at the University of Nevada, Reno.

In 1990, after 31 years he retired from the Department of the Interior (BLM) and he and his wife purchased a small ranch near Midvale, Idaho. At that time he began researching and writing a book titled ONLY ONE SURVIVED, the true story of a lone survivor of an Indian family that was massacred near Golconda, Nev. in 1911.

The Sweeneys retired from the ranch in 2003 and moved to Payette, Id. In the last 10 years Les has also written short biographies on three old time buckaroos, Albino Tais, a Yaqui Indian, Henry Harris, a black cowboy and Esador Munoz, old

time Calif. Vaquero. Les nominated two for the Buckaroo Hall of Fame in Winnemucca, Nev. and all three for the National Cowboys of Color Hall of Fame in Fort Worth, Texas. Two were inducted in Winnemucca, Tais on August 31, 2002, Harris on August 30, 2008 Munoz was already a member. All three were inducted in the NCCHF in Fort Worth, Harris & Tais in 2009 and Munoz in 2016.

Made in the USA
Columbia, SC
02 January 2020